G000061954

The
GUINNESS
Spirit

Also by Michele Guinness

Child of the Covenant
Is God Good for Women?
A Little Kosher Seasoning
Promised Land

The GUINNESS Spirit

BREWERS AND BANKERS, MINISTERS AND MISSIONARIES

MICHELE GUINNESS

Hodder & Stoughton
LONDON SYDNEY AUCKLAND

Copyright © 1999 by Michele Guinness

The right of Michele Guinness to be identified as the Author of
the Work has been asserted by her in accordance with the
Copyright, Designs and Patents Act 1988.

First published in Great Britain in 1999
by Hodder and Stoughton Ltd.
A division of Hodder Headline PLC

1 3 5 7 9 10 8 6 4 2

All rights reserved. No part of this publication may be
reproduced, stored in a retrieval system, or transmitted,
in any form or by any means without the prior written
permission of the publisher, nor be otherwise circulated
in any form of binding or cover other than that in which
it is published and without a similar condition being
imposed on the subsequent purchaser.

A CIP catalogue record for this title is available
from the British Library

ISBN 0 340 72165 0

Typeset by Avon Dataset Ltd, Bidford-on-Avon, Warks

Printed and bound in Great Britain by
Clays Ltd, St Ives plc

Hodder and Stoughton
A division of Hodder Headline PLC
338 Euston Road
London NW1 3BH

In memory of

Paul and Jean Guinness
who made me feel part of the family

As they would say: Backward look and forward march.

Contents

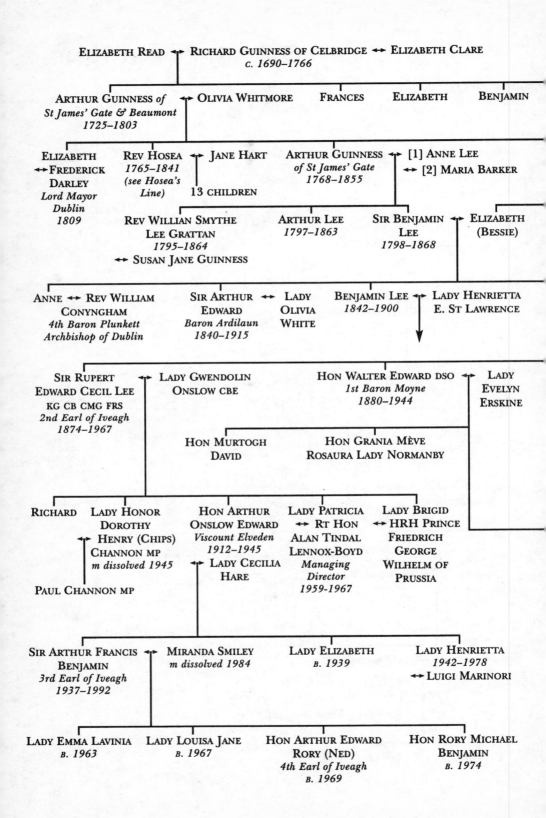

ELIZABETH READ ↔ RICHARD GUINNESS OF CELBRIDGE ↔ ELIZABETH CLARE
c. 1690–1766

ARTHUR GUINNESS *of* ↔ OLIVIA WHITMORE   FRANCES   ELIZABETH   BENJAMIN
St James' Gate & Beaumont
1725–1803

ELIZABETH   REV HOSEA ↔ JANE HART   ARTHUR GUINNESS ↔ [1] ANNE LEE
↔ FREDERICK   *1765–1841*   *of St James' Gate* ↔ [2] MARIA BARKER
DARLEY   *(see Hosea's*   *1768–1855*
Lord Mayor   *Line)*   13 CHILDREN
Dublin
1809   REV WILLIAN SMYTHE   ARTHUR LEE   SIR BENJAMIN ↔ ELIZABETH
                LEE GRATTAN   *1797–1863*   LEE   (BESSIE)
                1795–1864   *1798–1868*
                ↔ SUSAN JANE GUINNESS

ANNE ↔ REV WILLIAM   SIR ARTHUR ↔ LADY   BENJAMIN LEE ↔ LADY HENRIETTA
CONYNGHAM   EDWARD   OLIVIA   *1842–1900*   E. ST LAWRENCE
4th Baron Plunkett   *Baron Ardilaun* WHITE
Archbishop of Dublin   *1840–1915*

SIR RUPERT ↔ LADY GWENDOLIN   HON WALTER EDWARD DSO ↔ LADY
EDWARD CECIL LEE ONSLOW CBE   *1st Baron Moyne*   EVELYN
KG CB CMG FRS   *1880–1944*   ERSKINE
2nd Earl of Iveagh
1874–1967
                    HON MURTOGH   HON GRANIA MÈVE
                    DAVID   ROSAURA LADY NORMANBY

RICHARD LADY HONOR   HON ARTHUR   LADY PATRICIA   LADY BRIGID
         DOROTHY   ONSLOW EDWARD   ↔ RT HON   ↔ HRH PRINCE
      ↔ HENRY (CHIPS)   *Viscount Elveden* ALAN TINDAL   FRIEDRICH
         CHANNON MP   *1912–1945*   LENNOX-BOYD   GEORGE
         m dissolved 1945 ↔ LADY CECILIA *Managing*   WILHELM OF
                            HARE   *Director*   PRUSSIA
PAUL CHANNON MP   *1959-1967*

SIR ARTHUR FRANCIS ↔ MIRANDA SMILEY   LADY ELIZABETH   LADY HENRIETTA
BENJAMIN   *m dissolved 1984*   B. 1939   *1942–1978*
3rd Earl of Iveagh   ↔ LUIGI MARINORI
1937–1992

LADY EMMA LAVINIA   LADY LOUISA JANE   HON ARTHUR EDWARD   HON RORY MICHAEL
B. 1963   B. 1967   RORY (NED)   BENJAMIN
                                       4th Earl of Iveagh B. 1974
                                       B. 1969

THE BREWING LINE

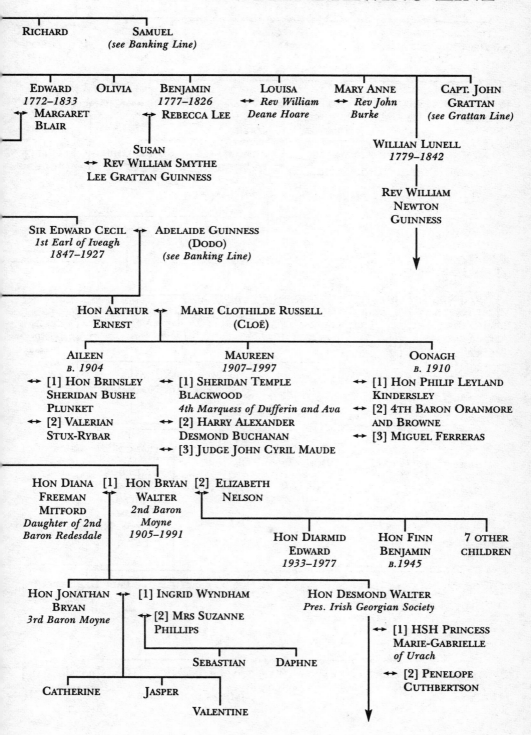

RICHARD   SAMUEL
(see Banking Line)

EDWARD
1772–1833
↔ MARGARET
BLAIR

OLIVIA

BENJAMIN
1777–1826
↔ REBECCA LEE

LOUISA
↔ *Rev William
Deane Hoare*

MARY ANNE
↔ *Rev John
Burke*

CAPT. JOHN
GRATTAN
(see Grattan Line)

SUSAN
↔ REV WILLIAM SMYTHE
LEE GRATTAN GUINNESS

WILLIAN LUNELL
1779–1842

REV WILLIAM
NEWTON
GUINNESS

SIR EDWARD CECIL
*1st Earl of Iveagh
1847–1927*
↔ ADELAIDE GUINNESS
(DODO)
(see Banking Line)

HON ARTHUR
ERNEST
↔ MARIE CLOTHILDE RUSSELL
(CLOË)

AILEEN
B. 1904
↔ [1] HON BRINSLEY
SHERIDAN BUSHE
PLUNKET
↔ [2] VALERIAN
STUX-RYBAR

MAUREEN
1907–1997
↔ [1] SHERIDAN TEMPLE
BLACKWOOD
4th Marquess of Dufferin and Ava
↔ [2] HARRY ALEXANDER
DESMOND BUCHANAN
↔ [3] JUDGE JOHN CYRIL MAUDE

OONAGH
B. 1910
↔ [1] HON PHILIP LEYLAND
KINDERSLEY
↔ [2] 4TH BARON ORANMORE
AND BROWNE
↔ [3] MIGUEL FERRERAS

HON DIANA
FREEMAN
MITFORD
*Daughter of 2nd
Baron Redesdale*

[1]

HON BRYAN
WALTER
*2nd Baron
Moyne
1905–1991*

[2] ELIZABETH
NELSON

HON DIARMID
EDWARD
1933–1977

HON FINN
BENJAMIN
B.1945

7 OTHER
CHILDREN

HON JONATHAN
BRYAN
3rd Baron Moyne
↔ [1] INGRID WYNDHAM
↦ [2] MRS SUZANNE
PHILLIPS

HON DESMOND WALTER
Pres. Irish Georgian Society
↔ [1] HSH PRINCESS
MARIE-GABRIELLE
of Urach
↔ [2] PENELOPE
CUTHBERTSON

SEBASTIAN   DAPHNE

CATHERINE   JASPER

VALENTINE

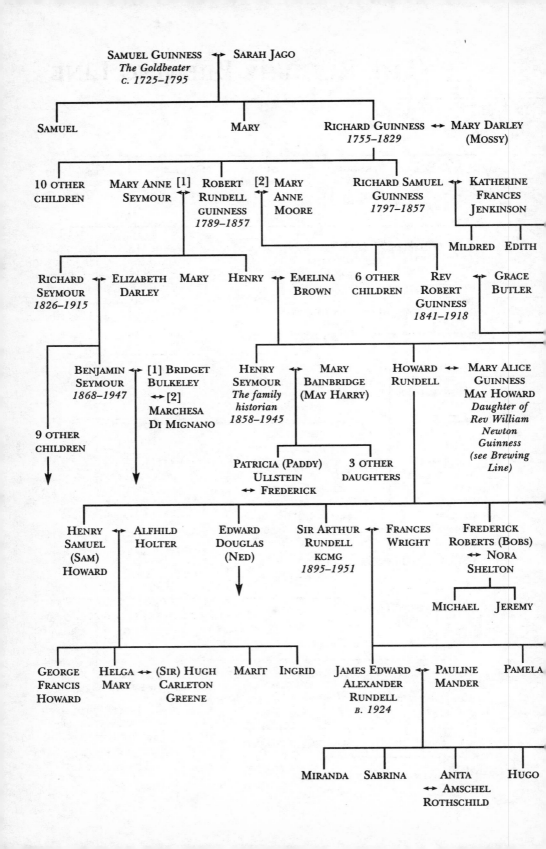

The Rundell Banking Line

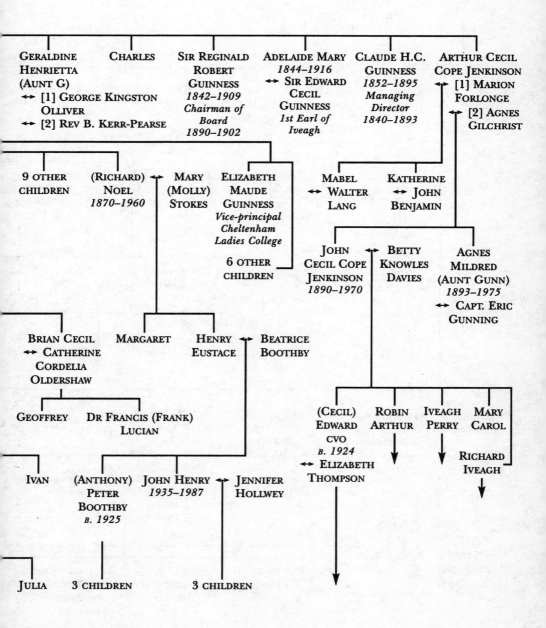

Geraldine Henrietta (Aunt G)
↔ [1] George Kingston Olliver
↔ [2] Rev B. Kerr-Pearse

Charles

Sir Reginald Robert Guinness *1842–1909 Chairman of Board 1890–1902*

Adelaide Mary *1844–1916* ↔ **Sir Edward Cecil Guinness** *1st Earl of Iveagh*

Claude H.C. Guinness *1852–1895 Managing Director 1840–1893*

Arthur Cecil Cope Jenkinson ↔ [1] **Marion Forlonge** ↔ [2] **Agnes Gilchrist**

9 Other Children

(Richard) Noel *1870–1960* ↔ **Mary (Molly) Stokes**

Elizabeth Maude Guinness *Vice-principal Cheltenham Ladies College*

6 Other Children

Mabel ↔ **Walter Lang**

Katherine ↔ **John Benjamin**

John Cecil Cope Jenkinson *1890–1970* ↔ **Betty Knowles Davies**

Agnes Mildred (Aunt Gunn) *1893–1975* ↔ **Capt. Eric Gunning**

Brian Cecil ↔ **Catherine Cordelia Oldershaw**

Margaret

Henry Eustace ↔ **Beatrice Boothby**

Geoffrey

Dr Francis (Frank) Lucian

(Cecil) Edward CVO *b. 1924* ↔ **Elizabeth Thompson**

Robin Arthur

Iveagh Perry

Mary Carol

Richard Iveagh

Ivan

(Anthony) Peter Boothby *b. 1925*

John Henry *1935–1987* ↔ **Jennifer Hollwey**

Julia

3 Children

3 Children

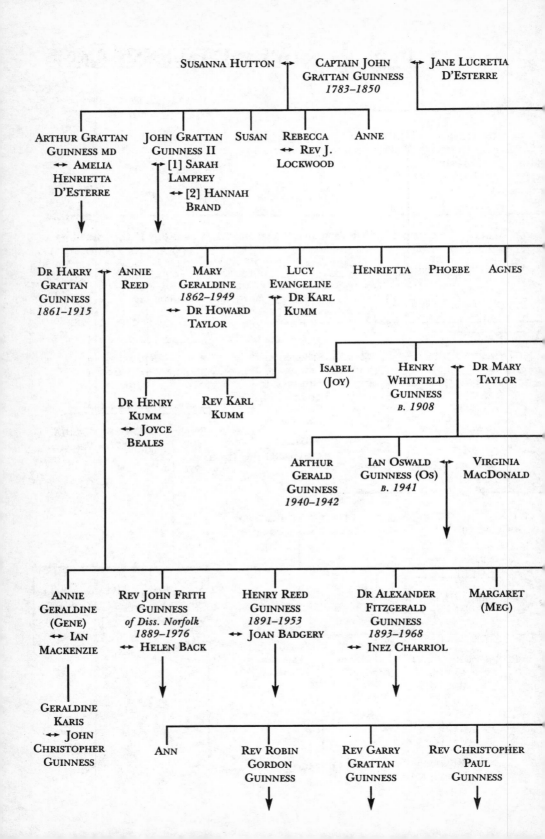

THE GRATTAN LINE

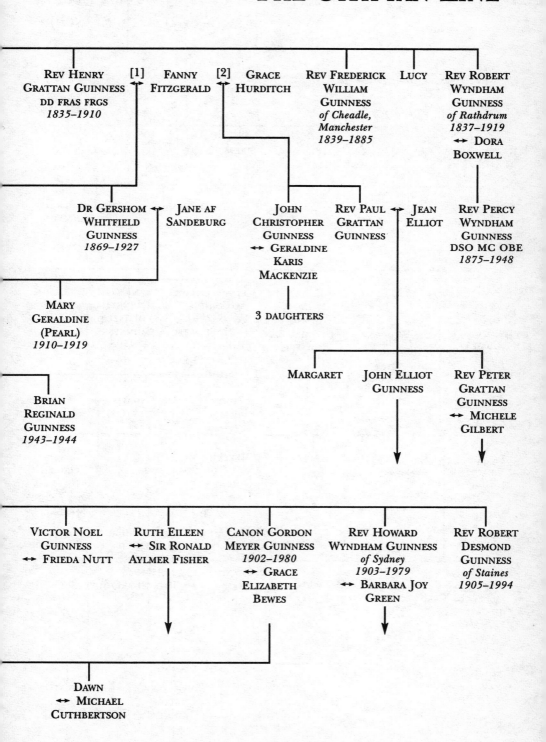

HOSEA'S LINE
(NEW ZEALAND BRANCH)

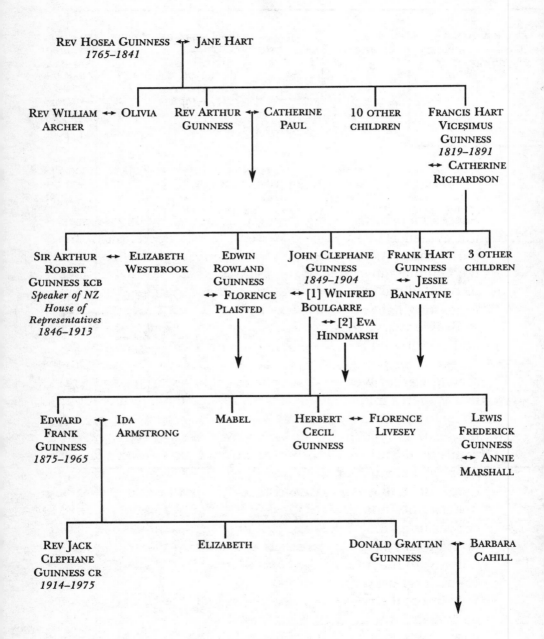

REV HOSEA GUINNESS ↔ JANE HART
1765–1841

REV WILLIAM ↔ OLIVIA   REV ARTHUR ↔ CATHERINE   10 OTHER   FRANCIS HART
ARCHER   GUINNESS   PAUL   CHILDREN   VICESIMUS
                                                            GUINNESS
                                                            1819–1891
                                                            ↔ CATHERINE
                                                            RICHARDSON

SIR ARTHUR ↔ ELIZABETH   EDWIN   JOHN CLEPHANE   FRANK HART   3 OTHER
ROBERT   WESTBROOK   ROWLAND   GUINNESS   GUINNESS   CHILDREN
GUINNESS KCB   GUINNESS   1849–1904   ↔ JESSIE
Speaker of NZ   ↔ FLORENCE ↔ [1] WINIFRED   BANNATYNE
House of   PLAISTED   BOULGARRE
Representatives   ↔ [2] EVA
1846–1913   HINDMARSH

EDWARD ↔ IDA   MABEL   HERBERT ↔ FLORENCE   LEWIS
FRANK   ARMSTRONG   CECIL   LIVESEY   FREDERICK
GUINNESS   GUINNESS   GUINNESS
1875–1965   ↔ ANNIE
                                                      MARSHALL

REV JACK   ELIZABETH   DONALD GRATTAN ↔ BARBARA
CLEPHANE   GUINNESS   CAHILL
GUINNESS CR
1914–1975

Acknowledgments

Successful detective work requires the testimony of witnesses, the evidence of eavesdroppers and the co-operation of the participants. As I scoured the country for clues to help unravel the Guinness mystique, many people either kept me on track or pointed me in a new direction, and I am indebted to them for casting light along the way.

Twelve years ago, when I first began my research, the writer and historian Piers Brendon allowed a complete stranger access to his home and to his book on Rupert Guinness, the second Earl of Iveagh, despite his own bitter disappointment that Rupert's immediate family would not agree to the public circulation of the fruits of his hard work, insisting on private publication. When, to my dismay, I discovered that the archives at Park Royal were empty, the files on the family missing, he came to my rescue and allowed me to use the notes he had made from Farmleigh manuscripts. Those manuscripts, and indeed, most of the family archive material concerning the brewing side of the family, are still mysteriously missing, vanished into thin air. Piers Brendon's notes, with the insights they provide, are now invaluable, and I remain grateful for his help.

Many of the people who helped me all those years ago are no longer with us: Rev. Desmond Guinness of Staines who wrote me a long account of his childhood; Dr Henry Kumm of Pennsylvania who shared his recollections of his parents; Jim Broomhall, archivist of the China Inland Mission, who sent me every reference he could find to Henry and Fanny Guinness from what he affectionately called 'Hudson Taylor's Bones'. But many new protagonists in the drama have emerged to take their place: Henry Kumm's daughter, Joey Alexander, who kindly photocopied a mass of Lucy Guinness's love letters to Karl Kumm, kept in a trunk in the family home at Chocorua, New Hampshire; Christof Sauer, a German pastor preparing a doctorate on the Guinnesses and faith missions, who spent a weekend in our home to continue his own research and ended up filling in all the gaps in my knowledge, particularly of African geography. I am immensely grateful that Karl Kumm III dared to entrust his grandmother's precious diaries to the postal service and an unknown cousin across the Atlantic, and that yet another unknown cousin, Stewart Darley Ogilby, sent me a photocopy of an invaluable diary, having traced me with dogged determination through the Web.

I have particularly enjoyed meeting several doughty Guinness women whose memories and anecdotes have provided a thoroughly enjoyable, entertaining lunchtime, teatime or supper, as they opened up new areas of Guinness family life hitherto unknown to me: Jennifer Martin, Mary Graham and Paddy Ullstein, daughter of Henry Seymour Guinness who compiled the first family tree, and her daughter-in-law, Pam. At ninety Paddy's brain is still a computer file on the Guinness family. She is her father's daughter. Genetics are a powerful force in a powerful family.

Which brings me finally to Edward Guinness, whose devoted service to the Brewery, when combined with that of his godfather, the Honourable Ernest Guinness, spans almost a hundred years. Though, strictly speaking, descended from the banking side of the family, yet linked to the brewers by the marriage of his great aunt 'Dodo' to the first Earl of Iveagh,

Acknowledgments

he was the last executive family member to serve on the
Board. There is nothing about the last fifty years of the
Brewery he does not know. I am immensely grateful to him
and his wife Elizabeth who have taken me in and treated me
as family, Elizabeth cooking, washing up and retiring alone –
all uncomplainingly – while Edward and I talked Guinness
into the small hours of the morning! Edward provided the
photographs of the family portraits, countless anecdotes and
insights, and vital contacts. Every request was always treated
with graciousness and courtesy. I have been inspired by his
wholehearted, though not uncritical, admiration for his family
– in its broadest sense. With his warmth and generosity of
spirit he typifies all that is best in Guinness, and, knowing
him, I doubt there is any compliment he would prefer.

Introduction

I was walking down O'Connell Street in Dublin, enjoying an hour of therapeutic shopping before speaking at a Women's Luncheon Club, when the strap on my sandal snapped. They were the only pair of shoes I had with me, and my meagre resources in those early-married days could not possibly rise to a new pair. My hostess, an American missionary, shared my state of impecuniosity and we rushed into the first shoe-repair shop we could find.

'Could you repair them for me now?' I asked, urgently. 'I have nothing else to wear.'

The assistant shook her head impassively, unmoved by my predicament, or any other emergency which might cross her path that day. Time has no meaning in Ireland.

'There's a long waiting list. Sure, it'll take two days.'

'Two days!' I expostulated. 'It only needs a stitch.'

There was still no response and I would have marched out of the shop with my head in the air, were it not for the fact that you cannot go far – let alone with dignity – wearing only one shoe, a fact which appeared to dawn upon the young woman gradually, as she observed with some surprise that I was still standing, or rather, perching on one leg, on the other side of the counter.

'Name?' she asked suddenly.

'Guinness,' I said.

1

There was a moment's silence, and, when she lifted her head, a perceptible change of expression on her face.

'Your shoe will be ready in five minutes, Mrs Guinness,' she whispered deferentially. And it was.

My companion was awe-struck.

'Oh gee,' she gasped, as we walked back out into the street, 'it's just like being with one of the Kennedys in New York.'

I felt slightly punch-drunk. My name had never had that effect before. Admittedly, when my husband, Peter and I got engaged and he handed me a copy of his pedigree, I was duly impressed. Not many girls are given an official, published family tree, containing three peerages, two baronetcies, and a heavy smattering of royalty – foreign admittedly. It was heady stuff for the granddaughter of working-class Jewish immigrants. But though the *Daily Express* claimed in 1969 that 'all the members of the world-famous Guinness family are reputed to be worth a fortune in the region of £200 million', I had never seen any of it. Great-great-grandson of Arthur Guinness, founder of the Brewery, Peter may well have been, but he was a comprehensive schoolteacher in Stockport when I married him, a fact not lost on my father. When I tried to soften the blow of marrying out of the faith by telling him he would have his place in the Guinness family tree, where I would be described as 'daughter of', he replied, 'And did you have to pick one of the poor members of the family?'

During the early years of our marriage, in the evangelical church circles in which we moved, I discovered, to my surprise, a certain prestige attached to the name even of those 'poor relatives', pronounced Guin-ness, with the emphasis on the 'ness', to dissociate it from its other, less acceptable spiritual connections. This kudos stemmed from the long involvement of the Grattan line of the family in church and missionary enterprise. At conferences I was forever being asked how my husband was related to Canon Gordon Guinness, Howard Guinness of the Inter-Varsity Fellowship, or Desmond, ex-Vicar of Staines, or other clergy like Robin, Garry and Chris, or Os Guinness, the theological writer – so much so, I threatened to pin a copy of the family tree to my back.

But a sense of belonging to the wider clan was reserved for that moment in the Dublin shoe repair shop. In Dublin the name is inescapable, emblazoned on illuminated clocks and signs. Statues of Guinness benefactors look proudly down on the buildings, parks and cathedral so bounteously bestowed upon the people. Pilgrims pour in to St James' Gate, and are poured a mystical pint as part of 'The Guinness Experience'. The name, the firm, the family, are deeply embedded in the history of the city, and I felt as if I had come home. For the first time I understood something of my husband's pride in his heritage.

Since then, in time-honoured tradition, not only in the Grattan line of the family, Peter became a clergyman, one of more than twenty in the family, as well as the other twenty or so acquired by marriage. But the family pride, resting on its reputation for uprightness and honesty, generosity and philanthropy, has been severely tested by an apparently endless stream of scandals and tragedy. In fact there were so many bizarre Guinness deaths in the 1970s and 1980s, that my parents began to wonder if their son-in-law had been watching the film *Kind Hearts and Coronets* on the television, and was making a bid for a peerage by removing the obstacles one by one.

Scandal is the twentieth-century term for the skeletons our forebears hid in the cupboard, and the Guinnesses, like any dynasty, have had their fair share from the moment the first Arthur went forth into Dublin and multiplied. Procreating was a more hazardous business than brewing beer. Three of his grandchildren became alcoholics. Two more ended up in mental institutions. Some were reduced to insolvency and begging. *Guinnessty* would make a more exciting, if less

3

credible soap opera than any shown on television. Truth always provides a better story than fiction.

Much has been made of a possible Guinness curse. 'The love of money', says the Bible, 'is the root of all evil.' For some members of the family, wealth was undoubtedly a curse for it destroyed the impetus to survive. Others used it wisely and well. According to the Old Testament the children of Israel's survival depended on the choices they made between life or death, blessing or curse. 'Therefore choose life, that you and your descendants may live.' The sins of the fathers could be visited on successive generations. The early Guinness patriarchs made decisive moral choices, guided by their Christian faith. Then the struggle between God and mammon began to take its toll – though who served which is not always very clear. Some of the business Guinnesses have been devout, some of the clergy very worldly.

And the tribe multiplied and spread unto the ends of the earth, so much so that updating the family tree, let alone writing a biography, is a logistic nightmare. Difficult decisions have had to be made to avoid writing a magnum opus of *The Rise and Fall of the Roman Empire* proportions, while maintaining a sense of Hollywood epic. I have therefore chosen to focus on one branch – the Grattan line – revolving the story of their brewing and banking cousins around their extraordinary hair-raising missionary adventures. The determination which earned their brewing relatives their millions was alive and well in the Grattan line – though serving another kind of spirit. In 1880 few ordinary people in England would have heard of Lord Iveagh, owner of the Guinness brewery. Everyone would have heard of Henry Grattan Guinness, the legendary preacher, whose influence was more extensive than Guinness beer imports, the catalyst for most major faith missionary societies, Barnardo's Homes, the World Council of Churches, A. B. Simpson and New York Bible College, the Moody Bible College, to name but a few.

The discovery of the raw material was in itself the stuff of storybooks. On honeymoon in Ibiza in my parents-in-law's retirement home, I wandered up to my father-in-law's rooftop study during siesta hour when all the house was quiet, and idly began to explore his bookshelves, looking for something to read. An old, musty-scented biography caught my attention. I took it down – and was still sitting on the floor several hours later when Peter came to find out where I was. 'I had no idea of the risks your relatives took,' I said to him. 'Why does no one read these books today?'

As I enthused over dinner, my father-in-law mentioned in passing a trunk in his study cupboard, 'full of bits and pieces', he said with a dismissive wave of the hand, poems, letters, the memorabilia his mother had collected over the years. He wasn't sure what was in it. He had never been terribly interested. She was a great hoarder.

I rushed to the top of the house as soon as the meal was over, heaved a large, antique trunk out of the study cupboard, prised it open and could hardly believe what I saw. It was stuffed to the brim with papers, withered with age and the drying effects of the heat. There were letters dating back to the eighteenth century, some in packs tied up with ribbons, newspaper cuttings from as early as 1815, volumes of poetry, postcards, diaries and notebooks. Grandmother Gracie had married Peter's grandfather, the famous preacher, Henry Grattan Guinness, in 1903, when she was twenty-six, and he was sixty-seven. They had two sons and a mere seven years together before his death. Everything in her possession relating to her marriage and her husband's family history had been carefully preserved – as if she knew that one day someone would recognise their importance.

I knew then, in 1975, that I would write their story. Had I known the work involved, I might have thought again. In the last few years a vast amount of new material has come to light – another trunkful of letters discovered in Chocorua, New

Hampshire, providing fresh insights into the relationship between Lucy Guinness and Karl Kumm; a diary in the USA written in 1840, describing a visit to Uncle Arthur at the brewery, giving the only real glimpse into how the family related to each other in those days; mounds of correspondence from countless Guinness relatives and friends, clarifying certain mysteries, opening up many more; new research, largely in Germany, into nineteenth-century faith missions. Two peers have died, a whole generation of familiar Guinnesses has gone and the name has lost some of its lustre in the aftermath of events surrounding the Distillers' takeover.

Contrary to the impression conveyed by newspapers, the Guinness story consists of much more than brewing. Brewing is hardly the most fascinating subject in the world. And though some would disagree, it is not as life-enhancing as brain surgery, or even proper waste disposal. But away from the brewing centre, on the dynastic fringes are a host of fascinating characters reflecting the quintessential Irish Guinness charm. And of course, there are the wives – Bessie, Jane Lucretia, Fanny, Dodo, Lady Ardilaun (no one ever called her Olive), Gwenny, Annie and Grace, exceptional spouses whose relationship with the leading men turn them into flesh and blood. While they give us the facts, men don't always record what they felt. Their women fill in the gaps, and weave many of the coloured threads through the story. But then, being a Guinness wife myself, I would say that.

Prologue

December 1, 1986 was a cold and grey winter day in the capital, on the face of it, indistinguishable from any other. Events, however, at the Guinness offices at 39 Portman Square, and the subsequent scandal unleashed upon the City, were to mark it out for ever in the annals of financial history. It was the day officials from the Department of Trade and Industry entered the premises and initiated a major investigation into one of the United Kingdom's most well-known companies, a family firm renowned for its exemplary attitude to its employees, for public-spirited munificence, and for its hitherto impeccable reputation.

The Guinnesses were supposedly 'almost oriental' about losing face. 'They would do anything rather than admit to another member of the family that they had made a mistake,' said Sally Brompton in the *Daily Mail* in 1978. 'And while they will be relieved when someone else takes the responsibility from them, if they find the most minute indiscretion – such as a mistake in the milk bill – they hit the roof.' This was a great deal more than a mistake in the milk bill. Certain irregularities had appeared in transactions leading up to the takeover of Distillers' Scotch whisky earlier in 1986.

Staff entering the building discovered DTI inspectors had placed a chair across the door to the office belonging to the Finance Director, Olivier Roux. In their search for vital documents, no one, it seems, thought to seal off the office belonging to the Chief Executive, Ernest Saunders. There was ample opportunity to shred evidence.[1]

Saunders, Chief Executive of Guinness since 1981, Chairman for a few months, did not seem unduly concerned. He appeared that evening, relaxed and genial, for a typical act of Guinness benevolence – the presentation of Raeburn's painting of a *Colonel in the Highland Regiment,* to the National Portrait Gallery. It had been hanging, largely unnoticed, for many years in a distillers' regional district office, but now took its place in the newly built, domed Rothschild extension at a glittering reception attended by Leo Rothschild himself and at least one distinguished member of the Cabinet.

At a Board meeting the following morning the auditors, Price Waterhouse, stated that at that stage of their audit there appeared no undue cause for alarm and Saunders left for a business trip in the USA. On the face of it, despite the unwelcome intrusion, all was well. Share prices from Tokyo and the USA at the end of the month were expected to show a record high. Nothing prepared Board members for what was to come. Perhaps it was simply too terrible to contemplate.

Edward Guinness was the last remaining executive family member on the Board. Descended from a junior branch of the family, rather than one of the peerages, he had worked his way up from apprentice brewer to Director of Public Affairs. Loved by the old employees, respected by his business colleagues, a committed charity fund-raiser and member of his local church, Edward had been with Guinness for over forty years, had chaired the powerful Brewers' Society, exemplified old Christian ethical values, and was referred to by Saunders with a mixture of affection and irritation as 'the company conscience'.

'What do you make of all this?' Saunders asked him, the day before Christmas Eve over lunch at the Inn on the Park Hotel, after one of the almost daily briefing meetings. As the days passed nerves were beginning to fray, the façade of calm was slowly crumbling. Journalists sniffed and snapped like wolfhounds at the heels of every Guinness director. Pressure mounted. With his secretary Margaret McGrath handling the press invasion of Portman Square, Saunders and his wife had taken a suite at the hotel. It began to resemble Hitler's bunker in Berlin.

'My one concern is for the integrity of the company,' Edward replied.

'You may find that in their concern for the company one or two people have been a little over-zealous in the execution of their duties.'[2]

'Has this compromised us?' Edward asked, seriously alarmed.

'No, no, of course not,' Saunders reassured him, and left shortly afterwards for a skiing holiday in Switzerland, which was uncharacteristic of him, as on a number of previous occasions he had cut short his holiday if he felt Guinness interests were threatened.

By Monday 5 January there was no longer any doubt in the City that the company was seriously compromised. Members of the Board returned to work after a troubled Christmas break to receive a copy of a letter written by Olivier Roux containing disturbing information about Guinness dealings in the acquisition of Distillers. The thirty-five-year-old French accountant, recruited by Saunders from Bain and Company, the expensive US management consultancy, appeared to have succumbed to the strain. 'Roux's gone off his head,' Saunders told his colleagues. Edward Guinness, like the other Board members, appointed before the Distillers' takeover, wanted to believe in Saunders's innocence. He had saved the company at a very precarious time, increased its profitability beyond imagining, ensured its continued success. They felt they owed him considerable loyalty.

Norman MacFarlane, however, one of five new Board

members appointed after the Distillers' takeover, felt no such allegiance, and insisted on a meeting of the full Board the next afternoon at the offices of Sir David Napley, the company solicitors, near Covent Garden.

As it happened, Edward had booked seats for his wife and two guests for an evening at the ballet. Instead, he found himself playing a part in a traumatic, real-life piece of drama. Macfarlane challenged Saunders about Roux's letter and demanded to know if there was any truth in it. When Saunders persisted in maintaining his unawareness of the transactions Roux described, Macfarlane told him Roux was in the next room, and asked if Saunders was prepared to let him come in. As Roux materialised Edward felt he was participating in some kind of ghastly fantasy. By the time he took his seat at the *Nutcracker* he had missed the first two acts, and the third passed before his eyes because of the shock of what he had just experienced.

On Thursday 8 January Howard Hughes of Price Waterhouse rang the Park Royal Brewery to express his concern that Benjamin Guinness, the third Lord Iveagh and President of the company, was ill yet again and unable to take any leadership role. 'It's essential', he told Edward, 'that at least one member of the Guinness family understands the issues at stake.' He refused to explain them over the phone and arranged to meet Edward that evening. It was a long and worrying meeting. Further work on the audit had shown Price Waterhouse that they could no longer be as sanguine about the company's affairs.

Friday 9 January was a day to end all days, as the nightmare sequence of events rattled disjointedly but irrevocably on towards their inevitable climax. In the morning all the directors were handed instructions from a firm of independent solicitors on their duties to the shareholders in a crisis such as this. Edward read his in the car on his way back to Park Royal and the enormity of the responsibility compounded the terrible conflict growing inside him. By the time he reached the Brewery it was no surprise to find a summons back to London waiting for him, to a meeting at Lazards, the merchant bankers.

It was here that the decision was finally taken to ask Saunders to stand aside so that a proper investigation could be undertaken. But who should relay that information to Saunders? He had always claimed that if he were toppled, his four loyal, long-standing executive directors would resign *en bloc*. There was effectively no choice. They were the ones to perform the deed. And since Edward was the most senior in terms of long service, he was delegated to take the lead.

Later, in court, he described the encounter as 'loathsome', so awful he would feel the cold sweat on his back and the nauseous sensation in the pit of his stomach whenever he thought about it for years to come. Conflicting loyalties made it highly emotional. Saunders insisted on bringing in members of his family. As far as he was concerned he was 'suspended pending investigation', therefore entitled to full pay. He fully anticipated being back at work before long, though it was made clear to him that this would have to be ratified by the full Board. And circumstances were to change within days. There was a farewell drink in the bar. Everyone tried to maintain some pretence of normality, but the four directors could hardly hold up under the strain and were longing for the chance to escape. Carole Saunders was obviously distressed, which upset Edward greatly. He had always had a high regard for her.

'The company conscience,' Saunders said to him again reassuringly.

'How can a conscience operate, when it doesn't know what's going on?' Edward replied sadly.

'It hurt,' Edward said quite simply, recalling that evening during the trial. Had forty-one years of loyal service come to this – to be forced to ask the Chief Executive to stand down, a man who inspired admiration and should have commanded absolute respect? It was the most terrible thing he ever had to do, a reversal of the natural business order. It seemed to Edward that evening that everything he worked for and stood for – the good name of the company, its august history, its credibility as a caring family business – was in considerable jeopardy.

Furthermore, since Saunders was Chairman and Chief Executive, the company was without a leader, a ship without a captain in a merciless storm. Where did authority and direction now lie? Who should take the initiative in informing the staff and preparing a statement for the press? It was a frightening position to be in. Something had to be done, and quickly.

On Sunday, at a meeting attended by a weak and frail Benjamin Guinness, who had flown in specially from Dublin, Norman MacFarlane was appointed Chairman. From that moment the investigation spiralled like a whirlwind, dragging in its wake some of the most powerful names in the City, threatening London's financial reputation and the integrity of the government itself. On Monday 12 January, following a report by Price Waterhouse confirming the contents of his letter about irregularities in the Distillers' takeover, Roux resigned. On Tuesday, in a damage limitation exercise, Morgan Grenfell, Guinness's advisors during the takeover, formed a committee of directors to look at ways of improving its management controls. On Wednesday it emerged that Bank Leu of Zurich, chaired by Saunders's former boss, Arthur Fuerer, was involved in £100 million of Guinness share-buying during the Distillers bid as part of a £200 million support operation. Saunders was officially fired without pay or compensation, and on Thursday, an embarrassed Prime Minister, Margaret Thatcher, hinted at the possibility of introducing statutory control in the City. The involvement of business magnates, Ronson and Jack Lyons, emerged gradually in subsequent days and was a complete revelation to members of the Board.

While Saunders disappeared into a private clinic suffering from stress, the executive directors were left to cope with their personal trauma and help the new Chairman try and pick up the pieces. At a meeting at Park Royal the following Monday, several of them publicly affirmed their personal commitment to the company and their faith in its future. That Guinness lost none of its most gifted senior directors at a time when headhunters smelt blood, is a tribute to their success. Edward said later, 'When I joined the company as a young man, the senior members of the family, Rupert and Ernest, had impressed upon me more than anything else the importance of integrity. Now, in the eyes of the world, it was in tatters. Yet I never ceased to believe that the situation must somehow be redeemable.'

The other, non-executive members of the Guinness family were equally distressed, though the press was quick to point out the immense financial benefits they had gained from the Distillers takeover, and criticised them for not taking a stronger hand. But their shareholding had been reduced from 22 per cent to 4.5 per cent and that whittling away of family power meant they could no longer exert any real influence. In the context of Guinness money, a few more millions made very little difference, while the loss of power and ownership did. Bryan Guinness, the second Lord Moyne, a previous vice-chairman, had always spoken out against any involvement with spirits, holding, like a prophet of doom, with an almost superstitious tenacity to the ancient legend which claimed that the first Arthur Guinness had created his brew with the express purpose of combating the negative effects of spirit-drinking in Ireland. Destroying the sacred cow was bound to reap its own rewards.

Saunders was finally arrested in March 1987, on charges relating to insider dealing, encouraging people to buy shares

in order to force up the market artificially, promising remuneration in the case of any losses sustained. His trial was
one of the lengthiest, most complicated and most costly in
history. Witnesses like Edward Guinness were in the box for
up to five hours, analysing moment by painful moment the
nature of their professional relationship with their erstwhile
boss and colleague. Defended by the barrister who sub-
sequently defended the mass murderess, Rosemary West,
Saunders was finally found guilty and sent to prison, then
released ten months into a thirty-month sentence on the
grounds of ill health and frailty, to take up a successful and
remunerative career as a management consultant.

And while the nation shook its head in disbelief, Arthur
Guinness of Dublin, brewer of distinction, stalwart of the
church, who in 1759 created the thick, black liquid – now
consumed worldwide in seven and a half million pint glasses
every twenty-four hours – was probably turning in his grave.

Chapter 1

1759–1803

Arthur the First, Founder of a Dynasty

1.

He was laid to rest on 23 January 1803, aged seventy-eight, a merchant of considerable means, owner of the largest brewery in Dublin. It was a dignified occasion, befitting such a respectable, public-minded citizen. This was a very satisfactory end for a man who had started life as a servant with £100 in his pocket.

The bier, draped in crimson and bearing the familiar crest of the Magennis family, was escorted by the carriages of the wealthy city burghers from Beaumont, his elegant white Georgian country house set in extensive grounds overlooking the north side of Dublin Bay. On a clear summer day the Welsh hills rise majestically from the horizon on the other side of the bay. In winter the churning Irish Sea merges with the grey of the sky, releasing a damp fret which hangs over the city as a dense, clammy mist. Brewery employees venturing out to show their last, silent respect, the men in rough shirts, their women huddling in woven shawls, would have found it hard to keep the chill from penetrating their bodies and their bones.

The procession made its way to the parish church of

15

Oughterard in County Kildare, several miles west of the city, where the brewer was buried next to his mother, Elizabeth Read. This was a strange last wish, for in his lifetime he never referred to his past, never spoke of his ancestors, not even to his children. He was as much of an enigma the day he died as the day he arrived in Dublin intent on making his fortune.

Yet he chose to be buried in the rich country soil where he was born, long before he acquired wealth, distinction and an aura of respectability, before there were sons to run the Brewery, take the funeral service, defend the country, before the prominent Dublin middle classes like the Darleys, Smythes and La Touches would have deigned to share his company, let alone attend his departure.

These were clergy, builders, bankers, members of some of Dublin's long-standing, well-to-do Protestant families, close relatives of the grieving widow. Even those who disliked his views, too liberal for some, too narrow-minded for others, could not question Arthur Guinness's standing. Whatever his birthright, he had done well for himself, taken a prominent part in public affairs, married heiress Olivia Whitmore, who brought him the prestige and society of her illustrious cousin, Henry Grattan, Ireland's greatest orator and foremost politician. If he was not quite well bred enough to mix with the Anglo-Irish aristocracy who danced to the tune of the English Viceroy, garrisoned safely in Dublin Castle, then neither were they. He at least was purveyor of the Castle beer.

Brewing was becoming an increasingly respectable trade. So when Arthur Guinness quietly adopted the coat of arms of the Magennises of County Down, one of Ireland's oldest and most powerful Catholic clans, the hereditary earls of Iveagh, no one questioned his right to do so. At his wedding the Whitmores presented him with a silver cup engraved with the Magennis crest, a right hand and a lion, superimposed upon their own. How and when his name became Guinness and he a Protestant, no one knew for sure.

Gossip, of course, filtered from the country to the city, whispered by one Dublin worker to another, elaborated as it travelled. Breaking her parents' hearts, Elizabeth Read had eloped with the family groom, a Richard Guinness of Celbridge. After their marriage he became agent and receiver to the Reverend Dr Price, Vicar of Celbridge, a happy appointment in the light of his employer's subsequent preferment to Archbishop of Cashel. By birth or choice, Richard Guinness was manifestly a Protestant. He may have been descended from the Magennis tribe, but locals in Celbridge, where the vicar built his residence, Oakley Park, preferred their own story, that he was the illegitimate son of a country girl and an English soldier called Gennys left behind in 1690 after the Battle of the Boyne. The girl, they said, left her bastard son to be raised at the foundling hospital in Leixlip. The rumours were never substantiated and rent collectors are notoriously unpopular. Richard Guinness was, however, born sometime around 1690.[1]

One hundred and fifty or so years later, a La Touche, blind drunk in a Dublin bar, holes in the elbows of his jacket, and in the souls of the shoes stretched out on the chair in front of him, held up a pint of Guinness and declared, 'My ancestor's butler was responsible for this.'[2] Arthur Guinness was never a butler. Nor did he serve the La Touches. From sour grapes a bitter harvest of misinformation was born.

What is known is that when the old Archbishop of Cashel died in 1752 he left £100 to his faithful retainer, Richard Guinness, whose delicious home-made black brew had made the old ecclesiastic a favourite host with the local gentry. Richard became proprietor of the Bear and Ragged Staff in Celbridge, and established its reputation as a popular coaching stop.

As for twenty-seven-year-old Arthur, the Archbishop also left £100 to 'my servant Arthur Guinness, his son', little knowing what would sprout from such a small bequest.

17

Richard Guinness's son opened a small brewery in Leixlip and began to concoct a beer unlike any ever tasted before. It was a time of great experimentation in brewing, but according to public consensus this was by far the best. No one knew his secret. Some said it started as a mistake, that Arthur had been following his father's recipe, burned the malting barley, and that the caramelised result turned out richer and better than the brew he intended. Others said Arthur had stolen the recipe from monks whose home-made beer had been known to make hair grow on the chest – of a woman, let alone a man. Six years later, when Arthur left the small Leixlip operation in the hands of his younger brother, Richard, and bought a modest brewery in Dublin, they said there was magic in the holy water of St James' well, and that it was the River Liffey which gave Guinness its distinctive flavour. They may well have been right. The new extra strong beer known as porter, or stout, needed soft water.

Whatever the truth about his pedigree and his brew Arthur Guinness was never prepared to say, but took his secrets with him to the grave.

2.

The run-down state of the small brewery Arthur Guinness bought in Dublin in 1759 was fairly typical of the rest of the town. The preacher, John Wesley, who had visited Dublin on several occasions, was struck by the number of dilapidated or unfinished buildings and attributed it to 'the amazing fickleness of this people'.[3] The lethargy grew not so much from an inherent character defect as a lack of national pride.

Ireland had been occupied for over one hundred years, since Oliver Cromwell's invading army devastated the country, took possession of the great estates and gave them to his anti-papist British supporters. Absentee landlords, the aristocratic ruling classes, had the means, but not the will, to make Dublin a glittering capital city. Their tenants, peasant farmers, dependent on a subsistence potato economy, were Catholic, unable to buy or own land, caught in a vicious spiral of primitive methods, high rents, arrears and possible eviction. Great wealth for the few, great poverty for the masses – there was nothing to bridge the divide, no one to take an interest in public amenities until the growth in the cities of an increasingly powerful mercantile middle class. They were responsible for the sweeping boulevards, the dignified, imposing buildings, and spacious parks and squares, the elegant Georgian stylishness which would grace Arthur Guinness's Dublin in later years.

The Anglo-Irish landowners, bored by occasional visits to their property, gravitated towards the Viceroy's fashionable court at Dublin Castle, looking for entertainment. Their wealth began to stimulate a host of service industries – building, banking, brewing. Some made a small fortune. Others tried and failed. In almost every industry economic competition with England was stiff. The mid-eighteenth century was a time of unlimited potential – but only for a prudent and hard-working opportunist.

Closed for nine years, the poky little brewery Arthur Guinness acquired for 9,000 years at an annual rent of £45, may not have been the most imposing in St James' Gate, but it was larger than many of its rivals and, by Dublin standards, fairly substantial. It consisted of the basic minimum, all in need of some renovation – a copper vat, a mill, two malt-houses, stables for twelve horses and a loft to hold 200 loads of hay. But the dwelling-place was undoubtedly 'des. res.' with spacious gardens, a summer house and a fishpond. This was the first acquisition on the road to becoming a gentleman. The next was a wife, preferably with income enough to keep him in the means to which he intended to become accustomed. This he also managed in a mere two years.

Olivia Whitmore, ward of William Lunell, with an almost mouth-watering inheritance of £1,000, and her important connections, appears to have accepted his suit with surprising alacrity. Guinness was not a handsome man, but he was personable, aristocratic in bearing with a high forehead and aquiline nose. The glint of steel in the eyes, the finely chiselled chin, passed on to certain, select individuals in future generations, conveyed determination, a breed of men who knew their mind and stuck to it. The Lunells were no fools. Nor were the Whitmores. They were well-established Dublin families. The young brewer Olivia married on 17 June 1761 must have exuded potential, fulfilling their expectations two years later when he was elected Warden of the Corporation of Brewers. The following year he represented his corporation in the annual civic ceremony of 'Riding the Franchise', moved out to the suburbs, where he had bought Beaumont, his stately home in the country, and began to multiply. Young Arthur had heard the famous preacher John Wesley say, 'We must exhort all Christians to gain all they can, and to save all they can, that is, in effect, to grow rich.' Guinness was only fulfilling his Christian duty.

His rise had been meteoric. Within five years he had acquired status enough for an embarrassed *Freeman's Journal* to apologise that the 'eminent brewer' who had died in James' Street was a Mr Ennis, and not Arthur Guinness, as the newspaper had previously stated.[4] But eminence does not guarantee supremacy. Seven years after Arthur bought the brewery, an account of the excise duty paid by Dublin brewers shows that his output was still outstripped by his major rivals. Taylor, Thwaites and Phepoe paid over £4,000 each in tax, while Arthur Guinness paid £1,498. He had a long way to go.

However, entrepreneurial skills were evidently in the genes. While Arthur was building his business in St James' Gate, brother Benjamin became a well-to-do merchant and died unmarried in 1778, brother Samuel was a prosperous goldbeater, and Richard, the youngest, continued to thrive at his brother's Leixlip Brewery.

Success requires hard work and determination. Mastery needs flair in addition to shrewd business sense. From the moment he saw it, Arthur Guinness recognised the unmistakable advantage of the site on St James' Gate. From the Dublin mountains, ten miles out of the city, water flowed in plentiful supply into the River Liffey, and was carried by a system of pipes right up to the western side of his property into the city watercourse. A free supply of water – particularly soft water – was a brewer's dream.

When Arthur Guinness signed the lease he made absolutely sure that he had acquired water rights, and took his fair share – and a great deal more, according to an outraged City Corporation which discovered he had enlarged the pipes and made new breaches in the watercourse walls.

In April 1775 the Corporation decided to re-appropriate the watercourse beside the Guinness property. It belonged to the city and was never his to lease. The brewer must be prevented from tapping into a public supply, the channel filled in forthwith.

The might of the Corporation, mindful of the brewer's status, duly descended on St James' Gate one month later, 'desirous of treating every citizen with all possible respect and lenity, considering that by a sudden privation of water, Mr Guinness, as a brewer, must be considerably injured'.[5] Injured! He would have been ruined.

Far from being intimidated, Arthur Guinness was incensed. The obsequious offer of reasonable time for the accomplishment of their object only roused his fury further. Before God and man, his conscience was clear. The water was his. He would defend the channel by force if necessary. It was.

Days later the City Sheriff arrived with a body of men armed with spades, shovels and a host of other tools. One employee caused a lengthy obstruction, defeated only by the

21

threat of Newgate Prison. Suddenly, with a volley of language unknown in the polite society of his wife's relatives, the brewer appeared, snatched a pickaxe from a workman, and wielding it with menace, vowed that if they filled the channel from end to end he would re-open it. The City Sheriff decided that diplomacy might be the best course of action and beat a hasty retreat.

The legal wrangling continued for years, a delay which suited the brewer's purpose. In 1779 when the Corporation's officers went back to examine the state of the pipes, they were met with a brick wall – literally. It blocked the narrow passage of entry to the Brewery from the city. In 1785, to the immense relief of the Corporation, Guinness finally agreed to settle for an annual sum of £10.00. He was by then Master of the Dublin Guild of the Corporation of Brewers, official brewer to the Castle, and definitely, not a man to cross.

3.

Unlike many women of her time, Olivia Guinness's constitution stood up well to twenty-six years of pregnancy and childbirth. She provided the patriarch with six sons and four daughters. In 1790, the year Arthur Guinness extended his brewery, and built two flour mills at Kilmainham for between £4,000 and £5,000, he expressed his gratitude to God not only for material prosperity, but for his children, especially his second son, Arthur, now twenty-two, and 'grown up to be able to assist me in the business, or I would not have attempted it, though prompted by a demand of providing for ten children now living out of one and twenty born to us, and yet more to come'.[6]

Presumably, at forty-eight, Olivia was pregnant again. Arthur himself was sixty-five. Their eldest daughter, Elizabeth, was twenty-seven and married to a member of the Darley family. Their eldest son, Hosea, aged twenty-five, was making a career for himself in the Church. Since there is no record of any living children after the birth of Mary in 1787, Arthur's prediction of more mouths to feed obviously came to nought. Whether the couple were grateful for that or not remains unknown.

His ever-increasing standing in Dublin society, commensurate with his growing business and burgeoning family, is well documented. For a man of his serious religious persuasion, wealth brought responsibility, moral obligation and public duty. He was treasurer and later Governor of the Meath Charity Hospital. He began the long family association with St Patrick's Cathedral, lending the dean and chapter 250 guineas for repairs and alterations to the Chapel schools, refusing repayment, and requesting instead that it should be distributed among the pupils. Then, in 1786, he founded Ireland's first Sunday School.

A number of good causes absorbed his surplus energy – among them, penal reform. In 1765 a man was burned alive in St Stephen's Green for keeping a brothel. A year later a priest was hanged, drawn and quartered for sympathising with a peasant uprising. Guinness was horrified. Excess – even in punishment – was always deplorable. He lent his voice to the increasing volume of public protest, and witnessed, to his satisfaction, a gradual modification of the law.

An attempt to put an end to duelling was less successful. As secretary of the Friendly Brothers of St Patrick, he was one of an increasing number of Dublin citizens sickened by the way a ridiculous insistence on honour, providing an excuse for a deadly upper-class sport, was spreading in popularity among those who aped them in the middle classes. No ban was ever introduced in his lifetime, and ironically, his youngest son would marry a woman widowed by one of the most notorious Irish duels of them all.

Arthur Guinness adopted as his motto 'Spes Mea In Deo',

'My Hope is in God'. It could equally have been 'Moderation in All Things', for he believed that the guiding principles enabling him to make a private fortune should inform public life as well. But his abstemiousness was at odds with the spirit of Dublin in the latter part of the eighteenth century. In 1872 England granted Ireland an independent parliament. It had little real executive power, but that did not dampen the enthusiasm of Henry Grattan, who believed he was witnessing the first step towards an independent Ireland. Standing beneath the magnificent chandeliers in the House of Commons at College Green, he proclaimed, 'Ireland is now a nation', unleashing a burst of national pride, expressed in a time of unparalleled draining, planning, building and general frolicking. The professional and merchant classes were heartily sick of being treated by the English landowners as uncultured provincials in a backward colony, and began building a capital city worthy of their affluence and obvious fine taste.

The sophistication was skin deep. Elegance had a habit of giving way to a more Bacchanalian ribaldry where food and drink were concerned. Both Dean Swift and John Wesley criticised the Irish for gluttony and drunkenness. Self-indulgence, they said, was Ireland's besetting sin. It was a matter upon which Arthur Guinness felt he should take a stand, and, as a member of the Dublin Council, he was in a position to do so. Tradition held that a newly elected council alderman should lay on a banquet for the entire Corporation. Guinness thought it an indulgence of the worst order, carousing at the expense of deserving charities. Men in public office should set an example. Let the money be given instead to the Blue Coat Hospital.

The city fathers were not prepared to let a killjoy like Arthur Guinness spoil all the fun, and 'universally scouted' his suggestion on the grounds that 'good eating, and above all, good drinking, were strong bonds of good fellowship and unity'. Good living was at the very heart of their charter and they 'must stand or fall together'.[7] There was probably a great deal more falling than standing.

As a purveyor of good beer, Guinness may well have hoisted himself with his own petard, but he was no hypocrite. Unlike many of his fellow merchants, he lived a serene and quiet life in his stately home, surrounded by fine portraits, elegant furnishings and his ever-growing family, all tokens of divine approval. Religious piety was not an accepted convention among eighteenth-century Protestants. Church attendance was sporadic, a social convention for the landed gentry. The clergy, younger sons of landowners, spent their time hunting, shooting, drinking and gambling. When they did manage a sermon, it was hardly worth hearing anyway. Into that context blew a whirlwind of religious penitence and grace, the preacher John Wesley.

Arthur Guinness was not offended to hear that the heart of a gentleman was as black and sinful as that of any labourer. It appealed to his innate sense of equality and fair play. He must have been a very young man when he heard Wesley for the first time on one of the preacher's many trips to Ireland, and it profoundly affected his thinking. Throughout his life, he remained Church of Ireland in practice, nonconformist at heart. One satisfied his aspirations, the other his integrity. Although Olivia's cousin Edward Smythe was minister of Bethesda Chapel, the leading nonconformist congregation in Dublin, Arthur was not a Methodist. It was too new a movement, too radical for a man of conventional tastes, mixing increasingly with the Protestant upper classes.

But where justice required it he was not afraid to stand up to his Protestant peers. Unlike many, he was an enlightened and exemplary employer, treating his Catholic workforce with dignity and respect. More unusual, especially for a member of the Church of Ireland, he publicly supported the Roman Catholic majority in their struggle for equality, including full political emancipation, as long as they went about it the proper way, the way of non-violence, said the mighty wielder of the pickaxe. In 1793 Catholics were given the right to vote, but not to stand for parliament or own land. That was the year a mischievous report was circulated round the town that Guinness had opposed the election of a certain Valentine O'Connor to the Freedom of the City on the grounds he was a Catholic. Guinness issued a public denial, claiming that in keeping with his consistent support for Catholic claims to equality, he had not only voted for O'Connor, but went out of his way to solicit votes on his behalf.[8]

Arthur Guinness became adept at manoeuvring his way around religious and political pot-holes. That he managed to chart such a successful course, with so little damage to his reputation or business interests, was evidence of a man who knew when and where to bend to prevent his conscience from breaking. It was a skill which would help establish him as Dublin's foremost brewer within the next five years.

4.

In the second half of the eighteenth century success as a brewer in Ireland was by no means a foregone conclusion. Despite high import duties, London brewers could often undersell their Dublin rivals in their own city. The Irish brewers could not take advantage of large-scale production. Their market was limited to the few towns with a cash economy and a growing middle-class population – Belfast, Cork, Limerick, Galway. The peasants, the majority of the population, drank cheap spirits.

By 1773 the industry was on the verge of collapse. In the ten previous years a quarter of the brewers had gone out of business, crippled by the cost of raw materials, high taxation and a host of petty regulations surrounding the brewing process. There were even penalties on brewers' draymen who used bad language.

Since 1766 Guinness had been one of a group of merchants acting as intermediary with Parliament on matters of trade. As Master of the Guild of Brewers he now spearheaded a twenty-year campaign to get a better deal, delivering petitions, testifying to the brewers' many grievances, demanding the repeal of all taxation on beer. He had a powerful political ally in his wife's cousin Henry Grattan, who was able to articulate the brewers' demands with a verve and eloquence which convinced the toughest opponents.

In 1791 he accused Parliament of double-dealing, of claiming to encourage Irish industry while discriminating against brewing with excise duties and excessive regulation. The Chancellor of the Exchequer, John Beresford, however, a reasonable man, knew that without any regulations, the brewers would brew lousy beer. It was as clear, he said, as the sun at noonday, that the backward state of Irish brewing did not arise from the increased consumption of spirits, nor from the increased importation of English beer, but from the poor quality of the drink.

On 14 February 1792, Arthur Guinness gave evidence to the Irish Parliament. Never, he said, had the brewing industry been at such a low ebb, and it was all due to the taxation advantages enjoyed by the distilleries, and the increased spirit consumption which ensued.

The debate continued and was interrupted on 27 February by confused noises overhead. The clerk was sent to find out what was happening and returned to inform the House that the roof was on fire and the dome likely to collapse in five minutes. A motion to adjourn the debate was carried *nem. con.* In less than two hours, the beautiful Parliament building, admired throughout Europe for its fine architecture, lay in cinders. Whether they thought it an act of God, or more likely, because the witness at the time – an Englishman – let it be known that there were profits to be made in brewing in Ireland, the Commons decided only to reduce, not repeal the taxes when they met in the Coffee House the following month.

Nothing short of the end of taxation would suit Guinness and his fellow brewers, and the campaign continued for a further four years. With Grattan's help they learned how to maximise political sympathy. Drunkenness, they pointed out, was rising at a disturbing rate. There was no doubt of the real culprit – the demon whisky, robbing the working man of his senses, making him lazy, unproductive and indolent. Whisky was the cause of turbulence, violence and factions. Beer, on the other hand, was wholesome and healthy, a sensible alternative. Distilling should be taxed – not brewing.

However profound the influence of Wesleyanism on Arthur's life, it never seemed to tempt him to teetotalism – unlike his youngest son, John Grattan, who would grow up with a profound distaste for the family business. Had it really never entered Arthur's head that men would drink themselves into a Guinness-induced stupor?

John Beresford, the Chancellor, saw beyond the moral protestations of public service, to the gleam of gain in the brewers' eyes, and expostulated with Henry Grattan, 'It is of very little consequence to the morals of the people if they will get drunk, what they get drunk with; it is however the duty of the legislature as much as in them lies, to make the means of intoxication as difficult to come by as they possibly can.'[9]

To be fair to Arthur Guinness, perhaps a man who deplored excess of every kind assumed that no one else would be able to drink beer in enough quantity to get drunk. Perhaps the very idea was too upsetting to contemplate, and he simply chose not to see it. It certainly was not the habit of the time. Beer was the middle-class man's drink – a fortified lemonade.

With all of Ireland's major problems – health, moral, social and economic – attributed to strong spirits, Parliament finally yielded in 1795, repealing all the taxes on beer, along with many other minor regulations. In a letter to the brewers, which smacks of the irony of hindsight, Henry Grattan hailed it as a major piece of social reform. 'It is at your source the Parliament will find in its own country the means of health with all her flourishing consequences, and the cure of intoxication with all her misery.'[10]

If the social aspirations were doomed to failure, the more pecuniary ones were not. British brewing had begun to suffer the disastrous economic effects of war with France. Imports into Ireland dwindled. The Irish brewing industry was about to come into its own.

But another part of the Guinness legend was born – popular especially with the descendants of the teetotal Captain John, founder of the missionary branch of the family – that Guinness was brewed in the spirit of true altruism, with a view to combating the worse excesses of whisky drinking. 'Beer', said Henry Grattan, 'was the natural nurse of the people', a sentiment echoed by many an Irishman over the years, as he sat, finding comfort for his sorrows, in a pint, or two, or three.

If Arthur Guinness stands convicted of diluting Wesley's warnings on the evil of drink to suit his conscience, judgment followed. For future generations alcohol would be an elixir of life, or their poison. Four of his grandsons had to be dismissed from the brewery for drunkenness and drink-related problems. The patriarch never lived to see it, which was just as well. It would have broken his heart.

5.

In the turbulent history of the Irish people, 1798 was a crucial year. Fired by the French Revolution, Presbyterians in the north and Catholics in the south joined forces and rose up against English domination, attempting for the first time to establish a democratic Irish republic. Dublin immediately raised a yeomanry to defend the city. Two of Arthur's sons, Edward and William Lunell, volunteered immediately, while young Arthur and Benjamin were left behind to look after the Brewery. Twenty-two-year-old Benjamin was not pleased to miss the excitement, especially since William was three years his junior, and wrote rather pompously, 'I think myself unfortunate that I am so situated at this time that I cannot join the yeomanry, but really attendance required now in Dublin is such that if both Arthur and I went into the yeomanry the Business here must be entirely stopp'd.'[11]

The French reinforcements expected by the revolutionaries failed to materialise, and the uprising was quickly suppressed – not without causing a certain amount of chaos and disruption, which old Arthur Guinness, for all his liberal attitudes, could not condone. Besides, it was far too close to home. Guinness had a country trade with Athy in County Kildare, sending supplies of beer forty miles down the Grand Canal. Foreseeing the trouble ahead, the day before the start of the 'Disturbances', as Benjamin called them in his letter, he and his brother had sent £80 to Athy to tide them over. With a tone of moral outrage, Benjamin described how it had been intercepted by the rebels and vanished.

What was more, hot-headed young John, at fifteen, desperate to see some action, had ignored family warnings to stay away from the defences, and was severely wounded carrying dispatches. Arthur Guinness never thought he would see the day when one of his sons lay wounded in his own city, attacked by fellow citizens. Enough was enough.

On the whole manufacturers like Arthur Guinness had supported a majority in the Irish House of Commons, led by Henry Grattan, agitating for Irish separation, religious emancipation and tithe commutation. But the insurrection seriously worried all the monied classes, not to mention the British government. The French Revolution had been an object lesson in the dangers of unchecked insubordination.

With a heavy-handedness which characterised most of its dealings with Ireland, the British government used the anxiety to seize an opportunity to pass the Act of Union in 1800, abolishing the Irish Parliament and uniting the country with the rest of the United Kingdom. The consequences would have a disastrous effect on Anglo-Irish relations for years to come.

They had little immediate effect on Arthur Guinness. He seemed hardly aware that the brewers' easy capitulation to Union showed a remarkable lack of gratitude to Henry Grattan for the lasting service he had done them. At seventy-five he had no personal cause for dissatisfaction. He was as vigorous as ever, would spend two hours or so every morning at the Brewery, keeping an eye on his sons, then ride out to his mills in Kilmainham on the western edge of the city. There he could stop, look down, and watch the River Liffey winding its way towards the Brewery, slow and sluggish, thick as rich pea soup, dark as full-bodied stout, and enjoy his sense of achievement to the full. He had arrived a nobody in the big city stretched out before him. He would leave it a man of substance and property. Had he not always fulfilled his God-given responsibilities? Industry, public duty, charity and family had been his preoccupations, in that order. Righteousness had reaped its own rewards.

All was as he would have wished, including the ceremonial attending his own departure in 1803. The Rev. Hosea Guinness, presiding at the funeral, was a solid, dignified and liberal-minded man, if a little lacking in fire and imagination. He had married a colonel's daughter, Jane Hart, and would, within eight years of his father's death, become Rector for thirty years of the prestigious St Werbergh's in the city centre. Arthur had never anticipated the Church depriving him of his natural heir to the business. In his will he bequeathed Beaumont, the family home, to Hosea and Jane and their children, his son, he remarked drily, 'not being in any line of

31

life whereby he is likely by Industry to enlarge his Property'.[12] One clergyman in the family, for form's sake, might be a blessing – but one was enough.

Arthur, to his relief, already the father of three young sons, was as like his father in nature as in name and had inherited what would become the quintessential Guinness flair for business. Physically the resemblance was remarkable, the same long, pale face, emphasised by a receding hairline and aquiline nose. The eyes, more hooded than his father's, glinted warily beneath the heavy lids. The set of the jaw gave an impression of dignity and determination, and only a slight curve of the mouth hinted at a carefully concealed store of compassion and generosity. To Arthur his father bequeathed the treasured silver salver, presented to him by the Corporation of Brewers of the City of Dublin, to keep in perpetuity as a sign of particular respect, and 'to go to the Eldest Male Branch of my Family . . . who shall be in the brewing trade'.[13] Arthur the second, wearing his father's mantle, stepped into the role which should have belonged to his elder brother, assumed the running of the Brewery, and with it, the headship of the family. For the first but not the last time God had come between a Guinness and his earthly inheritance.

Edward, his third son, was weak and indecisive, easily enticed by gracious living, without the self-discipline to earn it. Unimpressed with brewing, he tried a career in law, but at thirty-one had not yet distinguished himself in any way. Life, he would later complain, had not been kind to him. Every family has a black sheep – or two. Edward was the first of a long line.

His two younger brothers, William Lunell and Benjamin, had proved their fitness for business, and John, undeterred by the wounds he received during the uprising, had joined the 12th regiment native infantry of the Madras Army. Their father left them £1,500 each. Edward had frittered his legacy away already.

His daughters were not forgotten. Elizabeth Darley received £1,000, and his unmarried daughters, Louisa and Mary Ann, £2,000 each, in trust. Both married clergymen within the next few years. A fourth daughter, Olivia, had died in childhood.

To his wife, who would outlive him by eleven years, he bequeathed £200 a year, together with the £200 of their marriage jointure, the use of his house in Gardiner Street, and the coach and horses. She evidently was expected to live a quiet kind of a life, befitting a respectable widow, with occasional social visits, of course, to her ever-growing number of grandchildren.

Most importantly he had left behind a host of charitable and philanthropic works which he hoped would make his good name live on. He could now sink peacefully to rest in the family vault. 'The worthy and the good will regret him,' said an obituary in the Dublin *Evening Post*, 'because his life has been useful and benevolent and virtuous.'

The entire estate was valued for probate at £23,000, a small fortune for the time. In forty years Arthur Guinness had turned a white elephant into the biggest business enterprise in Ireland. Other brewers were astute. Others were hard-working and determined. What was the secret of his success? How did he manage to outstrip all his rivals? The reason was very simple. Arthur Guinness made the best beer.

Decent beer was not easy to come by, and it took him a while to perfect his art. Around the middle of the eighteenth century, British brewers had begun to manufacture a new kind of drink, highly hopped, stronger and darker than ordinary beer, whose flavour actually improved on keeping. It was known as porter, because its London punters were primarily porters or manual labourers. Later, because of its extra strength, it became known as stout. Its popularity in England grew, until in 1745 it was being hailed along with bread as 'one of the two pillars of life'. It took a while longer for the drink to catch on with the Irish working classes, who had always had access to cheap, locally distilled spirits, and it was not in the first Arthur's lifetime. His sons would reap the benefit of that particular sea change. Meanwhile, the new beer became very popular at the Castle, and with the merchant classes. Arthur Guinness had the foresight to recognise its potential. He stopped brewing pale ale altogether. Instead, he concentrated on producing an exceptional quality of stout. And it was that particular accomplishment, rather than any virtue, which would one day make his name famous worldwide.

Chapter 2

1803–1842
Captain John, a Soldier and a
Gentleman

1.

India was the place for an adventure, home from home for
many an Irishman with military ambitions. By the turn of the
century the 250-year-old Mogul Empire had collapsed, and
the country was divided into a number of warring, princely
states. It was a prime opportunity for European imperialism.

The East India Company, which recruited the young John
Guinness almost as soon as his wounds had healed, had been
created as a trading company in the reign of Elizabeth I. By
1765 it ruled the vast province of Bengal, reducing its mighty
princes to mere dependants. Every rapacious director, civil
servant, merchant or army officer grasped at a piece of this
exotic land. Every Muslim sultan, Hindu rajah, every thug
and bandit marauding the villages, was equally determined to
make them release their grip.

When war broke out between England and France, Tippu
Sultan, Rajah of Mysore, a clever and powerful prince,
recognised a chance to exploit the situation for his own ends,
and made a treaty with the French. In 1798 the English sent

one of their most famous Irish soldiers to bring him to heel.

Arthur Wellesley, later Duke of Wellington, had been Viceroy of Ireland and was excruciatingly bored at Dublin Castle, where, apart from the republican uprising, life consisted of little more than handing the ladies of the Anglo-Irish ascendancy in and out of their carriages. He was no doubt unaware that his brewer's youngest son, also desperate for action, had followed him out.

In India the tall, dark, rather good-looking seventeen-year-old found plenty to satisfy his appetite for excitement. Fighting methods were mean and underhand by gentlemanly British standards, stretching every nerve until it was taut. An unwitting soldier might have a nail driven into his skull, or his neck wrung by Hindu strongmen known as Jetties. A prisoner was subject to prolonged torture.

After a lengthy siege, Wellesley took Tippu Sultan's capital, Seringapatam, installed himself as governor, and appointed a new rajah. One of Tippu's supporters, a brigand from Mahratta with the unlikely name of Dhoondiah Waugh, managed to escape during the English assault, and gathering a band of Tippu's men around him, made a series of successful guerilla raids across the border from Mahratta into Mysore, inflicting serious losses on the English army. Wellesley was instructed to hang him from the highest tree.

In years to come John Grattan would regale his children with romantic tales of following the great General in the chase which would make Wellington's military reputation. The reality was very different – mile upon mile of marching in intense heat, freezing nights, and constant danger from bandits. But Dhoondiah and his untrained thugs were no real contest for the English, and his mission fulfilled, Wellesley led his victorious fighting force back to Seringapatam.

John Grattan's two years in the garrison there, restoring law and order to the province, were among the most difficult he had ever known. The natives were easy to manage compared with the troops who bullied and threatened them, engaged in looting, drunken brawling and debauchery as soon as Wellesley's back was turned. The youngest son of Arthur Guinness was deeply disillusioned. The Honourable East India Company was honourable in name only. This was not the glorious victory he had painted in his vivid imagination. He longed for action, and was relieved when, in 1803, Wellesley decided to deal with the violent princes of the Mahratta states once and for all. He assumed it would be as easy as the defeat of Dhoondiah Waugh, but he was wrong. In two years the French had transformed the marauding hordes into an intelligent, well-disciplined fighting force, equipped with skills in military intelligence and the latest weapons. As the English tried to navigate a treacherous system of river tributaries, the Indian troops advanced, inflicting huge casualties at Assaye. John Grattan survived the carnage, helped to subdue the enemy princes – and won his commission. His greatest disappointment was that his father had not lived to see it.

In 1805 Wellesley was recalled. Captain John stayed on, determined to live the kind of upright life his hero commended to his officers. One day he received a letter from brother Edward enthusing about the potential of two large ironworks in Palmerston and Lucan. Edward wanted to buy them, but had not enough money. Arthur, William and Benjamin were too committed to the Brewery to help, but John still had his inheritance. He didn't need it in India but, well invested, it would be worth a great deal more when he came home. Captain John, naïve in all but military matters, unaware of his brothers' lack of confidence in Edward's business ability, willingly handed his legacy over. Whatever shrewd financial good sense old Arthur possessed had been absorbed by the rest of the family before it reached the youngest of his sons.

When Captain John came home on leave in 1810, he met

and married Susanna Hutton, daughter of a local alderman, but any thoughts of settling down to a quiet life were shattered when the iron works collapsed. Local newspapers apportioned Edward no blame:

> He was the first trader who could claim the merit of rendering his native country not only independent of, but superior to, her neighbours in this branch of manufactures. He gave bread to several hundred fellow creatures who prospered under his auspices; his establishment turned out annually more than £170,000; he was candid and honourable in his dealings; highly esteemed and respected, not only as a merchant but as a private gentleman; he was enterprising and successful in his speculations; yet even this man is now made a bankrupt.[1]

Edward's correspondence with his elder brother, Arthur, however, reveals a weaker, more feckless character. As a lawyer expert in bankruptcy proceedings, he knew the penalties he could incur. Hounded by creditors, he fled to Dundalk with his wife, Margaret, and their five children, where, in terror of debtors' prison, he besieged his brewing brothers with demands for money. His letters were full of a sanctimonious self-pity and piety. 'I must wait for the Lord's good time and use reasonable means to save my person.'[2] He certainly wasn't concerned to save brother John's skin, and in 1813 left him, Susanna and their two baby sons in Scotland,[3] while he escaped to the Isle of Man, a safe haven from the Insolvent Act.

The two sons of Uncle Samuel Guinness the goldbeater, Samuel and Dick, both barristers, acted for him, appealing to their cousin Arthur as the head of the family, yet clearly, very anxious to do 'whatever Arthur G approves of'. That Edward was presuming on his brother's good nature was abundantly clear, and they did not particularly enjoy being party to it.[4]

Arthur could hardly watch his brother's family starve, and sent regular monetary gifts. By the time they were living in the Isle of Man, however, he had some rather stringent questions about their extravagant standard of living. Edward explained deferentially that he had moved out of a more modest property into an expensive house with two servants, 'having so many children within so few square feet and no yard or garden, and a tanner's yard immediately under our back windows, the offense of which by this hot weather and his increase of business daily becoming greater'.[5] Money matters, he went on to say, were making his wife ill – an overt request for more. Edward's needs were fast becoming a bottomless pit.

Worn down and more than a little irritated by the constant barrage of requests, Arthur finally paid off his brother's debts – an exorbitant sum of £5,900, at a time when the Brewery could least afford it. In 1815 Wellington defeated Napoleon at Waterloo. For Ireland the end of the Napoleonic wars heralded a time of major economic upheaval. The very future of Guinness was in jeopardy.

He found his brother a job at the Brewery as a clerk, a position Edward regarded as beneath him. He spent his latter years complaining about his elder brother's mistreatment to anyone who would hear him. As for the destitute Captain John, father of two small sons, John Grattan and Arthur Grattan, he had no alternative but to return to India where the army would divest him of his health and another fourteen years of his life.

2.

In 1815, as Wellington advanced upon Napoleon, and John Grattan sweated out his days beneath the scorching Indian sun, an event occurred in faction-ridden Dublin which would have lasting consequences for the young captain in the Madras

Army. Such was the impact on the Irish capital that over a hundred years later, when Catholic folk gathered around their fireside, they would still tell the story of O'Connell's duel with D'Esterre with as much relish as any account of the Liberator's great struggle for the emancipation of his people.

In the icy winter of 1814–15 frustration ran high amongst the Catholic population of Dublin. Political equality seemed an impossible dream. The Protestant-controlled Dublin Corporation was opposed to any kind of concessions. But the Catholic majority had found a leader and a voice – the lawyer Daniel O'Connell, a large, genial Irishman whose gift of the blarney was combined with a brilliant legal mind. At a meeting of the Catholic Board on 22 January, he described the Corporation as 'beggarly'. Given the man's reputation for deadly invective it was hardly the worst term of abuse he could have employed – but it hit the bull's-eye.

It was a time of severe economic depression. The Guinness Brewery was not alone in facing pecuniary disaster. Arthur's brother-in-law, Frederick Darley, Lord Mayor in 1809, was bankrupt. So were eight of the aldermen. The city treasurer's accounts were under investigation, and the Corporation was in debt and could not pay its bills.

One of the Corporation's most recent members, John Norcott D'Esterre, in grave financial difficulty himself, saw a report of O'Connell's remark in the *Carrick's Morning Post*, and took exception to it. Ironically, D'Esterre was one of the few members of the Corporation who had actually spoken up for Catholic emancipation. The previous edition of the same newspaper had published a letter in which he said, 'Though I did not and probably never shall oppose the Protestant religion, at the same time I shall consider it the duty of religion and loyalty to concur cheerfully in any relief Parliament may think proper to concede to the Catholics.'

D'Esterre was not a bigot. Nor was he 'gallant, but unfortunate',[6] as his wife's family would say of him in future

40

years. He was hot-headed and naïve, a political nonentity standing for City Sheriff, a post which would confer almost instant relief from his financial worries. After his apparently pro-Catholic pronouncements, a show of anti-Catholic muscle would not do his cause any harm.

Three days later D'Esterre sent O'Connell a letter demanding an apology. O'Connell replied that there were no doubt one or two invaluable persons on the Corporation, but in view of its treatment of the Catholic community, 'no terms attributed to me, however reproachful, can exceed the contemptuous feeling I entertain for that body in its corporate capacity.'[7] All future communication was returned to D'Esterre unopened.

The word spread quickly. In a city already deeply divided, tempers flared and tension began to rise. On 31 January D'Esterre swaggered down the centre of Dublin with a whip and pistol in his hand, threatening to shut the mouth of the great O'Connell for ever. The lawyer was twice the size of the wiry little merchant and Dublin Catholics might have been amused were it not that D'Esterre was reputed to be a crack shot. In 1793 he had joined the Marines, and four years later, as first lieutenant, played a heroic part in suppressing the mutiny of the Nore. Legend had it that the mutineers had put a rope around his neck and threatened to hang him if he did not join them. 'Hang away and be damned,' he cried, and his bluster changed their minds.

Crowds turned out to witness the confrontation. Up at the Four Courts, where he practised law, O'Connell and his supporters waited. But D'Esterre only put in a brief appearance before he set off for Grafton Street, where the Unionists were ensconced in the shop windows to watch the fun. O'Connell and his followers chased after him, but a riot was brewing and D'Esterre dodged into a house. O'Connell took refuge in a shop, where he was bound over by a judge and ordered to keep the peace.

The following day at Morrison's Hotel in Nassau Street, Sir

Edward Stanley, a colleague of D'Esterre's on the Corporation, called on O'Connell's friend, Major MacNamara, a wealthy Protestant from Clare with Catholic sympathies, once again demanding an apology. MacNamara, a practised duellist, refused, and with a speed which left Stanley breathless, accepted the challenge and insisted a duel be fought that day at three o'clock. Stanley tried to negotiate a postponement, but the only concession he was given was that since this was not a private quarrel a single shot would suffice.

'No, Sir,' he cried, 'if they fire twenty shots each, Mr D'Esterre will never leave the ground until Mr O'Connell makes an apology.'

MacNamara replied, 'Well then, if blood be your object, blood you shall have!' and stormed out of the room.

D'Esterre does not appear to have been prepared for this outcome. In all probability he never intended having a duel at all, but had dug a hole for himself so deep he could not climb out. After all, it had taken him three days to demand an apology, and a further six before he went out into the streets to confront O'Connell. But his colleagues egged him on, bolstering his ego by telling him that a man who had challenged O'Connell two years previously had got away without firing a shot, and had been made a judge for his pains. The Unionists were set on destroying the man they hated, and rash D'Esterre, junior Corporation member with lofty aspirations, was so obligingly malleable. With such tragic consequences.

It was a bitterly cold February day and snow lay thickly on the ground as O'Connell's carriage rolled slowly into the field in Bishop's Court, County Kildare, a spot some twelve miles west of Dublin chosen for the fight. D'Esterre arrived almost an hour late, at four o'clock, accompanied by Sir Edward Stanley, Mr Peile, the Surgeon-General of the Dublin Garrison, and his brother, Henry D'Esterre, the Recorder of Limerick. As the seconds wrangled over details, carriages and gigs poured into the field. Word travelled fast. Virtually the entire Dublin Corporation had turned out to watch the sport.

The two men appeared to be in high spirits. D'Esterre walked around nonchalantly twirling his cane, and O'Connell, seeing his tailor in the crowd, shouted, 'Ah, Jerry, I never missed you from an aggregate meeting.' MacNamara instructed the inexperienced O'Connell to remove his white neckerchief as it made him an easy target, and take off his fob, for if it were hit, it would inflict a more ghastly wound than the bullet.

D'Esterre won the toss and the two men moved into place, ten paces, approximately fifty feet, from each other. As the handkerchief fell, D'Esterre stepped to one side and fired. His shot fell short and ricocheted off the ground at O'Connell's feet. O'Connell lifted his pistol, fired and D'Esterre fell writhing to the ground, shot through the hip. Surgeon Peile, and O'Connell's doctor, Surgeon Macklin, who had been asked by O'Connell to help D'Esterre should he need it, rushed to his side. He was bleeding profusely, a large reddish patch spreading out into the snow, but his wound did not appear to be mortal.

O'Connell was in a state of shock. He stood motionless, muttering, 'I aimed low, I aimed low' over and over again. He wanted to see that D'Esterre was all right, but MacNamara led him quickly away.

That night the city erupted into a frenzy of joy and relief. Bonfires burned in the street, but O'Connell refused to join the celebration, and kept demanding to know whether his friends thought he might have killed a man. His brother went to Dr Murray, the Archbishop, to tell him the outcome. 'Heaven be praised,' he said, 'Ireland is safe.'

D'Esterre died two days later. A press release issued by the Corporation disclaimed all involvement in the affair. It was D'Esterre's pecuniary embarrassment and overriding ambition which led to such tragic circumstances. 'I was egged on by no one,' he is supposed to have said, uttering a few dying words of forgiveness, like a true Christian gentleman.

But O'Connell never forgave himself. Consumed with a guilt which haunted him for the rest of his life, he never took the sacrament again without wearing a black glove on the hand that had killed a man, so as not to bare it in the Saviour's presence. It was well known that whenever he passed D'Esterre's house in Bachelor's Walk on his way to the Four Courts, his lips would move in silent prayer, begging mercy for the dead and forgiveness for the living. He went to see D'Esterre's widow to offer her half his income and was greatly struck by her dignity. She refused his help, which did little to assuage his conscience. Eventually he persuaded her to accept a small annuity for her daughter, Amelia, which he paid until his death thirty years later.

3.

The first Jane Mary Lucretia D'Esterre knew of the duel was the moment her dying husband was carried home to her. She was eighteen years old, mother of one little girl, penniless and pregnant. This was hardly the glittering future the successful actress and society beauty had been led to expect.

Described in an early life of O'Connell as 'the beautiful Miss Cramer of Dublin', she looked, according to one of her sons,[8] as if she had been 'formed to win admiration and affection . . . Waving locks of dark hair falling over a high, fair forehead; the eyes dark brown and bright with intelligence; the eyebrows arched; the nose slightly aquiline; the mouth fairly large with mobile lips full of expression'. There was a definite resemblance, he thought, between his mother and her half-brother, the world-famous pianist, Johann Baptist Cramer, mentioned in Beethoven's letters as the only pianist the great composer truly rated. By comparison, 'all the rest went for nothing'.

Like her brother, who became a founding partner of the successful music publishing company, Cramer and Addison, Jane Lucretia was a brilliant piano player. But despite similarities in looks and character, they were not close. They had not been raised together.

The Cramers had been musicians for generations. They hailed from Sachau in Silesia in the south of Germany, where her father, Wilhelm Cramer, had shown exceptional brilliance on the violin as a child, and was accepted as a pupil by Johann Stamitz and Christian Cannabich, the foremost violin teachers of the day. When Johann Baptist was still a baby, the family sailed for England. King George III quickly recognised Wilhelm's outstanding musical ability and made him leader of the Court Band, the Opera and the Pantheon. But it was his role as lead player in the Handel festivals at Westminster Abbey which brought him real recognition as a virtuoso performer. For a while he was without rival – until his son outstripped his father's reputation.

It was rumoured the Cramers were Jews. If this was true, they never made it public. It probably accounted for Wilhelm's lack of good fortune in Germany, and he had no desire to suffer the same disadvantage in England. When his first wife died, he married Maria Madden, daughter of a well-established Dublin Protestant family, and many years his junior. Jane Lucretia was born in 1797 and Wilhelm died two years later. Her mother took the little girl back to Dublin and raised her there as a member of the comfortable but solid Protestant bourgeoisie.

The genetic mix of Irish wilfulness and Teutonic artistic flair would never allow Jane Lucretia to settle for respectable mediocrity. At fourteen she appeared on the stage at the Theatre Royal and took Dublin by storm. Her stunning looks and brilliant musical gifts made her a prize at any soirée. Warm and vivacious, clever and cultured, she was just native enough to be accepted in society, and just foreign enough to exert a certain fascination. But the attention did not make her happy. A career on the stage was hardly reputable, and six months after her debut, the dashing, worldly naval officer D'Esterre, richer in swagger than common sense, swept her off her feet.

To Jane and her mother, it seemed an entirely desirable match. The young merchant came from a well-established Limerick family, mainly lawyers. His brother was a judge. In 1811 his ships' chandlery business was thriving, and his home in Bachelor's Walk bespoke a certain affluence and success. In fact, port trade was being undermined by the deep economic depression, and there were money problems from the beginning of their short marriage. D'Esterre's untimely and unnecessary death left her virtually destitute.

To add to her problems, her husband's name was anathema. Rumour and gossip were rife. Protestant newspapers disowned his actions, attributing them to self-interest and greed. Catholic newspapers with unlikely titles such as the *Irish Magazine and Monthly Asylum for Neglected Biography*, bent on destroying what remained of his reputation, recounted with relish a tale passed on for posterity, that the bailiffs moved into his house before his body was cold, impounded his goods and would have had his body for medical science, had not Jane Lucretia stolen it away and buried it by candlelight in the dead of night somewhere outside the town.[9]

According to the register, he was in fact buried in the parish church of St Mary's two days after his death. His posthumous child, stillborn six months later, was buried close by. Some years after, a preacher, denouncing from the pulpit the perniciousness of duelling, reminded the congregation that one of its most famous victims lay within the sound of his voice.

The house on Bachelor's Walk remained in the family for several generations, passed from Amelia D'Esterre to her son, Henry Cramer Guinness. When he died in 1902, it was inherited by one of his actress daughters, Nora, who, according to family legend, had nothing to show for it in the end except a row of empty champagne glasses and a feather boa.

Thespianism and financial misfortune appeared to run in the family line. The poet Byron asked a friend in Dublin to see if he could tempt Jane Lucretia back on to the stage at Drury Lane in London, but his efforts to dictate her future were no more successful than Daniel O'Connell's. The young widow was determined to brave it out alone, however difficult that might be.

And it was extraordinarily difficult. A great deal of her time was spent in futile litigation. She and her late husband's executors brought an action against a certain Christopher Taafe who had owed D'Esterre more than £7,000 since 1807. Though judgment was made in her favour in 1817, the debt still was not paid in 1821. When he heard that Mrs D'Esterre was at law in Cork, O'Connell dropped another lucrative case and went to plead on her behalf.

The strain inevitably took its toll. The combination of gossip, poverty and legal wrangling wore her down and began to drive her close to despair. Events over which she had little control seemed as if they might blight her life for ever. One day, in Ecclefechan in Scotland where she had taken a house to get away for a while, sitting by a river, too listless to read the novel she had taken with her, she was overcome by an almost overwhelming temptation to plunge herself into the deep waters and find peace at last. The sudden appearance of a farmer's lad merrily ploughing a field in the distance jolted her out of her morbid contemplation. He was totally unaware of her presence, completely caught up with the task at hand. She watched him for some time, marvelling at his concentration and determination, at the evident satisfaction he gained from performing his simple daily labour.

She felt rebuked for her maudlin self-pity. The young lad

was probably about her age, had none of her responsibilities as a mother, but performed the necessary chores to the best of his ability. The very least she could do was plough her own furrow with application and dedication, and perhaps, finally, she too might discover the 'blessedness of work'.

Weeks later, back in Dublin, another ostensibly insignificant event would have profound repercussions on her life, providing her with the moral and spiritual stamina to carry out her goal. Sitting in the gallery of St George's Church, as she did every Sunday, listening half-heartedly to the preacher, she was suddenly struck by his text as never before. 'God so loved the world that he gave his only begotten son.' It was as if she were hearing the familiar words for the first time, that God loved not 'the world' in general, but Jane Lucretia in particular, that this was a love which would not let her down, and could perhaps make life less of the intolerable burden it had become.

With new confidence she applied herself to providing for her child by giving music lessons. The severe widow's weeds she wore, with stand-up white collar framing her face and flowing black veils from the top of her head to the tip of her toe, did little to deter an army of would-be suitors, but she managed to ward them off successfully for fourteen years. When she eventually did succumb, it was to the attractions of a military man again. Once more she followed her heart, rather than the dictates of financial good sense.

4.

Jane Lucretia D'Esterre and Captain John Grattan Guinness were married in 1829 at the York Street Chapel in Dublin. In many ways the match appeared a romantic happy ending. Life had not been any kinder to Captain John than to his new bride.

For fourteen years, in gruelling conditions, the young

infantry captain had led his mercenary Indian troops against the Mahratta princes until each and every one, including the Peshaw, Rajah of Poona, was subject to British control. The conquest of northern Burma in 1824 under Lord Moira almost broke him. He could no longer cope with the climate, his wrecked digestive system, or the constant massacre of human life.

Fighting had lost its appeal. Wesleyan teaching was having a profound impact on an ever-increasing number of officers in the mess, and Captain John was no exception. The preacher had in fact been dead for some time, but his message was as productive as ever, propagated by a new generation of ministers and their large, dissenting congregations. Established churches, watching their own dwindling congregations and revenues with dismay, persuaded the government to outlaw Wesleyanism in 1810. Meetings were broken up, their leaders beaten and imprisoned. Under pressure the movement spread like wildfire – all the way to India, where disillusioned, unhappy British officers provided it with a highly fertile environment.

Raised as an Irish Protestant, even if his religion had been a mere formality in recent years, the youngest son of Arthur Guinness was very susceptible to notions of justice, morality and decency. Like Jane Lucretia, he experienced a revelation of God's love which changed the direction and values of his life. The Bible appeared a much more effective weapon in dealing with the ills of mankind than the sabre or the gun.

Captain John arrived home unwell in 1825, with a wife, two sons, two daughters, and an army pension of £1,000 a year, modest by Guinness brewing family standards. Like the rest of his brothers and sisters he expected brother Arthur to provide, and Arthur complied. He was in the process of expanding Guinness exports to England, and there was a vacancy for an astute young businessman at their agency in

Liverpool, run by his partners, Bewley and Neville, at 29 Manesty Lane.

Captain John's brief was to make the agency self-supporting as quickly as possible. The retired soldier did his best, but it soon became apparent to Bewley and Neville that their new manager was not made of the same stuff as his elder brother. Despite his recklessness in battle, the captain was a mild-mannered man without the tenacity needed in economic warfare. Nor had he the heart for it – for there was one other major problem.

The agency's main trade was in whisky, not beer. Alcohol of every kind, but especially spirits, was anathema to the nonconformist. In Liverpool the family attended the Methodist Chapel, where the minister, Dr Raffles, was well known for the power of his preaching. John Grattan was the first in the family to become Wesleyan in worship as well as persuasion, and effectively snub brother Hosea and a host of clerical brothers-in-law by leaving the established church. He was also the first totally teetotal Guinness.

He suggested to Bewley and Neville that they might like to replace whisky with another commodity – food perhaps. They were understandably concerned. Noble principles do not always make sound financial sense, but how could they complain to the boss about his brother? In the end, Captain John understood their dilemma, and rather than ruin their chances, withdrew from the partnership.

A few months later Susanna died. With his usual compassion Arthur agreed to take on their eldest son, John Grattan junior, as an apprentice at the Brewery.

Having finished his military career and failed in business, Captain John decided he was suitable for very little other than to lead the life of a retired officer and Christian gentleman. In middle age he was still the most handsome of the Guinness brothers with an erect, military bearing and a strong, dignified face, set off by the high collars and cravats he wore. There was no hint of grey in the dark hair, or even in the long sideburns, and the only suggestion of the trauma of past years was in the unusual pallor of his complexion. His youthful drive and bravado had long since burnt out, leaving a shy man, who often hid behind spectacles, and preferred the simple, solitary pleasures of reading and walking to the high life of Dublin society. In this refined, gentle man Jane Lucretia D'Esterre found the qualities she most admired. Elegant and vivacious, she bowled him over at once, but he saw beyond the mystique of her notorious past to the depths of her character, moulded by hard experience and her evangelical Christian faith. In many ways it was an ideal partnership. He needed her to stir him from his phlegmatic temperament. She needed his quiet strength. But that was all he had to offer. Jane Lucretia was destined to marry men without the capacity to earn a reasonable, regular income.

After their marriage they led a nomadic existence, living at first in Dublin, then Edinburgh, Cheltenham and Clifton, constantly looking for cures for his fragile constitution. For six years there were no children, but to their delight, in 1835, Captain John Grattan's second son, Arthur, married Jane Lucretia's daughter, Amelia. In the same year, when he was fifty-two, and she thirty-eight, while they were still living in Kingstown (now Dun Laoghaire), six miles from Dublin, they produced a son, Henry Grattan Guinness. Born in the year of Halley's Comet, a propitious omen for a future astronomer, the baby was dedicated to God at York Street Chapel. And while John Grattan II and Amelia were providing them with grandchildren, the older couple produced three more children themselves, Robert Wyndham in 1837, Frederick in 1839 and Lucy in 1841.

Captain John's favourite occupation was house-building, a vital necessity since he moved his young family so often. Cheltenham was their favourite place of residence and they settled there for some time while the children were growing up. Its sheltered position and mild climate made it an oasis for retired officers from the East India Company. It was said 'you couldn't fire a shot-gun in any direction without hitting a colonel'.[10]

Cheltenham was a gracious, beautiful old town with exclusive clubs and villas whose verandas and porches overlooked wide, tree-lined avenues, in many ways a replica of life in India. The spa waters were reputed to do wonders for a liver and stomach disordered by years of unwholesome food. If that were not enough to attract Captain John Grattan and his wife, the Madras army officers had also imported their piety, making the town the English gentleman's evangelical Mecca.

The most powerful local figure was the Rev. Francis Close, Vicar of St Mary's parish, known locally, because of his authoritarianism, as 'the Pope'. Though he was Low Church and evangelical he was too establishment for the son of Arthur Guinness, who passed him by in favour of Dr Archibald Brown, minister of the Congregational Chapel and a liberal politically.

The couple were very happy, he at his pottering, she chivvying him along, reminding him of his responsibilities to both his first and his second family, taking upon her own shoulders all the practical details of running the home. Guinness men were either practical and rational, or spiritual and other-worldly, and when they were the latter, they were hopelessly impractical.

According to his son, Henry Grattan, Captain John was a man of 'decidedly religious turn'. One abiding childhood memory was reading to his father in their home in Clifton, where they moved some years later, from the 21st and 22nd chapters of the book of Revelation, 'the light of the street lamp shining into the quiet room where we sat together, and the solemn, beautiful imagery of the chapter relating to the New Jerusalem seeming to shed over the scene a purer and loftier light'. Though he was still young, he felt as if he had entered into his father's profound admiration for the passage, and felt with him 'the vibration of a soul attuned to eternal realities'.[11]

There were great similarities between father and son. Both lived half in this world, half in the next, leaving the lesser, mundane necessities of basic survival, such as food and finance, to the practical good sense of their spouses.

On more than one occasion Jane Lucretia gently teased her husband for his lack of common sense. One surviving letter between the two, written on 9 August 1842 from 5 Carlton Place in Clifton to Captain John in Ireland visiting his children, Arthur, Rebecca and Nan, and his sister Mary Anne, married to the Rev. John Burke, MP for Ballydugan in Galway, reveals an affectionate couple who obviously did not find separation easy.

> Although I so much wish to see you again, yet I would not on such a selfish account have you shorten your absence from home even one day when so many and such urgent claims are heaping upon you. I shall be much more satisfied when I think you are in the path of duty and of pleasure and shall patiently wait until you find it suitable to come to your little wife again.

He had asked her to leave everything and join him. She appears to have found the proposition rather romantic, if wildly impractical. Decent child-minding arrangements were obviously as much of a problem then as now.

> As to your affectionate invitation, would you really like to see the house, which I believe is yours, completely turned outside the windows and the children after it! 'On Horror's head, horrors accumulate'. I would as soon put a little lap dog over my house and family as the lady you

mention . . . 'Tell it not in Gath' that a lady of my sapient time of life should elope without ever the temptation of a lover's attendance. I have the Demon of Ruin to wave his wand over my domicile.

Jane Lucretia appears as charming and coquettish in middle age as she was when she first dazzled Irish society with her wit and vivacity. Wherever they lived, she was also well known for performing acts of charity all over the neighbourhood, visiting the sick, gathering poor children into ragged schools, reclaiming fallen women, reasoning, Bible in hand, with the Jews, and stopping to talk to people in the street about their eternal destiny. In the evening, while he read, she wrote letters and poems, painted in oils, produced an illustrated book on flora and fauna, recited poetry to her children, and sang hymns accompanying herself on the harp.

By the time of Henry's birth she had already produced a book of religious poems, dedicated to the Right Honourable the Viscountess de Vesci, 'calculated to excite the best feelings of the heart', its profits 'to be devoted to the aid of a respectable family in reduced circumstances'.

For someone of Jane Lucretia's brilliant temperament and artistic gifts, life in Cheltenham and Clifton must have been a little dull after Dublin. She never complained of frustration, but was determined nonetheless to inspire her children with a love of the arts. Years later, Henry Grattan wrote, 'Whatever love I have had for nature, for history, for literature, has been derived from her, and also whatever gift I may possess as a public speaker.'[12] His gift was exceptional, but then his mother's conversation was never dull. She certainly had a very unusual way of expressing herself. Even her account of the trivial goings-on at chapel, which she admits is the sum total of excitement in her life and hardly worth repeating to her husband, reveal a woman without an ounce of sham or pseudo-piety, capable of self-mockery, and of finding amusement in the most mundane, everyday events.

She and 'Gregory', possibly a visiting minister to Hope Chapel from abroad, have had 'a desperate quarrel', and Gregory has expressed his extreme annoyance in a letter. 'I was vexed of course and was determined not to speak to him. At the singing class accordingly I was making my way out of the room by a circuitous route in order to avoid him, but no, he intercepts my way, squeezes my hand, smiles in my face and says, "I hope you all very good".' This provokes a letter from her, a funny letter, ridiculing the whole affair, 'saying that notwithstanding all his explosions there is nothing in all the artillery he lacks against me but powder, and the noise has frightened me into good behaviour'. Gregory's access to the pulpit appears to have given him the upper hand – temporarily at least – for he preaches on the words, 'and will ye also go away?' levelled unashamedly at her. 'I have expected my forgiveness since then, all the while I mean to make him smart a little.'

The only real threat to their serenity was the behaviour of John Grattan junior, Captain John's eldest son by his first marriage. In 1838 he arrived on their doorstep in deep disgrace. His Uncle Arthur had dismissed him from his brewery apprenticeship for drunkenness and mixing in degraded company, insisting he leave Dublin altogether. It was the first they knew that a child of theirs was going astray and it came as a severe shock. Captain John persuaded his brother this was a temporary aberration, and begged him to give his son another chance. There were new brewing opportunities and family contacts in Bristol. Wetherman, the Bristol agent, was duly instructed to buy the young man a small brewery in the town, but there was no evidence of any reforming of John Grattan junior's character, and the brewery collapsed in 1845.

Chapter 3

1815–1855
The Life and Times of Arthur the Second

1.

Arthur Guinness the Second was afflicted with a host of difficult relatives. Since the bankruptcy of his brother, Edward, a steady stream of brothers, sisters, nieces and nephews tugged at his heart, as well as his purse strings. As the tribe spread throughout the land the patriarchal mantle hung ever more heavily on his gentle, gracious shoulders. He was advisor, counsellor, benefactor and banker. In fact, he felt, he said to one of his nephews, 'pressed upon by claims on the part of the multiplied branches of our family (and from various circumstances needy family) to an extent of which even you, though not altogether ignorant, can hardly form adequate conception'.[1]

An instinctive sense of duty and decency would not allow him see any of his family destitute. Besides, he was not unfeeling. He was close to his nine brothers and sisters, and genuinely wanted to do his best for them and their offspring. An army of nephew-apprentices was now working at the Brewery with a view to developing their managerial and business potential. They were carefully supervised by John Purser Junior, a formidable Guinness partner, and woe betide them if their behaviour did not enhance the Brewery's reputation and moral standing in the community. Arthur Guinness's charitable nature would not stretch to anyone whose conduct impugned the firm's good name.

Ingratitude upset him. It was unjust, when he went to such lengths to be accommodating. In 1821, although he did not find it easy, he remonstrated kindly, yet firmly with his elder brother, Hosea, for interfering in his treatment of the bankrupt Edward, who, despite having all his debts paid, obviously felt entitled to more than the basic salary of a company clerk.

> My dear Hosea
> I feel myself placed in a painful and delicate situation when called upon to address my Elder Brother, and a Brother who I so sincerely love and respect upon the subject of his pecuniary concerns, but my situation by which I am unavoidably obliged to act as Family Banker forces me to speak plainly . . . What claim had Edward upon the Trade? Had he rendered any service to the Trade to entitle him to an annuity and was it given for a period of years? Certainly not.[2]

To Hosea's daughter, Olivia Archer, another ongoing beneficiary of his bounty, he wrote patiently, yet with a certain amount of exasperation, 'May I recommend, my dear Olivia, that you keep a systematic account of all your expenditure for in that way you may more easily judge . . .' Learning the art of good budgeting was a recurrent commendation in his letters to the younger members of the family.

Even Hosea was not above asking for a supplement to his stipend. Times were hard for the clergy in Ireland. They were accustomed to a high standard of living, but stipends were drawn from the compulsory tithe, imposed since the Act of

Union on Protestant and Catholic alike. Understandably, the Catholic community bitterly resented being forced to support a church they despised, and as relations deteriorated, withheld the tithe as a means of protest, leaving a host of clerical Guinnesses in pecuniary distress.

In 1819 Arthur's eldest son, William Smythe Lee Grattan, announced his intention, like his Uncle Hosea, of forgoing his natural inheritance in the family business to enter the Church. Such was the pivotal nature of Arthur's faith, he could hardly be surprised or disappointed, and once again, there were still two sons at home to join their father at the Brewery.

Arthur had married Anne Lee in 1793. William was born in 1795, Arthur Lee in 1797 and Benjamin Lee in 1798. After a gap the couple also had six daughters between 1804 and 1814, raising them at Beaumont, which Arthur had bought from Hosea, who could not afford to run it, and needed extra financial help when his daughter, Olivia Archer, became mentally ill.

It was a very happy marriage. An affectionate husband and father, Arthur was devastated when his wife died. Two years later he married her closest friend, a respectable spinster by the name of Maria Barker. Unlike her future sister-in-law, Jane Lucretia, the thirty-eight-year-old Maria did not provide her husband with a second family, which was probably just as well, as Arthur had more than enough family claims on his time and his bank account already.

The potential he expected from his apprentice-nephews failed to materialise. Like the young John Grattan, Richard Lyons Darley, his eldest sister Elizabeth's son, left Dublin in disgrace. Arthur and John, the sons of his youngest sister, Mary Anne Burke, and her MP clergyman husband, were constantly drunk, as was Hosea's son, John. If that were not enough, one of brother Edward's sons, Richard, had to be committed to a mental institution, like his cousin Olivia. Small wonder Arthur wrote to his sister-in-law Jane Lucretia, who was starting with a young family all over again, 'Early control can alone secure, under God's blessing, obedience and steady conduct.'[3]

Unfortunately for Arthur, the family seemed to be acquiring as many clergy as black sheep. His own eldest son, Hosea's eldest son and William Lunell's only son had all chosen careers in the Church. Three of his daughters married Church of Ireland clergymen. It was becoming increasingly difficult to ensure a succession of reasonable, let alone feasible managers for the Brewery. And if that were not enough, both sorts of Guinness, clerical and lamentable, pursued him as if his pocket were bottomless. Any tussle for his soul between God and mammon was doomed from the start by a clan who knew how to manipulate his Christian conscience. When outsiders also asked to be remembered in his will, his generous spirit was stretched beyond the bounds of reason.

> It appears from your letter to be your opinion that I am extremely wealthy and my children so independent that on making my will I shall have much property to spare for others. Now you have formed a very mistaken estimate on both points. I have from various casualties, which have in the act of the Lord's Providence fallen out, chiefly affecting the property of my many dear Relations, had several individuals depending on me solely or partially for support . . . so although the Lord has been pleased to prosper mine and my sons' industry, I could not have been accumulating as you suppose, and indeed, I think I could not have done so acting as a Christian man . . .[4]

Like his father, the second Arthur Guinness was immensely charitable, a man who did what he felt was right whatever the cost. That combination of integrity and concern for his family caused the Brewery one of the most precarious moments in its history.

The early years of the nineteenth century were boom years for the brewer. He took advantage of the war between England and France to extend imports across the Bristol Channel. What better way to put strength into the young men resisting Napoleon's steady advance across Europe?[5] The defeat of Napoleon in 1815 and subsequent unemployment created a severe economic depression throughout the whole of Britain, particularly in Ireland. To make matters worse, in 1817 and 1819 the potato crop failed.

The Guinness brothers were appalled by the poverty and human misery it produced. They already served on a host of charitable committees, Arthur as founder member of the Society for Improving the Conditions of Children Employed as Chimney Sweepers, William Lunell on a committee to end begging, but charity appeared to do little to alleviate the distress. A radical economic policy was called for.

As Governor of the Bank of Ireland nothing could deter Arthur from introducing whatever stringent measures he deemed necessary – not even what today would appear a blatant conflict of interest. With his banking, rather than his brewing hat on, he united the Irish to the English currency, causing widespread deflation and ten very lean years for the family business. Settling brother Edward's debts compounded the problem. Surviving against overwhelming odds was a close-run affair, but Arthur had proved that he was a man of principle, prepared to put his country and his family before his own material prosperity. Writing to his teenage son, Benjamin Lee, he noted with pleasure the improvement in young Ben's handwriting, and the care he was taking with his schoolwork, but added this proviso: 'but my dear Ben ... recollect that although diligence in our worldly calling is our indispensable duty as Christians, yet we have a higher than these to engage our attention, for we have a heavenly calling in Christ Jesus and to this our supreme diligence is required.'[6]

His colleagues at the bank were very pleased with their

Governor's fiscal skills at first. Their pleasure diminished rapidly when he vetoed a rise in salary – his and theirs. Heaven knew his own financial situation could have benefited from such a boost, but he was only too aware of how it would seem. The public would presume the directors had an ulterior motive for the currency reforms. Self-interest had no interest for a man immersed in the biblical principles of Wesleyanism. 'Abstain from all appearance of evil.' Virtue would bring its own rewards. As far as Arthur Guinness was concerned he would not be the beneficiary of a nineteenth-century equivalent to a 'fat cat' pay-out. Like his father before him, he was austere in his standards for men in public office. The difference was that he was now in a powerful enough position to enforce them.

In 1821, the state visit to Ireland of King George IV included a tour of the Bank, and it was Arthur Guinness who welcomed him and showed him round. This was the first crossing of the ways for the Guinness family and British royalty, and in typical fashion for a tradesman who knew his place and had no time for cant or social climbing, Arthur was not unduly impressed. Years later he declined the privilege of becoming 'Purveyor of Porter' to Queen Victoria, on the grounds that it was 'a useless feather, and, I think, not even a respectable feather'.[7] Future generations did not share his disdain for royal patrimony. They coveted that token feather, and a great deal more besides, as wealth propelled them swiftly up the social ladder.

2.

Arthur Guinness was what is untruly called 'a liberal'. But while he developed those views, partly it might have been from his associations, partly from his circumstances, and with a judgement not yet fully enlightened in divine truth, and, therefore, without the perception of their error and evil tendencies, he yet manifested much of his natural character in the firmness with which he carried out his convictions. (Rev. John Alcock, Bethesda Chapel, Dublin, 17 June 1855)

Rev. John Alcock was the master of the back-handed compliment. Rarely has any funeral sermon said more about the bigotry of the preacher. The eulogy certainly did not reflect the deceased. Arthur Guinness was a true liberal. He believed in Catholic emancipation. Enlightenment, on the Rev. John Alcock's terms, never finally dawned. Had he been in a position to do so, Arthur would probably have got up and denounced the sermon as codswallop. The man who said, 'Although always a sincere advocate for Catholic freedom, I never could look my Catholic neighbour in the face. I felt I was placed in an unjust, unnatural elevation above him; and I considered how I would have felt if placed in a different position myself. Sorrow always excited my mind by such a contemplation', would have been appalled to hear it said publicly that he eventually 'recognised the error of his ways, passed over, and took his stand on the opposite side – on that side which shall ultimately be pronounced true liberality by the voice of God'.

In his lifetime he publicly repudiated any suggestion that his views had changed. He was, however, deeply opposed to the use of force. Herein lay the Guinness brothers' ambivalence to the Act of Union. On the one hand, they had a strong sense of national pride, identifying with the Irish people rather than the English landlords, unlike most of their social set. They supported their cousin Henry Grattan who had served the cause of brewing so well. On the other hand, the uprising, following so closely behind the carnage of the French Revolution, was a frightening warning of how small a spark would light the fuse. Basic human rights were one thing, an independent republic quite another.

On the whole, however, their innate belief in justice prevailed. The second Arthur never ceased to ask himself how he would feel in a Catholic's shoes. He fought for their right to admission to the Court of the Bank of Ireland, at the cost of a great deal of popularity among his Protestant colleagues.

But his stance did not win him the warm acceptance of the Catholic community either. Factions were far too deep. Steering an even course across the shark-infested waters of nineteenth-century Irish politics was bound to be a bloody business. With increasing regularity the Guinness family felt the fangs – and it always hurt.

In 1812 an extreme anti-papist group sent a petition to the British government begging them not to grant any concessions to the Catholics, signed among others by Arthur Guinness. His signature had been forged. Try as he might to clear his name, offering a £500 reward for information about the instigators in the *Dublin Evening Post,* Catholic newspapers continued to recall certain unpopular remarks he had made during the uprising.

The Catholic Board, anxious not to lose such influential goodwill, passed a rather deferential-sounding resolution saying the signature was an obvious forgery, and the brewing family entitled to the 'confidence, gratitude and thanks of the Catholics of Ireland'.

Humbug, said an editorial in *Cox's Irish Magazine* in June 1813. Must the Catholic Board fawn on its 'superiors'?

We hope that Mr O'Gorman does not mean to interweave brewing into the Catholic bill, nor make it the terms of our emancipation that we do give security to drink Guinness' porter . . . If Councillor Guinness will get us porter for nothing, as he gave us character for nothing when he called us a 'felonious rabble', we may deal with his porter, but until some domestic arrangement is agreed on, we will drink what we like, and whenever we can.

To the dismay of both sides the saga rattled on. In October 1813 the *Milesian Magazine*, a nineteenth-century Irish *Private Eye*, published this little piece of doggerel:

> To be sure did you hear
> Of the heresy beer
> That was made for to poison the Pope?
> To hide the man a sin is
> His name is Arthur Guinness
> For salvation he never can hope.

According to a certain 'Dr Brennan', Guinness beer was impregnated with heresy because 136,000 tons of Bibles, and 501,000 carloads of hymn books and Protestant catechisms were poured into the brew. His analysis of the liquid proved beyond all doubt that anti-popery porter was subverting all good Catholics by inducing 'a disposition to bowels particularly lax, an inclination to pravity, and to singing the Lord's praises through the nose'. Protestants, it appears, were lampooned as spending too much time on the toilet or in illicit sex, while singing evangelical hymns with an English accent. However, Dr Brennan concluded, there was an antidote to the effects of too much Guinness: Pim's ale.

Little trade was lost but the Guinnesses were not amused. Inflaming prejudice was dangerous. It was Hosea the churchman, aware the wind was blowing increasingly glacial, who decided it was time to take certain matters in hand. In 1814 he wrote to Sir William Bethan, deputy Ulster King of Arms and Herald of all Ireland, and asked for official permission for all the descendants of Richard Guinness of Celbridge to use the Magennis crest and coat of arms. Sir William replied tartly that there were *no* records to suggest he was entitled to them, which was exactly as Hosea suspected, but since the first

Arthur had been using them anyway, as a concession he would grant a new coat of arms. Except for a minor change or two it happened to be the Magennis crest.

Hosea was more than satisfied. An Anglo-Irish pedigree would do the family no good. But now they could confidently claim Irish descent from the hereditary earls of Iveagh.

But Hosea's efforts could not spare the family further political difficulties. In 1829 the British government passed the Catholic Relief Act, granting Catholics the right to sit in parliament. Arthur Guinness was delighted. He had helped Daniel O'Connell win a by-election in County Clare. 'I am much joyed', he said, at a public celebration, 'at the final adjustment of the "Catholic question" as it is wont to be called – but more properly the Irish question.' His joy was premature. Qualification for voting was immediately raised from a two-pound to a ten-pound freehold and most of O'Connells' supporters were disenfranchised.

Undaunted, Arthur Guinness was convinced full emancipation would come in a matter of time. Reason, sound common sense, a distaste for oppression and the love of liberty demanded it – and that was only what he would expect of the British government. The Reform Act giving Catholics the right to vote was eventually passed by the Whigs in 1832.

But the brewer's satisfaction was slowly eroded in subsequent years by what he saw as the increasing fanaticism of O'Connell's Catholic Association. They were calling for an end to the Act of Union, and Arthur Guinness saw no advantages in hot-headedness or republicanism, in that order. In the General Election of 1835, a mere five years after he obliquely accused the government of being oppressive, he not only opposed O'Connell, but seriously considered a request to stand against him. 'I think', he is reported to have said, 'that the time has come when it is the bounden duty of every man to speak his sentiments and to declare whether he is for the destruction or preservation of the constitution.'[8]

O'Connell was devastated. His newspaper, *The Pilot*, described how for years Arthur Guinness had publicly resisted the intolerance of the Orange system. He was a man 'who never committed but this one public error', and they were at a loss to know why.

Guinness loudly denied any change in political allegiance. He was not, and never would be, an Orangeman, however it might appear. It could not have escaped their attention that his youngest brother had just married the widow of the Protestant loud-mouth, John D'Esterre.

O'Connell's only explanation for his friend's betrayal was that his hard-done-by clergy relatives had 'got about him'. It was a stab in the dark, but it may well have hit the bull's-eye. In all probability Arthur Guinness was less disturbed by O'Connell's 'extremism', which had always been there had he cared to see it, than by the Whig government's plans to separate off the Church of Ireland. Eight of Arthur's relatives were clergy, dependent on tithes no longer paid by Catholics – dependent therefore on him. He can hardly have been pleased.

In the end projected reforms in Ireland led to the collapse of the Whig government and a General Election brought the Tories back into power. Arthur Guinness heaved a sigh of relief while O'Connell bitterly regretted the end of their long association. Some of his supporters demanded a boycott of Guinness beer and made several attacks on the Brewery. O'Connell deplored their behaviour, reminding them in *The Pilot* that revenge was counter-productive. Guinness was insured. They were not – against a guilty conviction for wilful damage. The brewer's behaviour, he said, in tones reminiscent of the funeral sermon preached in Bethesda Chapel – though from a Catholic perspective – was the senile aberration of an old man, who had been on their side 'when in the full strength of his intellect, and in the youthful vigour of his mind'.

While Protestants smugly claimed Arthur had seen the truth

at last, O'Connell referred to him as 'that miserable old apostate'. It was as well he was not a man who courted popular approval, for his balancing act on a ridge between two valleys satisfied only his own sense of tolerance with moderation. The narrow middle path did not allow for the slightest shift without the risk of a fall – and great was the drop on either side. Small wonder that some years later, when his son Benjamin Lee was invited to stand for a Dublin seat, his father urged him to decline.

> You will recollect that on two occasions a similar suggestion was conveyed to me . . . I then felt, and now feel, that the office of sitting in Parliament for a great city and especially such a city as Dublin where party and sectarian strife so signally abound, and more especially if filled by one engaged in our business, is fraught with difficulty and danger.[9]

However his actions appeared, Arthur Guinness always believed he kept to the narrow path. Others moved. O'Connell shifted left which pushed him to the right – just far enough to impair the balance for posterity. Never again would the Guinness family climb their way back into the Liberal fold, and one potentially moderating voice in the Catholic and independence cause was stilled for ever.

3.

In 1838 Arthur Guinness celebrated his seventieth birthday. He was as alert and sprightly as his father at the same age, fulfilling his public engagements with an energy which would put a much younger man to shame. He wore his sideburns thick and long according to the fashion, and dressed in black, having had the misfortune to lose a second wife.

His lifestyle, like his dress, was simple, almost austere. He never took advantage of the position his civic responsibilities bestowed upon him to climb the echelons of Dublin society, but lived quietly at Beaumont with his five unmarried daughters, except for an occasional extended visit to Rathdrum, where his eldest son had his first incumbency. William had married his cousin Susan, Benjamin's daughter, and the couple had three sons, Arthur's only grandchildren at that time.

While he was away his two younger sons managed his business affairs. Arthur Lee, aged forty-two, was a bachelor living alone at St James' Gate, and Benjamin Lee, at thirty-nine, had just married his cousin Bessie, daughter of the begging, bankrupt, recently deceased Uncle Edward. His father's wishes were Ben's command, and despite her impecunious state, Arthur positively encouraged the match. Devout Bessie, who shared her uncle's preference for the style of worship at Bethesda Chapel, was his favourite niece, and Benjamin Lee was not getting any younger. The Brewery needed an heir – or preferably two for good measure, since the Church had a tendency to entice them away – and a Guinness could do a great deal worse than look inside the family. Intermarriage was becoming a family tradition.

If family was Arthur's main source of pleasure, it was also his only source of real pain. They made too many demands upon his purse to allow him to lead a life of unbridled luxury, not that it was ever a real temptation. He was far too abstemious for that. His deeply evangelical Christian faith, based on the Bible, left permanently open on the desk in his study, and given a new lease of life by the preaching of Whitefield on the need for new birth, saw no point in worldly pleasure or waste. But neither did it reduce him to a grudging insensitivity. 'Later generations have seen members of this persuasion as narrow-minded bigots, killing joy and generous instincts wherever they were to be found. Fortunately, the evidence given by the letters written at a time of crisis in all their lives

68

enables us to refute this. The Guinness' faith was a generous broadening one. It comforted and strengthened them.'[10]

One particular family crisis, coming as it did out of the blue, was a major blow. Business at the Brewery was booming. 'The Guinness Persecution', as it was called in the Protestant press, had fizzled out, with no noticeable decline in sales, the Nationalists evidently preferring their porter to their principles. Father Matthew's national temperance campaign in 1839, though remarkably successful, barely dinted beer sales. Spirits were usually singled out for condemnation. Nonetheless, the old brewer, who closed every interview with 'let us pray', heard his precious porter called an affront to Christianity right outside the Brewery itself. He had the wisdom to keep silent, knowing, in the end, that for the Irishman total abstinence was one leap too far. The campaign finally achieved more than advertising ever could. It established beer as the working-class Irishman's drink. The Brewery had reached another major milestone.

A tranquil retirement was on the horizon. His two middle-aged sons were running the business successfully. Or so he thought. In 1839, a few months after he sent John Grattan the younger back to his parents, his own son, Arthur Lee, came to his father and confessed he had been leading a double life. Not only was he incompetent at managing the Brewery, he could not manage his own affairs and was hopelessly in debt. Mortified by his failure, he admitted that he could not actually bear trade at all. It was a daily affront to his artistic nature, and he begged not only forgiveness, but to be released from the business immediately. 'Believe me,' he wrote to his father, 'that "for worlds" I would not hurt your mind, if I could avoid it – of all the living. Your feelings are most sacred to me. This situation, in which I have placed myself has long caused me the acutest pain and your wishes on the subject must be religiously obeyed by me . . .',[11] and he signed the letter, 'your dutiful, grateful, but distressed son'.

Arthur was deeply shocked. It appears he had never had the slightest inkling of Arthur Lee's emotional or economic struggles. Overspending and financial mismanagement were beyond his powers of comprehension, yet he put aside his own strict personal code of conduct, never once reproached his son, and dealt with the situation as thoughtfully and even-handedly as he knew how.

The practicalities of enabling his son to withdraw from the Brewery were complicated. If Arthur Lee took his half share it would leave Ben and the business in a parlous state. In fact there was some discussion about winding it up altogether. Arthur Lee was deeply moved that his father should even consider such a drastic course of action, but wrote to his brother that it would be a pity, 'that so well-established and prosperous a Business should be given up when one in every way suited to conduct it is already so much at the Helm'. He would therefore be willing to continue with a moderate allowance, rather than increase it and risk destroying the goose that laid the golden egg.

It is not only the letters which reveal the generous, open and loving nature of relationships within the Guinness family at that time. A diary written by Frederick Darley Ogilby, which has only recently come to light, contains a rare account of the daily doings of the Guinness clan. It reveals a close-knit extended family network of cousins, who, with the Darleys and other in-laws, spent a great deal of time calling on each other, breakfasting, lunching and dining together, while stopping at various intervals throughout the day to chat to each other in shops or from passing carriages.

Frederick was the middle son of Eliza Darley, daughter of Alderman Frederick and Elizabeth Guinness Darley, Arthur's eldest sister. Eliza married Leonard Ogilby of Ulster and they sailed to America with their three young sons in 1816. Fred, now in his late twenties, and a very earnest young clergyman in the making, sailed to Dublin on the packet ship *Oxford* in

March 1840, to pay a visit on the family he had heard so much about, but could only vaguely remember. The journey took over a month. At seven o'clock in the morning of 24 April he is on deck to catch his first glimpse of 'the green sod of my dear native land', trembling with excitement.

Nor is he disappointed. The Darleys press the young American to the bosom of their family, as do the Guinnesses, though their welcome is a little more restrained, befitting their loftier status. The first Arthur thought it distinctly advantageous to marry his eldest daughter to a Darley. Now apparently, the Darleys benefit most from the match. Like John D'Esterre and brother-in-law Edward, Grandfather Frederick Darley, Lord Mayor of Dublin in 1809, was bankrupted by the economic recession of 1814, and dependent for his financial survival, like many other in- and out-laws, on Arthur Guinness. The Guinnesses, meanwhile, have prospered and risen. In the social snakes and ladders, the players have changed places. And young Fred finds it all rather overwhelming.

On his very first afternoon in Dublin he rides with his Aunt Susan Darley into the centre of town for a sight of the fine squares and noble buildings, and his first encounter with his Guinness relatives. Taking his afternoon constitutional in his carriage is his august elderly uncle, the Rev. Dr Hosea Guinness. A rather ingratiating Frederick is duly introduced, then passes on to greet Rebekah and Mary Ann, two of his maiden aunts,[12] occupying their father Arthur Guinness's carriage, which is parked outside a shop. Life for Dublin's well-to-do appears to consist of these pleasant daily encounters, with little else to relieve the monotony.[13] Frederick is manifestly charmed by the wealth and gentility of his Irish relations, by the elegance of Dublin, where they are treated with such deference and respect, and by their gracious, sophisticated lifestyle.

A visit to St Anne's Clontarf, country home of his Guinness

cousin, Benjamin Lee, now brewer-in-chief, reduces him to his most sycophantic. Ben, his senior by just a few years, lives in greater luxury than anything Frederick has hitherto experienced in his short, very different life on the other side of the Atlantic. St Anne's 'is situated on Dublin Bay most beautifully. The house has a castle-like appearance being of irregular Gothic construction with a high tower rising from the centre. The prospect from this is very extensive and commanding.'

The interior is even more impressive. In one of the most magnificent rooms he has ever seen, the fretwork ceiling alone cost £1,500! 'There is a splendid organ and the greatest profusion of the costliest furniture.' But the ceiling barely compares with the exquisite landscaping of the grounds, where rural bridges cross and recross the Serpentine and long, straight, terraced walks end in breath-taking vistas of the sea.

At seven thirty the Beaumont single aunts arrive for dinner, accompanied by Arthur Lee, 'a very pleasant addition to the party'. Fred must have received an invitation to visit Arthur Lee's bachelor pad at the Brewery, for he and his jovial uncle, Arthur Darley, breakfast there on 2 May. It is, Fred grudgingly admits, as sumptuous as Benjamin Lee's accommodation, but decidedly more eccentric.

> His house is crowded with knick-knacks, statuary, painting, stuffed birds etc. His drawing-room is furnished in Chinese style and most richly. In the yard there are plenty of gods and goddesses etc. There is a fountain which plays into a willow tree and on one side, with foot in brink, sits a little figure of ambiguous character which Uncle Arthur [Darley] very contemptuously denominated 'a little angel or a devil'.

Given this description of Arthur Lee's lifestyle, it seems strange that his father should have been so unaware of his eldest son's unsuitability for the brewing profession. The signs were there. This was the home of a man profoundly influenced by the new Romantic movement in literature and poetry, who identified with Byron or Wordsworth, and lived in a quasi-Gothic world of his own creating, a world at odds with the harsh industrial reality of brewing, as described enthusiastically by Frederick. 'It is an immense establishment altogether, everything on the grandest scale. We saw vats which would hold 100,000 gallons.' Frederick does not appear aware of any discrepancy. Evidently, nothing has been said about his cousin's plans, or the tensions they have caused in the family.

An invitation to spend a few days at Beaumont, Uncle Arthur Guinness's residence, is accepted with alacrity, and the house 'all I expected'. Fred spends a great deal of time describing and comparing the merits of the respective Guinness properties. 'Beaumont is situated in the midst of a fine park, elegantly laid out, with a noble mansion and has about it a look of highest gentility.' Uncle Arthur, at close quarters, also lives up to his nephew's expectations. 'I was delighted with Uncle Arthur, a perfect specimen of a Christian gentleman.' After dinner, 'he showed that he was determined his should be regarded as a Christian household. The clergyman of the parish, the Rev. Mr Brown, was called upon to lecture and have prayers before the party separated.'

One of the guests, Tom Burke, a Guinness brother-in-law, was renowned for falling asleep at the dinner table. Fred is told how on one occasion he was so soundly unconscious at his Grandfather Darley's house, that Uncle Arthur Darley encouraged everyone to creep away from the table, leaving him there while the dishes were cleared away and the lights blown out. While prayers are said, 'Poor Tom Burke made an exhibition of his old infirmity', but in Arthur Guinness's home 'the steward aroused him with a hearty shake by the shoulder'.

Beaumont seems to render Fred his most parsonical and

ingratiating. He spends his days reading to the ladies, or walking with them, the very picture of a perfect prospective clergyman. But then, plans are afoot. An important meeting has been arranged by his prominent relations with the Archbishop of Dublin. Presumably Fred has discussed with them, or they with him, the possibility of his finding a living in Ireland. It would appear to be an attractive proposition. 'There seems to be more of a disposition to make religion a concern of life here than I have often observed,' he notes in his diary, after being invited one Sunday evening to give a short homily in the Darley home.

The interview with the Archbishop is remarkably informal by contrast with life at Beaumont, the ecclesiastic making a jocular, and rather embarrassing attempt to put Frederick at his ease. 'Come Mr Ogilby, set by, as you say in American, set by.' Frederick is not impressed with this attempt to speak his native language and cannot bring himself to call the Archbishop 'My Lord' or 'Your Grace'. All that will come out is plain 'Sir'. Fortunately the Archbishop does not appear affronted, gives him a 'regular pumping' for personal information, and invites him to preach at St Ann's, his own church, on the following Sunday morning. Whatever the Archbishop's assessment of Fred's performance he cannot have failed to have been impressed by the way the whole family, Darley and Guinness, turn out in force to support their protégé.

Beaumont is constantly overrun by relatives, Uncle Hosea Guinness and Minnie his daughter-in-law, a widow with five children; cousin Ben Lee and his wife and children; Uncle John Guinness, his second wife and their young family, with whom Fred was evidently very popular. 'How the cousins flow in upon me,' he exclaims. Another very regular visitor and close friend of Arthur Guinness is the lonely widower Robert Rundell Guinness, son of Dick the barrister and grandson of the first Arthur's brother, Samuel the goldbeater.

Robert Rundell has just founded the Guinness and Mahon Bank and Land Agency.

On 16 May, after three weeks of intensive socialising, Frederick heads north to Ulster to visit his father's relatives. Whether the Archbishop ever offered Frederick a living is unknown,[14] but he returned to the USA, taking the diary with him, returning only for a brief visit to marry one of his father's cousins. The ceremony was performed in Dublin by old Uncle Hosea, 'almost in his dotage and can hardly walk', according to Fred, but capable of performing the task satisfactorily, it would appear, nonetheless.

In 1840, shortly after Frederick returned to the USA with his Irish wife, a new family agreement was drawn up, enabling Arthur Lee to take what he called 'a moderate £12,000' out of the business, enough to buy Stillorgan Park on the outskirts of Dublin.

There he exchanged materialistic pursuits for aesthetic pleasures, rebuilding the house, and indulging to the full the romantic, neo-Gothic lifestyle he had begun to indulge at his home at the Brewery. At last he had the proper setting for his paintings, for composing pantheistic verses and writing letters, sealed with the design of a young Greek god. Dark, slim and good-looking, his attempts to play the part made him look more of a dandy than a classical deity or a Byron. Nor was he other-worldly enough to avoid embarrassing his father and brother with his recurrent financial problems.

Arthur was mystified by his son's behaviour, and wished that his veneration of the Romantic poets could be replaced by 'some token of his being awakened to a sense of the value of the Gospel of our Lord Jesus Christ'. He urged him to self-discipline, particularly in his passion for beautiful objects. They were all very well, but he ought to 'lay something by for the evil day'. But Arthur Lee had inherited his father's generosity of spirit without the prudence and discretion which made it feasible. When the 'evil day' finally came in 1845 with the failure of the potato crops and widespread famine throughout the country, he, more than any of the landed gentry, did everything in his power to look after his tenants, and they loved him for it, erecting a small obelisk in green Connemara marble, 'to mark the veneration of his faithful labourers who in a period of dire distress were protected by his generous liberality from prevailing destitution'. His memory would 'ever remain green in Irish hearts', but it was Guinness beer money which made it possible.

The family crisis was the making of Benjamin Lee, who now took over as the senior brewer, showing exceptional flair for the task. Arthur stepped back into an advisory role, watching the Brewery's rapid expansion with evident satisfaction. Guinness's unique black stout was beginning to find its way all round the world, thanks to its many influential converts. In 1837 the future Prime Minister Disraeli recorded eating oysters and drinking Guinness at the Carlton Club. That brought the elderly brewer less satisfaction than a letter from his old friend, Michael Solomon Alexander, first Anglican Bishop of Jerusalem, whose appointment he had encouraged as key member of the Hibernian branch of the Church Missionary Society. 'We are daily enjoying your excellent porter, which I think has done much to keep up our strength. I regret to say we have lost some on the voyage. I have no doubt that you will be pleased that your excellent beverage has found its way to Jerusalem.' It must indeed have warmed the cockles of the old man's Christian heart, and brought him some amusement, to know his beer was on a vital mission to the Holy Land.[15]

4.

Shrewd Arthur may have been, hard-hearted never. The appalling famine resulting from the potato blight in the late

1840s which left whole families homeless, starving and destitute, exercised his compassion to the limit. Like many of his social class living in protected seclusion in Dublin, he had no idea of the extent of the disaster until he read about it in the *London Record* while on holiday in Torquay. The English newspapers contained graphic descriptions of children lying dying on the waysides, of bodies left unburied where they had died, the stench filling the countryside, while wealthy landlords did nothing. Thousands of Irish immigrants were pouring into Britain off crowded boats, riddled with the plague and countless other diseases.

Horrified, Arthur dashed off a letter to Ben at once. 'How awful do the accounts from Ireland continue and how evident is it that the exertions of the Government need to be aided by those of private individuals.' He could hardly tell a man of nearly fifty what to do with his money, even if he was his son. But Ben evidently did not take the hint, so Arthur wrote again, this time more explicitly. 'May the Lord in his infinite mercy direct our Government and all individuals possessing means to do so the use of measures to relieve if possible the sufferings of our wretched poor people. I wish to know of any mode in which we might be able to aid in the work. You know my dear Ben that my purse is open to the call.'[16]

But in Dublin the usual well-heeled, well-fed, bourgeois lifestyle continued, and merchants like Benjamin Lee never bothered to look beyond their own social boundaries. It was as if there were a war in a neighbouring country, while they remained on slightly anxious neutral territory. They chose to assume that if there really were a problem, the Government must be dealing with it. The Government in fact did very little, and Arthur was left with the problem facing any individual committed to famine relief – what can be done which does not constitute throwing drops into a boundless ocean? He lamented the fact that 'a fair honest movement independent of party spirit is not working towards relief . . . if there were, I know our Firm would stand forward.' In the end, he did what he could, but only Arthur Lee at Stillorgan Park, in contact with peasant farmers first-hand, used what resources he had to save their lives.

Had he been able to look into the future, Benjamin would have known he could have done a great deal more for the starving. The Great Famine did not do the Brewery any harm. Ironically, it actually turned a highly successful business into a potentially million-pound wonder almost overnight. There was a sudden dramatic improvement in rural living standards after 1850. The population had been drastically reduced by emigration and death. Agricultural labourers began to be paid in money. Some, at the wealthier end of the scale, opened shops. The railways were developed. Dietary habits changed. And more people than ever began to drink porter. Guinness had been given its great Irish market, and Benjamin Lee was just the man to exploit such an advantage.

In 1851 Arthur handed his big estates in Wicklow and Wexford to a new agent, George Waller. Letters from Waller to Arthur's solicitor, Robert Rundell Guinness, founder of the Guinness and Mahon Bank, speak of introducing arterial drainage to improve farming conditions for the tenants. There were good and bad landlords. In keeping with his character, Arthur Guinness was one of the former, benevolent and caring, at a vital time in Ireland's rural history.

As the years passed his mental faculties and physical energy remained undiminished – to his obvious surprise. 'My bodily health and my mental vigour are both preserved to a degree very unusual at the age of nearly 84.'[17] He still served on numerous civic and charitable committees, the Farming Society of Ireland, the Dublin Ballast Board which managed the docks, an exclusive business club known as the Ouzel Galley Society, the Meath Hospital, the Dublin Society, the Dublin Chamber of Commerce of which he had been president for many years. 'We have much cause for continued thanksgiving to our God, who giveth us all things richly to possess,' he wrote to a highly prosperous, ever-expanding Benjamin Lee, now father of a daughter and three sons, and in 1851, Lord Mayor of Dublin. In 1855 *Freeman's Journal* described him as 'our most distinguished citizen'.

A slight cloud moved across the horizon shortly before Arthur's death, when a certain Captain Edmund Henn-Gennys of Whitleigh House, Plymouth, suddenly invited himself to Dublin, claiming to be a distant relative. Fortunately, Hosea had died some years earlier and was therefore spared a visit which would have probably brought on a stroke. Arthur consented to have dinner with the man along with other senior members of the family – not in Dublin itself, which was too close for comfort, but out in the country, at Stillorgan, Arthur Lee's home. He listened carefully to the Captain's claim, that Richard Guinness of Celbridge was descended from the ancient Cornish family of Gennys through one of Cromwell's senior officers, then dismissed it quite happily on the grounds that there was no evidence to suggest any connection at all.

When he died peacefully some months later the Magennis crest was in evidence, as usual, at his funeral. In many ways it was in keeping for a man who always instinctively felt himself more Irish than English. With successive generations that sense of national identity would begin to wane, as increased prosperity urged them on to a more glittering lifestyle.

'God brought wealth also to his hand – and herein lay the greatest danger,' said the preacher at his funeral. For a man of Arthur Guinness's convictions, riches never constituted any danger at all. But it was a prophetic warning for later generations. The trap was set. At the death of the second Arthur Guinness his family had arrived at the crossroads.

Chapter 4

1855–1860
Henry Grattan and Sir Benjamin Lee:
Stars in their Ascendancy

1.

The second Arthur Guinness was valued for probate at £150,000. He left each of his nephews and nieces £400 in trust for their twenty-first birthdays. Some young men might have been impressed, but not Henry Grattan Guinness. Throughout his life money would never be more to him than a tiresome necessity, best left in anyone's hands but his.

Of all his uncles Arthur Guinness made the deepest impression on the child during occasional visits to Dublin with his father. There was something about the old gentleman's dignified bearing which defied contradiction and commanded respect. Yet he was kindly, and paid the child attention. He always commented on Henry Grattan's namesake, to the effect that if he grew up with a fraction of the force of character and gift of oratory of his illustrious cousin and forebear, Ireland's foremost politician, he would go far.

The child listened carefully to the many conversations in the family home about religion, business and politics, and especially to any mention of the notorious Daniel O'Connell, discussed in hushed voices only when his parents were out of the room. With such genetic history to nurture a vivid imagination, he grew up with a strong sense of Irish identity and a deep love for the country of his roots.

After Captain John's death in 1850, contact with the Dublin Guinnesses was more sporadic. Arthur rightly assessed that his youngest brother would not have left generous provision for his family, and offered the fourteen-year-old Henry Grattan an apprenticeship at the Brewery. But the boy had been raised in the society of military gentlemen, who whiled away the hours recounting fantastic adventures in faraway, exotic places. Henry's dreams were made of far more exciting stuff than brewing, and he turned the offer down.

His father's death was an enormous blow. Henry Grattan suddenly realised that he had never really known this reserved, quiet man, and now the chance was gone for ever. Their similar temperaments, essentially introspective, had kept them apart. Encouraged by his mother, Henry loved collecting fossil ammonites and belemnites. He could spend hours wandering, reading or daydreaming, completely absorbed in the rays of sunshine falling on the walls of a romantic old castle, solitary pleasures he never shared with his father. For much of the time he was away at school in Exeter.

But the bereavement left him feeling bereft and cheated. Drowning his sorrows in some of the seedier local taverns, he fell into what he would later refer to in deep, dramatic tones as 'evil company' and 'evil ways'.

Jane Lucretia's anxiety about her eldest son was compounded when at seventeen he decided to follow his younger brother, Robert Wyndham, to sea, sailing to Mexico and the West Indies as a midshipman, transporting thousands of pounds worth of precious cargo for owners who would never dare hazard the dangers of the ocean themselves. If Henry Grattan was looking for adventure he found it. Some of the crew deserted on the way home and it was largely due to his presence of mind that the ship was saved. He battled at the wheel for four hours at a stretch, fighting to keep the vessel on course in gale-force winds. Years later he would still be able to feel in his hands 'the jerk of the wheel as the vessel bounds over the billows, leaning to leeward before a stiff breeze', and vividly remember 'the exultation of battling single-handed with the top gallant sail when sent aloft to furl it before the rising storm'.[1]

Any thought of settling down was now firmly out of the question and as soon as he was back he set off for Lough Corrib to train as a farmer in preparation for emigration to the colonies. But an unexpected event one night in 1854 changed, not his passion for travel, but his course of direction.

At home in Cheltenham, at two o'clock in the morning, he, his mother and her visitors, all fast asleep in bed, were suddenly awoken by a loud banging on the front door. Wyndham had arrived home after sixteen months at sea on the *Francis Ridley* in a state of high excitement. The only available place to sleep was next to his elder brother. Instead of regaling him with tales of the countries he had visited and sights he had seen, as Henry hoped he would, he told him instead about the ship's chief mate, a man called Peek, who had been laughed to scorn for his outspoken Christian convictions by the loud-mouthed, abusive crew – until a storm such as Wyndham had never experienced in his life threatened to capsize the ship. While the hardened crewmen clung to the masts, terrified for their lives, Peek knelt calmly down on the deck and asked for the storm to cease. When his prayer was answered, mockery turned to grudging respect. Wyndham was his first convert. Who, in extremis, had not remembered his mother's prayers?

His voiced tailed off as he fell into a deep sleep, but Henry lay awake tossing and turning. It was inevitable that, under Jane's instruction and example, both brothers would see more to admire in the brave and honourable Peek than in the seamen whose aggressive behaviour they once thought it clever to emulate. Henry suddenly recalled having measles when he was ten, lying in a darkened room, while his half-sister Rebecca talked to him of the beauty of heaven. He vividly remembered the way her face became illuminated with a strange, other-worldly glow. He had wanted that 'mental vision of moral loveliness', but it had always eluded him, leaving a deep, yawning pit at the centre of his being which none of his adventures had been able to fill.

At breakfast the next morning his younger sister Lucy discerned that despite the bags under his eyes, her eldest brother was a changed man. He started to read *Hawker's Morning and Evening Portion*, scribbling notes about the Bible passage of the day in pencil in the margins.

But a deep restlessness inherited from his father was unabated, and when the news reached them that Captain Peek was looking for a crew to accompany him to the East Indies, he and Wyndham set off together on a new adventure. Henry only got as far as Hartlepool, where he was put ashore and sent home to Cheltenham, apparently dying. Whatever the mysterious illness, he recovered, and in the spring of 1855 set off for his beloved Ireland to become a farmer's assistant in Tipperary.

Farming was tedious. There was more fun to be had wandering the countryside with his gun – until he fell in a ditch, sprained his ankle and found himself with time for serious reflection.

What if his series of misadventures were not coincidences at all, but divine judgment, God's personal intervention to stop him in his tracks and turn him in a different direction? How could he have ignored the voice for so long, frittering away twenty precious years on his own selfish pursuits? But what did God want of him? He spent hours alone in the woods, crying out for inner peace and new vision. And gradually, the longed-for revelation came:

> Nature itself seemed transformed; earth and sky wore a
> new aspect; sun and stars were brighter, and flowers more
> beautiful; the song of birds was sweeter, and echoed by
> interior harmonies. The future was lighted with hope.
> The gates of glory and immortality opened to my mental
> vision and there shone before me an interminable vista
> of pure and perfect existence in the life to come. It was
> ... the union of the creature in appropriating and self-
> yielding love with Him who is uncreated, eternal love.[2]

Inspired by his new vision he now saw that he was surrounded
by 'the miserable and abject slaves of Romish superstition',
without spiritual enlightenment, and he began to preach in
the marketplace, in fields, on street corners, anywhere simple
countryfolk would stop and listen. And they did, in such
numbers that a local priest Henry called Father H was so
annoyed, that he set off on horseback with a whip in hand
to silence the young Protestant upstart. He found most of
his congregation giving the handsome preacher their rapt
attention. From being a gawky boy, Henry Grattan had turned
into a striking young man, tall and slim, with a mane of
shoulder-length dark hair and large dark eyes.

'How dare you disturb the peace of the countryside,' the
priest raged at him. Henry said he didn't intend to disturb the
peace, but offer the people real peace.

'Your religion is false,' the priest retorted, 'a cursed lie. I
challenge you to prove the truth of the Bible on which you say
it is founded.' Henry was about to do so when Father H
turned his horse and galloped off in fury, promising, over his
shoulder, to denounce the madman from the pulpit that very
Sunday.

True to his word, the priest instructed his congregation to
kick the young preacher if he tried to gain entry to their

cottages, to splash him with sink water or throw him into the nearest puddle. Henry's employer was warned that if he did not silence his assistant, his farm would be attacked, his hayricks burnt to the ground.

The opposition was music in Henry's ears, confirmation that he had found his life's work, especially as many of the local folk still flocked to hear him, tears pouring down their faces as he preached. He was appalled by the ignorance of rural Catholics, steeped in superstitions which kept them in grinding poverty. They told him that Protestantism had been invented by Henry VIII who had imprisoned Mary Queen of Scots and married his own daughter. 'These people are unconvertible,' warned the Protestant governess at the farmhouse. 'Thank God,' Henry wrote in his diary, 'she was, through my poor testimony, converted herself shortly afterwards.'

Henry now needed a bodyguard and could not leave the farmhouse after dark. He was little help on the farm, and constantly borrowing money from the farmer. His presence was becoming increasingly unwelcome. It was time to move on. The story of the great Captain Gardiner who had died in an attempt to take the Gospel to the Patagonians of South America had fired his imagination. He could shoot, fish, ride, sail a boat on a stormy sea, and was a passable carpenter, the perfect omni-competent missionary, now that he was taking lessons in cobbling. What did his mother think?

South America was definitely not what Jane Lucretia had in mind for her son. She replied from Cheltenham on 11 August 1855, his twentieth birthday, urging him 'to seek in constant prayer, guidance as regards your future course'. Uncle Arthur had just died, and 'it appears that you now have a prospect when of age, which is new and encouraging. The sum of money which by your late kind uncle's will is in reserve for you will enable you, if you are desirous to make a favourable commencement in a line of life for which you are now preparing.'[3] If not farming, then what? She couldn't see why the Patagonians needed to hear his message more than his fellow countrymen. Why not, she suggested, with more than just a touch of maternal self-interest, be a missionary at home? 'In this happy and favoured land – England – the towns and villages especially are so many moral deserts. The towns corrupt, the villages in a state of brutish ignorance.' Studying theology might therefore be a sensible option.

With the birthday money she sent he paid off his debts as she told him to do (how could any son of hers incur debts?), packed his bags and went home to Cheltenham, to be built up on a diet of 'farinaceous' food – his mother's latest nutritional fad, her vegetarian phase.

Word arrived from Wyndham almost at once that he and Peek were almost home. If Henry wanted a pleasant surprise he should meet the ship in London when it docked.

Henry was staggered when he saw the crew again, as Wyndham knew he would be. Some of the worst blasphemers he had ever met were 'singing the songs of Zion with such stentorian strength that it seemed to me they might have meant to blow the roof off the deck cabin in which they held their prayer meeting'. If hardened sailors could be transformed like that, anything was possible. There was no time to lose.

In January 1856, on the night before he left to take up a place at New College in St John's Wood, Henry Grattan paced the streets of Cheltenham in a state of utter dejection, convinced he was taking a wrong turn. He was terrified that theological study would rob him of his zeal and dampen his spirit, and only made his way to bed in the small hours, having determined to walk in the ways of Wesley and White-field. Nothing would be allowed to extinguish the sacred fire burning in his soul.

As he suspected, prolonged bouts of academic study did not come easily to someone as impatient as he was. He balked at what appeared to be wasted time, and at weekends and in the evenings, when fellow students were settling down to write their essays, was out in the streets holding open-air services. Gathering a crowd was never a problem. The dynamic young student with the penetrating eyes and intense expression had magnetic appeal. But if the ordinary people were enthralled with his preaching, local church leaders were not. After his first official sermon at the Congregational Church in Kentish Town, they said 'his voice was too loud', and 'people would not be frightened into heaven'.

'I am sure I should not attempt to do any such thing,' Henry replied, 'but if I could be enabled to point out their danger, scare them away from the pit, I should rejoice.' No further preaching invitations from the Congregation Union were forthcoming. It was disappointing, until he remembered no one could deny him a congregation in the open air.

To his fellow students he was a familiar sight, hobbling back late at night after tramping miles around the district, his feet crippled by blisters, especially on the Sabbath day when he refused any form of transport. By the summer, having completed his first year and gained a second-class certificate of honour, he was preaching more and more, attending classes less and less. He never finished his second year.

At home in Cheltenham he started preaching every evening on the Promenade. Thousands gathered to hear him. 'He'll be a very useful man when he cools down,' said his pastor, Dr Morton Brown. 'Did he say that?' Henry asked Wyndham indignantly. That made him more determined than ever there would be no cooling down. The proof of it would be in his preaching.

Every night he invited anyone who wanted a private discussion about the state of their soul to come to his house. As many as seventy 'enquirers' might be queuing up to see him at any one time. Jane Lucretia could not move in her own home. It had to stop. So Henry moved into a room at the

Town Hall, where he preached regularly, packing the place to the doors.

On his twenty-first birthday he noted in his diary that his only ambition was 'to live preaching and to die preaching; to live and die in the pulpit; to preach to perishing sinners till I drop down dead'. Uncle Arthur's bequest of £400 was now his to do with as he pleased. He gave it to his mother, and set off for Birmingham with a half a crown in his pocket.

After three weeks in Birmingham where huge crowds turned out to hear him night after night, he went to Wednesbury, descending a 600-foot shaft into a coal mine with brother Wyndham so that they could preach to 'these poor, benighted men'.[4] From the Midlands he travelled to many English towns, attracting ever larger audiences as his fame grew. In Exeter hundreds had to be turned away. The more he preached the more he became aware of his growing ability to hold a congregation in the palm of his hand. But acclaim did not bring material comfort. It was a hand-to-mouth existence. He never knew where he would eat his next meal or find a bed for the night.

In April 1857 he was invited to preach at the famous Moorfields Tabernacle in London, once the base of the great Whitefield himself. Henry Grattan Guinness now stood in the pulpit of the most prestigious nonconformist church in the country, overawed at the thought of his illustrious predecessor whose life-sized portrait hung in the vestry, arms reaching to heaven, and whose presence still seemed to pervade the place.

Wyndham sat at the back of the gallery, waiting anxiously for the reaction to his brother's first sermon. In front of him sat two elderly ladies, one of whom turned to the other and said, 'My dear, there ought to be a committee appointed to choose a suitable wife for this young preacher!'

There was no doubt that Henry Grattan now constituted a serious risk to unattached young ladies. Well-to-do women with marriageable daughters invited him to tea. According to

The Christian World, his attractions were immediately evident:

> The moment you observe him you cannot fail to be struck
> with his appearance. It is decidedly singular and rather
> prepossessing. In person he is tall and slender, and of an
> easy, graceful manner. The long, thin face, not altogether
> destitute of healthful hue, but sometimes tinged with a
> hectic flush, bears, in repose, a grave and studious aspect;
> and when lighted up as it frequently is, with a quiet smile
> of pleasure, indicates the presence of a genial spirit. The
> long, dark hair, parted in the centre and thrown back-
> wards, gives to the preacher a rather womanish aspect;
> but his voice is by no means feminine, for it is full and
> loud. Indeed, we do not suppose that there is a church,
> chapel or hall in London, or elsewhere, in which he could
> not make himself heard to the remotest corner; albeit he
> is sometimes so rapid in his utterance, that the words
> unite and become indistinct ... That which strikes you
> most, perhaps, in his preaching, is the thoroughly natural
> and unstudied style of address he employs; and it is to
> this fact, we believe, may be attributed much of his power
> over the people, which, despite the frequent want of logic
> that is displayed, and the lack of connexion that is
> observable to the critical eye, between the different
> parts of a single discourse, rarely fails to melt and move
> the hearers.[5]

It was whispered that a Wesley and a Whitefield were about to
have their parallels in a Spurgeon and a Guinness. But not
everyone shared that view. Some were bitterly disappointed
and thought him decidedly eccentric, for example, in keeping
his seat for several minutes after the end of the hymn-singing
before getting up to read the lesson, or in the long pauses he
would interject into his address, which made his audience
think he had lost his place.

The pastor of Moorfields Tabernacle, Dr Campbell, felt that these were merely signs of immaturity and was so impressed with the young man that he invited him to stay on as a permanent minister. It was a very tempting offer, holding out security and prestige, but after a lengthy inner struggle Henry Grattan declined. He could not be tied to one church. On 29 July he was, however, ordained there in front of a large congregation as an itinerant, interdenominational evangelist by five different denominations. The following day he went to Cheltenham to say goodbye to his mother, then set off on a three-year preaching tour which would take him half way around the world.

The rumblings of the mighty religious revival which would shake most of the USA, and large parts of the United Kingdom and the Continent in 1859 were just beginning. Crowds thronged to hear the young preacher, breaking down and weeping openly as he spoke. In Wales Henry preached in eighty different locations, 140 times, to a total of about a hundred thousand people. In Aberdare, when he invited members of his audience to come forward in repentance, all ten thousand of them responded at once, mobbing the platform which promptly collapsed. He was dragged to safety, fortunate to escape with a minor leg injury.

In Scotland, where he packed the churches of famous past preachers like Haldane and Murray McCheyne, he met well-known ministers, 'Rabbi' Duncan of Edinburgh and Dr Candlish, and hobnobbed with one or two 'titles', staying at Keith Hall with the Earl of Kintore, and at Huntley Lodge with 'the dear old Duchess of Gordon'. His brewing cousin, Benjamin Lee, would have no doubt been impressed with such important social conquests, but Henry's values were rather different. 'I think I can still hear the rustling of the leaves of the Bible at Bannockburn on a Sunday morning as the whole congregation turned simultaneously to the chapter read.' *The Glasgow Examiner* approved of his zeal and fervour.

'He appeals directly to the feelings in the soft tones of affection, or the stern voice of warning, suiting his features to the sentiment and moving his hands and arms to heighten the effect.' But regarding the power of his voice, felt 'a little modification of its tones would make a still deeper impression'.

In January 1858 Henry Grattan travelled to Paris, where his most influential convert was the future, doughty female evangelist to Algiers, Jane Bonnycastle; then on to Boulogne and Geneva, up into the Alps and across frozen streams on mule-back to Chamonix. While he was in Switzerland Henry received the most enticing invitation of all – to Dublin.

2.

Meanwhile, back at the Brewery, in the Dublin of 1857, Benjamin Lee Guinness, compliant son, dutiful husband, and responsible, recognised leader of the city's merchant classes, was recreating himself after his father's death. He was fifty-seven, but until that moment had lived a prescribed kind of existence. At sixteen he became an apprentice, at twenty-four a partner, and at forty the undisputed head – as prince regent, deferring in all major matters to the king. Once the kingdom was truly his, a cautious policy of steady growth was suddenly upgraded into determined expansionism. Within a few years the growth of the Guinness export trade would make him the richest man in Ireland.

His private life mirrored this subtle, but definite change in style. In his father's lifetime, he lived fairly quietly with his growing family at St Anne's, Clontarf, opulent by his young American cousin Frederick's standards, but on a comparatively small estate for such a wealthy man, about two miles from Dublin, four from the Brewery. He used a modest town house, 1 St Thomas Street, for ease of access to his work.

The year after Arthur's death he bought a property much more in keeping with his aspirations, in the most fashionable of Dublin's elegant Georgian squares, 80 St Stephen's Green. This imposing, three-storey Palladian mansion with a projecting portico, supported by four columns, the first to be built in Dublin, cost him a mere £2,500 as its previous owner was bankrupt. As soon as number 81 became available he acquired that too, dismantling the adjoining walls to make one large dwelling with thirty bedrooms, accommodation for twenty servants, and its own expansive gardens, later known as Iveagh House. It was here he began to entertain on a lavish scale, and the legendary Guinness hospitality was born.

Family fortune was obviously increasing at a considerable rate, as he then thought of investing 'a small sum (say £20,000 to £30,000) in the purchase of land',[6] and bought an estate in Ashford, County Galway, on the shores of Lough Corrib, the ultimate seal of the slow metamorphosis of a family of tradespeople into the landed gentry. All Benjamin Lee needed was a title.

He could afford to look a little pleased with himself, as his portrait suggests. He had the same determined chin, prototypic Guinness jaw and aquiline nose as his father and grandfather, the same tight-lipped smile, but his face was fuller altogether, and there was something about the way he held his head which suggested a man confident enough to look the Irish aristocracy firmly in the eye.

The rise of Benjamin Lee after his father's death might appear swift and sudden, like a greyhound from a cage door when the signal is finally given, but in fact there were earlier signs that he might not strictly concur with Arthur's disapproval of ostentation and extravagance. His inauguration as Lord Mayor in 1851 was a magnificent occasion. The Dublin correspondent of *The Times* wrote on 3 January that 'it was conducted with more than ordinary civic pomp. The municipal procession altogether eclipsed anything that had been seen since the palmy days of the old "Orange" corporation and the day, so far as business was affected, was to all intents, observed as a holiday.'[7]

A sumptuous civic banquet twenty days later, attended by the Lord Lieutenant and every important dignitary in the city, was reminiscent only of one given thirty years earlier when King George IV himself visited Ireland. There were no scruples about the self-indulgence of men in public office here, no determination to set an example in simplicity like his father and grandfather. And the Great Famine was barely over.

Arthur had the wisdom to keep quiet. Bessie however struggled with her husband's apparent enjoyment of luxury and status, being a stalwart nonconformist and attender at Bethesda Chapel. Raised in relative penury by parents on the run from creditors, she knew and feared with prophetic foresight the seductive, destructive power of riches, and worried continually about the effect of such a lifestyle on her children.

There were a daughter and three sons, Anne Lee in 1839, Arthur Edward in 1840, Benjamin Lee in 1842, and Edward Cecil, the future first Earl of Iveagh, in 1847. Benjamin Lee appears to have adored his wife and children, and liked nothing better than to spend time alone with his family at St Anne's or at Ashford. He would never give himself over completely to unabated or frivolous socialising. It was not in his nature. Temperamentally, he manifested the uneasy ambivalence which haunted successive generations of heads of Guinness. Success necessitated gregariousness, but innate shyness drove them to take refuge in privacy and solitude. He seems to have convinced an uncertain Bessie that entertaining was at best his duty, at worse, a necessary evil.

She remained 'frail' after the birth of their children, a common euphemism for all sorts of conditions afflicting women at the time. In 1852 Arthur turned down a request to persuade his son to stand for Parliament as a Conservative on the grounds that he was 'a devoted husband of a wife suffering extreme delicacy of health'. Benjamin Lee bowed as ever to his father's wishes and refused the invitation, either to give his undivided attention to his wife or, more likely, because he was far-sighted enough to see that the time for a Guinness MP had not yet come. Outspoken Conservative political allegiance could damage trade in a nationalistic Ireland.

Though Bessie was never taken in by the fast and fashionable society in which they were now established leaders, she was never that sure of her husband. She lived in daily fear for his eternal soul, painfully aware of the moral dangers waiting in snare for a man of his wealth and prestige. If she were to die, where would he or her children be without her spiritual protection and guidance? To her growing son, Arthur Edward, she wrote:

> Do my darling avoid bad company, I mean worldlings, for there will be plenty anxious to come here, and do guard darling papa from designing, worldly women, for he will be much set on and might easily be taken in. I do not mean that he should not marry, but that he will get one who will help him on to that future world and not lead him to think of or live for the present.[8]

Her anxiety was compounded by the fact that along with the other changes in his life, Benjamin Lee was becoming less nonconformist, increasingly conservative in religious observance. He would say to her that a Church of Ireland threatened with disestablishment needed a staunch defender. And, after all, they were surrounded with clergymen – one of his brothers, and all but one of his brothers-in-law. But she saw that evangelicalism and increased sophistication was a mixture which easily curdled. Nonetheless the atmosphere in which she raised her children remained distinctly pious, serious without being repressive. Prayers were said morning and evening attended by family and servants alike. Benjamin Lee would hardly throw off overnight the influence of his low church childhood, now reinforced by his wife.

Like his forefathers, he believed wealth was a sacred trust. To squander money was a sin, to use it wisely for the good of others, a cardinal virtue. But although the family motto was 'My Hope is in God', Benjamin Lee's reliance on a gospel of self-help appeared greater than his trust in any outside force. The 'serene equipoise between God and Mammon', the very 'hallmark of the family',[9] as Bessie saw only too well, was now in jeopardy. Work, discipline and duty were what mattered, a concerted effort to get Ireland back on its economic feet after the famine by providing ample employment with fair remuneration.

Christian duty implied responsibility to the workforce. Like the Quakers, Benjamin Lee was a benevolent employer, providing job security, pensions, decent housing and amenities. As the Brewery expanded, propelling him from the safe base of a wealthy man to the dizzying heights of millionaire, he never abused his employees. Wages were higher than at any other company. A job at Guinness was gold indeed.

Not surprisingly, when, on 15 January 1858, the *Daily Express* announced the imminent arrival of another, very different kind of Guinness, saying, 'We understand our fellow citizens will shortly have an opportunity of hearing this now celebrated preacher', Dublin began to buzz with the news. 'Is he a meteor or a star?' the newspapers asked. Dr Urwick, minister of York Street Chapel, who had baptised the young man twenty-three years earlier, could not wait to find out. Neither, no doubt, could Bessie. Benjamin Lee might have been a little less enthusiastic at the idea of having a cousin-preacher renowned for collecting more temperance pledges than any other, right on his doorstep, but no doubt he comforted himself with the reminder that his young relative had just turned down the most prestigious nonconformist pulpit in the country.

3.

Henry Grattan Guinness arrived in Ireland in February to huge acclaim. Dr Urwick noted in his diary, 'Unwonted excitement possessed all classes of what is called the religious public, and spread fast to numbers beyond it. To prevent serious disorder, admission was regulated by tickets; yet under that restriction the chapel was thronged to its utmost capacity of even standing room, long before the hour for commencing the worship.'

Only 22 per cent of the population was Protestant, but Dublin was proud of her successful sons, particularly a Guinness – even if he was the son of D'Esterre's widow. The pro-Catholic *Dublin Evening Post* was not going to let anyone forget the fact, but nonetheless showed a great deal of interest, weighing him up against other Protestant preachers like Spurgeon as if they were professional boxers. On 28 January it referred to a glowing account of one of his sermons in the *Liverpool Mercury*. The Concert Hall there had been full to capacity, albeit a crowd 'of very mixed character', since many left their heads uncovered. It described him as 'a modest unassuming young man . . . wearing a frock coat that reaches to the knees and is buttoned almost up to the neckerchief', which was really rather quaint and old-fashioned, since everyone else was wearing high collars and cravats. His shoulder-length hair framing his face, gave him 'a classic or poetic grandeur, intensifying as it does every expression'.

It would have been easy, after the press build-up, for Henry Grattan Guinness to have been a major disappointment, but he more than fulfilled expectations. The drive and forcefulness of the entrepreneurial Guinnesses were blended with the artistic flair and magnetic quality of the Cramers, and it was an irresistible combination. He had merely to walk into a room to command attention. But his intensity, 'the deep earnestness' everyone found part of his personal charm, meant he found it difficult to laugh and even harder to relax. He was a man who would push himself to the very limit.

On 8 February the *Daily Express* carried a full report of his first public appearance. It described his rather singular looks, the long dark hair thrown back from a pale, interesting face, and went on to say, 'In the pulpit his manner is quiet and unaffected, and characterised by an earnest simplicity which forcibly impresses itself on the listener. His gesture is re-markably graceful and appropriate, without the smallest approach to elocutionary display, and in addition to these, his voice is musical and well-modulated.' He had evidently learned to modify his volume.

All the newspapers referred to his abstinence preaching. 'Mr Guinness is not for Guinness' became, and remained, a popular catch phrase in Dublin for many years. The publicity attracted the cream of Dublin society. The ruling Protestant ascendancy, the leading professionals of the town and the clergy, deigned to grace a nonconformist chapel with their presence, determined to have a look at the latest phenomenon lest they might be missing something. By Monday 15 February, after nine sermons, he had captured the front page and the headlines.

Few preachers have ever addressed congregations more select. They consist of the elite of all denominations, including a considerable number of the Established Clergy. The wealth, the respectability, the cultivated intellect, as well as the evangelical piety of the city, have been represented in a measure unprecedented, we believe, on such an occasion in this country. Judges,

Members of Parliament, distinguished orators, Fellows of College, the lights of the various professions, and, to a considerable extent, the rank and fashion of this gay metropolis, have been drawn out to a dissenting chapel which was thronged, even on weekdays, by this new attraction. On Wednesday morning the Lord Lieutenant was present with the gentlemen of his excellency's household; and yesterday morning we observed among the audience the Lord Chancellor, the Lord Justice of Appeal, and Baron Pennefather.

No mention was made of whether Benjamin Lee came to hear his cousin preach on the folly of drunkenness and riches, but there seems little doubt they met. The family remained very close. There was however a slight embarrassment on both sides – not just because of Henry Grattan's temperance preaching. Playing on his half-brother's acclaim, John Grattan the second, living in penury for twenty years since he bankrupted the Bristol brewery his Uncle Arthur had given him, picked this particular moment to sue Benjamin Lee for wrongful dismissal.

The reception Henry Grattan received in northern Ireland was even more euphoric. The Dublin social élite had remained very much on their dignity and in control of their faculties. In Belfast the classic signs of religious revival broke out, thousands lying prostrate on the ground for hours after he had preached. The large Catholic community, some forty thousand strong, found it very disturbing, scoffing loudly at first, then shunning the Protestants in terror, in case they should catch 'the thing that's going'.[10] The priests distributed holy water and consecrated medallions as protective measures, but many succumbed to the disease. Dr Urwick noted, 'Altogether, nothing to compare with it had been known in Ireland within living memory. An announcement that he was to preach was enough to put the population on the move.' The largest buildings available were too small to accommodate the masses who wanted to hear him. 'A tidal wave of popularity bore him along day after day', and the press followed him about, commenting on his sermons as if they were leading topics of interest.

There is no doubt that in an era before the cinema and television, a handsome young preacher was wonderful entertainment, happily fulfilling the role of the later screen heroes. But that alone cannot explain Henry Grattan Guinness's popularity. The *Daily Express* admitted there was no 'cunning exhibition of oratorical fireworks, a dazzling stage effect or theatrical contrivances to work up a "galvanic" revival'. In fact, his sermons were almost childlike in their simplicity. Henry Grattan would say in later years, 'it was hardly a matter of preaching'. There was no need for 'hanging back', for taking care over what he said lest he gave offence to one side or the other. 'Everyone wanted to hear.'

The year 1858 was one of intense political turmoil. The Industrial Revolution had intensified a sharp divide between rich and poor. The established church had little to say about the evils of sweated labour, slum housing and appalling deprivation. It offered little spiritual satisfaction to the prosperous middle classes with no goal other than the accumulation of wealth, or to the working classes committed to a life of drudgery to provide it. A population sunk in despondency and gloom, with no hope, was ripe for religious revival, and it came, sweeping through England, Scotland and Wales, affecting every rank and class of person, giving birth years later to some of the greatest pioneering movements for social reform.

Ireland, for sectarian reasons, had always been resistant to Protestant-style religious expression, but Grattan Guinness heralded a new dawn. He was bold enough to criticise Protestants for denouncing Romanism when they were manifestly in darkness themselves. A gratified *Dublin Evening*

Post quoted him at length in an article entitled, 'The Rev. Grattan Guinness on religion in Ireland'.

> In the North I saw a great deal of rancour and Orangeism, but very little true Christianity. One clergyman told me that a man applied to him for Church membership and to be allowed to take the sacrament, stating he believed himself to be a Christian. The minister said to him, 'What makes you think you are a Christian?' 'Ah well, Sir,' said he, 'I think I could eat a Roman Catholic.' (laughter)

What, asked the Catholic newspaper, would Lord Eglinton, the Viceroy make of that, when he had just appointed two loyal Orangemen as his chaplains? 'The Rev. Grattan Guinness will however have accomplished a great deal for society and religion, if his disinterested advice be followed . . . Before Protestants seek to convert Roman Catholics, let them seek to convert themselves.'

He left Ireland for a few months in the summer of 1858. While he was away his half-brother's claim for compensation was dismissed. Benjamin Lee himself gave evidence. The press had conveniently forgotten this difficult little episode by the time Henry made his triumphant return the following year. This time he dispensed with chapels and ticket systems altogether. They tended to limit his hearers to the well-heeled, so he preached in the open air instead, so that no one could be disappointed.

In Ulster he had to be hoisted on to the roof of a cab, so that the twenty thousand who had turned out could all see him. Certain English newspapers including *The Times* and the *Lancet* were highly indignant that riff-raff should be allowed to attend his meetings. Filling the streets of Belfast with prostitutes and drunken revellers was nothing more than 'a moral epidemic and contagious hysteria'.

At the end of 1859 he set off for the United States, where a similar 'moral epidemic' was about to break out. In Philadelphia he preached on average thirteen times a week for several weeks – to groups of firemen, sailors, medical students, to seven hundred boys and girls from a House of Refuge, to violent prisoners in the County Gaol. All 246 prisoners were kept in solitary confinement, locked behind double doors, one of which was opened slightly, so that they could hear him. He had to shout to his invisible congregation down a 400-foot iron framework corridor. It was a gloomy December day and there appeared to be little response to his message. Afterwards, he sat in the twilight of one of the cells for some time with a wife-murderer who was 'filled with the gloom of mental wretchedness and despair and only stared at the floor, shook his head, and said, "I believe all that" '. It was not what Henry wanted to hear, and he allowed himself to be discouraged by the apparent failure. For months he had kept up a punishing schedule. There was little spare energy left to burn.

Unaware of his diminishing resources he spent seven weeks in New York, preaching a minimum of nine sermons a week, then travelled across America and Canada, stopping in many towns along the way. Everywhere he went the crowds turned out to hear him. Henry Grattan had never known anything like it, nor would he again in his lifetime. Looking back at those days, remembering the deep hush which would fall upon his listeners, their rapt attention, and tears of repentance, he would say wistfully, 'I can almost listen to him, that evangelist of other days, and wonder, WAS IT I?'

Returning to Ireland in June 1860 he expected to continue where he had left off but was by now utterly exhausted and on the verge of a breakdown. A holiday was imperative. The inveterate traveller decided upon Norway, but when plans fell through, settled reluctantly for Ilfracombe. It was one of the most fortunate disappointments of his life.

4.

On an Ilfracombe down one sultry summer afternoon, three sisters in wide-brimmed hats are lazing on a grassy cliff top. Beneath them, the cliff falls away sharply in a sheer rocky drop to the sea shimmering in the August sun. Mabel, the eldest, is engrossed in a book, while Laura, the youngest, conscious of her attractions in the new muslin dress she has bought specially for the holiday, is unable to settle to anything and determined to distract the other two. Fanny, the plainest of the three, puts her sketch pad down with a sigh, and gazes out to sea.

She and her sisters have not been raised in the same household. Compared to them she seems a pale, insipid flower, a slight, sallow-faced woman, well past the first bloom of youth, wearing a dark, unfashionable dress, buttoned to the neck in the plain, simple style of the Quakers. Her dark hair is parted in the middle and dragged austerely into a bunch of ringlets on either side of her face, emphasising a high fore-head, almost permanently creased by the difficulties life has forced upon her.

Gradually the glorious expanse of azure blending into the distant skyline, the rhythmic murmur of the waves, the taste of the salt on her lips and the warmth of the sun on her back begin to work their charm, soothing away some of the tension. It is not such a bitter blow to be in Ilfracombe after all, and not in Paris, as she had hoped. A poor second best, but it will do.

She has been vaguely aware that Laura is enthusing – again – about the dynamic Mr Guinness (she has talked of little else since she heard him preach on their first Sunday), and smiles to herself as she picks up her sketch pad and gets to work.

Laura, noticing the smile, says, with a slight edge in her voice, 'Well you missed something, Fanny. Why on earth didn't you come?'

Fanny felt like saying there was hardly any point since she had been given such a detailed, blow by blow account, but thought better of it. The humour would have been lost on Laura.

'Such speaking, such a voice, such a manner! You never heard anything like it in your life, I am certain. And you didn't even care enough to go.'

Fanny laughed and shook her head: 'Oh, I've no doubt I shall hear him one day', and then, teasing her younger sister, added loudly, 'and after all, it doesn't much matter whether I hear him or not.'

Fanny was so busy sketching, she didn't notice Laura's sudden silence, or see the way the colour had drained from her face. Directly below them a boat suddenly shot into view around the corner of the cliff, close enough for Laura to identify the lone rower at once.

'It's him!' she whispered to Mabel, aghast. 'Do you think he heard her?'

The oarsman did not look up, and the irrepressible pair studied him with interest as he vigorously pulled his way past them through the silvery water, giggling uncontrollably as they noted his muscular prowess.

'Do look, Fanny,' Laura urged her, 'there he is!'

'Who?' Fanny asked, without looking up, obtuse to the end. 'Mr Guinness!'

With a sigh of resignation, Fanny glanced down at the sea and caught a fleeting glimpse of a slight, dark-haired young man disappearing round the far side of the cliff.

'That youth!' she said dismissively, and got on with her sketching.

Years later, that was how Fanny would describe to her children the first sight of her future husband.

Born in 1831, Fanny Fitzgerald was descended from one of most distinguished families of the Irish Protestant ascendancy, their Irish roots dating back to the time of Henry II, when they had crossed over from England and played a leading part in the conquest of the country. In recent years they had not been unsympathetic to Catholic emancipation and a Fitzgerald was even involved in the 1798 uprising. Marrying outside the faith was another matter, and Fanny's father, Edward Marlborough Fitzgerald, had been disowned when he took a wife from the Catholic lower middle classes. So great was the ill feeling, that even after an early divorce, a distinguished military career, and prestigious second marriage to Mabel, daughter of Admiral Stopford, they refused all reconciliation.

The second, very happy marriage was cut short by Mabel's tragic early death from tuberculosis, leaving her grief-stricken husband to raise a son and four daughters alone. Fanny, the second daughter, had a vague recollection of being held in her mother's arms, an impression of long, wavy brown hair and beautiful eyes. She also remembered her wonderful papa, so handsome with his twirling military mustachios, coming home to her in a garden near the Thames, and she, about three years old, running to meet him in a shining white dress, to show him her new ribbons.

Here the happy memories end. Fitzgerald never got over the death of his wife and rarely socialised. Nonetheless he made a name for himself as a journalist and reviewer, writing from home so that he could care for his young family. Fanny remembered the large front room at their home in Buchanan Street in Glasgow, lit by dozens of tiny, twinkling candles on a big square dining table, and 'Papa writing, always writing'.[11] But it did not pay well and there were financial difficulties.

To compound his problems the children all succumbed to a smallpox epidemic. Fanny was desperately ill for weeks, and in the haze of a high fever was aware of bells pealing louder and louder, and of some stiff and unfamiliar object being carried out of the room. When she was well enough to ask for her brother, her father took her into his arms and told her that ten-year-old Gerald had died the day the bells rang out for the wedding of Queen Victoria. The pain of losing his only son was more than he could bear.

Some months later, Arthur West, actuary and dignified Quaker gentleman, was sitting at his desk in his London city office reading the paper as he did every morning when a particular story caught his eye. A certain military man had taken a one-way ticket on a Channel steamer, and halfway across, had thrown himself overboard, leaving four orphaned little girls without any financial provision. As West was reflecting on how sad it was, his partner came into the room, waving a letter he had just received in the post. 'I cannot understand this, West,' he said. 'What do you think it means?'

The letter, addressed from a Channel steamer, contained a few words of farewell from Fitzgerald, begged his solicitors to see to the needs of his children, and ended with, 'Before this reaches you, I shall be out of reach of any answer.' West handed his partner the morning paper, then folded the letter and put it in his pocket.

That night he showed it to his wife, Mary. The Wests were childless and it had always been a source of sorrow to them that there were no little ones to enjoy their pleasant home and garden in Stamford Hill. Mary read the letter in silence and in true Quaker fashion, refrained from comment until the following morning. Before her husband left for work, she put her hand in his and said, 'My dear, I have been thinking that thee and I perhaps might help to care for those fatherless little ones.'

'I had thought the same myself from the first moment,' he said to her. 'God bless thee for thy loving heart.'

Mary West put on her bonnet and paid a series of calls on leading members of the Tottenham Friends Meeting House. Before the day was out homes had been found for three of the girls. Eight-year-old Fanny would live with them.

The Wests were a kindly, though reserved couple, grave and old-fashioned as many Quakers were, and young Fanny, raised in a freer kind of environment, with the passionate blood of Anglo-Irish barons in her veins, often balked at their strange, rather narrow ways. Fortunately, however, the Friends were also cultured and well read, enjoying open debate and discussion on a wide range of contemporary issues which fed and satisfied the literary and intellectual abilities Fanny had inherited from her father.

In the 1840s the family moved to Exmouth, where they became involved with a new religious movement known as 'the Brethren' from its emphasis on the equality or brotherhood of all believers. Not many years had passed since Methodism had broken away from the established church, setting a precedent for other reactionary groups to found new Christian denominations. Brethrenism began in Plymouth where a group of dissatisfied evangelical Anglicans, wanting to dispense with the hierarchical divide between priest and people, set up a church with a simple communion service, where everyone could participate on an equal footing. The movement spread rapidly through the country, revitalising church life for thousands of people from aristocrats to the working men and women. It presented a radical challenge to the social as well as the religious establishment and had a profound influence on the embryonic Trade Union movement.

Twenty years later, with no central leadership, the Brethren movement became hidebound by restrictive rules and regulations, dividing into 'open' and 'exclusive' factions, but in the early days it seemed to herald a new social order, breaking down the divide between rich and poor. It was similar to Quakerism in that members of the congregation would wait to be 'led by the Spirit' before they read a scripture, prayed, or preached. But it was also more dynamic and exciting, appealing to Fanny's enquiring mind and offering a faith which would sustain her through a very difficult time in her life.

When she was in her late teens, Arthur West, exhausted by years of over-exertion in the Quaker struggle against slavery, had a stroke which left him severely disabled. Mary and Fanny nursed him devotedly but there was no money coming into the house, and Fanny was forced to combine her studies with a teaching job. They were living in Dublin at the time, and though she could well have done with their help, pride prevented her from making contact with the Fitzgeralds. She would rely on her own resourcefulness.

Eventually Mary West's emotional health broke down beneath the strain. The family moved to Widcombe Crescent in Bath where Fanny held a class for young ladies, earning a modest £200 a year, while taking care of both her adoptive parents. It was a terrible, almost personal blow when Arthur West took the same step as her natural father and ended his own life.

By the time she was twenty-nine, hard work, slender means and sorrow had taken their toll. Brilliant mental powers and a loving, vivacious personality were hidden behind a wan, rather sober appearance. Fanny was robbed of her youth, but not of her warmth. There was too much of the Irish fire in her soul to be extinguished altogether. Wherever she went it was noted that she had a way of enlivening the company, particularly the rather dull little tea parties of the Quaker or Brethren circles in which she moved. One old lady was once heard to say, 'My dear, I do assure thee when Fanny Fitzgerald comes into the room she breaks the ice in a moment. Thou knowest the way she has with her! Sets everyone talking and puts the stiffest people at ease.'

Henry Grattan Guinness felt completely at ease with Fanny Fitzgerald the moment they were introduced by a mutual Brethren friend in Ilfracombe. She blushed, remembering her comments on the cliff top a few days before, but he gave no sign of recognising her, and asked if he could call on the sisters one evening before he left. Fanny was convinced he was interested in Laura who stood next to her trembling with excitement. She herself had long abandoned any hope of matrimony, but at twenty-five, Laura was his age, beautifully dressed and lovely to look at. Laura's adoptive parents were wealthy enough to have provided her with every accomplishment necessary for the wife of a man like Grattan Guinness.

But when the young preacher did call, to the amazement of all three sisters, it was obviously Fanny who was the centre of his attention. His criteria for a future wife, like his attitude to money, did not conform to the usual expectations, but Fanny, interesting, capable and devout, more than fulfilled them. After that one evening with her he could say with simple joy rather than great passion, 'I felt that I had found, for the first time in my life, a woman with a mind and soul that answered to my own. With her I no longer felt alone.'

When she received his proposal within a day of returning home it came as a complete shock. It was hardly the most romantic of letters, for he made no secret of the fact that his calling must come first, and marriage to a man in his position, with no home, no official employment, and no financial security, would not be easy. But Fanny's life had never been easy, and that, she now realised, had prepared her for what lay ahead. 'It is a life worth living, worth suffering for, a life worth resigning all else for,' she replied, almost at once. 'Were it to cost a hundredfold more than in all probability it will, I would not resign the prospect or exchange it for the brightest lot earth could offer.'

On 2 October 1860, a mere two months later, they were married at the Princes Meeting House in Bath. At home that morning Fanny had risen early and supervised the preparation of the wedding breakfast. Mary West was too frail and in a state of some distress at the thought of losing her daughter. She became distraught at the sight of the wrong tablecloth on the top table. 'No one will notice it,' Fanny assured her. 'They will be thinking about Henry, not of the tablecloth!'

'My dear, thee should have put here the cloth that I selected.

108

This pattern is the wrong one. We really ought to change it.'

At that moment the maid announced the arrival of the old gentleman who was to stand in as father and give Fanny away. She heaved a sigh of relief, and radiant in her plain white dress, ran down the stairs to meet him. For the first time in years the heaviness lifted from her shoulders and she felt relaxed. Nothing was going to spoil her day.

The meeting house was packed to capacity, crowds filling every available space on the plain, unpolished benches. The women sat expectantly in their shawls and poke bonnets, their tightly curled ringlets nestling neatly beneath the wide brims. This was to be a simple Quaker ceremony. There were no flowers, no decorations, no organ, no platform, pulpit, or minister, no bridesmaids, nothing except a table in the centre of the room and two vacant chairs for the bride and groom.

A hush descended as they walked in together and took their seats in silence. Someone suggested a hymn, and after it had been sung, unaccompanied, the bridegroom rose to his feet and began the service with prayer. Other hymns and readings were selected by various members of the congregation, and then a long pause gave the bride and groom their cue. With a quick nod at each other they rose to their feet. Henry took Fanny's hand and placed a gold ring on her wedding finger, announcing in his resonant voice that this was to signify that hereafter she would be his wife. Fanny, in turn, made her promises, then the couple knelt down together, while the meeting united them with prayer.

'Did no one marry you? Nobody at all?' her children and grandchildren would ask incredulously, as they gathered round her lap, begging to be told the story of their wedding once again. And Fanny would reply with a radiant smile, pointing to heaven, 'Father married us, darlings. Father did everything – except the registrar's work. We didn't need anybody else.'

Chapter 5

1860–1872
Ups and Downs

1.

The honeymoon in Clevedon on the pretty north Somerset coast was a short, blissful interlude, the calm epicentre of a tumultuous period in Henry's life. By day the couple wandered hand in hand along the sandy beach at the entrance to the Bristol Channel watching the vast expanse of churning sea stretching to the distant, grey horizon, wondering where it would carry them. At night, in their very basic lodgings, they shared the few simple provisions they had bought, revelling in the cosiness of being alone together in the gathering autumn twilight.

It was as well they had no glimpse into what lay ahead, the years of incessant wandering, of scrimping and scrounging, of raising children with all their childhood ailments in a variety of temporary, damp and inadequate lodgings, of never owning their own home. Their lifestyle was such a stark contrast with the serene, comfortable existence of their brewing and banking cousins that it is hard to believe they were part of the same family. It developed inevitably from a sense of calling rather than deliberate choice, and eventually brought its own rewards – though they took some time in coming. Immense acclaim of the kind Henry enjoyed could not last indefinitely, and though neither of them knew it, the tide was beginning to turn.

Henry himself underwent a profound change of direction in the early days of their marriage. Fanny introduced him to the Plymouth Brethren. He had always been impressed by their zeal and earnestness, but it was their fascination for analysing political history in the light of biblical prophecy which fired his imagination.

This was not an entirely new departure for Protestants. As early as the Middle Ages, and particularly at the Reformation, Christians breaking away from the Catholicism had interpreted the 'Great Beast' in the book of Daniel as the Church of Rome. The preface of the King James version of the Bible in 1611 clearly stated that 'the Man of Sin' in the book of Revelation was none other than the Pope. Indeed, the world had witnessed a succession of popes more corrupt and cruel than any temporal power. Prophecies of 'the Beast's' ultimate downfall enabled persecuted Protestants to stand firm in the face of martyrdom.

As Protestantism became acceptable, interest in biblical prophecy waned, experiencing a dramatic revival in the early nineteenth century when a triumphant Napoleon conquered the Holy Roman Empire, and made the Pope a virtual prisoner in the Vatican. His temporal power decimated overnight, it seemed to many Protestants as if the prophecies of Daniel and the book of Revelation were being fulfilled before their very eyes. The unthinkable had come to pass, and that being so, there must be other major political events the Bible had foreseen.

Throughout the whole of Europe 1848 was a year of revolution. Governments, and even empires, waxed and waned. People wanted some understanding of the great events changing their world almost daily, and wondered whether the Bible held the key. An Irish Protestant, who had experienced first-hand the superstition and fury of the Roman Catholic

Church, with a passionate love for the Bible, Henry was predisposed to take an interest in redefining past and current events. He now lamented his lack of formal theological education, and taught himself history, Greek and ancient Hebrew. Early in 1861 he produced his first pamphlet on biblical prophecy and world history, then set off immediately for a preaching tour of America, scene a few months earlier of some of his greatest triumphs.

But there too a social earthquake had begun to rock the country to its very foundations. An inevitable consequence of religious awakening, the American government was in the process of banning slavery, as Britain had done in 1833. Eleven southern states refused to accept the legislation and asserted their right to secede from the Union. Revival fire had given way to war fever.

The change of moral climate was not the only reason for the more restrained reception he received on his second visit. The people responded as warmly as ever, crowding into church halls to hear him. The church ministers did not. The exclusivity of the Plymouth Brethren was provoking widespread suspicion in both Britain and the USA. Their democratic method of church government was a threat to church ministers, and provoked accusations of sectarianism. In her book *Silas Marner*, where the hero is falsely accused of theft by the diaconate and driven out of the chapel, the novelist George Eliot warned of the dangers of believing that consensus of opinion could inform moral judgment.

Rumours had filtered across the Atlantic that Henry Grattan had become a member of the sect. After all, he had taken a Brethren wife. When he began to baptise his own converts it confirmed ministers' worst fears, and they slammed their doors in his face. Of the thirty churches in Philadelphia which had welcomed him so warmly months before, only three allowed him to preach. Henry was mystified. Certainly he admired aspects of Brethrenism, but he was also aware of their shortcomings and had never allowed himself to be associated with any one denomination.

But his Brethren contacts had influenced him more than he cared to admit, even to himself. They had told him his great gift of oratory, linked in Irish newspapers with his illustrious namesake, a great political hero, was not divinely inspired. It stemmed from a need for popularity and attention. Young, naïve, terrified of human pride, and desperate for real holiness of character, Henry believed them. He would trim away any suggestion of histrionics, assuming it would lend his words more, not less impact. But he was wrong. Like Samson after his hair was shorn, he had been deprived of his power. His style was cramped, and to some of his American audiences it seemed that all that was left of the fire in his belly were a few last desperate sparks.

In years to come he would realise he had been misled, but for the time, his confidence had been eroded and the quality of his preaching seriously undermined. It was a loss he would lament for the rest of his life.

Sensitivity to the prevailing climate would never be one of Henry's strengths. Unaware of his waning popularity, he launched into a full-scale attack on the emotional manipulation driving America inexorably towards the carnage of a civil war. He had no doubt that the abolition of slavery, achieved in Britain by the campaigning of the evangelical Wilberforce, was just. His own preaching had stoked the cause. But in an open letter published by the Peace Society, entitled, 'The Duty of Christians in the Present Crisis', he stated that whatever the provocation from the southern confederacy, Christians should never fight and were within their rights to disobey any government which ordered them to use the sword.

His pacifism, coming from a foreigner and an Irishman to boot, was greeted with howls of derision from the American press. Was the European so naïve that he had not learned from Napoleon that 'heaven was on the side of the strongest artillery'? Most parsons in North and South believed that 'while the New Testament may enforce a conviction, still the rifle is not to be entirely neglected'. They called him 'a cowardly poltroon', and suggested he be tried by court martial before the chaplain of the Brooklyn phalanx. *The World* demanded a public retraction or enforced removal to the Southern Confederacy.

No one had ever publicly questioned Henry Grattan's integrity before. He was devastated by such a bitter personal attack, realising, too late, that he had grossly overestimated his own influence. He had as much hope of altering public opinion as turning 'the current of Niagara with a pitch-fork'. It was time to leave. Fanny was pregnant and must not be further upset.

In America, with a great deal of reluctance, she had begun to accept speaking invitations, at first to groups of women. Initially the prospect terrified her and Henry had to use all his powers of persuasion to get her into the pulpit. Preaching was not a gift she ever anticipated or desired. In fact a woman preacher was a novelty and Fanny was not sure it was acceptable at all. But she was such a success that Henry encouraged her to preach at his side wherever he went, even as her pregnancy became increasingly evident.

Now that they were no longer welcome in America they needed a safe haven for the birth of their baby and accepted an invitation from Toronto. On their way to Canada news reached them that war had been declared. As Henry had foreseen, America tore itself apart in a futile conflagration for four years. In retrospect the article which condemned his stance almost sounds like a eulogy.

Reiterating our advice that Mr G had better depart for a more profitable vineyard, we place him on the record as among the first clergymen who advocated peace, and the only Irishman who ever so far forgot his nationality as to interfere to prevent a quarrel that promises in a military sense, to be in all respects so interesting as that we have now at hand.[1]

2.

On Henry and Fanny's first wedding anniversary, 2 October 1861, young Henry Grattan, known as Harry, was born in Toronto. To Fanny's relief he was a healthy baby, not adding to the burdens she already had to bear. Canada had greeted Henry with little more enthusiasm than America, and he was beginning to show signs of serious depression, disappointment and exhaustion, compounded by the rigours of a freezing Canadian winter.

With their new baby they crossed the frozen St Lawrence River by boat to Quebec, 'a frightful and exciting exploit', Fanny recalled in her diary. 'I was terrified, expecting each moment to be swallowed in the surging ice.' Now, for the sake of Henry's mental health, she knew she had to get him home to England as quickly as possible. The nearest embarkation point was Portland in Maine which would mean recrossing the treacherous St Lawrence and braving a country riven by civil war with a three-month-old baby. In the end she felt she had no choice. Travelling conditions would become more hazardous in the next few months as a thaw set in and the river flooded its banks. She wrapped up her tiny baby and they set off, reaching England safely in early January 1862.

Any hopes she had that Henry's spirits would be restored once he was back on familiar territory were soon dashed. A prolonged period of rest was essential and made possible by a financial gift from a generous friend. Leaving Harry behind in an English nursery, they set off for the Middle East.

In those days there were no personally conducted tours of

significant sites in Egypt and Palestine. Tourists made all their own arrangements, travelling in convoy on camel or donkey, camping overnight en route to their destination. They were largely at the mercy of local people, and the quality and conditions of the experience were extremely variable. Henry's horse, it would appear, left a great deal to be desired. It had a reasonable trot, but was somewhat bony and bit into the soul. He sold it before returning to Europe to Dr Henry Jessup, a veteran missionary in Beirut who lent it to visitors. 'Brother Jessup,' said one visitor, 'I would like to buy half of that horse.' Jessup asked him why. 'In order to shoot it.'

Despite the discomfort, Henry was overcome with awe at seeing so many sacred places. He had an overwhelming sense of walking on hallowed ground, particularly in the Judaean desert. It would have a profound effect on his later ministry, though initially, when they returned to England at the end of April, his emotional health seemed little better. The very thought of addressing a large meeting was enough to provoke a panic attack. Yet how could he support his family? Fanny was pregnant again.

Just as she was becoming seriously concerned about their means of survival without an income, a small chapel in the run-down Waterloo area of Liverpool offered him a temporary pastorate and he accepted with relief. It was there on Christmas Day 1862 that Mary Geraldine was born. Her father always called her Minnie and felt that her conception in the Holy Land had endowed her with heightened spiritual awareness and unusual strength of character, preparing her for a sacred destiny.

The warm, loving acceptance of the simple working-class congregation at Byrom Hall helped to restore Henry's confidence and after seven months he took to the road again, preaching all over England, Ireland and Scotland, taking cheap lodgings for his family wherever he went. In April 1863 in Bury in Lancashire, Fanny wrote inside the cover of her husband's large black Bible:

> We think it undesirable to determine beforehand on the length of our stay in any one place; this should be regulated by results. A definite period in view, especially if it be a short one tends to hinder earnest, whole-hearted labours and preclude large expectations. It may also tend to longer tarriance in a place than is wise (as at Boston). One step at a time!

But the response to his preaching was not what it had been in the old days. Any preacher of reputation was invited by the Earl of Shaftesbury to preach on a Sunday evening to the packed Exeter Hall in London. The man hailed nationally as Spurgeon's rival a mere four years earlier received no such invitation.

In Edinburgh in the bleak November of 1863 his preaching tour came to a sudden standstill. A distinguished Irish minister accused him publicly of bribing his converts with Guinness Brewery money. Most of the newspapers covered the story and all further speaking engagements were cancelled forthwith.

It was a bitter and cruelly ironic attack on someone who deplored alcohol and had given away his own Guinness legacy. Henry was stunned by the vilification of his character, and even more that a flagrant untruth should receive unquestioning acceptance. The shock made him ill again. He had no home, no money, no means of defending himself or now, of earning an income. Fanny did her best to comfort him, but she went into labour prematurely and gave birth to a stillborn little girl.

These undoubtedly were the worst months of his life. One day in March 1864, he found himself in Dundee with his wife and two small children crammed into damp, freezing cold lodgings, the cheapest available, 'strangers amongst strangers, with only seventeen shillings in hand'. It was he wrote later, 'most exercising'. But many of his supporters did not desert him, and a month later the family were offered no less than three country homes free of expense for as long as they liked.

Fanny chose Mount Catherine, a beautiful house in glorious surroundings three miles from Limerick. Here at last she could create a measure of normal family life and a proper Christmas. Nonetheless, she was forced to concede that their extra-ordinary upbringing would mean her children were always rather quaint. At a local party she was bemused by Harry who marched up to a boy teasing a little girl at the Christmas tree, and said, 'I'll tell you what sir, if you tease that fair lady, I'll put you in prison or shoot you dead.' Where he had heard such an expression she had no idea. It sounded absurdly gallant on the lips of a three-year-old. But Harry was a knight errant by instinct, a defender of the weak and dispossessed, and the child would be father to the man. Each of her children reflected certain aspects of the circumstances of their birth and early childhood. Son of their Canadian adventure, Harry would always be the most audacious and extrovert.

Life for Fanny was never too settled at Mount Catherine. Against her better judgment, Henry was risking life and limb preaching to the Catholic community of Limerick. It was a matter of time before the tolerance of the church authorities was pushed beyond its limit. One day she was called out of the women's meeting she was addressing and sent home to find Henry had been badly beaten. He had not even told her where he was going. Apparently, a large crowd had gathered to hear him as they usually did, but this time one or two planted ring-leaders urged the people to hustle and stone him. He tried to get away, but two burly men, one a butcher, hit him repeatedly on the head. Providentially he had fallen into a low cart. Had he not, the police informed her, Henry would have almost certainly been trampled to death. At that very moment an army officer rode past, his uniform covered in medals for gallantry in the Crimean War. He leapt down, collared the butcher, and harangued the crowd for their cowardice in attacking one defenceless man, giving Henry a chance to make his escape. According to *The Times*, which reported the incident on 6 May 1864, Mr Guinness had been saved from the vengeance of the populace by a Captain Jones of the depot battalion.

Despite being severely shaken, Fanny wrote bravely, 'We trust some good will come of it, in attracting Roman Catholics to the theatre services, and in making Protestants take more decided ground.' They had no argument with individual Catholics but with a church institution which kept the people in poverty and ignorance. Fanny was even more incensed by Protestants who claimed to have the truth, but were not prepared to stand by her husband when he shared it. 'There was not, I dare say, a Protestant in the crowd.'

Henry began to wonder if he were not travelling on the wrong track. He was almost thirty, and for some time now every door had slammed shut in his face. The great religious revival had passed its peak, some of its ardour dampened by the publication in 1859 of Charles Darwin's *On the Origin of Species*. Henry was concerned that the book appeared to be rocking the moral and religious foundations of society, undermining those too weak in faith to marshal their theological arguments. What was needed to fight off an enemy invasion was an army of young men adequately equipped to proclaim the evidence for Christian truth. Instead of preaching himself, perhaps the time had come to train others to do it.

Fanny's heart sank. She knew what that would mean. How could they set up a training class for would-be missionaries and preachers in the heart of the Irish countryside, miles from civilisation? If this was their destiny there was only one option, to give up Mount Catherine and head for Dublin, the city of Henry's birth.

3.

Dublin in 1865 had changed very little in the seven years since the young evangelist had caused such a stir. It was a deeply divided city, the wealthy, largely Protestant minority, living in elegant mansions and country houses in the suburbs, the poor, largely Catholic majority living in relative squalor. Henry's first student, Tom Barnardo, a young man of Italian extraction whose orphanages would eventually make his name a household word, described his first impressions:

> Whisky drinking, added to the vicious tendencies of the people who dwell in these wretched hovels, have demoralised them to the lowest degree. The Corporation of Dublin have reason to be utterly ashamed that such fever dens and loathsome sources of moral contagion are allowed to remain in a city which boasts of so many noble streets and imposing public buildings.[2]

The first Arthur Guinness's dream of a moral victory for stout over spirits in every part of society had evidently yet to be fulfilled. His grandson Benjamin Lee had the matter in hand. He understood that for maximum growth in trade, pursuing a policy of rapid expansion was inadequate. He had to create a new market, transforming Guinness from a good drink, but one of many, into the natural heritage of the Irish people – an institution in its own right. The committed Unionist achieved his goal with a stroke of pure genius, exploiting nationalist pride and the growing demand for Home Rule by appropriating one of the most abiding legends of the people.

In 1014, at the Battle of Clontarf, the site of Benjamin's first country residence, the great Irish hero and chieftain Brian Boru had conquered the pillaging Norsemen. With undisguised irony it was Boru's harp, symbol of nationalist victory over unwanted invading foreign powers, which Benjamin now adopted as the Guinness emblem. Instinctively, he had grasped the potential of clever advertising and good public relations. All that was required was a simple, inspired gesture.

Although it was now the most lucrative business in Ireland, the Brewery was not the only burgeoning Guinness enterprise in the Dublin of the 1860s. Guinness, Mahon and Co., bank and land agency, was becoming so successful that it was about to expand its operations to London. The banking Guinnesses were descended from Samuel, the first Arthur's younger brother, who followed his elder brother to the big city at the end of the eighteenth century. He gave up brewing and became a goldbeater after his marriage to Sarah Jago, a goldsmith's niece.

From that moment it became a tradition that divergent family members, step-brothers, half-sisters, third cousins twice removed, would make their own mark as entrepreneurs, inventors, trailblazers and business magnates, each in their own field, with varying degrees of success. Inventive flair is in the Guinness genes, unawakened only, as Benjamin Lee's Bessie foresaw, when a seductive sense of entitlement to status and wealth stifled the lack of incentive to earn it.

Samuel the goldbeater and Sarah his wife were responsible for a long line of financiers, often with the middle name of 'Rundell', just as 'Lee' identified the brewers, and 'Grattan' the missionary branch of the family. But the divide is not that straightforward. Some of Captain John Grattan's descendants opted for worldly pursuits like a career on the stage, while some of the Lees and Rundells exchanged their earthly inheritance for eternal rewards.[3]

More than in many family trees, the lines overlap and criss-cross. Despite the proliferation of family members, the early generations followed each other's progress and remained fairly close, united largely by a love of Ireland and their Christian faith. The brewers and bankers moved in similar circles, employed each other's services and, ultimately, intermarried.

From time to time members of the banking side of the family ran the Brewery.

Samuel the goldbeater's two sons were the barristers Sam and Dick, who had acted for their bankrupt cousin Edward. Sam died without progeny, but Dick and his wife Mary, known as Mossy, one of the ubiquitous Darley family, produced twelve children. Only two of their five sons, Robert Rundell and Samuel Richard, survived infancy. In many ways the salutary tale of the two brothers symbolises in embryonic form the triumph and tragedy of the entire Guinness clan.

Born in 1789 and educated, like his father, at Whyte's Academy in Grafton Street,[4] Robert Rundell was apprenticed on leaving school to his uncle the brewer, Henry Darley of Stillorgan. He was a quiet, industrious man, evidently well thought of, for by 1821 he was Master of the Guild of Brewers and a member of the Dublin Corporation. In 1825 he bought the leasehold of 'The Farm', opposite the Darley brewery, a large, rambling property, where he installed his wife, a clergyman's daughter by the name of Mary Anne Seymour, and their two sons and a daughter.

A disagreement with his uncle in 1831 brought their working relationship to an end, leaving Robert Rundell with £10,000. His younger brother Richard Samuel (he reversed his first names to sound a little more stylish) had meanwhile set up a modest land agency and banking business at 5 Kildare Street. Robert Rundell was invited to become a partner and invest his capital, while the younger brother contributed his name – which says a great deal about their respective characters. Private banking was a risky business. There were no laws in Ireland protecting investments and banks tended to rise and fall overnight. Nonetheless 'R. Guinness and Co.' did modestly well until 1836, when a cautious Robert Rundell, who had become increasingly concerned about the extravagance which surrounded his younger brother's social climbing, withdrew from the partnership.

It was a shrewd, far-sighted decision. At 'R. Guinness and Co.' he had also noted the potential of a young apprentice by the name of John Ross Mahon, a young man with exceptional business flair, from a good Irish family, and with invaluable connections with the rural landed gentry, vital for any land agency.

Recently widowed, his young sons at boarding school, Robert Rundell tired of living in splendid isolation in the large candle-lit house in Stillorgan, rented out the property and bought 26 South Frederick Street in the centre of town. It was an elegant, regency, four-storey house, a stone's throw from College Green, 'central and convenient for business' according to its new proprietor. He invited the twenty-two-year-old apprentice to join him there, and together they formed a new firm, Guinness and Mahon.

The two men were as unlikely a partnership as could be found, in age, looks and personality. Robert Rundell was tall, stately and reserved, John Ross Mahon round and genial, fond of children, though sadly, he never had any of his own. From a business perspective the combination worked well. The merchant bank and land agency was a satisfactory, if not startling success, weathering the economic menace of the Great Famine, acting as an agency to distribute charity and relief. An old school friend of Robert Rundell, General Sir John Rowland Eustace, went out of his way to use his influence to bring in business.

Life for the lonely widower, whose main source of society appears to have been his cousin, Arthur Guinness the second, took a decided turn for the better. In 1840, following an apparent penchant for daughters of the clergy by the name of Mary Anne, he married Mary Anne Moore and sired a further seven children.

Meanwhile, the teenage sons of his first marriage arrived home from school and were ready to join the family firm. Richard Seymour Guinness became an apprentice in 1841,

Henry Guinness in 1844. Both were made partners at the age of twenty, and with a new name, Guinness, Mahon and Company moved to new premises in College Green in 1854. It was a psychological, if not actual improvement in status, reflected in its new position in the shadow of that established part of city life, the Bank of Ireland. When Robert Rundell died suddenly in 1857, having been taken ill at lunch after a Board Meeting of the Great Southern and Western Railway Company, he left his two sons £42,000 and a very viable business. According to his grandson, Howard Rundell, he was a charitable, hard-working, religious man, director of two of the railway companies in the process of transforming Ireland's trade network. It was just a pity that he had spent most of his life in banking, a profession he did not particularly enjoy.

Richard Samuel, his pretentious younger brother, died the same year. But his was a very different story. Richard was as ambitious as Robert was cautious, as worldly as his brother was devout. In 1833 he became the first member of the Guinness family to marry into the landed gentry. Katherine, second daughter of Sir Charles Jenkinson, 10th Baronet of Hawkesbury in Gloucestershire and MP for Dover, appears to have been an inveterate snob with a profound distaste for trade. Nonetheless, she condescended to marry into a family already dependent upon its benefits for respectability and status in Dublin, enduring her husband's profession, ignoring his more successful, bourgeois brewing cousins.

Nor were the Guinnesses impressed with the match. From a letter written by Richard Samuel to his mother on 9 December 1835, two years after his marriage, which begins, 'As the Ice is broken which prevented you writing to me from the time of my marriage to the other day', it would appear that Mossy was very displeased with her son, for reasons he finds hard to understand.[5] He promises to steal a day to go and see her next time business takes him to the west, 'which I was prevented doing the last time I was in the country by the circumstances of never having heard from you either upon my marriage or the birth of my child and not being able to account for this'. He would also like her to visit them in Dublin, so that he can show off his child and my home, which Katherine's taste has made remarkably nice and comfortable. So much so that all our English friends remark it for its air of elegance and comfort.'

Mixing with English company in Dublin was sign alone of a man bent on being upwardly mobile. The whole letter reeks of snobbery. It is a study in name-dropping. At the time of writing they are staying with their friends Mr and Mrs Tighe (Mr Tighe is related to the Duke of Richmond, of course!) at Woodstock Montagne, their magnificent home in County Kilkenny, where the cream of society has gathered for a weekend, Lord Arthur Lennox, Lord and Lady Crofton, Lord Rokeby, and so interminably on. 'All here as well as everywhere we go seem to like Katherine, at least those sort of people with whom we live, for to say the truth, we have decided to have no society, or the best.'

The decision was their ruin, as Robert Rundell had so clearly foreseen. He deplored his sister-in-law's lavish tastes. But her sister Eleanor Mary had married the 2nd Duc de Montebello and Katherine was intent on living like a duchess too, albeit in Dublin not Paris, in a manner way beyond her husband's means. In 1849, following the Great Famine, the R. Guinness and Company Land Agency finally gave out.

Universally resented for his airs and affectations, nicknamed 'Old Pel', because the stiff, highly starched collars he wore forced his chin up, emphasised his pointed nose and made him strut like a pelican, Richard Samuel was now a bankrupt. Katherine does not appear to have been unduly concerned. Her husband was now free from the taint of commercial pursuits. Brother Robert Rundell, the boring banker, and cousin Arthur, the tradesman, paid off some of the debts, enabling Richard Samuel to turn his full attention to politics, an eminently more suitable occupation for the husband of a woman of her background and refinements.

He had already won the seat for Kinsale in the 1847 General Election, but was divested of it shortly before his business collapsed because of certain irregularities in the voting papers. Now, to Katherine's relief, there was nothing to keep them in uncultured, unworthy Dublin. They could live like other sensible, well-to-do families, in London, whence Richard would lobby the government for a seat worthy of their status. In 1854 he managed to become MP for Barnstaple in Devon, fielding charges of malpractice in his election campaign until his dying day three years later.

Katherine and her four sons and four daughters were left virtually penniless. But Katherine had learned to survive – without forgoing the basic necessities of servants, a carriage and the entertaining of the right kind of people. The social graces she taught her children would stand them in good stead one day, for they would reign over a world more lavish and luxurious than any she had ever visited in her wildest dreams, playing host to kings and princes – all thanks to those deplorable Guinness trade connections.

It may have reached Katherine's refined and delicate ears from the gentlemen of her acquaintance who frequented the fashionable Brooks's Club in St James's Street, that on the day that Prince Albert, the Prince Consort died, the wine steward announced with due solemnity that even the champagne would be in mourning, and added a touch of Guinness. From this respectful gesture of solidarity with the Queen in 1861 came 'Black Velvet', the champagne-Guinness cocktail which would become so popular with 1920s London socialites. Guinness was making its mark in London.

Benjamin Lee and Bessie, however, remained in Dublin where their children received a comfortable, rather sober upbringing. Anne Lee, their only daughter, brought the first title into the brewing line of the family when she married

William Conyngham, the treasurer of St Patrick's Cathedral, who would become the fourth Baron Plunkett on the death of his father. She, like many Guinness women, had opted for a clergyman, only this one would become the Archbishop of Dublin.

Though Ben was delighted it was not exactly the kind of match Bessie had planned for her children. She simply wanted them to be happy, and as far as she was concerned, that meant living as plain and simple a lifestyle as possible with partners who truly cared for them. She worried incessantly about her three boys, all young men in their twenties, wondering whether the 'worldliness' of their upbringing had not done them more harm than good. Constantly ill, and faced with her own demise, she wrote with some urgency to her eldest son, Arthur Edward, 'All tho' the Lord has given me peace and joy in believing . . . if I were well assured that my darling children were safe in Jesus, oh how happy I should be – well, I think they are the Lord's, but I want to SEE it.'[6] Evidently there was room for doubt. Though none of her boys could ever be classed as 'wild' (they were all in fact of a fairly serious turn of mind), as far as their mother was concerned, they were not leading a godly enough life either. 'We are lonely without our children on New Year's Day,' she wrote again a little later, adding, 'I do hope you do not smoke, and that if Lee must smoke sometimes, which I wish he would not, it is not vile tobacco or cigars.'[7]

It was as well Bessie never lived to see successive generations indulge in a great deal more ungodly pursuits than smoking. She died in September 1865, a few weeks before Henry and Fanny arrived back in Dublin. The renovation of St Patrick's Cathedral, personally supervised and completely financed by Benjamin Lee at a cost of £150,000, had just been completed. It was characteristic of a man whose faith was becoming more formal to express it in the grand gesture. The city's Protestant wealth, unable or unwilling to save the cathedral from dilapidation, now hailed their benefactor as a national hero. One of Ireland's greatest monuments, once home to Dean Swift, had been saved for the nation. Lord Wodehouse, the Lord Lieutenant of Ireland, said that 'work which had been too great for the Knights of St Patrick, or for the Ecclesiastic Commissioners, or the Bench of Bishops, which the Irish Parliament had refused to undertake and which the British parliament never entertained the thought of executing, has been accomplished within four years by a single merchant'.[8]

The Dean, the Rev. Dr Leeper, apparently saw no incongruity, no human appropriation of divine glory in the claim that Benjamin Lee Guinness, 'with the eye of an architect, the resources of a Prince, the public spirit of a true citizen and patriot, and above all, as an earnest, practical, Christian man, has reared a temple on whose every stone and cornice, on whose every embellishment, his name might be inscribed'. Nor did he foresee that one particular cathedral window would become the most fitting tribute. Inscribed with the text, 'I was thirsty and ye gave me drink', it never failed to amuse successive generations of visitors.

Bessie's fears that her husband might be snapped up by an unprincipled, grasping woman (did she have her cousin's wife in mind?) were unfounded. Benjamin Lee did not marry again, but embraced the political life instead, as Conservative-Unionist MP for Dublin. The restraint advocated by his father was now irrelevant. Fourteen years earlier it may have been prudent from a business point of view to forgo public political allegiance. But the Brewery was now so successful that he no longer feared antagonising prospective customers. His father had been a Liberal at heart, whereas he, the most prominent businessman in Irish life, was instinctively Conservative and Unionist: Conservative as this was the official 'liquor party', Unionist, because there were few Protestants who did not fear the Fenian movement and their republican demands.

The Fenian uprising when it finally came in 1867 was a half-hearted affair, quickly suppressed. But for 'services to his country', namely the restoration of the cathedral, Ben was made a baronet. It must have been particularly galling for the penniless widow, plain Mrs Richard Samuel Guinness, to see her brewing cousin by marriage arise Sir Benjamin Lee, even if his poor wife had not survived to become Lady Bessie. But then, with the typical irony which pursued Guinness fortunes down through the years, Bessie would not have appreciated a title anyway.

4.

Henry and Fanny returned to Dublin at the end of 1865, this time with no fanfare or publicity, but with a new baby, Lucy Evangeline. 'We called her Lucy – from lux, lumière, light,' Henry explained, for she was a symbol of their own hopeful new beginning, a glimpse of light at the end of a very dark tunnel. Several times the light was almost extinguished. She was a frail, fretful baby, causing her parents a great deal of anxiety. Henry carried her everywhere. 'When she was a child there was no place she loved better than her father's arms,' he wrote, 'and to him, the delicacy of her frame and sensitiveness of her mind were no mystery, for trials which preceded her birth seemed their explanation.'[9]

Lucy was something of a child prodigy, inheriting the brilliant musical flair of the Cramers, mastering complex Chopin and Mendelssohn piano pieces at an unusually early age. Emotionally she was always finely tuned, unusually sensitive, capable of such intensity of feeling that as she grew, Henry would worry for her sanity, an anxiety which one day proved well founded – with tragic consequences.

Like their mother, Harry and Minnie were hardy, vigorous plants compared to Lucy, 'a frail and clinging woodbine, that hangs its blossom on a supporting bough'. Harry was a strong, sturdy little boy, full of mischief, while Minnie was grave and prim, the perfect lady from the first. On Christmas Day 1865, her third birthday, her first portrait was taken. She is wearing a voluminous pink dress with five deep tucks in the waistband and tiny puff sleeves trimmed with blue ribbons. Two enormous eyes stare solemnly into the camera. With a slightly worried expression and hair parted demurely in the middle and curled around her ears, she looks almost thirty-three, a miniature of her mother.

Though his cousin Benjamin Lee, saviour of St Patrick's, was now the undisputed defender of the established church, Henry accepted the position of elder at Merrion Hall, a newly built, socially unfashionable Brethren chapel. Living in the same town, their paths had so diverged that it was hard to believe their fathers were brothers, and close. There was contact between the two men, but Bessie, who would have made a tremendous fuss of Henry and Fanny, was dead. Nonetheless, if their views on alcohol were irreconcilable, the cousins were united in their passionate love for their homeland, and an abiding hatred of Fenianism.

In the two years before the Fenian uprising the rumbles of revolution struck terror into the Protestant establishment. It was presumed with growing paranoia that groups of exiles in America were plotting a full-blown attack. In a response to the 515 employees who pledged their undying support, Benjamin Lee referred to the Irish Republican Brotherhood as

> wicked and worthless adventurers who would not only deprive our country of the advantages, which, as a part of the British Empire, we enjoy, but who would break the ties which bind man to man, and, by a reckless destruction of property and of human life, would deluge our country in bloodshed and reduce the industrial classes to

want and misery, and take from others the ability of
advancing the onward progress lately so evident in our
beloved country.[10]

Their intention, he claims, succumbing to a certain amount of
emotional hype, is 'by deception and by pillage to grasp from
its owners their property', and 'to escape with their plunder'.
How, one might well ask, would a small, ill-equipped band of
revolutionaries have made off with the largest Brewery in the
world?

Henry and Fanny were occupied with a far more pressing
revolution – the defence of the eternal soul against the ravages
of Darwinism. They rented 31 Upper Baggot Street, a large
Georgian house just beyond the eminently fashionable Lower
Baggot Street, in a more run-down part of the town, intending
to turn it into a 'Training Home for Evangelists and Missionaries'. It occurred to them that expecting young men to give
up their employment and move in was asking a great deal.
Better not be too rash and provide evening classes at first –
giving them a chance to test out their calling.

About eight men gathered at the house to study Paley's
Evidences of Christianity four evenings a week. There were
Charles and Edward Fishe, the dashing sons of a retired
colonel of the East India Company's Horse Artillery, and
John McCarthy, a thoughtful older man, married with three
children, all of whom would make pioneer missionary
explorers one day. The Guinness children's favourite was Tom
Barnardo, their Sunday School teacher at Merrion Hall. He
was a small, bespectacled, almost monkey-like little man
whose unprepossessing appearance hid an irrepressible sense
of fun. He was a great talker, waving his arms around
energetically as he held forth on the subjects filling him with
righteous indignation – usually the injustices suffered by the
poor. He was a source of fascination to three-year-old Minnie,
and even her parents, aware in a new way of the deadening

effect of poverty on the human spirit, could not fail to be moved by Barnardo's passionate outbursts. The young student developed in turn a deep respect and abiding admiration for the tall, striking man with an inspirational teaching gift. The house on Baggot Street became his second home.

The evening of 19 February 1866 was a turning point. During a visit to Liverpool Henry Grattan had heard and met the renowned missionary explorer, Hudson Taylor, who had accepted an invitation to precede his tour of Limerick, Cork and Belfast with a talk to the Dublin Bible class about his adventures in China. That evening the students waited in anticipation for Guinness to return from the Kingston Ferry with his special guest whom he had arranged to meet at 'half past six Irish time, seven o'clock English'. In exchange for this favour Henry Grattan promised to escort Taylor to his other meetings, 'being better known in Ireland at present than you are'. It was a genuine offer of support, not a put-down, but Henry was always immune to the subtleties of language.[11]

Hudson Taylor had sailed to China in 1853, spent ten years there, and since his return had enthralled the country with tales of that exotic land. Throughout the 1860s the world map altered almost daily. Voyages of exploration expanded geographical horizons and revealed hitherto unknown, mysterious parts of the globe. It was a source of immense fascination to the general public. All travel was an adventure, but China, with its ancient dynasties, strange traditions and colourful culture had a fairy-tale mystique.

To add to Taylor's appeal, the religious revival of the 1850s had also stimulated a rush of new missionary activity. He was, however, radical in his opposition to British expansionism in the Far East. Preaching the Gospel was not an excuse for colonialism. Missionaries must lay down their creature comforts, accept no salary, and identify with the people, as far as they were able, in lifestyle, customs, diet and dress. It was a hard and difficult path to tread, but true Christianity demanded a total rejection of the twin scourges of imperialism and denominationalism with all the self-interest they implied. Not everyone was inspired by Taylor's rhetoric or his vision.

Inside the large drawing room at Baggot Street waited Barnardo, McCarthy and the Fishe brothers, sitting stiffly in their sombre, tight-fitting frock-coats, their collars barely visible above their coats. One or two members of the group still adhered to the high-wing variety, loathe to make any concession to fashion. The door flung open. Framed in the doorway, filling it in fact, was Guinness's magnificent figure, totally shielding Taylor from view.

'Where is the great man?' Barnardo whispered to McCarthy with a twinge of disappointment.

'I suppose he hasn't come,' McCarthy whispered back. But when Henry Grattan stood aside, they all saw a slight, slim, fair-haired man in a dress coat with an abundant white kerchief knotted at his neck. Bemused at his dress, they ogled him for some time. Taylor was even less fashion conscious than they were. Eventually Barnardo broke the silence. As he took stock of Taylor's height, or the lack of it, he said loudly, 'There's hope for me yet!'

Barnardo volunteered for China almost before Taylor had finished speaking. The missionary was unsure. He liked Barnardo enormously, loved his ebullience, but wondered whether he wasn't a little impetuous. He suggested a course of study at one of the London hospitals to improve Barnardo's medical knowledge. If then he still felt called to China, he could join a party leaving on the *Lammermuir* later in the year.

Taylor had no qualms about McCarthy, whose only stipulation was that his wife should be safely past her fourth confinement by the time they sailed. Nor about Charles Fishe, who, still very young, promised to go as soon as he had his father's permission. Taylor's greatest surprise was reserved for the journey to Cork, when Henry told him that he and Fanny were seriously considering joining him on the *Lammermuir*.

Taylor promised to give the matter serious consideration as he travelled on alone to Belfast and by the time he called in at Baggot Street on his return, had reached a decision. As gently as possible he tried to explain to them that since they were past thirty they were too old. They would find language study too difficult. 'Stay here,' he said to Henry, 'and train me the men and women.'

While Henry and Fanny were struggling to come to terms with the idea, Hudson Taylor noticed a little girl standing at his side staring up at him with her enormous, almond-shaped eyes. If Tom Barnardo said this was a very important man, he must be.

Taylor bent down, picked her up and sat her on his knee.

'And how old are you?'

'Three,' Minnie said.

'I have a three-year-old,' he told her, 'a boy, called Howard.'

Minnie forgot her shyness and bombarded Taylor with questions about his son. A bond was sealed that day between Taylor and the Grattan Guinness family, and especially with the little girl who sat on his knee, who forty years later would become his best-known biographer and greatest comfort at a time of almost unbearable trial.

Fanny could not simply set aside her newly inspired passion for China and days after his departure wrote to Hudson Taylor, making the best of her disappointment, 'We see our way clearly now, I think, to aid the work not *directly* but indirectly ... *Here* we may do much and be the means of sending you more efficient labourers than ourselves.'[12] She went on to propose the immediate establishment of an Irish Auxiliary of the China Inland Mission, 'to disseminate information and stir up interest ... to promote prayer and liberality on its behalf ... and provide funds for passage and outfit money'. She enclosed a notice they intended to disseminate throughout Ireland.

Taylor took fright. He was seriously alarmed at the proposition and wrote back to say so. Formidable supporters they might be, those high-powered Guinnesses could be a little overwhelming, especially if they intended fund-raising. Since God knew his needs, Taylor's policy was never to ask for money, and he explained so as gently as he knew how. To her credit, Fanny graciously took the point, and learned a lesson which would prove invaluable in her own missionary enterprises in the years ahead.

Nonetheless, Taylor needed a substantial amount of money before the sailing of the *Lammermuir*, and invited the Guinnesses to share in the limelight at a special reception given for him at the home of Lord and Lady Radstock at 30 Bryanston Square in London. The Radstocks were inveterate supporters of all kinds of missionary work, using their influential position to relieve many of their social circle of their extraneous income and guilt. They would one day prove invaluable friends to Henry and Fanny.

But on this occasion, her first sally among the upper-class London élite, Fanny felt gauche and faded. Henry was in great form, exuding his usual magnetic charm, speaking with what Taylor referred to as 'marvellous power', in contrast to his own measured presentation of the facts. But Fanny standing at Henry's side, could not get over the revealing décolletage of the ladies, or decide whether covering her neck and shoulders in true Quaker fashion made more of a statement about her modesty or her provinciality.

The spring of 1866 was a gloriously happy interlude. Hudson and Maria Taylor invited the Guinnesses to share their last few weeks in England at Saint Hill, a lovely country house in East Grinstead, set in acres of rolling farmland, with its own lake and lush lawns, lent to them by a generous farmer called William Berger. The sun seemed to shine every day, and while their parents planned the evangelisation of China, the seven children romped and played together and got to know each other fairly well. One day, ignoring her nanny's instructions, Minnie rushed out on to the porch and fell headlong down the stone steps, cutting her arm quite badly. As it was bandaged up she was mortified to see the two fair-haired little Taylor boys, Herbert and Howard, so handsome in their long pinafores, watching her in shocked silence. She knew she had been naughty. Their look said it all.

When the Taylors finally sailed for China in May,[13] Henry and Fanny and their family felt bereft and out of sorts. Henry was once again in great demand as a preacher and decided they should give up the house in Baggot Street, say goodbye to Dublin and set off on their travels. One evening, as he wandered through the streets of Keighley in Yorkshire, he noticed a poster on the wall of a house announcing a series of lectures by a Mrs Harriet Law, a well-known exponent of Darwinism who would prove beyond doubt that the Bible and its claims were false. His high-crowned hat pushed to the back of his head so as not to obscure his view, hands clasped firmly behind his back, he stared at the poster with mounting indignation. Up to that moment he had presumed the new scepticism was limited to the intelligentsia. If they chose the path that leads to spiritual destruction so be it, but they had no right to drag down with them those whose limited education left them without powers of argument.

When Mrs Law delivered her first address, Henry Grattan Guinness was in the front row, ready for the first round of a mighty theological battle. By the second night most of the town turned out to watch the sport. Keighley had never had such entertainment. Mrs Law was no match for a man of Henry Grattan's verbal genius. The people loved him and she bowed to his popularity, if not to his theology. A few miles away, alone in a draughty parsonage after the death of his three famous daughters, lived the blind, elderly Rector of Haworth, Patrick Brontë. News of Henry Grattan's victory must have brought some cheer to his twilight existence.

Henry noted in his journal that in 1866 he preached 230

136

times and was ill only twice. By the following year, which
included a very successful mission in Sunderland, the
travelling was wearing Fanny out. She desperately wanted a
base for herself and the children, and persuaded Henry to let
her buy their own home, their first in seven years of marriage.
They opted for Bath so that she could take care of her mother.
It was also near enough to Cheltenham for Henry to spend
time with his own mother who was becoming very frail.

Fanny began to preach again regularly too – to both
genders, still feeling very ambivalent. From around 1858,

> women (the daring of it!), *women* began to take part in the
> revival meetings, though with trepidation at first, and
> after long searchings of heart and much anguished prayer.
> There was an outcry of course. There were quotations
> from the Fathers, from St Paul. But the broader minded
> among the revivalists soon came to see that resistance to
> such compelling sincerity would be in vain.[14]

Fanny, however, maintained that she could never presume
women were called to work *equally* with men. 'We believe, on
the contrary, that the *rule* is men – the *exception* only, women;
and that, as always, the exception only proves the rule.'
Catherine Booth, wife of the founder of the Salvation
Army, William Booth, soon to become close friends of the
Guinnesses, and an increasingly successful preacher, had few
qualms about whether she was an equal or an exception – as
long as congregations responded to her appeals. By the time
Fanny met Catherine Booth, she had already been convinced
of the validity of women's preaching by the extraordinary
Geraldine Hooper.

Raised in a well-to-do family and converted to Christianity
in 1861 at the age of twenty, preaching publicly from that
moment in the more deprived parts of Bath, Hooper was the
subject of much local debate. Some thought her eccentric and

excitable, others condemned her as fashionable and worldly. But on the whole Fanny's correspondents described her as something of a marvel. Back in Bath one of the first things Fanny wanted to do was discover the truth for herself.

Watching Hooper preach was an unforgettable experience.

It was at eight o clock on a Sunday morning in a low back street where tramps, sweeps and costermongers live. She stood on a chair, surrounded by a rabble of the lowest kind, but who formed a most attentive and respectful audience. Wretched women sat at the widows of the surrounding houses, and the tears rolled down many a black and hardened face as she sweetly commended to them from the story of the prodigal the free and boundless love of God.[15]

When Geraldine Hooper died in childbirth four years later at the age of thirty-one after her marriage to Henry Dening, Fanny was devastated. She had lost a close friend and inspiration. But never again did she question a woman's right to preach.

Her children were her greatest fans. Returning from one meeting to which Harry had accompanied his mother, he said to the maid, 'Ah, Susan, if you were to go with Mamma like me, then you'd know what *preaching* means.'

In the September of 1867, Henry and Fanny's fifth child, Henrietta, was born and lived only a few months. Harry, Minnie and Lucy had their clothes edged in black crepe. It was unlike Fanny to be morbid. Her approach to raising children was fairly free and advanced for the time, but she did not cope at all well with this bereavement. She blamed herself for Henrietta's death and, though she never said so openly, felt she was being punished for her materialism. The three children deprived of a cosseted existence had thrived, while the only baby born in the security of their own home had died. It could mean only one thing – time to uproot again. What did it matter that China was denied them when just across the Channel was a continent gripped by a spiritual darkness as dense as in the great Eastern Empire?

5.

The Dublin cousins, meanwhile, were contending with an unexpected bereavement of their own. Sir Benjamin Lee Guinness caught a chill and died on 19 May 1868, enjoying his title and parliamentary seat for only a few months. Although he had only had complete control of the Brewery for the last ten years of his life, he had made it the most successful in the country, becoming the most prominent figure in Irish business life. His estate was valued at £1.1 million, making his will the largest in Ireland to date. There were bequests for Anne, his daughter, and for Lee, his middle son, who was only twenty-six and a captain in the Royal Horse Guards, but the bulk of the estate went to his eldest and youngest sons, Arthur Edward and Edward Cecil, who were both working at the Brewery.

With his usual far-sightedness, Sir Benjamin Lee managed to do what many a rich man longed to do and failed – to control the future of his fortune from beyond the grave, ensuring it would be neither dissipated nor dispersed, but remain in the family business. The Brewery was to be divided equally between the two young men, with the proviso that if one of them should ever withdraw from the partnership he would receive not the value of his share, but a mere honorarium of £30,000. Ben remembered only too well the family trauma provoked by his elder brother, Arthur Lee, whose preference for artistic pursuits put the Brewery in jeopardy and almost cost him his livelihood. The capital must be left in the business so that the surviving partner could

139

continue without fear of liquidation.

In an uncanny way he appears to have foreseen the future. Perhaps he knew that history tends to repeat itself in genealogical lines. Perhaps he simply knew and understood his sons better than his own father. He certainly seems to have had a shrewd idea which of the two most closely reflected him in character. Educated at Eton, twenty-seven-year-old Arthur Edward was a grave, rather serious young man, old before his time, fond of his creature comforts, conservative in his opinions, a politician not a visionary. He inherited St Anne's Clontarf, the gracious Ashford Estate – and his father's parliamentary seat. Edward Cecil, on the other hand, though only twenty-one, was apprenticed to the Brewery at the age of fifteen, educated himself at Trinity in his spare time and had already shown instinctive business flair. His father left him 80 St Stephen's Green, the real symbol of status and prosperity.

The family intended a small private funeral, but that was not to be. Many lamented the passing of Sir Benjamin and wanted to share in the family's grief. The occasion was described in *The Times* as, 'one of the most impressive demonstrations of public feeling ever seen in this city'. Five hundred Guinness employees, dressed in black, marched at the front of the cortège. Behind the hearse and family coaches, in 239 private carriages, were the Lord Lieutenant, the Lord Mayor, representatives of the gentry and of every aspect of the civic and professional life of Dublin. All along the route from St Anne's to the family vault at the Mount Jerome Cemetery shops were closed and the streets lined with silent mourners. It was a remarkable tribute to an avowed Unionist, yet Sir Ben was also known for his courtesy and kindliness. Despite wealth and status, he remained, like his father, unassuming and approachable, sensitive to the needs of his employees and his family. The bronze statue by Foley erected in his honour within the precincts of St Patrick's is of a merchant prince, dignified yet benevolent.

The only discordant voice at his departure belonged to the Temperance Society, which made a barbed attack not so much on the brewer as on the Bishop of Cork who gave the funeral oration. How dared such an outspoken teetotaller say with impunity, 'God did bless Sir Benjamin's untiring endeavours with great prosperity' – this man, 'who in the course of his life had made more drunkards at home and abroad than, perhaps, any other in these lands'?[16] Had the great wealth of the Brewery blinded the Bishop's eyes?

Did Henry Grattan agree with the Bishop or the Temperance Society? No record exists of whether he attended the funeral, though he may well have done so, for he was once again receiving many preaching invitations to the country of his birth. There was no doubt he regarded all alcohol as devilish, but giving away his legacy was a severance with the Brewery, not of his family ties.

Sir Benjamin's death marked the end of an era for the entire Guinness family whose lives would never be quite so closely entwined with the city of Dublin again. For brewers, bankers and missionaries the great metropolis beckoned. London would increasingly become the hub of the wheel. But while brewers and bankers maintained their links with Ireland, gravitating between their Irish and English homes, depending on the social season, Henry Grattan simply went wherever he felt called, wherever he was provided with a house.

There were other family deaths in the year 1868. In September, at the age of sixty-nine, weeks before Henry and Fanny were due to sail to France, Jane Lucretia died suddenly in Lyme Grove in Manchester while visiting Fred, her youngest son, who was a curate there. Unlike Bessie, Jane Lucretia had no qualms about the eternal destiny of her three boys. Both of Henry's brothers, Fred and Wyndham, were Anglican clergymen, and she gave thanks to God for such a benevolent answer to her prayers.

Henry missed her dreadfully at first, despite the excitement of the move, and gave himself little time to grieve. He and Fanny settled in Paris where Napoleon III and his beautiful wife, the Empress Eugenie, held court in the glittering splendour of the Palace of Versailles. As ever, it was the challenge, not the sophistication of life in Paris which attracted Henry. There had been no religious revival in France. Resistance was nationally ingrained. Home of the philosopher Voltaire, France was riddled with rationalism and scepticism. Like Ireland, it was also a stronghold of 'Romanist superstition'. And Protestantism, without a Wesley or a Whitefield, was turgid and dreary. This was pioneer work and though he barely spoke a word of French, Henry threw himself into it with his usual gusto, preaching in the market place to Catholics as they came out of Mass. The French had never known anyone foolhardy enough do that before, but then, they said, Grattan Guinness was a 'true Englishman' (even if he was Irish), and used to free speech.[17]

In a few months he addressed some seven hundred meetings, and soon a combination of exhaustion and a recurrent eye infection brought on the familiar 'black dog' depression. Fanny sent him off to Switzerland for a rest, and during his journey back through Spain he had a bizarre experience which would sharpen the focus of his life.

While he was in Madrid he heard that workmen, constructing a new road on the outskirts of the city, had cut through the top of a hill and discovered, sandwiched between the usual layers of red gravel, an unfamiliar stratum of soft black dust. On examining the dust more closely they had found to their horror bits of bone and hair. Suddenly the realisation hit them that this was the site of a vast human grave – the legendary Quemadero, where the Spanish Inquisition had tortured and burned thousands of Protestant heretics.

Henry could not resist a chance to see the site for himself.

As the workmen went on digging they unearthed more gruesome remains, evidence of the most barbaric form of cruelty – rusty chains, two hands clasped tightly in prayer transfixed by a huge iron nail, a ribcage penetrated by a spear. Touched by living hands the relics simply crumbled away into the dust.

Henry stood watching, tears of sorrow, helplessness and fury welling up inside. So many martyrs! Never had the history of the Church touched him so profoundly, filling him with a mixture of grief and revulsion. He collected a heap of ashes, folded them in a Spanish newspaper and took them back to his hotel. That night, as he meditated on their implications, he poured all his outrage and anger into a poem, lambasting the Church of Rome for her heartless cruelty. 'Tell me, thou murderess black, what mean these bones?'

At home in Paris he told Fanny and the children of his find and showed them the ashes. Minnie caught something of his emotion, and always felt in awe of the pile of human ashes which sat on his desk from that day on. In years to come, whenever Henry was tempted to feel depressed and down-hearted, they would symbolise his life's work and calling, a constant reminder of the need to fulfil the dreams and vision of those who had laid down their lives for their faith.

The spring of 1869 was a happy one. Paris was breath-takingly beautiful at that time of the year, the tree-lined avenues heavy with almond blossom. There was no presage of the disastrous political events which threatened its serenity. On 25 April Gershom Whitfield was born – Gershom meaning 'stranger in a strange land', though Paris hardly seemed strange at all. The family loved the accommodation they had been given at the Chateau Foicy and settled down well, the children chattering away in French like natives, and Fanny addressing meetings with a fair degree of fluency. 'Love reigned in our home,' Minnie wrote, looking back at those early years. 'Life seemed free and generous. All the changes didn't matter, there was home and happiness everywhere as long as we were together.'

That sense of security was mainly Fanny's influence. Neither beautiful nor particularly creative, she nonetheless had some indefinable charm which made people notice her. She was calm and capable, essential for the wife of a man with as tempestuous a nature as Grattan Guinness. One young caller never forgot her visit. She was asked to wait for Fanny in the nursery which had a commanding view of the Parisian sunset from its west-facing window. Whitfield began to scream and neither the visitor nor the nanny were able to placate him. Fanny swept into the room, picked up her son, carried him to the window and said, 'Look!' He was only a few weeks old but he did as she said. 'It was not a vacant stare but a look of beautiful intelligence which lit up his eyes as he gazed at the glowing sky.' Mother and baby stood bathed in the sunset glow for at least three minutes. 'Then, without a word, she handed the quieted child back to the nurse and turned to me to speak of other things, not at all aware that she had given me one of the finest object-lessons of my life.'[18]

Fanny never forgot the lesson she felt she had learned from Henrietta's death in Bath. She would never allow any home to be completely hers again. It would be shared over the years with a variety of people needing her motherly care. To the devastation of all who knew and loved her, Maria Taylor died in China. Hudson, unable to care for his three children, sent them with their nanny, Miss Blatchley, to stay with the Guinnesses in Paris for a prolonged holiday on their way back to England. He knew that only Fanny could provide the extra security and love they needed at that time. They were all fitted with French suits.

By the time Phoebe Canfield was born, a year after her brother, the halcyon interlude in Paris was almost over. Day after day the city was filled with ugly demonstrations, angry workmen in their caps and overalls demanding war with

Prussia. The narrow cobbled streets were virtually impassable. Harry, Minnie and Lucy were returning from a walk one day with their nanny who was carrying fifteen-month-old Whitfield in her arms, when their way was blocked by a noisy procession. As they tried to squeeze past, the nanny and Whitfield were thrown to the ground in the path of an oncoming carriage and dragged to safety just in time.

The children were extremely upset and Fanny decided there and then that they had no choice but to return to the safety of England. With a heavy heart Henry handed over responsibility for the chapel he had founded in the Rue Royale between the Madeleine and the Place de la Concorde to Pastor Armand Delille. Throughout the war with Prussia, and the terrible months of the siege of Paris which followed, the chapel doors would stay open, making it a refuge for thousands of suffering soldiers and civilians.

By then the Guinnesses were back in Bath, following the harrowing accounts in the newspapers. They could hardly believe the photographs of the city they loved, surrounded by the Prussian army, an ever-advancing ring of artillery fire, and Napoleon III and his empress fleeing for their lives. 'Ma guerre', Eugenie had called it proudly, the war which would be her downfall.

From Henry's perspective, events began to take on apocalyptic significance. The day before France had declared war on Prussia the Pope decreed his infallibility. This was not simply heresy, it was blasphemy. The pile of ashes on his desk cried out for justice, and vindication was swift. The French troops in Rome, sorely needed at home, evacuated the Vatican, leaving it at the mercy of King Victor Emmanuel who intended being the sole monarch of a united Italy. By the end of 1870, in a matter of months, the balance of power in Europe had shifted radically. The temporal authority of the Pope had been destroyed for ever, France was in ruins, and Bismarck's Germany was a force to be reckoned with. Henry was convinced this was significant for the history of civilisation. There must be an overall plan, but what was it?

When Fanny broke her leg badly and was confined to a couch, pregnant again and unable to care for her five children, travelling for any of the family was out of the question. For Henry this proved an invaluable opportunity to study biblical prophecy and begin the successful writing career which would exercise a profound influence on government policy in the Middle East even after his death.

Every night Harry, Minnie and Lucy would climb into his arms as he sat in the huge armchair in his study, and in the firelight glow he would read what he had written that day, excerpts from what was to become *The Approaching End of the Age* which would sell in thousands. He told them not to be afraid of what was happening in Europe. It all pointed to the certainty that Christ would soon return, 'perhaps not in my lifetime, but in yours'. The idea fired the children's imagination. It would become a driving force in their lives.

Subtly, the dawn of a new era in Europe had heralded a new beginning for Henry Grattan Guinness. The preacher was becoming a teacher and would influence the nation in a more far-reaching way than he had ever done before.

Chapter 6

1872–1880
To the Great Metropolis

1.

Henry walked round and round, underneath the beautiful old trees in Armagh city centre, muttering half to himself, half to God, about the various possibilities for his future, oblivious of passers-by who stopped to stare. The way ahead finally came into focus. After years of uncertainty, of groping his way through a fog, of banging on doors which remained uncivilly shut, he felt as if a path was materialising out of the mist. 'The cloud moves,' he wrote in his diary in 1872 with undisguised relief, 'may I have grace to follow.'

The vision he shared with Fanny was of the world's first interdenominational missionary training college run on the same faith principles as Hudson Taylor's China Inland Mission. The few theological colleges which existed at the time were tied to one particular denomination. They were expensive and exclusive, reserved for those who had access to paid education. Attendance at Henry's college would not depend on denomination, gender or financial wherewithal. There would be no fees. God would provide the location, the staff, the students – and the food to feed them.

Fanny did not share his enthusiasm. After twelve years of

147

marriage she was used to her husband 'brooding on great schemes'. There was no doubt that young men and women were desperate for training to prepare them for mission overseas, and Henry could inspire and teach. But he did not have the practical ability to turn the vision into reality. That, she knew for certain, would be left to her. And she had six children to raise, Agnes having been born in 1871.

But such were Henry's powers of persuasion that one cold December evening she found herself alighting from a horse-drawn tram on to East London's teaming Mile End Road to look for an appropriate property. The road itself, a broad thoroughfare, was thronged with weary, work-grimy labourers heading for the comfort of home, manoeuvring their way around cabs and horse dung. Every tenth building was an alluring public house, its garish lighting holding out the promise of warmth and solace. Cocky factory girls in jaunty feathered hats dallied in the doorways looking for fun. Under the flickering, hissing blue naphtha flares barrow boys and pedlars competed loudly for the attention of the passing crowds.

Fanny was disoriented by the noise. Along with the clatter of the cabs on the cobbled street, the jingle of the tram bells, the neighing of the horses and the raucous shouting of the costermongers, she could just detect the sound of a barrel organ. An occasional mouth-watering smell of an evening meal wafting past on the night air quickly gave way to the all-pervading odour of burning hops emanating in sulphurous clouds from the vast dark edifice of Charrington's Brewery, casting its giant shadow down the entire length of the road.

The squalor and deprivation captured by Charles Dickens for posterity in his novels was painfully evident. Huddling in doorways for warmth, shivering women drew threadbare shawls around their shoulders, some clutching babies, little more than filthy bundles of rags, to their shrunken breasts. Starving-looking children dressed in tatters played in the gutters. Fanny was appalled. They stopped to stare at her as she passed, but then, she reflected, she and Henry must have made an interesting spectacle – an uneasy little woman hanging on the arm of a large, striking man.

They turned into a narrow, ugly little street with brick houses on either side semi-hidden by rows of tall spiked iron palings. Hayfield Passage was the approach to Stepney Green, popularised in the writings of Walter Besant which Fanny knew well. Besant's quaint descriptions however were penned before the East End sprawl swallowed up every open field and meadow, and when she saw the square of dilapidated three-storey mansions unadorned by tree or shrub, Fanny's disappointment was acute. Number 29, inevitably, was the shabbiest of them all.

Henry's excitement failed to raise her sinking spirits. This was a major test of her faith. 'I felt just like a would-be swimmer longing to strike out and feel the water up-bearing him, yet fearing to trust himself to do it,' she wrote in her diary, then added with her usual determination, 'But I shall swim yet.'

She moved her family from Bath to London at the end of 1872 under a siege of criticism from friends and acquaintances. How could she take her children to such an unhealthy, unsavoury neighbourhood? Where would they play? What about their education? There were no local schools. Fanny replied that the noise was trying, the dirt and dust disagreeable, that they gasped for a breath of fresh air and sighed for sights other than a never-ending succession of omnibuses and market carts, and for sounds other than the shriek of the railway whistle. 'But when we recall the lot of our missionary friends in the narrow lanes and streets of undrained Chinese cities, unable to secure in their comfortless dwellings even privacy from rude and curious crowds, or freedom from fever-breeding odours . . . we feel that we have good reason to be content with such things as we have.'

Henry had chosen the East End because he honestly believed no man or woman could possibly cope with the rigours of missionary life if they could not cope with living among their own poor. Tom Barnardo, who had given up any idea of going to China, had alerted him to the needs of the people in the London slums. Conditions were far worse than anything Barnardo had seen in Dublin Bay. The plight of the children, starved, kicked and brutalised as if they were animals, haunted him day and night. So many died during the cholera epidemic of 1866 that their bodies were taken in barrow loads outside the city and shovelled into mass graves lest demand for cemetery spaces give rise to embarrassing questions in high places. Christian political crusaders like Lord Shaftesbury, exposing the cruel lot of child chimney sweeps, mine and factory workers, demanding tougher legislation to protect them, constituted a serious threat to the livelihood of many a factory and landowner.

Barnardo opened two small houses as a ragged school in Hope Place in 1868 and his first residential children's home in 1870. On the whole, the gentry who had seen the liberating effect of Methodism on the working classes and feared any shift in the social status quo, treated his efforts with scorn. Shaftesbury, however, managed to rally support for Barnardo and an increasing number of other 'dissenters' committed to humanitarian causes, from a small, but influential group of Anglican evangelicals.

Barnardo, like Grattan Guinness, thought up grandiose schemes by the minute and always managed to carry them off. In 1872, without a penny in his pocket, he attended the auction of one of London's largest gin palaces and bawdiest music halls – and bought it. The Edinburgh Castle had turrets and a flagpole and a garish, brassy interior filled with statues of scantily clad women. When the day came to pay the bill Barnardo handed over the entire amount, as he said he would. Out went the alcohol, the women of easy virtue, the comedy acts and the statues. In went Barnardo with tracts, Bibles, hymn books and a variety of soft drinks. He kept the décor very much as it was. The blazing lights, coloured glass and floor-to-ceiling mirrors appealed to his cheeky Italian temperament, and after all, the world's first soft drink palace would need to be as bright and gaudy as any pub, if it were to attract customers.

The music hall provided a ready-made auditorium and the Edinburgh Castle Public House was soon converted into the Edinburgh Castle People's Mission Church with a congregation of over three thousand. Barnardo could say with some satisfaction that 'those who tell us that the working classes are inimical to Christianity are wholly misinformed'.[1] Initially, it was the Guinnesses' church, and a wonderful world of make-believe for their children.

Barnardo, however, still needed somewhere to live, and Henry needed a college supervisor. The Stepney Institute, as he called their first training establishment, was a stone's throw from the Edinburgh Castle, so Barnardo moved in, enabling Henry to take a house for his family in nearby Clapton. It was a perfect solution and meant the Guinnesses could fill the institute with students rather than their children.

Accommodation at 29 Stepney Green was hardly luxurious, though Fanny became rather fond of the old place in the end.

Old and ugly though it be, 29 is not an uncomfortable house, as houses go in London nowadays: and it suits our purposes very well. In the first place, it is roomy; and as we want to pack a good many people into it, that is one great point. Why, it has a hall twenty three feet long by ten feet broad! There are not many houses in London at £63 a year of which as much can be said. Then the dining-room, though not lofty will dine a party of twenty without difficulty. And there are three good studies – no little matter in a house intended for students. A broad and easy old staircase leads to a spacious landing, off which are ten bedrooms. True, nine of them are but a ship's cabin in point of size, but each contains a bed and a chair and a gaslight, if not a candle, so they answer their purpose as prophets' chambers. The beds only measure two feet six in width; but as the Duke of Wellington said to the young officer, who, on seeing his Grace's camp bed, exclaimed, 'Why, dear me! your Grace, there's no room to turn round in it!' 'Turn, Sir, turn? When a man wants to turn, its time he turned out.' So we think. We provide beds, not to soothe the restlessness of the slothful, but only to give rest to the weary, and two feet six is enough for that.[2]

Number 29 also had its own garden at the front, 'a square of sufficient dimensions to admit a fair amount of exercise', and a timber yard at the back, which, compared to dreary slated roofs and blank walls, was, Fanny declared, the next best thing to 'a view'. It was furnished sensibly according to their limited budget, with strong chairs, well-stocked bookcases, warm coconut matting and serge curtains. Fanny could not abide extravagance.

While Henry set off on a recruitment drive all over the country, the three elder children settled down at a nearby school run by the indomitable Mrs Pennefather. Catherine Pennefather was the wife of William, Vicar of St Jude's, Mildmay, and together the formidable pair initiated a host of charitable works at a complex known as the Mildmay Centre, consisting of church, conference centre, school, evening classes, soup kitchen, and, following the cholera epidemic, a hospital. Years later, when Minnie was asked whether Mrs Pennefather wasn't something to do with Mildmay, she retorted, 'She was Mildmay!'[3]

The first theological student arrived from India at the beginning of 1873. Joshua Chowriappah spoke so little English that the Guinnesses decided he should live with them at Clapton. The children loved his sparkling dark eyes and mischievous toothy grin and he quickly became part of the family. When he left them several years later Chowriappah would become an outstanding pioneer missionary in his own country.

As Henry travelled and news of the Institute spread, potential students began to arrive. Along with the British candidates were French, German, Russian, Armenian, Spanish and black South African, a hundred in the first year. Each served a month's probation and was subjected to rigorous examination. Thirty-two were finally accepted, which meant the college was full.

Donations worth £1,500 were received, which was just enough, if Fanny managed the budget carefully. She wrote to their supporters, 'Deeming it wise that intending missionaries be trained to independent and active habits, we keep no servants.' This was revolutionary in a Victorian household. Men were never expected to do housework. But Henry and Fanny deplored the tendency of British expatriates to turn the natives into servants. The missionary himself should be the servant of those to whom he was called. If he could not respect the integrity of local people, better he did not go at all.

The Institute schedule reflected the Guinness's radical attitude to theological training. It was practical and spiritual, as well as academic and intellectual. The rising bell sounded at six. There was housework at six thirty for an hour, then prayer until breakfast at eight. Classes began at nine, and ended at one thirty with lunch at the Edinburgh Castle to save cooking meals at the house. During the afternoon students learned a variety of crafts, including mechanics, building, carpentry, basic medicine, cookery, botany, and reading the compass and sundial. At seven in the evening they were out in the streets learning to field the physical and verbal brickbats hurled at any open-air preacher, 'to counter the deadening

153

influence of study on their souls'. Henry never forgot the lessons he learned at New College. Local brewers, more paranoid than Arthur or Benjamin Lee Guinness about possible losses caused by temperance preaching, hired rabble rousers to disrupt the meetings. Letting students loose on the Mile End Waste would make or break them. The long day ended with prayers at nine.

Grattan Guinness was criticised by the academic institutions of the time for offering amateur, 'short-cut' theological education. This was probably pique, for the Institute provided first-rate, 'hands-on' missionary preparation, however gruelling, and applications for the course poured in from all over the world. It became abundantly clear that the house at Stepney Green was far too small. Fanny felt increasingly that the students were an extension of her own family and that she should be on hand to mother them, particularly after Barnardo left to get married in the summer of 1873, so a year after opening the Institute the Guinnesses also acquired Harley House in Bow. The ground floor would provide classrooms, a dining-room, and a study for Fanny – for as she had foreseen, her life was now absorbed with accounts and general administration – and the upper floor the Guinnesses' own accommodation. Number 29 Stepney Green became the students' residence.

A few days before they left Clapton, the doorbell rang, and ten-year-old Minnie, in frilly pinafore, ran to answer it. Howard Taylor was standing on the doorstep with a letter from his father to hers. Hudson Taylor had arrived from China to look after his children and was living with his family at Mildmay. At eleven Howard felt very grown up to be entrusted with such an important errand. Having successfully managed to find his way through the London streets, his confidence dissolved at the sight of the solemn little face with its large blue eyes, framed by two long blond pigtails, slowly appearing around the open door. The children stared at each other for some time before Howard finally found his tongue and explained why he had come. Minnie invited him in and as far as she was concerned, that was the end of the episode. Howard, however, would maintain for the rest of his life that from that moment there would never be any other woman in his life.

The whole family was thrilled with their new home. Although Harley House faced the Bow Road with its constant din, there was about an acre of land at the back, filled with shrubs and choice trees, separated from a spacious lawn by a bridge over a grassy ditch. It gave a sense of seclusion and tranquillity to Fanny, and freedom for the children who quickly converted a large, gnarled pear tree into a tree-house. Best of all, in the middle of the lawn stood a small fountain. Stopping to admire the garden, one local visitor said to Fanny, 'Shouldn't think, Miss, as 'ow you'd ever want to go to 'eaven with that there waterspout.'

As far as Henry and Fanny were concerned, Harley College was also ideally situated for student training. Bryant and May's match factory was nearby. So was the London Hospital where many patients died alone and abandoned, and the Tower with its garrisons of soldiers. The docks, where bewildered immigrants arrived daily were a mere stone's throw away. Directly opposite was the most imposing building in the area – the workhouse. Opportunity for practical pastoral care was virtually limitless here where thousands lived in hopelessness and despair.

The house was large and old-fashioned, dating back to the time when Bow had been a pleasant London suburb. There were disadvantages in living in such an area, particularly the almost deafening roar of horse-drawn trams in their tracks at the front, and the constant clack-clacking of cabs, so that even at midnight, 'sounds that never disturb the echoes of the West End squares are paining our ears'. However, said Fanny wryly, 'The noise is endurable when the windows are shut.' Fanny's remarkable ability to look on the bright side of any situation enabled her and the family to cope with the many demands inflicted upon them by her husband's visionary enthusiasm. She could still say, 'We would sooner live in the broad, cheerful, airy Bow Road than in many a dull, confined and built-up West End square, or in many an elevated cage-like apartment on the plane-lined Boulevards of Paris.' But Fanny could not know then how much the decision to take her family into such a confined, disease-ridden corner of England would cost her.

2.

In the year that Fanny and Henry moved into Harley House, Edward Cecil Guinness, youngest son of Sir Benjamin Lee, and the power behind the Brewery, married his cousin Adelaide Mary, youngest daughter of 'Old Pel', the late, little-lamented Richard Samuel Guinness, MP for Barnstaple, and his socially aspiring widow, Katherine, thereby uniting the brewing and banking sides of the family. Although 'Dodo', as she was known, was three years older than her groom, and, at twenty-nine, well on the way to confirmed spinsterhood, her mother was not at all pleased with the match. Katherine had sent all her daughters to be 'finished' at the court of her brother-in-law, the Duc de Montebello, with the intention of enticing a title or two into the family. But her efforts appeared to have been wasted. Mildred, the eldest, never married, Geraldine, widowed at thirty after three years of marriage to a soldier, then opted for a clergyman called Beauchamp Kerr-Pearse, Rector of Ascot, the brother of her younger sister, Edith's husband. And then Dodo picked one of those dreadful Guinness tradesmen. That he was Deputy Lieutenant of Dublin and one of the richest men in the country seems to have counted for little. Dodo had been groomed for the

156

aristocracy, not for one of the 'common branch of the family'.

The couple met in Fanny's 'dull, confined' West End. Katherine's disapproval forced them to conduct a fairly furtive courtship. Edward Cecil had been spending an increasing amount of time at the flat his father had left him at 5 Berkeley Square, particularly during the season. The dashing young bachelor had earned quite a reputation as a charming and entertaining host, but socialising never distracted him from his duties at the Brewery. On the contrary, despite his youth, he was a meticulous Chief Executive. Happy to delegate his authority, particularly to John Tertius Purser, whose family had faithfully served the firm for generations, he nonetheless expected to be kept informed about the daily running of affairs, however practical or mundane, and to be consulted on all matters of general policy. Throughout his life he tenaciously retained the ultimate control of the business.

While most of his managers appreciated the flexibility they were given, within the limits of Edward Cecil's absolute authority, his elder brother and partner, Arthur Edward, resented the apparent reduction in his status. Sir Arthur had neither his younger brother's vitality, nor his instinctive head for business, and whenever he did make an occasional foray into management, the disruption put the relationship under severe strain.

Arthur in fact seems to have regarded the Brewery primarily as a source of income. Both brothers had received a generous allowance from their father which more than quadrupled after his death. Edward Cecil tended to take less of the profits than his elder brother, though on the whole they both ploughed back as large a share as they could, which in many ways was the secret of the company's success.

Sir Arthur's real love was politics. He retained his father's Dublin seat in the General Election of 1868, but was divested of it the following year when it emerged that his agents had been bribing the electorate. He was never personally incriminated, but this second family brush with corruption tarnished his reputation. Five long years passed before he successfully climbed his way back into the political scene.

Meanwhile, in 1871, he married the formidable Lady Olivia Charlotte White, daughter of the third Earl of Bantry, converted St Anne's, Clontarf into an Italian palazzo and upgraded his property at Ashford by planting an extravagant larch forest to make it the best woodcock shoot in Britain – appreciated in time by no less than the Prince of Wales himself. With his brother, he also financed the Great Irish Exhibition of 1872. Though never as successful as its sponsors hoped, it nonetheless attracted a great deal of positive attention, and, of course, the gratitude of the Irish business world. An ingratiating article entitled 'What One Family Can Do For Ireland' appeared in *The Irish Builder*, and Edward Cecil was duly appointed Deputy Lieutenant of Dublin.

All Edward Cecil's decisions were careful and calculated and his choice of a wife was no exception. The marriage was compatible and affectionate, but that was a bonus. First and foremost, Dodo was the ideal spouse for a man who needed manners not money. Katherine's attempts at grooming had paid off. Not exactly beautiful, her daughter was striking nonetheless, petite, vivacious and neat, a charming and interesting companion, with a streak of determination to match her husband's. He intended to launch himself into the highest society. She knew how to provide the perfect base. As her husband had foreseen, Dodo's cultured ways acquired in France, her command of the language and her innate intelligence, made her the perfect hostess. The Edward Cecil Guinnesses quickly earned a reputation for the luxury of their beautiful homes, the lavishness of their hospitality and the glamour of their entourage.

They were, naturally, leading lights in Dublin, where it was easy to be an exceptionally large fish in a relatively small pond. Dodo converted their home at 80 St Stephen's Green into the most fashionable house in town, throwing sumptuous parties in the London style, making every other attempt at hospitality, including the Lord Lieutenant's, pale by comparison.

In 1874 they bought and renovated Farmleigh, a substantial property overlooking Phoenix Park, so that when they were in town for the season, as they invariably were, Edward Cecil could take a daily constitutional, walking briskly across the park to the Brewery. At Farmleigh they established a family tradition for large, jolly house parties, when, like the rest of their set, they opened their house for the Punchestown Races, the leading event in the Irish social calendar. Guinness house parties, however, tended to be bigger and better than the rest. Brimming over with restless energy, the master of the house occasionally showed off his own accomplished horsemanship, driving a four-hand with relays of horses all the way to Punchestown from St Stephen's Green.

The Dublin season was a little more showy, less sophisticated than its London equivalent, despite the pomp and ceremony of the viceregal court, now adorned de rigueur by the glittering Guinness couple. They were regularly invited to travel to the races on the viceregal train, and while the Viceroy had a distinguishing X on his carriage, Edward Cecil managed to have XX scrawled on his.

After the Dublin season there was the London season and Cowes, then back to Dublin for the Horse Show, Scotland for the shooting, and a trip to the Continent, if it could be fitted in. The arrival of their first child on 29 March 1874 at 5 Berkeley Square does not seem to have disrupted Dodo's social life in any noticeable way. She noted in her diary with an extraordinary lack of emotion, 'Baby born at quarter to six. Boy.' One month later he was christened Edward Cecil Lee Rupert at Ascot by his Uncle Beauchamp Kerr-Pearse. Rupert, the name by which he was known, seems to have been an afterthought.

Two more sons followed, Ernest born in 1876, and Walter in 1880. The upbringing of the three boys could not have been more different from their Grattan cousins. Although they were all left in the care of a succession of nannies, normal practice for most middle- or upper-class families, Henry and Fanny were constant visitors to the nursery, and easily distracted from their work when their children's needs required it. Edward Cecil and Dodo, however, might not see their boys, who were not allowed to impinge upon their parents' whirlwind social routine, for weeks, even months at a time.

When their paths did cross, Edward Cecil took a keen clinical rather than personal interest in his children's development. In his pocket book, where he kept an almost obsessive record of every detail in his life, even the tiniest purchase, he jotted down next to each other, 'Newspaper – 1d' and 'Rupert's height – 35½': He was methodical to the point of finickiness, a personality trait which would either irritate or please staff at the Brewery, depending on how much attention they welcomed from the boss.

Given her own tense and difficult childhood, her father's financial problems, his death when she was only thirteen, her mother's disappointment and self-indulgence, Dodo's lack of maternal instinct is understandable. But Edward's upbringing was warm, and it is strange that he had so little idea about how to relate to a child.

Though not the best of fathers, he was not a hard man. From his earliest days as head of the Brewery he had been appalled by the slum conditions he saw every day on his way to work. The one-roomed dwellings were 'veritable stinkpots'. If the Corporation would not do anything to improve the living standards of the poor, he would. In 1872 he began a home-building programme for Guinness employees, partly out of altruism, partly out of shrewd common sense. A healthy worker was a more efficient worker. This was the first step in a radical programme of social reform which would affect the lives of thousands of Dublin citizens, an almost inevitable response to the dictates of his Christian heritage and conscience. Besides, an inveterate hypochondriac, he was keen to put into practice any improvements which would remove disease from his near proximity.

Edward Cecil's notebooks reveal a man who did not suffer fools gladly. Tensions with his elder brother over the Brewery inevitably grew. When Sir Arthur won back his Dublin seat in 1874, it sounded the final death-knell as far as his interest in the business was concerned. The powerful Lady Olive was no more keen on trade than her sister-in-law's mother, and appears to have exerted a great deal of influence over her husband. Rumour has it that one evening she and her husband were taking a walk in Dublin. A labourer, disgusted to find his bottle of Guinness had gone off, slung it over a wall, where it landed at her feet. The following morning Sir Arthur resigned.

It is hardly likely that the Lady Olive would have deigned to go anywhere in the town without her carriage. It is more likely that Arthur's withdrawal from the partnership, which his father had foreseen, was a combination of his wife's distaste, and his own awareness of Edward's growing exasperation. He was beginning to feel pushed out. His impatient younger brother would never be satisfied with anything less than sole ownership.

Edward, who never felt any tension between his aristocratic aspirations and the means to make them possible, had balked for some time at the way responsibility was, in theory, shared, while, in practice, he did most of the work. But his father's will imposed heavy penalties on a partner who withdrew his shares. After the birth of Rupert he was particularly keen to draw up a new agreement, but his elder brother was reluctant even to discuss the matter. Finally, in 1876, he had a new deed drawn up which allowed a retiring partner to draw out compensation of almost £480,000, and Arthur, under pressure from his wife, snapped up the bait. Edward was so relieved he granted his brother a further £120,000, knowing he could afford to do so and that it was an advantageous investment. The policy of returning profits into the business had more than paid off. It was worth a great deal more than at the time of Sir Benjamin Lee's death. Besides, the intent of the will had been honoured. The Brewery remained firmly and safely in the family.

Sir Arthur was a man born to enjoy giving money away more than gaining it. A rich man, unshackled from the tiresome middle-class necessity of earning his living, he was free to indulge in the pursuits he and his wife liked best: politics, philanthropy and social climbing. Not to be outdone by the Edward Cecils, the future Lord and Lady Ardilaun chose 11 Carlton Terrace as their London base, where he entertained the good and the great, quickly establishing a reputation for magnificent dinner parties and glittering soirées.

Watching the meteoric social rise of her daughter's nearest and dearest, Katherine was forced to swallow her pride and admit that without any help from her mother, Dodo had made a brilliant match.

3.

Sir Arthur's father's first cousin Henry Grattan was living with his family in relative squalor at the other end of town, 'unnoticed by the world of fashion, business or pleasure', Lucy would write years later. The prophetic and scientific writings which would bring him the attention of government leaders were as yet unwritten. There was no organisation, denomination or society to fall back on, and nothing in hand for the needs of the missionary students.

Henry never took a salary from the college funds.

Looking back over the ministry of those days I recall the

fact that it was boldly undertaken in faith and largely unrecompensed in character ... Never, as far as I remember, in the course of a long ministry, have I made any bargain for fee or reward. £400 had been left me as a legacy by my uncle Arthur Guinness of Beaumont, and when my mother needed pecuniary help, I gave her this sum, and went down to Birmingham to preach the gospel with half a crown in my pocket ... and from that day I have never lacked a home to shelter in, or provision for daily needs.

It was a matter of principle to Henry Grattan that no matter how strapped for cash he would never approach his wealthy cousins. To ask would represent a singular lack of faith, to accept, a sign of double standards. His two elder half-brothers however, Captain John's sons by Susanna Hutton, had no such qualms. John Grattan, who had been dismissed from the Brewery for mixing with the wrong sort of company, had been set up in his own brewery in Bristol, and had then tried to sue Benjamin Lee for wrongful dismissal, was found dead in 1871, 'lying in the greatest misery and dirt imaginable'. His brother, Dr Arthur Grattan, saw an opportunity for a little gentle blackmail. He wrote to Edward Cecil telling him that he had had to bribe newspaper reporters with ten shillings to prevent them publishing the fact that the deceased was related to the rich Guinnesses of Dublin, 'feeling sure that you, knowing my present circumstances, would help me to pay it – it would indeed have been a terrible annoyance to have the particulars stated'.[4]

Edward Cecil's response is unknown, but with such step-brothers it is hardly surprising Henry Grattan became wary of social contact with his wealthy relatives. He himself tried to support his poorer relations financially and spiritually – with little degree of success. In later years two of Dr Arthur's stunning-looking granddaughters came to stay with him for a while, looking for a good time in London. They rejected his encouragement to become missionaries, opting for a career on the stage instead.

Fanny always found it difficult to rise to her husband's heroic heights of faith. She kept the account books. Feeding fifty young men with healthy appetites on very little taxed her abilities to the limit. Henry often set off on preaching tours leaving her with an empty cash box. She would write to him in desperation, 'In these days of high prices money rapidly melts away', and he would reply with maddening confidence, 'Let us go without meat in the Institute for another week, and give ourselves to prayer and searching of heart.' And Fanny would stand before the students, account book in hand, and explain why even more stringent economies were necessary.

Being of a more practical turn of mind than Henry she did not see prayer and effort as mutually exclusive. 'We cannot expect God to do by a miracle that which we can do for ourselves,' she stated firmly. That meant writing endless, time-consuming bulletins and reports to the Institute's supporters to attract the necessary funds. Yet time and time again, Henry was right. The tide would suddenly turn. Provisions would appear almost out of the ether, just as they were most needed. It was a faith-stretching experience for the students. From day to day there were great variations in the quality and quantity of food on their plates. Harley House was not 5 Berkeley Square, or 11 Carlton Terrace.

Nonetheless, it began to attract its fair share of high-profile visitors. Barnardo would bring the Edinburgh Castle's visiting preachers to the Institute for a meal, hardly the cultural élite, but probably a great deal more intriguing. There was Harry Moorhouse, Ireland's most notorious pickpocket until he was converted in the Irish revival. Henry loved telling his children the story of riding with Harry and several other, well-heeled travellers in an Irish jaunting car. No one could believe he was as bad as the stories suggested. 'Look to your purses, gentlemen,' he said, and divested them of the entire contents of their pockets by the end of the journey. The children would beg Harry to pick their pockets every time he came.

Other guests included Richard Weaver and his wife, rough diamonds but celebrated preachers, George Holland the wealthy businessman who gave up his comfortable existence to open a ragged school in Whitechapel in the George Yard Mission, and Amy McPherson who opened the first home for destitute children. Charles Haddon Spurgeon, pastor of the Metropolitan Tabernacle, the most well-known British preacher of the century, and William and Catherine Booth, founders of the Salvation Army, were regular visitors.

Occasionally, the gracious, elderly Earl of Shaftesbury himself would take time away from the demands of the House to sit on a bench in the shade of the gnarled pear tree with his old friends Henry and Fanny. In 1872 Lord Shaftesbury began what he called his 'regular tea-fight' for sixty heads of missions working in the lower parts of London, 'to come and give me information respecting the progress of Christianity under those forms'.[5] Barnardo, who was a great story-teller, claimed that it was he who had taken the Earl out at night to see for himself how hundreds of children slept rough in freezing temperatures. Shaftesbury is supposed to have said, 'All England shall hear of this!' He probably did utter those words, more likely in response to tales of poverty and despair he heard at his tea-parties. He was an invaluable ally for the Grattan Guinnesses and their friends.

One visitor, unknown in Britain when Henry first befriended him, would quickly become their most famous guest of all. The American evangelist Dwight L. Moody arrived in London in 1873, initially for a few weeks, but stayed two years. By that time almost three million people had heard him preach. He enjoyed an acclaim he had never known in America. His influence on the Guinness family, personally and on their work, was immense. Moody encouraged their public alignment with what was called the holiness movement.

The holiness movement grew out of the teaching of John Wesley, who believed there was a second spiritual experience after conversion, but completely separate to it, available to Christians determined to give their all to God. It entailed complete surrender to Christ, being filled with the Holy Spirit, freedom from habitual sinning, and power to serve God. In 1871, two years before he left the USA, two women urged Moody to seek this new experience himself. Disappointed with the apparent lack of response to his teaching, 'Moody locked the door and sat down on the sofa. The room seemed ablaze with God. He dropped to the floor and lay bathing his soul in the Divine.' It was such a profound, overwhelming revelation of God's holiness that in the end he had to beg God to 'stay his hand'.[6]

His preaching was transformed overnight. He said publicly, 'I was all the time tugging and carrying water. But now I have a river that carries me.' Suddenly, Henry's own experience in Ireland as a young man made sense. It explained his power to preach at the end of the 1850s, quenched by the seeds of self-doubt sown by the Brethren. The realisation had a profound effect on the way he taught his students.

Overseas students brought their own colourful traditions into the Guinness home. Unlike Edward Cecil and Dodo's three sons, protected from ordinary, let alone extraordinary society, Henry Grattan's children were exposed to a wide variety of different cultures. 'Robinson Crusoe, Robin Hood and Cinderella are all very well in their way,' Lucy wrote, recalling her childhood impressions, 'but you should see the war dance of our two Kaffir brethren.'

The family environment was stimulating. Social history, economics, politics and geography were everyday topics of conversation around the meal table. Stanley had just published his graphic, illustrated and rather glamorised account of how he had found Livingstone. 'Foreign missions were as real as

Guy Fawkes and quite as interesting. Curled up in a big armchair one can feel oneself fascinated still by the spell of Stanley's journey through the dark continent. He was only Hans Andersen with smaller print and a little more ponderous to hold.' Truth, Henry would say to them, is always more wonderful than fiction.

Fanny was forever at her desk. In the evening, before bed, there was always one last story, but then she returned to her work. It seemed to Lucy natural and proper that all people, children, nurses, governesses, servants, men and women should go to bed at night, 'but that mothers should stay up and start at about half past ten their hardest writing. I believed with a perfect faith that all mothers did this; that they worked on till one or two a.m. and came down to breakfast at eight o' clock the next morning as regularly as the sun went round the earth.'

It was Minnie who bathed and played with her two baby sisters, Phoebe and Agnes. She had always been a shy child, but at twelve was so withdrawn that it was hard to get a word out of her. She felt sluggish and stupid beside the rest of the family. Her parents were brilliant conversationalists, clever and gifted, Harry, her hero, so dashing and fearless, Lucy sensitive and interesting with her large brown eyes and pale, oval face. In fact, she felt so lacking in talent she persuaded herself she must be adopted.

Fanny was stunned. Distracted by the needs of the students she had not realised how distraught Minnie had become. She saw a great deal of herself in this gauche, unhappy child. She too often lamented her lack of looks and talents, and felt in the shadow of her larger-than-life, dynamic husband. It was time to make some changes. Minnie needed to stay at home for a while with an understanding governess while Harry was ready for school where his energy would be harnessed.

Shortly before he left for Tettenhall College in Wolverhampton, Harry, Minnie and Lucy were baptised at the

Edinburgh Castle by their father. Rubens Saillens, a French student at the college, said it was one of the most moving occasions he had ever witnessed. 'He did it in so touching a way, speaking to them with such tenderness and depth of meaning, in tones so vibrant, yet so calm, that there were few present who were not moved to tears.' For Minnie it was the most important day in her life. She had found the courage to demonstrate her convictions in public.

Harry was 'a most lovable boy, and a great favourite with masters and pupils', wrote one of his tutors in an end-of-term report, though he distinguished himself more on the sports field than in the classroom. Maths was a severe trial. He only scraped through because of a dogged determination to study medicine and be useful, one day, in one of the distant countries he heard so much about at home.

Bertie and Howard Taylor joined him at Tettenhall. Their father had remarried and returned to China with his new wife. Howard, known then as Fred, was a frail-looking, blue-eyed, fair-haired child, who looked as if he was born to be bullied.

'What does your father do, new boy?' a small, but menacing crowd asked him on the first day.

'He's a missionary,' Howard replied. The pack scented sport.

'What's your name?'

'Lazarus,' he replied, putting on a plaintive little voice. They began to jostle him.

'Have you brothers and sisters, Lazarus?'

'Two sisters – Mary and Martha.' At that moment Harry arrived in the playground.

'Hi, Fred,' he shouted.

'Fred,' jeered the crowd, 'Fred? This is Lazarus.' Harry caught Howard's eye and the pair burst out laughing. Throwing their arms around each other, they stomped off, leaving a very foolish gang of boys behind, who would never again rag Howard Taylor.

Despite their age difference Bertie and Howard were in the same class. Raised in China, where family honour was tantamount, Howard deliberately made sure he never gained higher marks than his elder brother, though he could have easily done so. He was an exceptionally unselfish child, happy to leave others in the limelight, a character trait he never lost in adulthood.

While Harry was at school Minnie and Lucy took lessons at home with Maud and Florence Charlesworth, the giggly, clever daughters of the Vicar of Limehouse. Maud would one day marry Ballington Booth, son of the founders of the Salvation Army. Minnie, fazed by the vivacity of the Charlesworth girls, thought them silly and giddy. They teased her for her earnestness, making a show of preferring Lucy, though in fact their real interest was the handsome, extrovert Harry.

They waited in great anticipation for school holidays. The Guinnesses kept their grand piano in the dining-room, as there were not enough rooms at Harley House to have the luxury of a sitting-room. At most meals Harry would leap to his feet and play a musical accompaniment. Florence would join him in a duet, and after the meal, organise charades and other enforced games. Minnie became increasingly withdrawn.

Fanny finally decided her children should have their own governess and a Miss Gardner was duly appointed. For Minnie it was the best decision her mother had ever made. She loved Miss Gardner from the moment she swept into the schoolroom in a trailing silk gown. But it took the governess a while to settle into her strange new surroundings. To find herself in such a dismal part of London was unnerving. To be confronted at breakfast the following morning by two swarthy-looking Syrians, one of whom was blind, was almost more than the sheltered Englishwoman could bear. But Fanny exerted her usual charm and Miss Gardner was soon put at ease and part of the family.

She remembered Minnie as a loving child, a second mother to her baby sisters. Lucy was frail but brilliant, while Whitfield, a rosy-cheeked seven-year-old, inseparable from his violin, was the darling of the students. When he first saw a map of London, he studied it for a while, then asked, 'Why are all the parks at one end, and the docks at the other?' Even Miss Gardner was hard pressed to answer that question.

At mealtimes the parents emerged from their respective studies, Fanny to listen to their children's progress, Henry, 'radiant with the light of heaven, absorbed in some fresh thought connected with the Second Advent'.[7] According to Miss Gardner, he was writing *The Approaching End of the Age*, and Mrs Guinness was 'putting it into more simple, popular form'.

Miss Gardner became an indispensable part of the Guinness household, helping Fanny with her correspondence, the students with their English, presiding at the meal table when Henry and Fanny were away. Encouraged by Fanny, an increasing number of match girls at the Bryant and May factory dropped in on their way home from work, and if the children were toffee-making, their favourite pursuit, joined in. Poor Miss Gardner was all but turned to toffee, and Henry was roused from his meditations by the laughter from the kitchen.

In the summer holidays the sun always seemed to shine, the garden beckoned and the boughs of the pear tree were laden with new fruit. Harry taught Whitfield to ride a one-wheel bicycle so that the four children could ride around together, playing their violins in harmony. Athletics was even more popular. Harry decided that five times round the garden was a mile and challenged the Taylor brothers to a fifty-mile run. Whitfield and the sisters were loud, encouraging spectators all day, until Fanny, summoned from her desk by the continual racket, finally stopped them at forty-eight miles. To Harry's chagrin the Taylor brothers quietly completed the full fifty miles when Fanny's back was turned.

From 1875 summer holidays took on a new dimension altogether. Henry Grattan Guinness acquired his own stately home and country residence. In Derbyshire there lived a couple by the name of Hulme, devout Congregationalists, who owned an extensive property consisting of a large, elegant country house, a farm and many outbuildings, to which they had added a small chapel, all set in twenty-one acres of rolling Derbyshire countryside. The Hulmes were elderly and there were no children to inherit the home they loved so much, yet they felt it should be put to positive use.

Driving home from the station one day, as he watched the house come into view, James Hulme had the strongest feeling that Cliff House should become a missionary training college, though he had no idea how that might be possible, and died before he could see the fulfilment of his vision.

Shortly after her bereavement Mrs Hulme happened to visit Harley College, and knew at once what she must do. The lease on Cliff House, then in the hands of a group of trustees, was offered to Henry Grattan so that he could set up a northern branch of the Institute.

Built around 1790 by Thomas Gardom, eldest son of John Gardom, owner of Calver Mill, Cliff House had been advertised in 1835, prior to its sale to John Hulme, as 'a very desirable investment'.

To gentlemen having families and desirous of spending the whole or part of their time in the country, Cliff House forms one of the most eligible residences in the country. The air is pure, remarkably dry, and calculated for health; the scenery is beautifully romantic and diversified. A range of lofty rocks, forming the boundary of the extensive east moors, is situated about a mile and a half on the east, and serves to shelter the house from the north-east winds. The

River Derwent is seen winding its course through the valley on the western side, and is overhung by a rich and extensive wood on the rising hill. The front of the house has a southern aspect, which is very extensive, having the beautiful grounds of Chatsworth with a view of the ducal palace from the upper rooms. A coach from Manchester to Nottingham to Newark passes immediately at the foot of the hill on which the house stands, and from Bakewell opportunities of travelling to almost all parts of the kingdom are afforded by London, Manchester and other coaches.

The Hulmes however had not been able to manage the property for some time. The floors were riddled with dry rot, most of the window frames had disintegrated, the plumbing had ceased to function and the roof was full of holes. Fanny groaned at the thought of taking on a white elephant. But Henry was adamant. Apart from a principal's salary the college would be self-supporting. Enthralled by news of recent exploration in Africa, an increasing number of students were feeling a sense of call to the great lost continent. But life there was utterly primitive. To survive they would need to understand the rudiments of subsistence farming. Where better to do so than in the wilds of Derbyshire?

The lease became theirs in December 1875, and Henry set off immediately with a working party of students, blessing the Almighty that among this year's intake were several carpenters, joiners, painters and glaziers. They camped in the empty shell of the house in freezing conditions, working from morning to night, breaking off only to eat and for chapel services. Once the basic repairs were complete, alterations began, the conversion of barns into dormitories, the building of additional staircases, windows, bathrooms and a large number of lavatories. Then there was the wallpapering, whitewashing and painting to do, all accompanied by the loud singing of the popular new hymns by the American Ira Sankey.

Inevitably, they caused a stir. The quiet, rural village of Calver had never experienced such an invasion before, and local people turned out to watch. Word got round that these were theological students, and some were foreign. They were soon in great demand in the surrounding chapels. 'The people expected us to be great guns, coming from a college in London and having attended Moody's meetings,' wrote one of the students, 'so we try not to disappoint them!'[8] That meant sitting up half Saturday night after an exhausting day of hard physical work to put a decent sermon together.

One day a local deacon arrived at the house in search of a preacher for some special services he had arranged. The students, dressed in sacks which had holes cut out for their heads and arms, were in the process of demolishing an old farm building and were covered from head to foot in dust and debris. The worthy deacon approached them and asked if he could speak to one of the students from London. They told him he already was. 'YOU, a student?' the deacon exclaimed incredulously, then seeing an acquaintance working in the farmyard, found an excuse to slip across and verify that these really were the students from Harley College.

While Henry acted as supervisor of works, Fanny in London had the task of justifying the expense to their supporters. Funds were urgently needed. The work of the Institute was expanding rapidly in many different directions. As well as buying two more East End houses as student residences, Fanny had publicly committed herself to creating ten new congregations in the area. She was appalled at the way established churches, Anglican and even Methodist, were moving out of the slums into more salubrious neighborhoods at a time when hundreds of the growing East End population were turning out night after night, sometimes in pouring rain, to hear the students preach.

For weeks, while Henry was in Derbyshire, she trailed the streets looking for possible venues for new congregations, but none of the abandoned churches and chapels she visited fulfilled her requirements. They were largely 'cheerless, desolate, dirty-looking structures ... with their high-backed pews and their formal religious associations sure most effectively to repel the very class we want to attract'. How could such dismal, sepulchral buildings compete with brilliant, beautiful gin palaces?

Fanny eventually found several possible mission halls, a sign-painter's shed in Old Ford, a little disused chapel in Bow, a Presbyterian iron church which she uprooted and moved to Stratford. She rented a local school on Sunday evenings for three hundred rough, uneducated children who poured off the streets into the established churches to keep warm and were ejected on the spot for being disruptive. Two oxy-hydrogen lanterns were bought so that the students could hold the children's attention by illustrating their talks with slides, or 'dissolving views' as they were called. 'Our men make the oxygen gas and work the apparatus themselves,' Fanny explained to supporters, 'so the expense is trifling, while the benefit and enjoyment they afford is great.'

One of their students, a former sailor who intended working among seamen, managed to persuade Fanny that one of her mission halls should be afloat. It could sail up and down the Thames, round the coast among British and foreign shipping, and anchor in the summer at seaside resorts. Early in 1876 a thirteen-ton cutter came on the market at the incredibly low price of £120 and was bought with the help of a single donation. The students lovingly repaired and repainted her, and launched *The Evangelist* the following spring with a captain and three students on board.

It was not difficult for Fanny to justify missionary work among London's poor, but how could she explain the acquisition of a property, not in squalid Bow, but in the lush

Arthur Guinness, the First, the family founding father.

Arthur Guinness, the Second, inherited the Brewery by default but was a shrewd and clever businessman. He always kept a Bible open on his desk.

Captain John Guinness, too much of a Christian
and a gentleman to be a brewer.

'The beautiful and talented Miss Cramer of Dublin',
Jane Lucretia D'Esterre, who married John Guinness.

Henry and Fanny Grattan Guinness, shortly after their marriage in 1860. Fanny still dresses like a Quaker.

Sir Benjamin Lee Guinness became rich, gave the family status and
dignity, and the Brewery its quintessentially Irish harp emblem.

Sir Benjamin's wife, Bessie, with their two eldest sons, Arthur and
Benjamin. She was a devout, gentle woman who worried
about the effects of fine living on her three boys.

Fanny Guinness and her six children,
Harry, Minnie, Lucy, Phoebe, Agnes and Whitfield, in 1877, shortly
before tragedy struck. She did not fear the effects of
riches on her children. Poverty was another matter.

Edward Cecil Guinness, the first Earl of Iveagh, who proved that trade could ultimately earn a man a title.

Adelaide Mary Guinness, Lady Iveagh, known as 'Dodo'.
Shy and aloof, yet a great socialite, she threw magnificent parties, but her illness was the best-kept family secret.

countryside of Derbyshire? It was, she wrote, an unimaginable release to escape from the noise and filth, to see a sky unobscured by a leaden pall of smoke, to hear the bird song and see the distant hills. 'Night brings real silence. Your whole being seems to expand with a sense of relief.'

Furthermore, learning experimental farming was providing an invaluable tool not only for the students, but for some of Tom Barnardo's boys, who were acquiring useful skills in a restorative environment for the first time in their lives. Altogether, Fanny concluded, despite her original misgivings, Cliff College was a gift from God not to be refused.

In the summer of 1876, however, overburdened by the tasks she had to bear, Fanny suffered from acute exhaustion. While she stayed at Harley House to recuperate, moving her couch into the garden to her favourite spot under the shady pear tree, Miss Gardner took the children to Derbyshire for the first time. They fell in love with Cliff from the moment they saw it. There had been occasional country holidays in Ireland to the home of their Uncle Wyndham Guinness, Vicar of Rathdrum, but this was different. All this was theirs, the wide open spaces and breathtaking views, the moors of heather and bracken climbing gently to the steep, gritstone cliffs, the gracious serenity of the house, the fun of life on a farm. Milking time was a source of endless delight to Phoebe and Agnes. And there was so much to explore – mushroom and calf houses, pigsties and store-rooms, a higgledy-piggledy rambling group of structures lending themselves to games of hide-and-seek, linked by quaint stone steps.

From that first summer Cliff was not only home to the Guinness family, it was an idyllic paradise, a summer retreat and a refuge at other crucial times from the pressures they would all face in the years ahead. The children were blissfully unaware of the tensions that periodically drove their mother to her couch under the pear tree, and Fanny was determined it should stay that way.

The expenditure exceeded her worst fears. While Henry became embroiled in the protest against the Bulgarian atrocities, speaking up and down the country in support of Bosnian Christians facing persecution at the hands of Muslim Turks and Bulgars, Fanny's time was absorbed in the mammoth task of finding carpets and curtains for Cliff. The floors were full of crevices, 'giving a peep of the regions below'. Something would have to be done before the cold weather set in – a covering of 'impervious and ornamental kamptulicon' at a mammoth cost of £50.

Other welcome gifts materialised – £15 worth of iron bedsteads, bedding for the Barnardo boys' dormitory, motley hand-knitted quilts – but it was never enough. Cliff House was a bottomless pit. The new principal, Henry Dening, widower of Fanny's friend, Geraldine, the exceptional preacher who had died four years earlier in childbirth, submitted a list of urgent necessities, including a cart, force-pump, two cows and half a horse. Some kind supporter had sold a pony on Cliff's behalf, and the proceeds represented half the price of a horse.

Begging lowered Fanny's spirits dreadfully. Why were they forced to scrimp and scrounge when £250 million, which could have been put to good use, lay untouched in the Bank of England? The years 1876 and 1877 brought 'almost unbroken financial pressure in consequence of the rather too rapid extension of our undertakings'. From time to time she made up her mind to get rid of Cliff, but every available space was filled with industrious students. James Hulme would have been thrilled to see it.

She kept an almost daily, painfully honest account of her struggles in her diary:

March 21st, 1876. Received this morning two SMALL donations and two LARGE bills, one for books, and the other for building and plumbing work, £75. Expenses are great!

April 28th, 1876. No money came in today; we have not a week's expenses in hand, with a hundred people dependent, in a sense, on us.

April 29th. £12 from two donors today is a help towards present necessities, and a cause for thankfulness. We were considering last night on how little it would be possible to keep the men for a week should it be needful to come down to dry bread!

May 1st. No funds came in today, only bills. We have never been so low before.

May 2nd. Nothing again this morning, save tidings they have the measles at Cliff!

The situation eased a little over the summer, but by December Fanny was urging both houses to give up meat for the foreseeable future. Henry, never willing to ask his students to do what he was not prepared to do himself, wrote from his preaching tour in Cornwall to say he would join them in their fast. But how, Fanny lamented, could they be vegetarians on Christmas Day? She so badly wanted to treat her Sunday School children to their first turkey dinner. 'Feeling cast down and tried,' she noted in her diary. On Christmas Eve a cheque for £50 was delivered to the door of Harley House, enough to provide Christmas dinner for the Guinness family, the Sunday School children, and any overseas students unable to return home for the festive season, not to mention a special Christmas tea for Fanny's Mothers' Group.

However close to the edge they pushed them, financial constraints were never allowed to interfere with Henry and Fanny's original vision. Small miracles were enough to help them rise to the next, major challenge. Harley House had manifestly become too small. The dormitory accommodation at Stepney Green was inadequate. Grown men did, after all, need a measure of privacy. A brand new, purpose-built college was out of the question until it occurred to Henry that if he built on the paddock beyond the garden there would be no land to buy. An immensely generous donation of £1,000, and the sale of Stepney Green house for £500, meant they had almost half the cost of the college before construction began.

Fanny's account of the slow, painful progress sounds strangely contemporary. Builders appeared to work very short hours – for very high wages. The cost of bricks went up by a third. To add to the many demands upon her, she was distracted from close supervision of the building site by a domestic crisis. Fifteen-year-old Minnie had been sent to boarding school in Weston-Super-Mare six weeks earlier and was so homesick she had made herself ill. She simply could not cope with separation from her two little sisters and cried until her eyes were so swollen she could not see. Fanny was summoned to collect her and take her home.

Neither Henry nor Fanny ever reproached her for her failure. Geraldine could not spell, the school informed them. So be it, said her mother. If she was backward at her lessons, Minnie was mature in other ways. Sensibly, they realised it was unwise to try and force her out of her reclusive tendencies. There was a time for everything – and time proved them right. Throughout a career which would take her all the way around the world and involve a lifetime of writing, Geraldine Guinness would never be able to spell.

By the time Minnie arrived home, the walls of the new college had almost reached their destined height and Fanny organised a supper party for the bricklayers as she promised she would. Henry, who had watched them from his study window balancing precariously so many feet above the ground, felt inclined to pray publicly for the safety of each and every man.

A few days later, during a freak, tropical storm, one of the labourers at the top of the scaffolding reached out an arm which was struck by a sudden flash of lightening. His blood-curdling screams brought Fanny and Henry running to the site. For a moment they thought his arm had been torn off. In fact it was completely numb, but intact. It soon became apparent he was suffering more from shock than any physical damage.

'If you 'adn't said that prayer, sir . . .' he whispered to Henry. Henry asked him if he knew how to pray himself.

'Oh yes,' he said proudly, ' "I can say, Our Father charten 'evn, allord be thy name", and "Matthew, Mark, look on John".' With a mixture of amusement and despair, Henry realised he attached no meaning whatsoever to the sounds he was making. He obviously thought his achievement impressive for he added for good measure, 'My little boy can say these prayers as good as I can, sir; that's just what I was teached, and I try to teach 'im the same.'

Harley College, the East London Institute for Home and Foreign Missions, was opened without debt on a biting autumnal day in 1878. It was an imposing red-brick building with a grey roof and large sash windows. The Venetian blinds were Fanny's pride and joy. As she handed out the tea, Minnie was as excited as her parents, thrilled to be a part of the buzzing life of Harley, but even happier to be in charge of her two small sisters again.

Every night she supervised Phoebe and Agnes's bathtime, then led them down to Fanny's study where they sat on the sofa playing chess as quietly as two little mice, less they disturb their mother's concentration. After an hour Minnie came back for them and took them up to bed. She resented any engagement which would take her away from them. Nothing prepared her, or any of the family, for the cruel blow to come.

4.

Missionary zeal was an integral part of life in the late nineteenth century. The Victorians were a self-confident race, religious, resolute and determined, unsettled but not undermined by the claims of Darwin, with none of the theological cynicism provoked by two world wars and the threat of a nuclear holocaust.

Missionary fervour has been subject to late twentieth-century criticism for confusing Christianity with imperialism, for exporting British culture and imposing western ways. For some, the early Catholic and Protestant missionaries, this was undoubtedly true. But a combination of deep ambivalence about religious certainty and contemporary cynicism about the 'grand gesture' has led to a disowning of the sacrifice many other missionaries made, and an undervaluing of their undoubted achievements. Britain's colonialising tendencies were wreaking havoc in India, China and Africa long before the missionaries arrived. Adventurers, traders, soldiers and government representatives were always in the vanguard, exploiting the natives with alcohol, drugs and guns for personal gain and to impose their own superiority.

The later, non-denominational missionaries like Hudson Taylor deplored colonial attitudes in China and tried to undo some of the harm already done, particularly by the opium trade. His missionaries were instructed to live and dress like the local people, the men shaving their heads and wearing pigtails, the women observing all the cultural traditions except foot-binding. There were to be no cathedrals, no monuments out of keeping with local surroundings.

In those days missionary adventures like those of Taylor in China and David Livingstone in Africa appealed to the public imagination. It seemed terribly romantic to sail off to unknown lands. Missionary magazines, with their engravings of regions and peoples never seen before, filled their readers with awe and excitement. These were lost souls. Christ would not return until they had had the chance to hear of his love. It was a driving compulsion to give up all and go, to die for the cause if necessary. This was the age of the Salvation Army, of hymns like 'Rescue the perishing', of Amy Carmichael and her vision of countless people hurtling over a cliff to endless damnation, watched from the banks by Christians making daisy chains. The end of the world was near.

In 1875 the first twelve students went out from Harley House, Joshua Chowriappah to India, the two black South Africans to their homeland, one to Burma, one to Japan, four to China, Arthur Douthwaite leaving his fiancée behind because he thought he could be more useful without a wife, and Rubens Saillens to Paris, where he founded a theological college at Nogent which exists to this day. On the day of their departure the 'Mother of Harley' delivered her last words of advice. Aware of the solemnity of the occasion, for who knew what destiny awaited them, one of the students sharpened a pencil and opened his notebook in readiness. She said, 'I have one piece of advice to give to you which I hope you will remember all your life.' The student gripped his pencil in readiness. 'Whatever part of the mission field you may be in, always be sure to keep your hair tidy.' There was, he decided, an unmistakable twinkle in her eye, masking the terrible wrench she felt at parting. After all, they had become *her* children, and she would never see some of them again.

'Our first twelve' always had a special place in her affections. She hung a photograph of them over the chimney-piece in the dining-room and at mealtimes allowed her vivid imagination to carry her to the countries they represented. Letters were read aloud to the children, who were enthralled with the descriptions of lively Japanese towns, of Chinese waters crossed in dozens of little boats known as junks, of scorching plains in India or Burma, of back-breaking work on Caribbean plantations.

The family also followed the daily newspaper descriptions

of Stanley's discoveries in the unknown continent of Africa. For years Africa had exerted an almost magnetic charm over a succession of hardy explorers, commissioned by the Royal Geographical Society to discover the sources of the Nile. The early pioneers, Speke, Burton and Baker, had no real interest in the African people. They thought them too barbaric to civilise. That, however, did not prevent Speke from bartering with guns. 'There is no such thing as love in these countries,' Baker wrote. 'Everything is practical, without a particle of romance. Women are so far appreciated as they are valuable animals . . . I am afraid this practical state of affairs will be a strong barrier to missionary enterprise.'[9]

An almost Stone Age system existed, brutal but valid in its own way, doomed long before the Westerners arrived, for they were preceded by Arab traders who pillaged and plundered and raped the land in search of human booty. African chiefs were only too happy to sell their fellows to the slavers and convert to Islam in exchange for weapons. Baker maintained that unless Britain stepped in quickly the whole land would be despoiled, and lost for ever to Christianity.

What was to be done? How could a civilised government enforce a ban on slave trading without resorting to the same aggressive tactics as the traders, rousing the suspicion and hostility of the natives in the process? The Royal Geographical Society sent out Dr David Livingstone, not to save individual souls, but with a commission to open up the continent so that others could follow. A gracious, gentle man, Livingstone, who refused to carry a gun, had a genuine affection for the people and became known to the Africans as a white man who treated them as brothers. 'The strangest disease I have seen in this country seems really to be broken-heartedness,' he wrote home, 'and it attacks free men who have been captured and made slaves.'[10]

Livingstone disappeared somewhere in the interior in the late 1860s. There was national rejoicing when the explorer

Stanley, who had been sent to find him, reported that coming upon a white man safe and well, he had ventured to ask, 'Livingstone, I presume?'

When Livingstone died two years later in 1873, natives lovingly carried his body overland so that it could be shipped home for formal burial in Westminster Abbey. Profoundly influenced by the great and godly man, Stanley went back to Africa, determined to take up where the doctor had left off, finally managing to reach the mouth of the Congo. His dispatches in the *Daily Telegraph* in 1875, gripping tales of danger and daring, captured the imagination of the public. Stanley was a journalist and an accomplished, compelling writer. *Through the Dark Continent*, published in 1877, was a real-life adventure story, full of graphic descriptions and emotional appeals to go and save a lost continent.

Shortly before his death Livingstone had written, 'All I can add in my solitude is may Heaven's richest blessings come down on everyone, American, English or Turk, who will help to heal this open sore of the world.' Dying on his knees, stretched out across his bed in an agony of prayer for Africa, he had thrown down the gauntlet to the enthusiastic students of the Harley Institute.

In 1878 Henry and Fanny set up the Livingstone Inland Mission. The aim was to establish missionary stations all the way down the swift-flowing Congo River to Stanley Pool, where it contracted to an unnavigable torrent, hurtling its way in a series of cataracts to the lower Congo and Atlantic Ocean. Many Harley students rose to the challenge. They knew the risks involved. Stanley had made it clear that the African waterways, the only real means of access into the continent, were treacherous, the climate unbearable, disease rife and the natives not only hostile, but cannibalistic. Hardly any of his own or Livingstone's party had survived. Africa meant almost certain death.

Nonetheless, a small party at Harley, led by an ideal

candidate, Adam M'Call, no stranger to Africa for he had spent seven years as a government official big-game hunting on the Upper Zambezi, was preparing to go. Fanny, for all her passion, felt a deep unease about encouraging 'her children' to make sacrifices that she, safe and secure in England, would never have to make herself. But before the little group sailed, events she could never have foreseen tested her own commitment and seemed to put her on an equal footing.

The Easter holidays of 1879 were fast approaching. Fanny planned to take her family to their Uncle Wyndham's rambling old vicarage overlooking the sea at Rathdrum for a good long rest. Some ten days before they were due to leave for Ireland, Henry set off for a series of meetings in Torquay taking Whitfield with him. Fanny was loath to let the child go, but he was not a robust little nine-year-old, and she thought the sea air would do him good. With Phoebe and Agnes, she stood on the porch at Harley waving them off until the carriage was out of sight.

The following morning, Wednesday, Agnes complained of a headache. Fanny thought little of it and made her stay in bed. She seemed better by the afternoon, got up and played as usual. By early evening she had a pain in her neck and ear and it hurt when she moved her mouth. Fanny, who was about to go out to speak at a meeting, thought she must have caught a cold and instructed Minnie to make sure Agnes had an early night.

In the small hours of the morning Fanny was awoken by the creak of her bedroom door. Standing by her bed, Agnes whispered, 'It's only me, Mother dear. I can't sleep and I've disturbed Minnie once or twice. I'm so hot I don't know what's the matter with me.'

Fanny carried her back to bed and in the morning sent for the family physician, Dr Dixon, who diagnosed tonsillitis, a condition unknown to Fanny, but apparently not serious. As the next two, endless days went by and Agnes showed no sign of improvement, Fanny found the diagnosis hard to believe. A terrible, sickening fear began to take hold of her, sitting on her stomach like a lump of lead. What if her little girl had diphtheria? How could she have contracted it? A picture formed in her mind – the meeting that evening before Henry left for Torquay, 150 Sunday School teachers and seven-year-old Agnes handing out tea and cake. Her friends and relatives so critical of her for taking her children into the disease-ridden East End, spoke some sense. Anyone could bring infection into their home.

By Saturday Agnes's throat was so sore it took her ten minutes to find the courage to swallow her medicine. There could no longer be any doubt about the nature of the illness. Dr Dixon urged Fanny not to worry about the students, but to get the other children out of the house. Meanwhile, he sent for a throat specialist called Mackenzie who managed to scrape away some of the membrane, leaving the tissue raw and bleeding. Fanny held Agnes and sang to her, and when she finally slept, scribbled a note to Henry begging him to leave Whitfield with her cousin in Torquay and come home.

Harry, mercifully, was still away at school, Lucy was dispatched to relations, but on the Sunday, before Fanny could finalise arrangements for the other two girls, it became clear that eight-year-old Phoebe had succumbed to the disease.

That was a night to end all nights. Agnes was desperately ill, Phoebe was incessantly and violently sick and Minnie, an invaluable source of support, began to develop the dreaded symptoms and was too unwell to help. Fanny struggled on, but by Monday morning her own throat was extremely painful. She told herself she was simply suffering from strain, and telegraphed Henry again. By the time he arrived home on Monday evening Dr Dixon had seen the characteristic membrane across her throat and sent her to bed.

Henry was in enforced quarantine downstairs with the students. Even if she couldn't see him it was a relief to Fanny to have him in the house. They communicated by notes, and on Tuesday, decided to send the students home for a prolonged vacation. The house stank of carbolic, but that was hardly a guaranteed protection against the spread of infection. Agnes was a little improved, Phoebe holding her own, and at seventeen, Minnie was old enough to fight the disease. Fanny was beginning to let herself believe the worst was over.

By Wednesday, however, Phoebe had deteriorated so rapidly that the two doctors held out little hope for her survival. Fanny begged them to let her go to her child, but they refused. Finally, in the evening, she could bear it no longer, and dragged herself to the nursery. Phoebe was labouring for breath. Her hand was cold and clammy. Fanny sat on the edge of the bed, sponging her brow. She opened her eyes and seeing her mother said, 'You shouldn't take that trouble. You'll make yourself worse.'

The following morning Dr Dixon performed an emergency tracheotomy, opening the windpipe and inserting a tube below the obstructive tissue. Phoebe's relief was instantaneous. She began to breathe freely. Fanny sent a message to Henry to say she had regained consciousness, and he was allowed to come and stand in her room, just inside the door. It was the first time they had seen each other since his return from Torquay, and they knew they must not go near or touch each other. All Henry could do was watch from the doorway while his little girl died in Fanny's arms. Fanny sat for some time without moving, too stunned at that stage even to cry. She kissed her daughter one last time, then went to look after Agnes.

Agnes and Phoebe were inseparable. It was impossible to think of one without the other. Dr Mackenzie was attending her. One look at his face was enough to tell Fanny that there was little more he could do. A tracheotomy would be of no use. The disease had spread to her chest. For several hours Fanny fought on, filling Agnes with medicines, willing her to live. Life was inconceivable without her bright, giggly baby dancing around the house like a sunbeam. But by late evening her breathing slowed and her pulse weakened. Henry came and stood just in the room again. Agnes could not see him, but recognised her father's voice. She died at ten o'clock, ten hours after her sister.

Fanny was distraught with grief and weakened by the disease. She longed for Henry, for the comfort of his arms, to share in his pain, but it would have been madness to take such a risk. Instead, she and Minnie cried the night away together.

The following day she wrote to Harry, Lucy and Whitfield, the hardest letters she ever had to write. To Wyndham and his wife, Dora, she said she could hardly believe that instead of joining them for a happy family holiday, she had news she could hardly bear to share. For the last years Institute work had left her little time for recreation. Her only relaxation had been brief moments snatched with her two little girls. They had been such merry, considerate, undemanding children. She had failed to remember that children are 'winged joys, ready at a moment's notice to take their flight'. She couldn't believe they wouldn't run in from the nursery or garden at any moment. She couldn't bear to think of the treats she would never be able to give them. Heaven had better treats, that was her only consolation. She thanked God they were in his presence, and that one day they would be joyously reunited. 'But oh, dear brother and sister, need I say, for the present, it is not joyous, but very, very grievous.'

The funeral took place without Fanny or Minnie on Wednesday 2 April at the Abney Hall Cemetery, Stoke Newington, where Fanny's sister Madeline and her four children were buried. Fanny was bewildered, full of questions about why God seemed to answer certain prayers but not others. Why had she and Minnie been spared? Why had Lucy not succumbed? Why was Whitfield providentially out of the way? Perhaps it meant God had some special work for them to do. A tiny ray of light penetrated the darkness threatening to engulf her. Perhaps, one day, there would be meaning in this apparently pointless bereavement. But for the time being it was a case of surviving one day at a time, when every ounce of her being seemed to scream, 'How can I ever go on without them?'

Chapter 7

1879–1882
The New Generation Grows Up

1.

Minnie cried herself to sleep for months. During the day she kept her feelings to herself. She had to be strong for Lucy and Whitfield's sake.

Henry and Fanny coped with their own bereavement by submerging themselves in work, and seemed largely unaware of the depths of their daughter's grief. Henry, who could not abide London and the mundane details of business – even missionary business – for any length of time, escaped on a preaching tour of Algeria. Within thirty-six hours' sailing time from France, four days from London, was a nation of ten million unevangelised Berbers. What was to be done about them?

Fanny, submerged beneath the endless demands of their burgeoning 'empire' at home, had run out of suggestions. But the following year they received a visit at Harley from Mr and Mrs George Pearse who came to consult Henry about their future. Mrs Pearse was the former Jane Bonnycastle, converted in Paris by Henry's preaching. She knew a little about the Berber people already, and felt excited at the idea of working in Algeria. With Henry and Fanny's support the couple set up the North Africa Mission and set sail.

The Guinnesses now had the oversight of three missions, two colleges and ten mission halls. A budget of £1,500 in 1873 had risen to £11,000 in 1878, and even that barely covered the running costs and salaries for missionaries, teaching staff and pastors. The college courses were still free and applications poured in, over a thousand in the first six years. Fanny found it hard to turn anyone down.

In the late 1870s the East End experienced its first major influx of Jewish immigrants fleeing the pogroms of Eastern Europe. They spoke little English, looked very strange, and their poverty made the Eastenders look wealthy. Local people treated them with a measure of suspicion, if not overt hostility, while indefatigable missionaries set up organisations dedicated to care, relief and evangelism.

One day in 1879, a minister from the Mildmay Mission turned up at Harley College with five young Jewish men, all destitute, with little command of English, but recently converted to Christianity and determined to study with Henry Grattan Guinness, who was establishing a reputation as an expert on biblical Zionism. There were no vacancies, but Fanny took them in all the same. One of them, David Baron, would later play an important part in the first international Zionist congress.

By the beginning of 1880 sales of *The Approaching End of the Age* had exceeded all Henry's expectations. Acclaimed by a variety of respected theologians including Professor T. R. Birks of Cambridge University, the book had been reprinted five times and greatly increased demand upon Grattan Guinness as a preacher. Lord Shaftesbury said he was 'so struck and moved by its contents . . . that I cannot resist the desire I feel to bring it under the immediate and serious attention of the public'.[1]

From his studies in the Old Testament Shaftesbury himself had long been convinced that the return of the Jews to their homeland in Palestine was a crucial part of the divine plan. As early as 1839 he had managed to persuade the Foreign Secretary, Lord Palmerston, that Palestine should become a national homeland with Jerusalem as its capital, under Turkish rule and British protection. The scheme came to nothing, but Zionism had evidently been a viable political proposition for some time.

There were other theological books on biblical prophecy and world history. Henry Grattan Guinness's distinctive contribution to the subject was largely due to a recently acquired interest in astronomy. Professor Birks had introduced him to the discoveries of a Swiss astronomer called Jean Philippe Loys de Cheseaux. Medieval astronomers had always maintained there was no possible convergence in the revolutions of the earth, the sun and the moon. In 1754 de Cheseaux, who had been trying to establish the exact date of the crucifixion, fell inadvertently on the fact that 315 years constituted a soli-lunar cycle, the sun and moon coming within three hours, twenty-four seconds of their relative positions in space. To his excitement he then realised that 315 was a quarter of 1,260, the number of 'days' mentioned in the books of Daniel and Revelation as significant for the end of the age. As a multiple of 315, 1,260 years must also be a soli-lunar cycle. More extraordinary, when he went back to his calculations he discovered that 1,260 years was the time it took for the sun and moon to complete a cycle in space to within one hour of each other. Just as the hour, minute and second hands of a clock all meet together twice a day at twelve o'clock, so here, in the biblical prophecies long before it was discovered by astronomers, was a 1,260-year convergence of the sun, earth and moon like a huge astronomical clock. This gave a vital key to understanding biblical prophecy. Twelve hundred and sixty years was a complete cycle of time, bringing the solar and lunar calendars into almost total harmony.

Henry Grattan was so enthralled by de Cheseaux's

deductions that he acquired a twelve-inch telescope so that he could continue the astronomer's work. It developed from amateur into serious academic pursuit, his painstaking research eventually earning him fellowships of both the Royal College of Astronomers and the Royal Geological Society.

For some months the telescope occupied pride of place in the Guinnesses' overcrowded dining-room at Harley House, until it could be equatorially mounted at a purpose-built observatory at Cliff. This was Henry's most treasured possession. At some stage in their course most of the students were invited to admire it. David Baron went back to the observatory time and time again, noticing on one occasion the Hebrew words scratched into the telescope's side, 'Holiness to the Lord'.

Henry would explain to students that just as the earth had its own cycles, the minute hand on a clock measuring an hour, the hour hand marking a cycle of twelve hours, light and dark denoting a day, and four seasons encompassing a year, so there were other cycles known to astronomers which measured very large periods of time. Henry was convinced that while most human beings were unable to think in any other than fairly limited cycles of time, God's time scale was measured by these huge astronomical clocks. Daniel, Revelation, the apocalyptic books of the Bible which spoke of the end times, must, then, be written in a kind of astronomical code. The books themselves spoke of being 'sealed up' until an appointed time. Unwittingly, de Cheseaux had broken the code. References in the text to days, weeks, years and 'times' were 'natural astronomic cycles of singular accuracy and beauty, unknown to mankind until discovered by means of these very prophecies'. The appointed time had come. The mystery of the last days was about to be revealed.

It was now relatively easy for Henry to establish that biblical time was often measured not in solar years like the Western calendar, but in lunar years. Many scholars of prophecy had long since realised that a biblical 'day' symbolised a year, and Daniel's '70 weeks' meant 70 × 7 'days' = 490 years. Henry's astronomical and historical studies on Daniel's 'seven times' (a week of years) namely, 7 × 360 'days' = 2,520 years was double the book of Revelation's 'forty-two months' (42 × 30 'days') or '3½ times' – each was de Cheseaux's figure!

Henry was convinced that the 'end times' of the apocalyptic books were the years referred to by Jesus Christ as 'the times of the Gentiles' – an era of Jewish degradation and dispersion, dating from the destruction of the great temple in Jerusalem. If this was to last for a period of 2,520 years, historical evidence showed that the 'end times' were fast running out.

But Henry Grattan was no crank with a presage of the end of the world.[2] He rejected any attempt to foretell the second coming of Christ. In fact he deplored every 'futuristic' approach to biblical prophecy which tried to use the Scriptures as a kind of an almanac. Historical facts were what counted, not speculation. In his own futuristic vision the prophet Daniel saw the world dominated by four terrible beasts for 'a time, two times and a half a time'. These beasts were the four great pagan empires of antiquity, Babylon, Persia, Greece and Rome. From the accession of Nabonassar, the first King of Babylon, to the fall of Romulus Augustus, last emperor of Rome, was a period of 1,260 lunar years. That was a fact.

Daniel's fourth beast, Rome, had ten horns. Once they were destroyed it would sprout another, very different in kind from those it followed. Henry believed that this horn represented the political and very corrupt power of the Vatican. From the moment it began to exercise a powerful influence in European affairs until its sudden collapse in 1870, which Henry and Fanny had witnessed, was another period of 1,260 years. From their perspective of history, that too was a fact.

In other words, 1870 must have been a turning point in world history, marking the end of 'seven times', a cycle of

2,520 years. The main indication that the 'times of the Gentiles' were slowly drawing to a close would be the end of the dispersion of the Jews among the nations and a return to their homeland in Palestine. According to Grattan Guinness, a key year in this process would be 1917.

Before 1870 no sensible person would have deemed that possible. Palestine had been controlled by the all-powerful Ottoman Empire for hundreds of years. Henry also calculated that a cycle of 1,260 years of Muslim occupation of the holy city would soon be complete. By 1870 Turkish might was beginning to fail. Its stranglehold in the Middle East had weakened, leaving a power vacuum which each of the European countries was only too happy to fill, seeking to out-manoeuvre each other in a series of political games known as 'the Eastern Question'.

Many politicians like Lord Shaftesbury believed that Jewish restoration was the obvious solution. He was not alone. Even the writer George Eliot, who had introduced liberal theology into Britain from Germany, claimed in the introduction to her pro-Jewish novel *Daniel Deronda* that 'the regeneration of the Jewish people is the great divine mystery of world history'. Only the Jewish people themselves remained impervious to their destiny, living throughout the diaspora in relative tranquillity. But on 1 March 1881 Tsar Alexander II was assassinated. The Jews of Eastern Europe became scapegoats overnight. Cossack soldiers rode roughshod over Jewish settlements, torching them as they looted, pillaged and murdered. Jewish refugees fled in their thousands, some to Palestine, some to America, most to Britain, particularly the East End of London. Now Henry's expectations began to have real significance. Along with several other early Christian Zionists, he and Fanny bought land in Palestine with the intention of handing it back to its historic Jewish owners when the opportunity arose. Neither could possibly know it would never be in their lifetime.

In a supplementary 600-page volume to *The Approaching End of the Age* Henry included his meticulous astronomical and historical charts, which even Fanny, in her popular précis of the book, was forced to admit looked rather daunting. Nonetheless, she said, they showed how every important world event fitted into an astronomical cycle in such a way that, 'any person of ordinary education and intelligence, reading it with attention will find no difficulty whatever in understanding and following its statements'. Now, she concluded triumphantly, the Christian student had found 'a new weapon where with to defend the Book of God against the oppositions of science falsely so called – a weapon with which, indeed, he may assume the aggressive, and challenge opposers to account for a fact which nothing but the Divine inspiration of the Bible can account for'.

While Henry and Fanny were absorbed in their own affairs, Minnie went on brooding. She refused to go out and began to complain of pain in her back. Part of each day was spent lying on a spinal board on a couch beneath the windows of the empty schoolroom – a room filled with aching memories. The combination of physical and emotional pain was almost more than she could bear and she longed for death.

Fanny took notice at last. Suicide had impinged too traumatically on her own past to be dismissed lightly. The child must be taken out of herself. Fanny insisted she socialise a little and accept a kind invitation to visit her Guinness cousins in the West End.

Although Edward Cecil was the head of the Brewery, Sir Arthur Ernest saw himself as the undisputed head of the family. He and Lady Olive took their responsibilities seriously. They were deeply shocked by the death of their cousin's two little girls. The inevitability of losing children in Victorian England did not make it any easier to bear. Lady Olive, childless herself, and given to great charitable gestures, began

195

to wonder whether she might not be of some service to the four who remained. After all, from their Fitzgerald mother the true blood of Irish nobility flowed through their veins. Grattan Guinness's reputation as a writer and preacher had reached new heights following the publication of his book. How could they raise their offspring in the dreadful East End? Youth was a tender plant to be nurtured and cultivated. Fanny must be encouraged to introduce her offspring to proper society.

Olive was more taken with the children than she expected. They were not the hoydens she feared. Harry had dash and charm. Geraldine was quiet and refined, pretty in a demure kind of way. Lucy's facial features were too strong to create an overall impression of beauty, but she had another, less definable quality, a certain luminosity, particularly when she played the piano. Lady Olive was too keen a connoisseur of the arts not to recognise brilliance when she saw it. They were all exceedingly well-mannered. In fact, growing up in the East End appeared to have had very little effect on the children's aristocratic accents and manners. Many years later, Geraldine's rich and plummy English voice would make her a popular speaker in America.

Harry, Geraldine and Lucy also began to spend time at the magnificent home of Sir Arthur's brother, Uncle Edward Cecil and his wife Dodo. Dodo never forgot her humble origins, the 'grinding poverty' in which she claimed she was raised. Years later she told her future daughter-in-law, 'I and my sisters all had to help in the house, my dear, and when I was a very small child one of my tasks was to measure out the tea from my mother's store cupboard for the servants' weekly tea allowance.'[3] Poverty of course is relative, but if she could rise to such heights, then who knew what might wait for the young people if they were groomed, polished and introduced to the right people? Her own three sons were obviously far too young for their Grattan cousins. Geraldine would have loved to spend time playing with them in the nursery. Rupert was six, the same age as Agnes when she died, but Aunt Adelaide, devoid of any understanding of a child's psyche, would not countenance the idea, insisting instead that they needed company their own age. Richard Seymour Guinness, her full cousin, had recently moved to London to expand the Guinness Mahon banking business. He had taken up residence in St George's Square, and established himself at the Carlton Club in St Swithin's Lane where he carried on business without a clerk or even an account book. That was hardly surprising, since Richard and his brother Henry had been denied any real education, but he wrote to Henry in Dublin every day, keeping him informed of the tiniest details.

Richard Seymour had sired ten children, of whom several were now in their teens. So the Grattan and Rundell branches of the family met up once again, played tennis, went on boating expeditions and picnics together throughout a long, lazy summer.

Once the season came, Harry and Geraldine retired from the fray. Unlike their Rundell cousins, and the Prince and Princess of Wales, they continually declined invitations to the legendary balls at Edward and Dodo's. Their evangelical piety forbade dancing, and to Dodo's irritation, no amount of pleading could distract them from their principles. Such serious-mindedness in the young was a mystery to her. After all, she herself was devout. Church attendance was more than a formality. She took the sacrament as often as possible. One society journal described her as a curious mixture of 'the puritan and the plutocrat',[4] but she was certainly not puritan enough to forgo dancing. That was a tradition of the Free, not the established high church.

Her religious devotion was nonetheless reflected in her cautious, sensible dress and manner. Her bustle was restrained, her neckline modest, her dark hair drawn neatly back into a bun at the nape of her neck. There was 'a touch of quaintness in her sweet, but prim little face'.[5] When she spoke it was in a rich, low voice. Her quiet, dignified manner was impressive. She was kindly, but distant, appearing much bigger than she actually was, the 'grande dame' in a small, slight frame.

When it came to entertaining however, she showed no such restraint. An onyx-studded ballroom at St Stephen's Green and one in Carrera marble at Farmleigh cost approximately £30,000 each. They were lit by an array of massive wax candles and kept cool by huge blocks of ice placed on the window ledges. Live parrots completed the spectacle. At each individual occasion the decorations were invariably breathtaking. She liked to weave a world of fantasy around her guests. Sometimes she picked an oriental theme, at other times the surroundings were lavishly exotic. No expense was spared. Augustus Hare, a professional socialite who would one day shock polite Victorian society when he published his diary which contained startling revelations about the private lives of the rich and famous, noted on 18 June 1879: 'In the evening I was with the Prince at Mrs E. Guinness' ball on which £6,000 are said to have been wasted. It was a perfect fairy land, ice pillars up to the ceiling, an avenue of palms, a veil of stephanotis from the staircase, and you pushed your way through a brake of papyrus to the cloakroom.' In today's money Dodo's ball would have cost approximately £300,000. She evidently had something to prove. Perhaps such extravagance was the chance to make up for the privations of her childhood, for the years of being passed by. It was claimed that when she sent out invitations she was almost paranoid about leaving anyone out.

But every morning and evening the servants filed into the library in their distinctive uniforms, the parlourmaids in their high white frilly collars, the footmen in red velvet breeches and white stockings, silver buckles on their black polished shoes, and sat in rows while Edward Cecil led the family in prayers.

While they found their aunts Dodo and Olive rather austere,

frightening figures, the young Grattan Guinnesses became very fond of their kindly uncles. Although he had rejected her strait-laced nonconformism, Edward Cecil appeared to have imbibed some of his mother's warnings about wealth, and never allowed it to turn his head. Totally lacking in pomposity, he had a quiet charm which put the young cousins at ease. A broad, muscular frame made up for his lack of height, and he had a pleasant face with strong, even features. Reserved and discreet in public, entertaining and witty in private with his friends, it was hardly surprising his company appealed to the future king.

Harry, Geraldine and Lucy's favourite, however, was the gentlemanly Sir Arthur, who seemed to have a permanent twinkle in his eye, except when he was involved in a heated discussion of Irish politics with their father. The children had all grown up with a strong sense of their Irish identity, but it was Sir Arthur, with his determined, and often unreasoned opposition to Home Rule, who rekindled their interest in the politics of the country, and taught them to mistrust that instigator of all trouble, the leader of the Land League, Charles Stewart Parnell.

Since his retirement from the Brewery, Sir Arthur had devoted himself to a career in benevolent philanthropy. That was an entirely acceptable thing for a man in his position to do, but Sir Arthur was a little unusual in that he 'gave the impression of giving money away, not to please others but to please himself. In his choice of objects for his munificence he showed imagination and an unconventional sense of discrimination.'[6] That is not to say he did not choose carefully and sensibly with the long-term benefits to the people of Ireland in mind. After all, there were generations of family tradition to maintain. But he was creative in his approach, financing the rebuilding of Archbishop Marsh's Library in Dublin, and the Coombe Lying-In Hospital, chairing the first organisation in Dublin to house artisans, and serving for sixteen years as the President of the Royal Dublin Society. As a boy, he had always had access to a large private park, fenced off from the public and overlooked by his home in St Stephen's Green, now Edward and Dodo's lavish town house. Sir Arthur bought the twenty-two-acre site from local house-holders, had it landscaped with walks, flower beds and an ornamental lake, and presented it to the city. This particular gift, the lovely St Stephen's Green Park, earned him a great deal of gratitude in Dublin, countering the unpopularity of his diehard politics.

In 1880, after Sir Arthur lost his Commons seat, Disraeli made him the first Guinness peer of the realm as Baron Ardilaun of Ashford. Unlike many of his class he was an enlightened, caring landlord, continually developing imaginative plans to stimulate industry for the tenants on his country estate in County Galway. He was one of the first in Ireland to encourage tourism in Connemara by establishing a ferry service on Lough Corrib between his large baronial castle at Ashford, Cong and Galway City. That, combined with massive afforestation schemes began to pay off, bringing employment and prosperity to one of the poorest, yet most beautiful parts of the country.

Lord Ardilaun was determined to prove that a manifest and confirmed Unionist could still love and serve the Irish people. His very openness about his political convictions earned him grudging respect. After all, had he craved popularity he could have been a little bit more reticent about revealing his views. But, like his grandfather and namesake, the new Lord Arthur saw no reason to pander to public sympathy with political games. Integrity demanded he please nothing and no one but his own conscience. He remained to the end a man of many contradictions.

In society however, thanks to the commanding Lady Olive, the Ardilauns so established themselves as the arbiters of good taste, that when a family member committed a social gaffe others would proclaim in mock horror, 'What would the Ardilauns say?'[7] She intended to present Harry and Geraldine at court. Fanny insisted she ask the children whether that was what they wanted. They were old enough to decide. Enlightened compared to many Victorian parents, she and Henry did not believe in overburdening their children with prohibitions. Some, like alcohol and dancing, were inherent within their religious tradition. Too many could be counter-productive. 'There are parents who in their desire to keep their children right,' Henry preached, 'are perpetually forbidding this and that. The word most commonly in the lips of those who have to do with children is DON'T ... They are constantly repressing, forbidding, prohibiting. Now there is another, far better, more useful word – that is DO.'

Radical words for the era in which Henry lived – but there is a certain irony about them too. One of his closest friends, a member of Harley's council of reference, was the naturalist, Philip Henry Gosse. A fervent member of the Brethren, Gosse had married late. His wife then died, leaving him with a young son. He had no idea how to care for the child, and appears to have been the very epitome of Henry's tyrannical parent. Did Henry have Gosse in mind? He never used the pulpit to attack an enemy, let alone a friend. But he had certainly observed the kind of parenting which Philip Gosse's son, Edmund, exposed years later in his classic factual novel, *Father and Son.* Shocking Edwardian society, it described in heart-rending detail the suffocating repressiveness of a religious upbringing and subsequent breakdown of a precious relationship.

None of the Grattan children appear to have given Lady Olive's offer serious consideration. Harry had just won a coveted place at the London Hospital to study medicine. Geraldine felt painfully out of her depth in her cousins' company. She was rather supercilious about their wealthy lifestyle, as only a teenager can be, dismissing the social whirlwind as 'the unsatisfying round of amusements'. She had more serious pursuits on her mind. The death of Phoebe and Agnes had strengthened her determination to do something about the tragedy she witnessed every day in the East End. She had started teaching a small group of factory girls to read and write, and found it satisfying to be 'useful'. It was one thing to daydream of meeting the Queen, quite another to give oneself over to the brash, superficial world of her satellites.

Lady Olive and her sister-in-law, more used to sycophantic, poor relatives demanding money and introductions than to rejection, were amazed, but continued to hold out hopes for Lucy. Minnie had one satisfaction. In years to come she would tell the younger generations with a smile of pleasure, that she could have 'come out' – and been quite a society belle – had she wanted to.

2.

Harry and Howard Taylor began their medical training at the London Hospital together. It was *the* place to study medicine. Their professor, Sir Frederick Treves, was one of the foremost physicians of the time. His reputation would be established for posterity some years later when he gave sanctuary to the famous 'Elephant man', protecting him from exploitation and the lurid fascination of the British public. Harry and Howard felt privileged to sit at the great man's feet.

While Howard Taylor was quiet and retiring, Harry was always brimming over with energy and *joie de vivre*. A born leader, brilliant sportsman, tall, dynamic and handsome, with his father's magnetic dark eyes and a hearty, ringing laugh all of his own, he was the kind of young man who inspired immediate envy in his fellow males, outweighed almost as quickly by their overwhelming admiration. He seemed totally unaware of his dazzling charm, a source of some anxiety to his protective sisters.

On his first day a fellow student canvassed the fresher for the Debating Society, meeting that very evening.

'We like to get new men,' the student said, then added, 'you needn't be a bit afraid – there's nothing religious about it. In fact, one of our rules is that no one is allowed to allude to a religious thing.'

Harry was amused, and wondered how the student would have felt had he known his background. At a bit of a loose end, he decided to go along. Sir Frederick himself was in the chair. The subject for debate was some medical matter about which Harry as yet knew very little. He listened in silence, until, for no apparent reason, one of the speakers made an offensive remark about Jesus Christ. 'I wondered what ought to be done,' he wrote. 'I think, as far as I know, that my brain had not made up its mind, but my legs had automatically made up their mind, and I found myself standing on my feet.' He asked whether a first year was allowed to speak.

'Hear, hear,' they said, and he needed no further encouragement.

'Well, I may be out of order, but I was informed when I came up here by the gentleman who invited me that it is against the laws of your society to allude to religious matters. Is that so?' They agreed it was.

'If that be so, Mr President, then I beg to protest against the words of the gentleman who has just sat down. He has spoken against one who is my Lord, my Saviour and my King in a way that has made my blood boil.' Harry sat down waiting for the laughter and the jeers, but what he heard, after a moment's stunned silence, to his utter astonishment, was thunderous applause.

As he was leaving the hall he felt a hand on his shoulder, turned and there with a hand stretched towards him, was Sir

Frederick himself. He asked Harry his name, then said, 'Now look here, Guinness, I'm glad to know you. You come back to these meetings, and if ever a man does what that man did tonight, you do what you did.'

From that day on Treves became a personal friend, as well as a wise and brilliant tutor. And Harry's popularity grew. He founded the Hospital Athletic Club, but never forgot that all his achievements, sporting and intellectual, were worthless if he had no moral fibre, if he was not brave enough to 'run his flag up to the masthead'.

From his circuit training days in the garden at Harley for the rest of his life cycling would be one of his abiding passions. The high bicycle, then in fashion, was almost impossible to ride at any other than top speed. To travel slowly was an art. On 10 June, 1881, at the Crystal Palace, cheered on by a large crowd of supporters from Harley and the Hospital, Harry won the world record for slow bicycling.

In any free moments left over after medical studies and sporting activities, Harry helped out at Harley College. The East End population was growing steadily, spreading out from Bow to Limehouse, Stratford and Hackney. What few support agencies there were could not keep pace with the rapid expansion. There were no educational facilities other than the few ragged schools set up by charities, little health or social care, no entertainment other than the gin palaces. Harley College tried to fill the gap. Whatever the time of day, it was always a hive of activity, with night schools of one kind or another, lantern lectures in the winter, garden parties in the grounds in the summer for women, cabmen or policemen. Harry could play the cornet and the piano, sing, organise games and even manage a passable conjuring or ventriloquist act. He was in great demand. When he was not involved in cabaret he taught local men to read and write.

Howard Taylor went with him, ostensibly to help, in reality to catch a glimpse of Geraldine. He was a shy, fair-haired young man whose gentle manner made him a great favourite with Henry, Fanny and the family servants. When Minnie was out riding, as she often was, the maids would tell him where she had gone so that he could bump into her by accident on her way home. But Minnie was not interested. She was totally absorbed in running the night school.

Fanny had planned to open a night school from the moment she moved to Bow. She and Geraldine would watch the girls pouring out of Bryant and May at seven each night, and occasionally invite them in. In dark skirts and dark shawls, the plumage of their hats providing the only splash of colour in their wardrobe, they looked for all the world like birds let loose from a cage. Clearly exhausted, their minds were active, hungering for entertainment, anything to deaden the terrible monotony of work, which would start again at six the next morning. 'Their often wretched homes afford nothing,' Fanny wrote to her supporters.

> They cannot get a country walk or a stroll on the sea shore; they are shut up to crowded, noisy streets, all aglow with gin palaces, and thronged with young men who are only too glad to take them into these hell-traps, or into the penny gaffs and dancing-saloons, or even to the cheap theatres. Small wonder they are led astray or end up on the streets.

Like many social campaigners, Fanny understood the power of education to keep them away from the many traps set for naïve, penniless young women. At the time of writing to her supporters she had just bought a little chapel down the road from Harley College next door to Bryant and May, and urgently needed the funds to convert it into a schoolroom. Harley Hall was brightly painted, fitted with cupboards, desks and forms, and opened in December 1876. Tea was provided, bearing in mind the girls would be coming straight from work.

An invitation was distributed offering free membership of 'The Working Girls' Improvement Association', dedicated to helping them become sensible mothers and wives. There would be classes on Tuesdays and Thursdays in reading, writing, dress-making, book-keeping and music. If they behaved nicely, were quiet, gentle and polite, they might talk and ask questions, for 'we quite understand that what you want, after a hard day's work, is a pleasant evening, "a good time" (as the girls in America say), and that is what we will try to give you'.

From the very first evening Harley Hall was packed to capacity. Two evenings a week were clearly insufficient, and once Geraldine joined Mrs Cole, the teacher, classes were extended to every night. In 1880 the night school moved into larger premises at the brand new Berger Hall, called after William Berger, who was as generous to Henry and Fanny as he was to Hudson Taylor and the China Inland Mission.

Teaching factory girls expanded Geraldine's horizons. She thought she knew all there was to know about how the people lived, but discovered there was so much more to learn. Fourteen-year-old Matilda was one of her special success stories. Matilda spent one evening at the Berger Hall trying to shield a black eye from Geraldine's hawkish attention. To no avail.

'I knocked it,' she said, without looking up, when Geraldine asked her how she had acquired it.

'It's a lie, Miss Guinness,' her neighbour shouted. 'Her father give 'er it.' Geraldine asked Matilda to sit out of the class for a while, and tell her more about her home life. The story visibly appalled her. Unused to such a sympathetic audience, Matilda started to push the boundaries a little. She turned up at Geraldine's Sunday Bible class, and proceeded to disrupt it completely, winking at her friends and making faces behind Geraldine's back.

'Close your Bible, Matilda,' Geraldine snapped. As she did

so, Matilda decided to make a quick getaway at the end of the class. She had heard how naughty girls were invited to take a walk around the garden at Harley House, where Geraldine would pick them a button-hole and attempt to 'civilise' them a little. She slipped downstairs, and was amazed to find her teacher waiting for her in the street.

Matilda found herself taking the inevitable turn around the garden, being invited to explain why she was being so difficult.

'Well, Miss, you know I can't read.'

'I am sorry, Matilda, I hadn't thought of that.' Geraldine leant forward and kissed Matilda apologetically on the cheek. The young woman shrunk away in horror. When Geraldine asked her why, she said, 'Because I thought you were going to hit me or something.' No one had ever kissed her before.

The incident left a deep impression on both women, and some days later Geraldine asked Matilda whether she would like to go into service in the country.

'No one would have me,' the young woman said. Geraldine insisted she go home and ask her mother's permission. Matilda laughed. She knew what her mother would say.

'She said I could go to hell for all she cared,' Matilda reported a few days later.

'Well that's exactly where you're not going,' Geraldine replied. So Matilda and two of her friends were sent to Guinness acquaintances who had a lovely home in the country. She never forgot the kindness of her first real friend, and years later, would more than repay her benefactress's kindness.

To free her mother who was increasingly absorbed in promoting missionary work in the Congo, Geraldine also took over the domestic reins at Harley College, acting as hostess to a number of important, influential guests. The society she spurned had come to her – Lord Shaftesbury of course, and his friends, Lord and Lady Radstock, Lord Poleworth, a member of the Congo Mission Committee, who always stayed a few days when he came to London from his stately home on the Tweed, Lady Louisa Ashburton, and Dr Karl Baedeker, the celebrated travel writer whose name had become synonymous with his European travel guide. No discerning traveller saw Europe without their 'Baedeker'.

When Charles Spurgeon brought the students of his Pastors' College to Harley for an athletics competition, Harry was in his element. So was Lucy, who had developed a sudden interest in male theological students – for their biceps rather than their brains. In December 1880 Spurgeon's College returned the invitation in the form of a pre-Christmas dinner, stipulating that Fanny should be the only female member of the Harley party. Spurgeon did not believe in exposing his students to the temptations of the opposite sex. Undaunted even by the most famous preacher in England, Fanny, to Lucy's great glee, ignored him and took along five female companions, including her two daughters. Never in her life, declared Lucy, has she heard such a deafening noise as the sound of all those young men eating and talking.

There was little privacy at Harley, but then privacy was a right denied most of the East End population. The children were happy simply to be together, however extended their family with students, foreign visitors, and foster children, especially at Christmas.

Christmas meant a family shopping expedition to Whiteley's Universal Emporium, the first department store in London. They emerged laden with presents, all beautifully wrapped and tied up with ribbon. Lucy described Christmas Day 1880 in her diary. 'After tea, Papa brought down some of his experiments, microscopes and electric machines, besides lots of others. It was great fun watching some of the students trying to get a sixpence out of the water. Of course, none of them could.' Harry then did a few conjuring tricks, Lucy organised charades, and Henry Grattan read from Byron, Cowper and Milton. The only cloud to darken an almost perfect day was 'darling Mother in bed all day with a very bad headache, brought on by riding in an omnibus'.

3.

> I think this diary must be a very stupid one . . . I wonder how most people write their diaries, not like mine, I am sure. Gracie's is the only one I ever saw, and that was all prayers and pieces of sermons and holy thoughts. Mine is not like that at all, because I am very afraid of anyone seeing it. Harry for instance! How terribly fearful that would be.

Lucy's diaries, which she began to write in 1880 when she was fifteen, are a delightful record of the emotional development of a young girl from adolescence to mature adulthood. Her writing is expressive and imaginative, her observations a fascinating commentary on the age in which she lived. And yet they are curiously contemporary. She was after all a teenager like any other in any age, analytical, intolerant, self-righteous and self-indulgent. There is no false piety. Her 'dy', as she called it, was her friend. To be less than honest would betray a friendship.

The first diary was written during her time at boarding school in Hastings, where, to her intense irritation, no one has any interest in the troubled situation in Ireland. 'Miss Byam did not even know what Boycotting meant.' That was strange since for weeks the newspapers had been full of little else.

In September 1880, to help protect tenant farmers from eviction and destitution at time of worsening economic conditions, Parnell had urged that any man taking on another's farm should be shunned in the streets and in the shops, in the market-place and at the fair, even at the place of worship. To all intents and purposes, he was to be a leper.

The first victim was not an Irish farmer, but an English land agent called Captain Boycott. The policy proved highly effective. He was ostracised completely. His labourers refused to harvest the crops, his blacksmith would not shoe his horse, his laundress wash his clothes, the shopkeepers serve him. His servants left, his mail was not delivered and wherever he went he was booed and jeered. By the time the *London Daily News* rose to his defence Boycott had been forced out of Ireland. And the Irish had discovered a deadly weapon they began to use freely on their landlords in an attempt to introduce much needed reforms.

Lucy was anxious about her uncle. On 30 January 1881, she wrote in her diary 'I wonder really what has happened there since I left and how Sir Arthur has been, and if his tenants have risen against him as they were expected to do; and if Parnell is imprisoned or punished in any way for rousing the people as he has, but no one can tell me.' Papa was coming soon, she noted, on his way to take some meetings. He would tell her because he knew everything there was to know about Ireland.

Lord Ardilaun's tenants did not arrange a boycott. Indeed, it would have been very strange if they had, given the advantages they enjoyed. Parnell was imprisoned for a time. No charges were brought and he was released to take his seat in the House of Commons.

A homesick Lucy went on hating school. Its only redeeming feature was a chance to improve her musical skills, and shine before staff, pupils and parents at the end of term concert. She knew she was the best in the school and was thrilled when she was invited to play two pieces instead of one, replacing a duet by her cousins, Dora and Edith Fookes, which simply was not good enough to inflict upon the public. The applause rang in her ears for days – until she discovered she had been awarded the drawing prize, which she did not deserve, instead of the music prize, which she did. Julia, 'who plays like a machine', had won it. Life wasn't fair.

Her concentration was disrupted the following term by the news that her old friend Florrie Charlesworth was engaged to be married to her father's curate, and Lucy could return home for the wedding. Mama thought Florrie too young, but Lucy noted, 'She is only a little older than Minnie, and I should laugh if Minnie were engaged.' Ten years later, in a red pen, she added in the margin, 'Minnie is engaged nowadays, and I don't laugh, but cry.'

The wedding was a great occasion. The streets of Limehouse were filled with cheering crowds waiting to catch a glimpse of the vicar's daughter. Lucy wrote that Florrie looked beautiful, then could not resist adding, 'The only thing that spoiled her was that she was laced most dreadfully tightly, which made her look like a doll. She is short and the tight-lacing did not at all become her figure which was never slight.'

The wedding breakfast was an even greater disappointment. She had been placed next to the boring Sidney Beddome. His sister had Harry for company. Judging by their laughter, Lucy was in no doubt about who had the better deal. Any potential suitor must at least possess the charms of her adored elder brother. That was an unattainable proposition.

Fanny and Henry took the opportunity of Lucy's visit home to launch their first Congo steamer. It was one of the earliest and most ingenious examples of flat-pack, self-assembly goods. The idea was that it would be carried in pieces by Adam M'Call's expedition up 230 miles of treacherous cataracts in the Lower Congo to Stanley Pool. At Stanley Pool the steamer would be re-assembled, taking the missionaries along a thousand-mile stretch of navigable river into the heart of Africa. The only problem was that so far, no one, not even the explorer Craven who had been struggling in appalling conditions in the Lower Congo, had managed to reach Stanley Pool. But the Harley students and Congo Mission supporters gathered at Forrest's ship-building yard on 8 March 1881 did not allow such trifling considerations to dampen their enthusiasm.

There had been pressure at Harley to name the steamer the *Fanny Guinness*, in acknowledgment of her sterling work, but Henry felt the *Livingstone* was more appropriate. Minnie and Lucy, who had been chosen to perform the launching ceremony, stood on a wooden jetty and shouted, 'God speed the *Livingstone*'. Cheers rent the air but the boat refused to move. 'This part of the performance', Lucy commented drily, 'was rather ignominious because the tide was too low for her to slide off gracefully in the correct manner and it took rather a long time to shove her into the water.'

A further cheer went up as Fanny climbed on board. She was terrified, and would have climbed straight off when the sails were hoisted if Henry had let her. 'There was really nothing to be frightened at,' Lucy observed, 'because there was not wind enough to make her go along, nor would there have been room amongst the torpedoes, barges, boats, steam-launches and cutters in process of construction that filled the cutting where we were.'

Henry however felt it incumbent upon him to try the steamer out. How could he provide student training without being certain of its effectiveness? And, after all, he had been land locked since his youth. Manoeuvring many a hazard on the River Lea, dangerous locks, low bridges and a profusion of vessels, he said to his children with satisfaction, 'If they can steer on this crowded narrow river, they can steer on the Congo.'

The call to Africa was suddenly and cruelly stripped of its romance when news reached England of the death of Mary Richards, the first woman missionary to the Congo. Mary had been one of the family at Harley House. She had recently married one of the Harley students and they had only been gone a few weeks. Her husband buried her and sent a drawing home of her grave. Lucy copied it into her diary. She was devastated by the young woman's death. It brought home to her the inescapable reality of missionary life in Africa. Beside the picture she wrote simply, 'How could M'Call?'

Meanwhile, her own overseas adventure loomed large. Lady Olive, with some encouragement from Lucy, had managed to persuade Fanny to send her younger daughter to a proper finishing school in Paris where she could acquire a good command of a foreign language and develop her music skills. Emerging from a dreadful winter of family ailments, Fanny could see the wisdom of it. Geraldine had a septic finger which needed lancing. Whitfield was constantly under the weather, and the doctor threatened to remove his tonsils, a barbaric piece of surgery, occasionally fatal, performed on the kitchen table. Fortunately, he was granted a reprieve at the last moment. Lucy herself suffered dreadfully from adolescence. She still hated Hastings and often felt too lethargic to study. On 28 March Fanny had written to her at Hastings,

> My darling child, You will I am sure have remembered today the sorrowful events of this day two years ago. Hour by hour as it has passed they have been present to me! It is now 5pm – just the time I crept up to the schoolroom for my last sad watch by our precious little Agnes' couch . . . You are spared to me my darling child. God preserve and bless you and spare you if he so pleases.

Time abroad might provide exactly the stimulation Lucy needed.

Lucy in fact was keen to find her own. Before she left for Paris a gentleman called Murray was given permission to escort her to the Saturday evening concert at the Bow and Bromley. 'It was nice indeed!' she commented in her diary. 'I like concerts.' The red pen addendum made ten years later said, 'And nice boys! I meant to write that in, I remember, but never had the pluck till now.' She promised to write to him and hoped Papa wouldn't think her 'inadvertent'.

At the end of December 1881 Henry Grattan Guinness deposited his youngest daughter at The Miss Ellerbys' Finishing School for Young Ladies on the elegant Boulevard Malesherbes. The two Miss Ellerbys must have thought there was much finishing to do, as Lucy had been violently sea sick all the way across the Channel, and by the time she reached Boulogne could hardly speak or walk. Henry the sailor insisted it had been a quiet crossing. 'How could he!' she wrote scornfully.

Lucy loved Paris from the first – the taste, the chic, the charm of the pretty shops. But the school was disappointingly dreary. Tucked away on the top two floors of a six-storey building, its elegant façade hid a penny-pinching, rigid, regimented routine which lacked imagination and real creativity. Christmas Day was a miserable affair. Laughter was strictly rationed, so she hid Minnie's letter until she had the chance to read it in private. Even that was difficult. The candle allowance was restricted to one every five days. She became a hoarder of stumps, hiding them in corners of her neighbours' washing-stand drawers so that at night she could at least read her letters and write her diary. On 1 January 1882, when the other girls were all asleep, she wrote by the light of a last spluttering piece of wax:

How strange it seems to put 1882 as a date for the first time in my diary ... How very funny it would be to put 1900 and something on one's letters! I wonder very much whether the world will last so long – I shouldn't think so – let me see how old I should be then – about 48! I can't imagine myself 48! What should I ever be like? Frightfully ugly and fat – I should think, with a nose something like Miss Ellaby's only worse, a great deal worse, I daresay, so there.

Lucy's mathematics were somewhat defective. She did live to see the new century, but not her forty-ninth year. And she was never ugly. At fourteen however, she did not feel attractive. She felt her hair was too straggly, her face too large, her eyes a nondescript grey, her mouth pale and ugly, her teeth frightful, her nose worse. 'She is, I believe, rather selfish, though this quality generally arises more from thoughtlessness, dreamy ways than anything else.'

The months in Paris represented that strange adolescent no-man's-land between childhood and maturity, when the former slips sadly out of our grasp while the latter is still a frightening substitute. Her 'bodily troubles' caused her a great deal of embarrassment. Womanhood both beckoned and repelled her. Florrie had just had a baby. 'A BABY! Florrie, who used to do lessons with Minnie and me only yesterday as it seems. How dreadfully old I must be getting. How happy Florrie must be to have a baby all of her own! But how CAN people do such things! I can't understand.' When yet another of her friends became engaged Lucy noted tartly, 'It seems that people are getting very unprincipled.' Fortunately for her own piece of mind, she was not aware that her own sister was on the verge of becoming 'unprincipled'.

Though Howard Taylor was always at Harley, happy to exist in Minnie's shadow, he noted with increasing dismay how positively she responded to a new young suitor, a doctor with a brilliant medical career ahead of him. Minnie was too serious, too busy a young woman to allow her heart to dominate her head, but there was no doubt the attention had brought a bloom to her cheeks.

Fanny watched with interest. She knew there had been a proposal, long awaiting a response. It was hardly fair of Minnie to keep the doctor hanging on while she sorted out the problems of the East End. The truth was Minnie knew the young man was not for her but could not bring herself to say so. Their aspirations were different. Professional success seemed his only goal. But breaking off the relationship was too terrible to contemplate. Wisely, Fanny sent Geraldine to Paris that summer to bring her sister home.

Lucy was excited, but apprehensive. Minnie always made her feel giddy and immature. Her sister was so unlike other girls her age, so much nicer. And her fears were well founded. From the moment Lucy ran out into the Boulevard Malesherbes to meet her sister, looking very chic in a new emerald, Parisian dress, Geraldine feared school had done her no good at all. She seemed superficial and her conversation with her friends confirmed Minnie's worst suspicions. She chided her sister for her cattiness, and Lucy felt duly chastened.

It was not that Geraldine was unduly sanctimonious. All her life she had an extraordinary capacity to see the qualities, or at least the potential, in other human beings, while remaining oblivious of their faults. Back-biting was beyond her powers of comprehension. But she was never sour and did not scold for long. In fact, in Paris she was jollier than Lucy had ever seen her, 'coiffing herself with a little bow of bright red ribbon in the middle of her arrangement behind, and singing, "Suppose, and suppose that your highland", etc . . .' in such a loud voice that Lucy could not concentrate on finishing her work.

Two of Lucy's closest school friends were the Dreyfus sisters. They lived in a flat on the ground floor of the house on the Boulevard Malesherbes with their brother, a colonel in the French Army. Lucy and Geraldine passed him on several occasions on their way up the stairs and developed a little more than just a nodding acquaintance. A decade later, when 'the Dreyfus affair' was emblazoned on the front of every French and English newspaper, Geraldine would remember a quiet, gracious man and marvel at the curious irony that she and Lucy, daughters of a leading Zionist thinker, had known the French army officer court-martialled for treason on no grounds other than that he was a Jew. With the support of the writer, Emile Zola, Dreyfus's was the cause célèbre which highlighted nineteenth-century antisemitism, and justified the Zionist cause.

4.

No summer was complete for Henry Grattan and his family without a month's house party at Cliff. Lord Ardilaun and Edward Cecil had their own country estates where they entertained royalty, Henry Grattan shared his with a motley collection of friends and ever-increasing family. There were adopted children like Fanny's teenage nieces, Edith and Dora Fookes, who had lost their own mother, and foster children like Ada, orphaned at birth and threatened with the workhouse.

Geraldine had the responsibility of supervising an advance party which transformed the college into a comfortable holiday home. It was a mammoth task. The main classroom was converted into a comfortable drawing-room. Desks were removed to make way for the summer furniture, kept in store from year to year. The piano was transported from the other end of the house, and vast arrangements of fresh flowers brought in from the garden.

The bedding and catering arrangements were particularly complex as visitors came and went. In the summer of 1882 all forty bedrooms were in use. One evening, Lucy counted fifty-three people sitting down to dinner. She did not mind the quantity, 'if they are select (which unhappily they are not always!)'.

Henry would have brought the entire world to Cliff, if he could. He never ceased to marvel that such a wonderful place could be his, and was too generous to keep it all to himself. Everyone who joined the Guinnesses found it an escape, a rare experience of the peace and purity of rural life. It was Lucy's favourite spot on earth.

Is there a pleasanter, sweeter spot in all England than Hulme Cliff? Behind it rises to a height of 800 feet a heathery upland moor. Before it winds a narrow, verdant valley. Up the moors the hills rise to perpendicular sandstone (they are gritstone) cliffs, with miles of moorland stretching from their summits. North, south, and east, down in the valley rushes the glittering Derwent, filling the air with the sound of ever-falling waters. Hill rises beyond hill all round and clefts open to narrow valleys and rocky gullies, with lovely, undulating country here and there. Close around are clustering trees, and beyond them cultivated fields and waving woods, but we see no roads, no dusty highways, and hear no sound of traffic. The woods are green with summer foliage, the far-off hills grey with mist and distance; the air is fresh and cool, for there seems always a breeze stirring here, and the voice of the waters, breeze and birds mingle from morn to night. As I write the latter are singing as though there were no sin and sorrow in the world. No other sound reaches me except these tranquillising voices.

We call this OUR GALILEE – our refuge from close, crowded, noisy, dusty, ill-savoured, enormous London.

Unlike his cousins at Ashford and Farmleigh, Henry Grattan may not have offered a decent shoot, but his house-parties were every bit as companionable. There were tennis and chess competitions, picnic expeditions to Haddon Hall in Castleton with its famous caves, boating parties on the Derwent, and hikes up Eagle Rock, led by Henry himself, hammer in hand, in search of interesting fossils. Few of the young could keep up with him.

The evenings were filled with music. Most years they could

muster a full orchestra. In 1882 there were eight violins. If there was not a concert, or organised games, there might be a lecture from Fanny on Central Africa, or from Henry on prophecy and Zionism. The older members of the party would groan if he happened to choose astronomy as his subject, for he would march the young people out to the observatory to spend half a night with the telescope. Harry, who often disrupted the proceedings with ghost stories so terrifying no one would go to bed, later claimed he grew up knowing more about the mountains on the moon than the geography of his native land.

As the holiday that year drew to a close Lucy was at a loose end. She wasn't sure what she wanted to do with her life. 'I don't want to be a young lady – I mean grown-up and charming and dangerous – like Minnie. Not that there is any need for me to be afraid of being charming – unhappily!' She did herself a great injustice. Over the years many men would find the large grey eyes in the pale oval face irresistible.

That very autumn in Bray, County Wicklow, where she spent several months, the son of the house took quite a shine to her. But the relationship was not a great success. Lucy had very high standards – intellectually and theologically – for any potential suitor. What's more, she seemed to expect equality in both between the sexes, no doubt a reflection of her parents' relationship, but hardly realistic at that time.

Oh, surely, men with great minds, powers of thought, and who are gifted with education and leisure – might, in these last days . . . find some better means of employment of their time than in speculating whether or no we are descended from monkeys, tadpoles and minute specs of protoplasm . . . I wish now that I had said so, who am not, being a girl, supposed – at Bray at least – to think on such matters.

Back at Harley in the spring she found her mother confined to bed with one of her dreadful headaches, 'brought on by certain anxieties and troubles with the students – creatures that they were!' Evidently, all was not sweetness and light. Lucy felt as if she was seeing her home for the first time. How could she have lived in the East End for so long and not noticed how dreadful it was, 'the degradation; dirt; defilement; noise; glare; atmosphere; people; houses; sights and sounds; all, everything combined to horrify and amaze me'.

Henry and Fanny had never sought to hide the desperate effects of poverty from their children, but the sheer misery of it all had never reached Lucy's inner sanctuary. That night, as she returned home from several months in the country, her eyes were opened, and all she wanted to do was escape.

Henry and Fanny let her go, alone, to Cliff. She seemed so sick at heart that Henry had given her a glass of port on the train at St Pancras before she set off. His teetotalism was evidently weakening a little. Or perhaps it was waived when health considerations made it necessary.

At Cliff calm entered her soul again. She revelled in the short, icy winter days, pinching frosty walks, bare countryside, the snow and snowballing, afternoon teas by firelight, the long winter evenings and howling windy nights. Spring melted the ice and the frosts and slowly gave way to a blistering hot summer.

Lucy counted over sixty visitors that summer, among them a commanding, regal-looking widow called Mrs Henry Reed. The Reeds were a wealthy Christian family, pioneers and founding fathers of Tasmania. Mrs Reed suggested to Fanny that Lucy and Whitfield accompany her home. Fanny was very much against the idea at first. She had her children's education to consider. But Mrs Reed was adamant and dismissed all her arguments. Lucy would go to school with her daughter Mary, Whitfield with her son Henry. The experience would broaden their minds, the climate do wonders for their constitutions. Lucy needed taking out of herself.

A woman used to getting her own way, Mrs Reed knew how to put her finger on Fanny's raw nerve. Reluctantly, she handed over her children. All was settled so quickly and in such a flurry of excitement, shopping and packing, she had no time to consider what a wrench it would be to part from her youngest son. And on Saturday 8 September they set sail.

Chapter 8

1882–1886

Adventures at Home and Abroad

1.

The 1880s were serene, satisfying years for Ireland's upper crust, and the Edward Guinnesses were the undisputed leaders of the social jet set. The glamour and intensity of their social life often belied the amount of hard work Edward put into the Brewery. He was determined to expand its influence, to make it one of the most respected and profitable companies in the world. He had also set his heart on a peerage, to be achieved, not by the usual route of philanthropy, which had served his brother well, but in recognition of his contribution to business, which he believed was equally beneficial to the community by raising industrial standards and increasing prosperity. He intended to take the social stigma out of trade and establish a tradition acknowledging the value of enlightened capitalism.

Many of his political machinations in the early 1880s appear to have been concentrated on that particular goal. In 1882 he waived the chance of a political seat, but subscribed £1,500 to campaign expenses instead, expecting due Tory gratitude. It never came, and in 1885, when urged to stand for the City of Dublin, he resisted at first, claiming undue pressure at work.

'To sit would be most distasteful to me in every way; the unpleasantness of it would be very great, for I was always to be found by anyone at St James' Gate.'[1] He finally acquiesced, but did not win the seat, nor did he stand again at a bye-election. It seemed a waste of time as far as the coveted peerage was concerned. In the end he asked the Prime Minister outright, and Gladstone granted him a baronetcy, 'in recognition not only of your high position in Ireland, but especially of the marked services rendered by you on the important occasion of the visit recently paid to that country by the Prince and Princess of Wales'.[2]

Taking charge of the delicate negotiations surrounding the visit of the future Edward VII, ensuring not only the protection, but the warm welcome of the future King and Queen of England was no mean achievement. Anti-British feelings were running high. Three years earlier two high-ranking government officials had been killed by terrorists in Phoenix Park. In the recent General Election, Charles Parnell's Irish Party had taken eighty-five seats. The Catholic Party in Ireland could scent Home Rule. Many in the Chamber of Commerce thought this was not the best time for a royal visit. Nor should they be seen to give the Prince too enthusiastic a welcome. But Edward Cecil, as High Sheriff of Dublin and the most respected member of the Council, used all his powers of persuasion to rally the city dignitaries to a fairly convincing performance.

When Edward Cecil's own great moment finally arrived and he stepped forward to receive his honour from the Queen, he realised, to his acute consternation and embarrassment, that he had not been informed of the proper etiquette. He had not waited for Prime Minister Gladstone to present him. The gaffe somewhat took the edge off his pleasure.

Their parents' social whirl meant constant upheaval for the three children. Rupert's earliest memories were of endless journeys from house to house accompanied by a retinue of nannies and governesses. Winston Churchill's grandfather was Viceroy of Ireland for a time and since Rupert and Winston were the same age, they shared a governess. The two future leaders had an uneasy relationship. On one occasion they were given a toy harness and coachman's whip and told to go and play together. 'You be the horse,' Winston commanded Rupert. The idea did not appeal to Rupert at all. Winston, who had the whip in his hand, lashed him across the face, catching his eye. A leading Dublin eye specialist was called in. He applied ice and a caustic solution which burned off Rupert's eyelashes and brows and left him with permanent scarring.

Years later when the two men, both in their eighties, met again at a rehearsal for the new Knights of the Garter at St James's Palace, Winston turned to the second Earl of Iveagh and said, 'I say, Rupert, do you remember that fight we had in Dublin?'[3]

Rupert was a shy, retiring boy. His apparent lack of academic ability was a source of bitter disappointment to his parents. Neither of the prep schools he attended, depending on whether his family was in London or Ireland, nor the tutors brought in to provide extra coaching, were able to help him grasp the rudiments of reading or writing. At first his parents thought he was educationally subnormal. Then they wondered whether he had eye trouble and took him from one eye specialist to another, none of whom could find a problem. Dyslexia was not a recognised condition.

Had they stopped to consider it, Edward and Dodo would have known their eldest son was not unintelligent. When Rupert was seven Edward Cecil acquired a microscope to study the effects of the yeast culture on brewing, as yet unknown. Rupert was fascinated and begged his father for a microscope of his own. It became his favourite toy in the nursery and the beginning of a lifelong fascination for the sciences, compensating for the fact that his parents showed more attention to Ernest because he was obviously clever, and to Walter, the cherub and their favourite.

The children admired, rather than loved their parents – from a distance. Rupert's letters home from Eton contain no reference to his feelings. They were to do with rowing, whether he could run faster than Ernest, and what subjects he preferred. In one, heart-rending letter, the nearest he ever comes to expressing any real emotion to his parents, he pleads with his father to let him drop German so that he can pursue scientific study in greater depth. Edward evidently neither understood nor particularly rated his son's passion and said no. Growing up was a hard and painful process for Rupert Guinness, with many knocks and setbacks. But a combination of public school stoicism and genetic determination refused to let him admit defeat, and in the end, adversity revealed the true metal in the man.

2.

Like most adolescents Lucy only fully appreciated the positive points of her upbringing when deprived of the security it had provided. She had never been exposed to anything vaguely resembling shipboard life before and the P. & O. line's HMS *Ballarat* seemed a veritable den of iniquity where, the passengers abandoned themselves unreservedly to the worldly pleasures of smoking, drinking, dancing, playing cards, flirting, gossiping and falling out.

Whitfield had a companion, the Reeds' youngest child, Henry, and like any teenage boys they fished and played, oblivious of the complex, tangled social interactions taking place around them. Lucy felt very much alone, left to survive or succumb to a frightening, hostile environment.

Mrs Reed, so charming at Cliff, turned out to be an autocrat, never explaining her motives for a command. Used to Fanny's sensible reasoning, Lucy was not surprised that the two younger Reed daughters, Maggie and Mary, were almost out of control, flirting with every officer in sight. Mrs Reed's constant haranguing drove them to it, and they had daily 'rowings-up' with her.

Her late husband, dead three years, had acquired wealth in the same measure as the second Arthur Guinness, thanks to a similar shrewd business sense. Henry Reed was also extremely devout, a preacher and philanthropist, ruthlessly honest and totally inflexible. Despite a stormy and difficult relationship with William Booth, he was one of the foremost supporters of the newly formed Salvation Army.

He had married Margaret Frith when he was 57 and she 35. The daughter of a well-to-do Anglo-Irish family, he had found her aristocratic elegance and evangelical piety an irresistible combination. One of her ancestors, John Frith, had been betrayed by Sir Thomas More for distributing Tyndale's Bible and duly burnt at the stake at Smithfield in 1533. This was a pedigree to be proud of.

Despite their maturity in years the Reeds produced three daughters and a son, raising them alternately in Tasmania and at Dunorlan in Tunbridge Wells, their English holiday home. They counted the Guinnesses as their closest friends. The two families had many interests in common and their children were of a similar age. In 1880 when Henry Reed died, Margaret Reed decided to make an extremely generous donation to the Livingstone Inland Mission, a second steamer for the Upper Congo, which would be called the *Henry Reed* in his memory.

In 1883 her eldest daughter, Annie, volunteered for missionary service, joining the Booths' daughter, Katie, who was trying to establish the Salvation Army in Paris. 'La Maréchale' lived up to her nickname and was a genius at handling crowds of lewd, drunken men. Annie was not. News of the innuendos and cat-calls she attracted reached her mother at Dunorlan who set off for Paris and brought her back to England forthwith. It was Fanny, thoughtful and practical as ever, who wondered whether a summer at Cliff might not be a way of defusing family tensions.

The Reeds were seasoned travellers, blasé about the journey home. Lucy was homesick at first, but soothed at last by the long, lazy tropical days in the sun, and warm evenings watching the moonlight sparkle on the sea. Occasionally, she gave a virtuoso piano performance, accompanied by Whitfield on the violin.

There were stops at interesting sights. The first, a trip to a Capuchin monastery on Malta, had a disastrous effect on the susceptible teenager and left her with nightmares for a week. As the party descended into the freezing cellars they became aware that propped up in niches gouged into the stone walls were the skeletons of dead monks. Some were still covered in bits of rotting flesh, their tongues hanging out, their eyes glaring in the torchlight. It was a terrifying experience, especially for someone who had experienced a painful bereavement. For days Lucy wrestled with the concept of eternity and the immortality of the human spirit, but no matter how hard she tried, every positive thought was swallowed up in visions of death and decay. It fired her Irish Protestant resentment of Roman Catholicism. 'What a pretence – what a system of man's invention!' she fumed.

Lucy was just as intolerant of the boring weekly Anglican service in the Captain's cabin, with its 'weary, meaningless hymns and prayers'. Worse still was to be forced by Mrs Reed to sit in the stern singing stirring hymns, 'in opposition' to the dancing in the lounge. Her reason accepted the command, but her feet and heart rebelled.

Is there anything wrong with dancing? Any harm? I see none. The thing itself is delightful, motion in rhythm and time and swing with music. I like it very much – with girls, like we used to do it at school, but here it is quite different, and though my feet keep time and long to go, I would hate to dance as they dance here – with these men – it is not good.

Men were a complete mystery to her – especially men without the gentlemanly Christian values of her elder brother and his friends. She set out to reform the men on board, encouraging them not to smoke, and was deeply disillusioned when they betrayed their promises. Maggie and Mary told her she was far too prim ever to marry, and went on having daily arguments with their mother over the ship's fifth officer – little Mr Arnold.

'I am just glad I am not unexperienced like they are!' declared a superior Lucy, whose pride would take a proverbial fall before the journey was over. When Mr Arnold removed himself from the girls' influence by announcing his engagement to one of the other passengers, 'short, pale, thin, ugly, badly-dressed, gawky, ungraceful, chattering, flirting, unaccomplished, unladylike, apparently uneducated . . .', she was amazed. 'I suppose there must be something in her which I have not found out as yet . . . Men are geese!'

A potentially disastrous fire in the engine room meant that the ship was detained for repairs in the Suez. At first the passengers were entranced by the sights, the small Egyptian cargo boats in parakeet colours, laden with their mysterious Eastern booty, beads, corals, muslins and shawls, passing to and from the port, but the novelty quickly wore off as the sun's rays bore down and boredom set in. The heat was so intense it was almost unbearable. People lay on the deck 'melting', being served endless amounts of ices, iced water, iced fruits and jellies by the overworked crew. Tensions rose as never before. 'Why must people wear clothes?' Lucy lamented. 'Mrs Reed and Annie dispense with the most necessary articles of clothing but I don't like doing this – it feels so shameful.'

More shameful still was to stand before the entire ship's company accused of stealing someone else's young man. What did she want with Haythorne anyway, Lucy said scornfully. She was no flirt. Her Mama had taught her how to behave. But Lucy would not have been human, had her female vanity not been susceptible to masculine admiration. The barriers she had so carefully constructed around herself began to crack. She felt the first flutters of romance. Now, like any other young girl, she longed to dress up in beautiful clothes, to dance, to shine – with one young man in mind. She was furious when Mrs Reed refused to allow them to go to the fancy-dress ball. Instead she sulked in the stern with Mary and Maggie watching Bo-peep, a fishwife, an exotic Turkish lady, an eighteenth-century belle, and a variety of other characters in exquisite costumes having a wonderful time.

> *October 19th.* They had their fancy dress ball last night, and I should expect they enjoyed it very much. It must have been amusing I should think – and well, why wrong? Am I very bad to question? I wish Papa and Mama were here to ask about these things. I want to understand and I can't.
>
> What I saw last night was not so bad, but on the contrary very charming, and I do so believe, in my heart, if I could have an easy conscience, I would love to have gone. There!

Mary Reed made up her mind that night to tear off that tiresome symbol of abstinence, her blue ribbons, at the first opportunity. She was going to parties, balls and the theatre as soon as she was old enough. But she was not going to tell her mother just yet for fear of another row.

Within the microcosm of time and space Lucy's love affair,

innocent by today's standards, was intense. Whether out of embarrassment or guilt, she kept it a secret from the Reed family, and had no one to turn to for advice. In the end, despite her new determination to be less rigid, she realised with a heavy heart that she would never have very much in common with a man who did not share her faith. H. had no intention of doing anything useful with his life. She cut off their relationship as the ship docked in Melbourne, and it almost broke her heart. 'You are on board – and so am I – and yet I cannot see you – cannot speak to you nor tell you what I want – nor say goodbye this last time – and forever! Have I done right? Yes, yes I know I have – but it is hard – oh, it is very hard.'

The family transferred to *The Flinders* for the last part of the journey to Tasmania. The sea was rough and she was so busy fighting her usual battle with seasickness she had little surplus energy for self-pity. Her letter home to Minnie was cheerful, describing with some amusement how passengers were divested of their dignity every time the boat lurched. 'An old gentleman will skim gracefully along on his back, or a lady will make a bow and then lie extended on the deck.' She made no mention of her real feelings, the unbearable pain which would haunt her throughout her stay in Australia.

Nov 1st, 1883. Seven weeks ago today – Thursday – we left England. Am I the same girl now as then?

If I wrote that letter – but I shall not – I might tell you one thing – you have opened my eyes – for better or worse? You would say for better I know – is it for better? Perhaps so. One cannot live in this world and do it good without understanding some of its evil – but oh – I would like to be as trustful and pure and innocent as I was before I came on shipboard.

Farewell to her first love had been a farewell to childhood.

3.

Mount Pleasant, the Reed family home, stood in a perfect setting against the Blue Mountains, high above the town of Launceston, commanding a magnificent view of the Esk Valley. The house was in its glory in the late Australian spring, the gardens a riot of colour, lush crops of cherries and strawberries waiting to be picked, apricots and peaches ripening slowly in their turn.

Whitfield was in his element. He threw himself with gusto into the Reeds quasi-colonial life in the outback, learned to ride, pole-vault, shoot rabbits and drive the pony and trap bought specially to take him and Henry to school in Launceston. Any local pupils who thought the white-skinned English boy with the plummy accent fair game regretted it when they discovered he had been having lessons in ju-jitsu and could toss them over his shoulder.

Lucy however was less resilient and missed the sophistication of Paris and the interests provided by the *Ballarat*. She conquered her fear of horses, but cows were another matter.

Reed family life was as spartan emotionally as it was physically. Mrs Reed seemed unable to show affection. Mary was often selfish and bad-tempered, Maggie flighty and temperamental, and Annie, the eldest Reed sister, nicknamed 'Cull' and the only one to show her any attention, was totally matter-of-fact and devoid of any sentimentality. It was a relief when the time came to accompany Mary across the Straits to the Presbyterian Ladies' College in Melbourne, Dame Nellie Melba's old school with a fine reputation for its music teaching.

For the first time in her life Lucy was a triumph. She excelled at English and composition. The other girls adored her. Years later Mary Reed was asked whether she was pretty. 'Pretty?' Mary replied. 'No! She was more than pretty, she was interesting to the last degree. She was small and dark with a clear, pale face and with something vivid about her. She had a way of getting herself up in the evening – a rose in her hair – a scrap of lace maybe – and the result would be charming.' On dark, wintry mornings, Lucy was always out of bed by the time the others awoke, sitting by the window huddled in blankets, reading her Bible as dawn spread its first eerie light across the dormitory.

Her classmates never found her pious. In fact she often managed to cajole them into doing her maths homework. Nor were the teachers immune to her charm. She broke any school rule she thought extraneous without reprisal, simply because she knew how to carry it off. Girls were instructed to collect all they needed for the day straight after breakfast, and not return to their dormitory before five in the evening. Lucy thought this nonsense and went up and down as she pleased. On one occasion she bumped into the superintendent on the stairs. With absolute calm, she engaged her in such a fascinating conversation that the woman seemed unaware that any rule was being broken. They parted pleasantly, and Lucy continued coolly on her way.

Her musical brilliance was recognised from the start and given every encouragement. She won the Senior Pianoforte scholarship easily. 'It is a fine thing to get,' Whitfield wrote proudly to his parents. 'They have to play before a lot of swell Melbourne musicians.' It provided her with an opportunity to play a solo at the Athenaeum Concert Hall. The music critic from *The Age*, a popular Australian newspaper, hailed her as a talent with a great future in the front rank of musicians. 'Miss Guinness' tempo was at times a little faulty, no doubt owing to nervousness in the young performer.' When she re-read the cutting years later, Mary Reed laughed out loud. 'Lucy Guinness was never nervous. Her tempo was often faulty, but it was because she preferred her own tempo to that of the composer! She was after all a great-granddaughter of Cramer, the composer, the first pianist of his day.'[4]

So impressed was the school with Lucy's musical ability that the great violinist, Remenyi, was invited to hear her play. He concluded that she was 'on the very threshold of the inner temple of classical music', and that a career as a concert pianist was indeed within her reach.

Mrs Reed quickly put a stop to such nonsense, deciding, after a year, that two marriageable young women needed no further formal education and should fill their time at home with domestic pursuits. It was a disastrous decision as far as Lucy was concerned. She tried her hand at jam-making, baking bread and saffroning lace,[5] but showed no aptitude for any kind of home-making. She promised herself faithfully she would keep up with her piano practice, but boredom and discouragement made her lethargic, and she soon lost the will to press for further lessons.

In January 1885 news reached them that Harry was coming to take them home. It was March before he actually sailed on the *Lusitania*. In the intervening month Fanny had a stroke. She recovered fairly well, though it left her with permanent facial paralysis, distressing for her and the family.

Harry made light of it in April when he finally arrived in Tasmania, not wanting to worry Lucy and Whitfield unduly. Mrs Reed was delighted to have such a personable young man around, a budding young preacher with all the charisma and promise of his father. She put him to work and he was soon in demand for his preaching all over Tasmania. To Lucy's dismay he consented to stay on another few months. It gradually became very plain to her that Mrs Reed's motives were not as disinterested as they appeared.

My eyes have been opened. Who would have dreamed of such things?

Well, the long and short of it is simply this – Mrs Reed wants Harry for a son-in-law! And he – is thereby perplexed!

How very awkward to be sure.

Harry doesn't want to marry anyone just at present, much less one of these girls. But Mrs Reed has given him to understand that poor Mag cares for him and that it is his fault, and that he can have her if he likes – terrible!

While Mrs Reed continued her game of 'throwing her daughters at Harry's head', they all set off together for a sightseeing tour of Sydney. Harry's reputation as a speaker had gone before him and requests poured in from Brisbane, Melbourne, Adelaide and Sydney itself. In particular demand were his talks for men only, entitled, 'Social Purity', or 'The Temptations of Men in the City'. As a newly qualified doctor he was concerned at widespread masculine ignorance on sexual matters. Many men were unaware of how their own body functioned, let alone a woman's. Ignorance led to fear, and fear enticed a man to underhand, illicit sexual activity.

In England men had fainted and were carried out of Harry's lectures. The Australians found it rather novel. No one had ever spoken in public about such matters before, and they admired his courage. 'The Admirable Crichton must have been such a man,' claimed one Melbourne newspaper. 'He has revelation in his right hand and science in his left, and can use both weapons freely.'

Lucy found the trip to the mainland a bitter disappointment. 'The men wear the same ugly coats and stiffest of collars and hats, the women have the same pretty faces and foolish fashions as they do at home,' she wrote to Minnie, who, at Mrs Reed's insistence, had reverted to using her real name, Geraldine.

I cannot be natural with dear Mrs Reed. I feel she does not like me; it shrivels me up; I am constrained and cold and dull. It is a wretched state. I wonder if when I am liberated and get back home again I shall be once more my old natural self? I think it has not been wholly good my coming out here; it has transformed me; and I would rather be like Mother than Mrs Reed ... these two loveless years have changed me from a merry, happy child into a small, dull, slow, pale, little woman.

By the end of 1886 Harry was still in such demand that Mrs Reed would not hear of his returning to England. Lucy and Whitfield were desperate to go home, and arranged to go on ahead without him, accompanied by Henry and Annie Reed. If Mrs Reed did not 'effectually catch him now, she ought to!' Lucy noted cryptically. She wrote a long, philosophical letter to Geraldine, trying to prepare her for the inevitable. Margaret was a nice girl, after all, a Christian, well educated, good at nursing and household matters. No one sewed buttons on better, even if she couldn't play hymns. But she was affectionate and useful, and made a good impression. But then, perhaps Harry would prove to be 'a wiser boy than I think he is', and manage to escape the snares of Mount Pleasant without committing himself. 'I only hope it may be so, but fear it may not.'

Harry urged Lucy not to send the letter. Even if she put 'private' on the envelope other members of the family might read it. Lucy bowed to his wisdom without question. It never occurred to her to wonder whether he might not already have an ulterior motive for staying in Tasmania. Not until 29 January 1886, when he announced his engagement to Annie Reed.

That Friday night everyone had arrived home late from a church meeting and gone straight to bed – except Harry and Annie. Annie was on her way upstairs when Harry called her to ask if she was coming back down.

She came into the dining-room and Harry evidently wanted to say something to her but could not. So they

two stood there (Harry describes his own experience at
that moment as that of having his tongue glued to the
roof of his mouth – unusual for him!) and at last Harry
said, 'Cull – I want a great many things –' and she
answered, 'So do we all' (in her blunt tone!) and Harry
said nothing more, so she said goodnight and went out
into the hall and had got up two of the stairs when she
turned round and Harry was behind her. So they two
stood again and then he said 'You will soon be leaving
the old home, Cull,' to which she answered, 'Yes – it was
very soon', and he said, 'I should like to make a home for
you in the old country, Cull, if you will let me', – and
Cull stood still feeling like a stone, and knowing now,
until she said, 'I will – if Mother will'. And the two turned
and went into the little room – and I don't know what
happened there exactly . . .

'This is a faithful record according to Cull's own account,'
Lucy wrote in her diary. 'I think they did it very badly myself!'

Lucy was asleep when Harry rushed into her room with the
news, Annie close on his heels. Roused by the noise, Whitfield
arrived, then Mary, and a very agitated Maggie. There was
much crying, joy and congratulations in the darkness.

Of the three sisters Annie was the most devout and the least
pretty. Her features were heavy, her nose long and thin. But
she was sensible, practical and down-to-earth, very like Fanny.
Unknown to Lucy, Annie had caught Harry's eye from the
first. 'Annie is just splendid,' he had written to his parents after
he had watched her organise tea for 1,500 people without the
slightest sign of fatigue or strain. Harry the charmer, the
incurable romantic, who could have had any one of a large
number of beautiful women in Australia or England, had
common sense enough to see that this woman, plain as she
was, had all the qualities he wanted in a wife.

Lucy was stunned. How had she been so blind? Even

Whitfield seemed to have known Annie was 'the real nugget'. But as the initial shock wore off she was forced to admit that if Harry had to have one of the Reed sisters, Annie was by far the best. 'Cull – dear, good, hard-working, unselfish, simple, humble, sober, practical, useful, devoted, brave, strong, kindly Cull.' The two were, Lucy decided, eminently well suited. She listed their contrasting qualities:

Harry a talker – Cull rather slow of speech.
Harry a writer – Cull not.
Harry extravagant – Cull careful.
Harry well fitted to shine in society – Cull not – as yet!
Harry musical – Cull unmusical.
Harry poetically inclined – Cull absolutely matter-of-fact.
Cull a mathematician – Harry not.
Cull a businesswoman – Harry not very practical.

The strong resemblance to her parents' relationship does not seem to have occurred to her.

For days the family moved in a dream, Harry 'suddenly grown, altered, completed somehow', Cull 'beaming and blissful', Mrs Reed 'overflowing with delight and satisfaction, unable to settle herself to anything, watching the two of them with glad eyes and laughing to herself, often right out at them'. Mary was astounded, 'half-pleased, half-vexed'. Only poor Maggie was devastated, and spent the evenings weeping bitterly, alone in the dark drawing-room. It was, Lucy had to admit, a fitting, if unexpected, end to that particular chapter in her life. After two years she was sailing home, bringing a new sister with her. 'When I began you,' she said to her diary, 'I never expected your contents to have been what they are. I thought you would have brought me home to England. My new diary must do that; but you have brought me in a good way, the best way, the shining way – and so, I thank you.'

There never was a new diary.

4.

While Lucy and Whitfield were away in Tasmania, Henry, Fanny and Geraldine, like everyone else at Harley College, had been following M'Call's progress, step by painful step up the 230 miles of cataracts in the Lower Congo. It was recorded with tiny markers on a huge map of Africa as it was then presumed to be, hung on the wall at Harley. The markers were moved each time news of the little party arrived in London. Stanley Pool, gateway to a vast, unexplored continent, lay just beyond their reach. They struggled on in desperate conditions, with inadequate supplies, no map or guide except Stanley's diagrams, no drugs, no understanding of the causes of malaria, dysentery or the fatal blackwater fever.

The arrival of the *Livingstone* in Africa in 1881 enabled M'Call to press on as never before, establishing mission stations all the way up the cataracts, at Banana, Mattadi, Minkanda, Pallaballa, Banza Manteki, Bembi, and Manyenga. Each station was consecrated with a grave. Husbands buried their wives and wives their husbands. Others sailed out, some dying faster than those they had gone to replace. At Harley each loss was a personal bereavement and they mourned. But there was still no shortage of volunteers.

Stanley Pool was finally reached in 1883 – but M'Call did not live to see it. The new steamer, the *Henry Reed*, arrived in Africa in 500 pieces and was transported up the cataract region, as Stanley's boat had been, on the heads of a thousand carriers, to be reconstructed at Stanley Pool. Sixteen thousand rivets were required to fasten the vessel's 160 plates. The men worked beneath a blazing African sun with no access to spare parts. Some died. Some were invalided home. But at last the *Henry Reed* was afloat on the upper river. A new adventure could begin.

The major development at home was the purchase of Doric

Lodge, a large house opposite Harley College, as the first missionary training institute for women. Within the social culture of the time this was a radical step to take and largely due to Fanny's insistence. Unlike the denominational missions, the faith missions had always taken on female missionaries, and, if they were single, accepted them in their own right. In 1878 a Harley student, Henry Craven, was accompanied to the Lower Congo by his fiancée, Miss Bossom, the first white woman the natives had ever seen. The North Africa Mission had been set up with Henry's encouragement by Jane Pearce, and many of its stations manned by women only. The Algiers Missionary Band was led by Lilias Trotter, a woman whose courage was universally admired.

Fanny was convinced it was time to offer women proper training. She and her fellow female preachers, like Catherine Booth, had begun to see there were no limits to a woman's ministry. They constituted a great, 'neglected force'. If society wouldn't provide real opportunity for their talents, she would. 'We are increasingly convinced of the importance of well-trained female agents among the heathen,' she wrote, appealing for her first students, 'and of the fact that multitudes of women who have the natural and spiritual qualifications ... are wasting their time at home here in England.'[6]

The extra administrative work took its toll on her health. She was fifty-four and had been feeling very tired since her stroke. The facial paralysis was upsetting, and made her feel uncomfortable about accepting public speaking engagements on behalf of the Livingstone Inland Mission. When she heard that Adoniram Judson Gordon, Director of the American Baptist Missionary Union, wanted to absorb the fledgling North Africa Mission, she offered him her baby instead, though with a heavy heart.

John Glenny, who now led the small North Africa Mission, resented the attempted American takeover, but Fanny saw there were obvious advantages in giving up the Livingstone Inland Mission instead, and not just for her personal well-being. It was unusual for a Bible college to have its own mission. Though students were told they were free to join the mission of their choice, it put pressure on their loyalties. Harley's independence would be re-established, (though not for long in fact). She also had the idea that new, more appropriate missionaries might be found for the future Zaire amongst America's black congregations. It was not an easy decision, but Henry and Fanny were never possessive about their work. It belonged to God.

Geraldine tried to shoulder as much of the Institute work as she could, but her teaching had expanded. Before he left for Tasmania Harry had begged her to take over his men's night classes. He was far too preoccupied with his medical studies and preaching. Geraldine refused. How could she cope with loud, rough working men, many of them the worse for drink? Harry was so irresponsible at times.

One Sunday afternoon he sent a message to the Berger Hall to say he had been unavoidably detained at the hospital. The men were waiting for their class. She could hardly disappoint them, and discovered it wasn't such a trial after all. They had been stunned into good behaviour by her appearance. 'I can see her now, standing on the platform with her white handkerchief on the rostrum,' one of them said in later years. 'She was like an angel.' None of them knew how frightened she was.

From that day the men's classes were taken by women. Edith Fookes, more academically minded than Geraldine, taught Latin, logic and mathematics to the advanced class, while Geraldine's special responsibility was the beginners and the drunks. Howard Taylor supplied her with some medicine which was supposed to sober up any miscreant she was forced to drag out of the classroom for causing disruption.

One night Geraldine was feverish and Edith went to Berger Hall alone. Despite her protestations, Henry insisted she

240

mustn't walk home alone. He would collect her at the end of her class. She waited, and waited, but there was no sign of her uncle. Eventually she set off. As she walked down Devons Road she noticed a small crowd underneath the flaring lights of a public house. Intrigued, she went to see the source of the curiosity and, standing on tiptoe, caught sight of her uncle, so absorbed in scribbling down astronomical notes, he was totally unaware of being the centre of attention. Edith pushed her way towards him and touched his arm, bringing him back to reality. He apologised profusely. He was writing *Light for the Last Days*, and could think of little else. Edith forgave him, but never waited for him again. Like Harry she had learned that for her uncle, 'sustained reflection on high themes was a necessity of life'. Harry had once travelled with his father on a tramcar from Bromley to Bow without Henry Grattan noticing he was there.

Strong-willed, widely read, an independent thinker, Edith Fookes had a profound influence on Geraldine. Edith encouraged her to get in touch with her own repressed romantic instincts, to swoon over poets like 'our friend' Robert Browning, to go to concerts and art galleries and discuss great novels. Edith insisted they take an evening off a week, remove the drab deaconess uniform they wore and do something 'normal', like attending a distinguished lecture in the city. But her new social life did not protect Geraldine from prolonged bouts of depression. She had inherited her father's intensity without his Irish expansiveness. She could never see the humour of any situation.

The pain of the East End oppressed her unbearably. She drove herself day after day as if its salvation depended on her efforts alone, and eventually developed acute back pain again. The doctor ordered a surgical corset to support the spine, and complete rest.

In Redhill, where she was sent to recuperate, she received a wise, loving letter from her father. She wrote on the envelope,

'To go with me wherever I go', and carried it in her handbag for the rest of her life, eventually publishing it after his death. He told her she was like him and so he understood her suffering. 'You have been brought face to face with sorrow, poverty, pain, death, miseries of many kinds. You see the world full of them. The problem presses upon your thoughts, it is too much for weary nerves and heart.' He too had once teetered on the edge of a complete breakdown and he apologised for not recognising the signs in her, for relying on her so much and appreciating her sensitivity so little. Now it was time for her to have a complete change. 'Give the brain a rest, give it sleep, give it fresh subjects. Read about other things, about natural history, and whatever interests and pleases you. Go out; let the sweet influences of Nature refresh your tired physical frame and mental nature too. Let sunshine and breezes, singing of birds, flowers and springtime, do their work.'

It was a perfect prescription and Geraldine arrived back at Harley in the summer of 1886 fit and well and ready to help Fanny with preparations for the arrival of Whitfield, Lucy, Henry Reed and their new sister-to-be. It was wonderful to have the house full of family again. She revelled in it, and when it became apparent that Annie Reed was at least as competent at supervising the domestic routine, if not a great deal more, she handed over the reins willingly. House management had been a necessity, not a pleasure.

In the autumn Whitfield and Henry Reed set off for the Leys School in Cambridge, Lucy accompanied her parents to Cliff where Henry could write in peace, and Annie was left in charge of the London house. At a loose end, Geraldine happened to pick up a pamphlet called *The Bitter Cry of Outcast London*, written by a crusading social reformer. It affected her deeply. She thought she knew all there was to know about conditions in the East End, but it was one thing to see them from the safe confines of Harley, it was another to experience them first-hand. How could she understand what it felt like to be poor when she was so sheltered and comfortable? Gradually the idea took root that the only way to get inside the skin of local people was by becoming one herself.

She saw no necessity to consult her parents. What they did not know could not worry them. Besides, she was twenty-three. But she did need an ally. Annie Reed was the obvious choice. As a Tasmanian Annie was free from English reserve and caution. To her it seemed a perfectly natural adventure.

Annie remembered that the kitchen maid, Sarah, had once been a factory girl, one of the wildest and roughest at that. Pledging the maid to absolute secrecy, they told her the plan and asked about suitable clothing and accommodation. Sarah thought Miss Geraldine must have taken leave of her senses! Her posh accent would give her away at once. Factory girls had ways and means of dealing with people who tried to ape them, like stripping to the waist and giving them a good hiding. With no disrespect, Miss Guinness was such a frail-looking little thing that they could blow her over in one puff. But nothing Sarah said would deter her and eventually the girl agreed to help, on one condition – that she went too. Geraldine consented. She was not as brave as she tried to pretend.

In a pawn shop Sarah found clothes for them both. Then she was sent to Colliers Rents, a turning off Long Lane, just south of London Bridge, to hire a furnished room. Geraldine could hardly preserve her incognito in the East End where everyone knew the family. South London was unfamiliar territory and Colliers Rents the very street mentioned by name in the pamphlet she had read. A triumphant Sarah returned with the news that she had managed to rent a room with a bed, table and a chair.

Factory hours were seven in the morning to seven at night, so Geraldine decided to move to Bermondsey on a Saturday evening. That would give her all day Sunday to get used to her new surroundings before she started work on Monday morning.

As the appointed Saturday drew near she was filled with an increasing sense of dread. She kept handling the strange, rough clothes, wondering why on earth she was taking such a step, yet convinced she had to do it. The moment to put the clothes on finally came. She had never felt so nervous in her life as she buttoned up the drab skirt, wrapped the ticklish woollen cross-over round her shoulders, then pinned on her apron. For some time she stood looking in the mirror at the transformation. Tentatively, she lifted up the hat with its large, gaudy, trailing feathers and put it on her head. The sight shocked her and she took it off quickly. Slipping a fur cloak around her shoulders, she ran downstairs, holding the awful hat in her hand. She could not bring herself to put it on until last possible moment.

Annie was waiting in the hall. For a moment their eyes met, Geraldine's as grave as ever, Annie's twinkling with unsuppressed amusement. Annie had to fight hard to stifle her laughter all the way out to the pony chaise. She was to drive Geraldine to London Bridge where Sarah would be waiting for her under a lamp by the church. They drove in silence. When they reached the bridge Annie slowed the chaise. With a rather desperate sounding, 'Goodbye', Geraldine dropped the fur cloak onto the seat, slapped the hat on her head, and stepped down. Annie shook the reins and Geraldine watched the chaise speed away, fading quickly out of sight in the murky October dusk.

Sarah was waiting for her and they walked down Long Lane together. Weaving their way around the stalls and barrows manned by yelling costermongers, Geraldine felt assaulted by the frenetic activity and the noise. As the dank chill of night began to enter her bones, the countless public houses looked increasingly inviting. She was pushed, shoved and jostled by swarming humanity out for a good time and reeking of drink.

It was a relief to reach the comparative quiet of Colliers Rents.

The door of their lodgings was locked and there was no sign of the landlady. A woman poked her head out of the next door window and said she had just gone round to the 'public', and would be straight back. They sat on the doorstep for hours. Mrs Tester appeared at last, considerably the worse for drink, yet kindly nonetheless. She showed them in and they climbed up a ladder to get to their room. Geraldine could hardly believe her eyes. It was far worse than anything she had seen in the East End. Sarah had tried to clean it up, but the dirt had defied all her attempts.

That night was the most frightening of Geraldine's life. A whole lodging-house of seventy men was involved in a fight underneath their window. Geraldine trembled so much the bed shook. That was no sooner over when a window was flung open nearby and a woman started screaming, 'Murder! murder!' until the police came and took her away. The drunken brawls in the street continued until the small hours of the morning.

As dawn cast a grey light over the drab little lane an uneasy, exhausted silence descended at last. Lying next to her, Sarah had managed to doze off. Beneath her Mrs Tester was snoring loudly. She got up to think and pray, sorely tempted to give up the whole idea. Then she remembered it was Sunday – she would have to find a church. Looking at her skirt and apron it suddenly occurred to her that her presence would not be acceptable in a 'respectable' place of worship. Only a mission hall would welcome her. This sudden awareness of how pernicious the class system was, how alien to true Christianity, strengthened her resolve to stick it out.

On Monday morning they started to work at the match factory. Sarah introduced Geraldine to the other girls as her mate from the country, which was half true as Geraldine had only recently come back from Cliff. She didn't say much because life was so strange down here and she was shy. The explanation was accepted. These country bumpkins did find city life hard at first.

Geraldine was torn apart by her experience in the factory. She was terrified of opening her mouth, yet longed to get close to the girls. Her heart went out to them. She was appalled by their conditions of work and angered at the way they were treated. Constant contact with phosphorus wore the skin around their chin away, a condition known as 'phossy jaw', which eventually caused the disintegration of all the surrounding tissue. Yet no one appeared to care. A girl was of no more value than an animal, her pay pitiful. At the end of the week Geraldine and Sarah had earned a mere four shillings and fourpence-halfpenny between them for piece work. It had been a slack week. On a good week they might have earned eight shillings.

After a fortnight Geraldine began to feel unwell. The pastor of the mission church she had attended urged her to go home and reluctantly she allowed him to send for Annie. It was a dejected-looking Geraldine who climbed into the pony chaise for the return journey. She felt a failure. Those girls had to put up with their lot for ever and she could barely cope with two weeks. And yet, in years to come, she was to see how formative they had been. The experience taught her that if necessary she could adapt to a totally alien culture. Had she known it, there could be no better preparation for her future.

She recounted every detail to an enthralled Lucy, just back from Cliff. Lucy had been feeling listless since she came home from Tasmania, wondering what she should do with her life. Unlike most well-raised young women of their time, both sisters intended being more useful than ornamental. There was no further talk about becoming a concert pianist, but writing had always appealed to her. She had a natural flair for using the appropriate word. Writing could inform, move men and women, and stir them to action. The popularity of Dickens proved it.

She decided to write up Geraldine's adventure in Bermondsey. But on reflection, felt that to write an honest, realistic account, she could not simply rely on her sister's version. She must experience the life of a factory girl herself. Poor Sarah was requisitioned again and repeated the whole process, this time with a determined, persevering Lucy, who in her quest for authenticity was prepared to go to greater lengths than her sister.

In *Only a Factory Girl* Lucy powerfully conveyed her impressions of life in the squalid end of London – piles of decayed vegetables, rags and bones, bits of papers and scraps of food, bunches of straw, oyster-shells, rotten eggs, fish bones fallen off the costermongers' barrows, the overpowering smell of the fish shops, the middle-aged woman in shabby, torn clothing with a red and bloated face, dancing about with a drunken man to the sound of a black, minstrel band while the children look on and laugh 'at the pitiful spectacle of degraded womanhood'.

The door of a public house swings to and fro and a rough working lad inside, seeing Lucy standing outside in the shadows, puts his head out and says kindly. ''E ain't 'ere, ole gal! 'E's gorn 'ome, 'e is.' Seeing she ignores him, he adds, 'Never you mind 'im, 'e ain't comin' back 'ere agen tonight. You just come into the warm, ole gal, you an' yer mate!' And Lucy takes her first faltering steps into a public house.

Inside, dozens of factory girls with pretty faces, half-stupid with drink, allow themselves to be fondled in turn by various men. 'We have often wondered at the language and uncontrollable wildness of factory girls. After tonight's experience, we shall never wonder again, but rather marvel that, seeing their lives are such, and that such places are open to them nightly, they should ever be content to come to our evening classes and sit and sew and spell!'

Out in the street large gangs of girls and lads lark about under the archways, shouting, swearing and singing music-hall songs. What is there to go home to? A wretched tumble-down tenement, cold, damp and overcrowded? Who is there to go home to?

Lucy had never felt so invisible in her life. No one noticed her. As a factory girl she simply did not exist. No one cared that she was cold and wet through, the rain beating down on her bare head. There was one way of keeping warm, the girls told her! 'If we listen to their suggestions, we shall never go home again – ! Pardon, gentle reader! We did not mean to shock you. We only wanted to tell you of things as they are.'

The booklet did shock its polite readership for all the reasons Lucy hoped it would. Its immense popularity led to the formation of the Shaftesbury Society, an organisation still committed to improving conditions among the poor more than a hundred years later.

In 1888, two years after its publication, the match girls went on strike demanding better treatment, and protective measures against 'phossy jaw'. They won their fight. Lucy's first opportunity to test the power of her pen had been a success, ensuring she would never again be less than outspoken. She had enabled some to see that the working classes were not inherently different from anyone else. There was no such thing as inbred respectability. All human beings were the same before God, sharing the same dreams and longings. The difference was that by birth some had the means to fulfil them. Others did not. This was where Lucy was a radical for her time, why no one could accuse her of patronising the poor. She did not believe they were inferior. Wearing their clothing, she was as much a factory girl as they were.

All the day long, all the year round, from early morning, standing ten hours a day, with weary feet and aching limbs, we work in the din of the busy factory. Often hungry – so hungry – even for a bit of bread! Often tired; always ill-clad; always poor; always tempted to sin;

always outcast and despised, for no fault of our own, but that we were born to it – never at peace, and never satisfied; intensely affectionate, yet unloved, except by those who would injure us, unloved by those who would aid us if they would.

THIS is how we live.

THOUSANDS OF US LIVE THAT WAY!

'Only a factory girl', people say when they see us misbehave.

'Only a factory girl', and they pass on.

ONLY A FACTORY GIRL – but that means SOMETHING!

5.

In 1886, while Geraldine and Lucy were trying their hand at factory work, news broke in the city that Arthur Guinness and Sons was to go public. Since most businesses were private partnerships this was an event indeed. Edward Cecil received £6 million, mostly in cash, about a sixth in shares. The new chairman could afford to be generous. The workmen received four weeks pay, there were cheques for the clerks and three months salary-worth of shares for the brewers. To brother Lee of the Royal Horse Guards, who had enjoyed none of the benefits of the family firm, he gave £150,000. Only John Tertius Purser, General Manager, who had worked for the Brewery for sixty-two years refused a handout. The old family retainer wanted nothing to do with a public company. He feared it would compromise his Moravian values. He was probably right.

After their issue the value of the shares rose steeply. Demand had been underestimated and the chairman was using his cash to make a killing. By February 1888 he had acquired more than 50 per cent of the shares. Today a chairman would be forced to reveal his hand. Then, 'insider dealing' was not an offence. No precedent necessitated legislation, and Edward Cecil had no qualms about the integrity of his dealings. He had said all along he intended retaining ultimate control of the company.

His bank however behaved in flagrant breach of any moral code. Baring Brothers had been his second choice. He had approached Rothschilds informally but they did not want to deal with beer.[7] As excitement in the City rose to fever pitch, the Baring Brothers' offices were in a state of siege. In an article entitled, 'The Boom in the City' in the *Daily News* on 26 October, a 'Disappointed Applicant' noted, 'nothing within the memory of living man had been quite like it'. Police tried to restrain the jostling crowds, but the mob broke through the cordon and Barings' door was broken down. 'It was said that one or two desperate applicants on the edge, despairing of getting in, wrapped their application forms around stones, and threw them through the windows.'[8]

Only 6,000 of the 13,000 applicants were successful. *The Times* was inundated with letters of complaint from frustrated applicants alleging a rigging, a fraud. Barings' handling of the matter was questionable throughout. Its valuation of the company at £6 million was a gross underestimation. Edward Cecil could probably have made £2 million more. Secondly, when the shares were apportioned it was evident that Barings had creamed off a huge profit for their directors, as well as large cuts for Rothschilds, Morgans and Hambros. Smaller fry had no chance. The law was bent but not broken, and Barings escaped with a dint in its reputation. This was not the best start for the new public company. The conception had been immaculate, but the birth messy, with City scandal as its midwife.

How could Barings have so underestimated demand for Guinness shares? The firm was one of the most thriving, well-managed companies in the British Isles. Sir Edward Cecil was committed to improving the living, as well as the working conditions of his employees. Given the standards Geraldine and Lucy witnessed at Bryant and May, it is hardly surprising that many industrialists, and not a few of his social set, thought him far too liberal. The *London Gazette* reported, 'Sir Edward Cecil Guinness is anything but an ostentatious man.' (Evidently the reporter had not been invited to one of Dodo's sumptuous parties.) 'Perhaps his failing is that he leans too much the other way – that he is rather retiring – if not timid. His wealth is boundless, and his enterprise is not less so.' Five thousand employees were treated like royalty.

> Emigration allowances, where men are silly, or wise enough (as fortune decides) to leave, are fixed on a large scale, widows are provided for, orphan children educated, and trained for business, and the whole order of things has reached such a pitch of princely generosity as well in the housing and care of the ordinary working man as in the upper commercial grades that it is probably not exceeded in Europe.

On the face of it Edward Cecil rebelled against the evangelical teaching he received as a child at his mother's insistence at the Bethesda Chapel and read Darwin with an open mind to prove it. But it affected his thinking more than he cared to admit. His religious principles were the guiding force of his life. He personally led family prayers in his home morning and evening, as his own father and grandfather had done. The upright example of the Moravian John Tertius Purser was also a constant reminder of his duty to humanity, and the necessity for good works. His was not the only company to renounce exploitation of the workforce. Firms like Cadbury and Rowntree were equally committed to applying Christian values to industrial practice. Where Edward Cecil excelled was in the scope and scale of the welfare he provided.

Unlike a factory girl in London, a Guinness employee in Dublin was a someone. His wages were the highest in Ireland. There was security of employment, and misdemeanours such as drunkenness, smoking on duty, late arrival, carelessness and wilful neglect, which would earn a man the sack elsewhere, incurred a fine instead. Posterity attributes to Sir Edward the saying, 'You can't expect to make money out of people, unless you are prepared to let them make money out of you' – a fairly radical statement for a Victorian employer, let alone an Irish Protestant with a largely Roman Catholic workforce. Despite his political stance Edward Cecil was not a bigot and numbered more than a few priests among his friends.

There had been pensions and holidays with pay since 1860, free medical services, midwifery, a dispensary and sick pay since 1869. A report to John Tertius Purser in 1888 from the two medical officers, doubling as welfare officers, claimed they had received 19,000 attendances at their clinic and made 2,260 home visits. They had prescribed 764 bottles of wine, 535 bottles of whisky and 213 bottles of brandy. What the teetotal Purser made of such medicine is not recorded, but sixty years later the chief medical officer, commenting on the report, noted, 'Today, none of such are ever prescribed, but only Guinness, which, it has been found in the process of time, is much better.'[9]

Like his Grattan cousins in Bow, Edward Cecil's social conscience was not immune to the slum conditions he saw every morning on his way to work. But while education was their solution, decent housing was his. After all, he had the means to provide it, and his motives were never devoid of good business sense. 'A man living in a well-ventilated, clean and sanitary dwelling is healthier, happier and capable of performing double the work of one who resides in an overcrowded house, not to mention the liability of the latter to contract disease, draw sick money, or perhaps die prematurely, leaving a widow and family to be supported by the firm.'

By the time he wrote that report in 1884 he had provided housing for a seventh of his workforce, with the Belview Building in 1872, and the Rialto Buildings in 1882. In 1885 as evidence to the Royal Commission on the Housing of the Working Classes, he described how he had provided 180 dwellings, mostly one- or two-bedroom flats, with living-room, scullery, running water and a lavatory. Tenants were regularly inspected to ensure they were complying with basic hygiene regulations.

Some members of the committee evidently thought Sir Edward far too benevolent. A handout of that magnitude removed incentive to personal effort and thrift. Sir Edward disagreed. His reforms were not far-reaching enough. 'I have some thoughts of erecting cottages perhaps outside the city boundary in the country and bringing my people in by train if I could see my way to do it, but I have not yet matured my point.'[10]

No further building schemes for the Brewery materialised, however. The Belview and Rialto Buildings were not an unqualified success. Workers complained the rents were too high, the coal too expensive, the shops too far away and the regulations too restrictive. Many of the flats remained empty. But Edward Cecil never admitted defeat, and constantly looked for imaginative ways of overcoming the difficulties. A shopping co-operative was set up at the Rialto Buildings. The firm subsidised allotments, classes in cookery for employees' wives, and gymnastic classes for their children. Despite repeated requests from Medical Officers, tenants were rarely evicted for living in unsanitary conditions. The Management Committee recognised that enforced cleanliness was a violation of basic human rights.

After the firm went public, Sir Edward felt less inclined to give his time to business commitments, more disposed to pursuing his philanthropic dreams. He was exceedingly rich, and that was, after all, his prerogative. The idea of relinquishing the chairmanship of the Brewery seemed increasingly attractive. After a trip to America he claimed it was a fine country, but no place for a gentleman as everyone worked. He had, after all, his health to consider. He was only forty-three, but a martyr to continual colds and sinus problems.

Securing the succession would be difficult. Rupert was only sixteen and, with Ernest, was still at Eton. His two nephews, Benjamin Lee's sons, Algernon Lee and Kenelm Lee, were younger than his own.

Instinctively Edward felt it should be a member of his side of the family, a direct descendant of the first Arthur Guinness. Loyalty to the family was paramount. But he had no full cousins either. All five sons of his father's only brother, the Rev. William Smythe Lee Grattan Guinness had died without issue. One, Frederick Darley Guinness, had taken 'poison by accident' in 1869, making him the first member of the family to die in mysterious circumstances. Edward would have to look further afield.

The first Arthur's eldest son, Hosea the clergyman, had thirteen children, but only two of his sons produced any issue. The younger, and more dynamic of the two, Francis Hart Vicesimus Guinness, went to India, then settled in New Zealand and started a branch of the family there. His eldest son, Sir Arthur Robert Guinness KCB, had embarked on a brilliant political career and was about to become Speaker in the New Zealand parliament. Hosea's eldest son Arthur, Vicar of Seaton Carew in Durham, had several sons, one of whom, Thomas Hosea, had married well and lived in style at his country house, Tibradden near Dublin. This branch of the family was very aware of its seniority. Thomas's eldest brother, Arthur Hart, had been taken on at the Brewery by Sir Benjamin Lee, and groomed for partnership. But Arthur Hart enjoyed the profits more than the making of them, and the relationship was not a success. Sir Edward decided not to repeat his father's mistake.

Of the first Arthur's other sons, both Edward and Benjamin had daughters only, and William Lunell's only son, William Newton, not only became a clergyman, but emigrated to Melbourne.

That left the line descended from Captain John – the Grattan Guinnesses – and Sir Edward had to admit that their teetotalism made them unlikely candidates for the Brewery Board. Although Henry Grattan was responsible for a large international company of his own, he had little practical business sense. Harry, who certainly had the qualities needed, appeared committed to a career in medicine. There was no doubt he and his brother and sisters had inherited the Guinness drive, but they had decided to use it for an altogether different purpose. They believed that all that was needed to change the world was not wealth, but one man or woman totally given into God's hands.

Sir Edward had no choice but to turn to his wife's side of the family. Dodo was extremely fond of her four brothers and had no qualms about pushing them forward. The elder two did not merit real consideration. Charles was a colonel in the 72nd Highlanders. Arthur Cecil Cope Jenkinson Guinness, known as Cecil, was a problem, the proverbial black sheep. He had inherited his mother's airs and graces, and lack of sense when it came to money. Stunningly good-looking with striking red hair, spoilt beyond reason, he seems to have had the notion that the grandson of a baronet should live like a gentleman, gave up his studies in law and became a remittance man instead. At twenty-one, permanently in debt with only his looks to commend him, he was packed off to Australia and fell on his feet by marrying Marion, the teenage daughter of his employer, William Forlonge the wealthiest sheep baron in the country. Conveniently, Rev. William Newton Guinness was available in Melbourne to conduct the service. To the temporary relief of his immediate family, Cecil remained in the wings of the Guinness story, though his offspring, and particularly his grandson, Edward, would have a major part to play.

Dodo's two younger brothers, however, showed a little more potential. In 1881 Edward took on Claude, the youngest of the two, with a view to grooming him to succeed John Tertius Purser as General Manager, installing him in Knock-maroon off Phoenix Park, a house which remains in the family to this day. Claude Guinness was intelligent and loyal, exceptionally astute in business matters, a man after Edward's own heart. When the role of Chairman became available, he had no qualms about turning to Claude's elder brother, Reginald. And so the descendants of Samuel Guinness the goldbeater found their way on to the Brewery Board. The Grattan Guinnesses had their chance and made their choice. Their vision involved a different kind of spirit.

Chapter 9

1886–1890
The Building of International Empires

1.

The Grattans had their own problems of inheritance. The empire was increasing as Fanny's strength diminished, but her four children had their own lives to lead. Shortly before he left Tasmania for home at the end of 1886, Harry received a letter from his mother which made his heart sink. 'How glad I shall be to have you to talk to. A man of action, of sociable disposition and popular sympathies.' Marriage to a man who lived as much in heaven as he did on earth, rich as it was, could be a lonely business. She was 'son-sick', she said. But it was not simply companionship Fanny had in mind. 'Darling Father, you inherit from him all your best gifts, but you also have a touch of your mother in you that will make you doubly useful, I hope.' This was Fanny's way of suggesting her son might take over her work when he came home.

It was the last thing Harry wanted. Treves had predicted a brilliant medical career. Or perhaps, after his success in Australia, he should be an itinerant preacher like his father. Marriage into the wealthy Reed family released Harry from ever having to earn his living. But sitting at a desk piled high with paper played no part in his dreams. Then who else would carry on his mother's work? She wanted to be free to help Henry with his writing. He struggled without her, unable to convey the great concepts in his head onto paper, in readable form. Yet she was convinced the work of the Institute had potential for further growth in the hands of someone with energy, vision and imagination.

Reluctantly, Harry gave way. His future was as carved in concrete as that of his brewing cousin, Rupert. There was room for personal development, but only within the confines of a prescribed destiny. It was the duty of the eldest son to take over the family business.

When he saw his mother again, so changed, so small, tired and shrunken, he knew he had made the right decision. Annie had already taken a great deal of practical responsibility for the daily running of the Institute onto her own capable shoulders. He would have the right woman at his side.

They were married on 17 March 1887, at the East London Tabernacle, followed by a reception in Charrington's Great Assembly Hall, the only room in the East End large enough to accommodate all their friends and family. The guest list was the oddest mix of rich and poor. Wealthy Institute supporters, elegantly and tastefully dressed, rubbed shoulders with the night-class students, a motley group of barrow boys, labourers and factory girls, all got up for the occasion in their gaudiest array.

The honeymoon was a trip to Egypt and the Holy Land. Annie's generous allowance was a novelty for Harry who could not resist buying his bride expensive gifts. But never was a woman more devoid of sentimentality. Annie Guinness had no taste for trinkets, and began a practice continued throughout their married life, of selling the jewellery and china he gave her and using the money for missionary work. Harry, whose memory was defective at the best of times, was never any the wiser.

His impetuosity was a constant source of irritation to her.

On the day after their wedding he left her in the Metropole Hotel and went off to conduct some 'business', presumably fund-raising for the Institute, although he never offered any explanation. The following morning he disappeared again on yet another venture, and they only just managed to catch the Paris train. Life with Harry would test her patience, but it would never be dull.

Their fellow pilgrims across Europe, through Lucerne, Milan and Brindisi, where they caught the SS *Siam*, were hardly conducive company for a honeymoon couple. A loud American woman monopolised the conversation at the dinner table. The ship's jocular surgeon regaled them with unintelligible jokes about Mark Twain. And an ill-mannered curate from Eyam attached himself to them, redeeming himself a little when he put his feet on the seat of the hot train to Cairo, his dusty boots almost reaching the insufferable American woman's shoulders. After the Nile and the pyramids, Jerusalem and Jaffa, they were relieved to part company with the tour, and travel on alone to Damascus to see Dora Fookes who was a missionary there. As they travelled by steamer up the Turkish coast from Beirut towards Greece, the honeymoon almost came to a tragic end. In her large new house in Hampstead, Mrs Reed received an alarming telegram from Harry telling her that Annie had been taken ashore at Smyrna to the Jews' Hospital, dangerously ill with typhoid fever. Mrs Reed packed her bags at once and set off with Mary for the Middle East.

As she vacated the house, Geraldine moved in. The pain in her back was almost unbearable and a new consultant recommended by Howard Taylor had again prescribed rest. Dr Anderson was a shrewd and kindly Scotsman from Aberdeen, one of the best surgeons at the London Hospital. He knew her symptoms were psychosomatic but did not dismiss them out of hand. During several visits to the house in Hampstead, he gently explained that she must learn to conquer the pain, or it would conquer her. The spinal corset had simply encouraged her to feel sorry for herself. She must throw it away, along with self-pity, or be an invalid for the rest of her life. Geraldine was shaken, but grateful for Anderson's honesty. He put steel in her soul, and by the time she returned to Harley six weeks later, she was determined not to be defeated.

Howard had watched her suffering from a distance for years. It grieved him he could do so little to help. Seeing his distress, his aunt Mrs Broomhall suggested Geraldine might be pining because he had not declared his love. Howard was unsure. She had given him no sign, and in her present state was hardly likely to receive a proposal with any degree of enthusiasm. Still, he knew little about the ways of women and would bow to his aunt's superior wisdom.

One beautiful June day when the sun was streaming through the windows of the dining-room at Harley House, Howard found Geraldine there alone. He told her quite simply that he loved her, that he had always loved her since he was a boy, and that there was no other woman with whom he would ever want to share his life.

Geraldine was appalled. She loved Howard as a brother. She had never considered him in a romantic light. The pain in his eyes as she declined his offer distressed her unutterably. The last thing she wanted was to hurt this dear, gentle man who had always been such a loyal and faithful friend. She tried to soften the blow by saying she and Edith had decided not to marry. They were going to consecrate themselves to serving the poor. But that robbed him of any hope and distressed him all the more. Summoning every ounce of dignity he possessed, he apologised for having embarrassed her and let himself quietly out of the house.

Annie made a slow but complete recovery, and when she returned with Harry to take over the running of Harley House, Geraldine escaped to Cliff, to spend a few weeks with her parents. One morning a letter arrived from Edith with a rather smug account of her rejection of an eminent suitor. Without thinking Geraldine read it out loud to her mother. Fanny was furious. How could any girl be so stupid? What did she mean by 'the life of self-sacrifice they had chosen was more exciting than the poetry of romance and the prose of the married estate'?

Geraldine felt she ought to tell her mother about Howard Taylor's proposal and Fanny was doubly aggravated. The girls were too pious for their own good. They were to be parted at once. Edith was sent to friends in Berlin, Geraldine to her Uncle Wyndham's in Rathdrum. That would give them both time to reflect.

The tranquil atmosphere of Rathdrum Rectory had a soothing effect on Geraldine's uneasy spirit. Daily rides on the long stretch of firm, white sand, the sea air filling her lungs and stinging her skin, made her feel more alive and at one with herself than she had done for years. One morning she arose particularly early and went down to the beach to watch the sunrise. A strange orange glow gradually lit up the sky, melting the grey first light of early morning. Suddenly, she became aware that another parallel light, an inner light, was flooding her whole being, driving the heavy greyness from her mind. In a flash she knew with absolute certainty that she was being called to go to China. On the distant horizon a huge red ball rose silently and majestically out of the sea. Her day had dawned.

She wrote to tell her parents at once. Fanny responded warmly but Henry was upset. He found it hard to let go of his little girl. Of all of his children she was the one who most feared launching out on her own. She always remained close to him. She was his soul-mate. He could not accept her decision without being absolutely sure she knew what she was doing. Since he had a preaching engagement in Ireland he went on to Courtdown Harbour to see her.

For two days they walked up and down the beach together,

and finally, Henry was convinced of her call. Writing poetry had become an outlet for his emotions, and that night, in an anguish of spirit, he wrote a poem entitled, 'I give thee up to God, my Geraldine'.

The Victorians were fond of sentimental occasions, and missionary farewells, strumming their emotional songs on finely tuned heart strings, were particularly entertaining. In 1885 the departure of the 'Cambridge Seven' for China had captured the public imagination. The seven, all Cambridge graduates from wealthy families, included C. T. Studd, captain of the first cricket eleven, Stanley Smith, stroke of the rowing eight, Montagu Beauchamp, Lord Radstock's nephew, and two officers of the British Army. This was no ordinary missionary farewell. The cream of England's manhood had put God before country. It caused an enormous stir.

Equally public, though not quite so exciting, Geraldine's farewell took place in a packed Exeter Hall on 23 January 1888. Every eye was fastened on the slim, pale, serious young woman in close-fitting black dress and black bonnet. Her long fair hair, parted in the middle and drawn neatly back from her forehead, hung loosely down her back. She looked much younger than her twenty-five years. Dr Barnardo described how he had watched her grow from a babe in arms to a fine young woman. Then Henry Grattan rose to his feet and said that this was one of the gladdest yet saddest occasions he had ever attended. As he looked at her he said, 'It is one thing to send out other people's children, but quite another to send out your own.' There was hardly a dry eye in the hall.

Outside, in the cold winter rain, the men and women of the night school were waiting to say goodbye. When Geraldine finally emerged from the hall, one old man, a tall, rough-looking pedlar, was too overcome to speak. He took her hands in his, work-toughened and calloused as they were, and with as much dignity as a prince, stooped and kissed them as tenderly as he knew how, sobbing all the while. It was only then that Geraldine let go of the control she had fought so hard to maintain and allowed herself a few tears.

On her last morning the family gathered in the dining-room at Harley. Henry read Psalm 121 from his large, familiar, black Bible. 'The Lord shall preserve thy going out and thy coming in from this day forth and for evermore.' Lucy noticed the wintry sunshine playing on the coloured glass of the window, painting mysterious patches on the floor. But then, she explained later, 'details are noticed in the presence of a great, overwhelming pain'.

A huge crowd gathered at the docks to wave Geraldine off. She could still hear the sound of their singing floating after her on the wind as she sailed down the Thames. In many ways it was a relief to be alone at last.

The boat docked at Naples to give passengers the chance to visit the Pozzuoli Palace. As Geraldine bent to sign the visitors' book, she noticed, with a mixture of horror and amusement, the name of the last entry: F. Howard Taylor. Howard had been to Pozzuoli the previous summer. No one had signed the book again until she came. It was an extraordinary co-incidence, but she made no mention of it in her letters home.

At Penang she made her first acquaintance with the people she felt called to serve, when a crowd of Chinese came aboard with boxes, bedding and household goods. She felt excited and nervous all at once. 'Real Chinese they are, with shaven heads, long pigtails and yellow skins – so strange!' As in the Bryant and May match factory, her inability to communicate with them was a source of major frustration.

The HMS *Deccan* sailed round the Malay Peninsula to the beautiful tropical island of Singapore where it made an extended stay when it became stuck in the mud. Geraldine could not resist going ashore, and was enchanted by the silent, moonlit, tropical jungle. The vegetation was so luxurious. Singapore town was five miles away, but the only means of transport there was a jinricksha, the human-pony-drawn 'hansom cab of China'. Nothing would induce her at first to climb into this baby's perambulator or bathchair, but if she wanted to see the town, there was no alternative. A jinricksha came to a standstill beside her. The coolie invited her and her companion to climb in. They stepped gingerly inside, convinced they were going to be tipped out backwards the moment they sat down. To their amazement they stayed upright – until the coolie lifted the shafts and they landed on their backs with their legs in the air in a most indecorous manner. Helpless with laughter they clung to each other as the coolie tore off at a terrific pace through the banana forest. Many times in the future, crossing China in a wheelbarrow, Geraldine would long for the comfort of a jinricksha.

The orient released rather than inhibited Geraldine. Thousands of miles from home she felt free at last. The reserve which hounded her had gone and she felt ready for any adventure. At the China Inland Mission home in Shanghai she put on Chinese dress for the first time. Some of the missionaries obviously found it amusing, but to Geraldine, unaware of how like a nun she sounded, it was 'a sacred and serious exchange – a sacrament'. She still refused to go out in her new clothes until it was dark.

On the steamer to the language school at Yang-chou, two days journey up the Yangtze River, she saw the effects of opium for the first time. Drowsy and apathetic, Chinese women lay out smoking in the hot sun all day. When she finally arrived at Yang-chou the school was so overcrowded there was no bed for her. She would have to make do with the table until one became available. It was a very short wait. That night she sat with a young missionary woman who had been in China five weeks and was dying of typhoid fever. Geraldine marvelled at her radiant acceptance of God's will and promised herself she would never give any room to self-pity again.

Language study almost defeated her resolve. She cried so

much with sheer frustration that her eyes began to trouble her. Nor, as ever, could she cope with the misery around her, the continual wailing and sobbing of beggars beneath her window.

One afternoon there was a loud hammering at the door and yet another urgent demand for the missionaries to come and save an opium suicide. There were several every week, usually women seeking to escape their terrible lot. They belonged to whatever man had bought them and were utterly dependent on his whims and moods. When he died they were as much value as refuse.

On that particular day the missionaries experienced at dealing with overdoses had dealt with two cases already and were too exhausted to go out again. Geraldine would have to stand in for them, with Lottie MacFarlane as interpreter. A guide led them through a maze of streets to a respectable looking house in a quiet courtyard. The darkened living room was crammed with excited women, shouting at the tops of their voices. From an inner cubicle off to the right Geraldine could just make out the sound of moaning and a struggle. As she pushed her way into the room and her eyes became accustomed to the light, she saw to her horror that the creature being held down on the bed, struggling like a tormented animal, was a child of about fourteen.

As she was dragged into the living-room, Geraldine and Lottie tried to calm the crowds. They prepared a strong emetic which the girl refused to take, swearing she would throw herself down a well if the overdose didn't work. It was obvious they could do little for her while she was the centre of attention. Gently, Geraldine led her away back to the cubicle and managed to persuade her to take the medicine.

In between bouts of vomiting she told them her sad story. She had been sold at six to a cruel family to be the wife of one of the sons. Her mother-in-law had beaten her regularly for eight long years. The only reason she had sent for the missionaries was because she didn't want to have to buy another wife for her son.

Whenever a man's face appeared at the window or in the doorway the girl shrank back in terror. Geraldine covered it with a makeshift paper curtain, but they tore it away and continued to leer at her and giggle. Eventually she lay quiet, her face a picture of utter despair. Geraldine wondered what had been achieved. Lottie was in the living-room, trying to tell the women about the great God who loved the people he had made, but when the man of the house appeared, he sent the missionaries on their way.

Back at the mission house Geraldine was horrified to discover that the girl's story could be repeated thousands of times, throughout the entire Empire. She ran up to her room, threw herself down on her bed and wept. 'Oh, God – China! The whole vast empire, million-peopled – all its suffering, sinning, anguished hearts; its women, its little children! The long years of darkness, the few to bring them light!'

2.

The 1880s established Henry Grattan Guinness as one of the foremost authorities in the world on history, astronomy and biblical prophecy. His books, which sold in their thousands and had to reprinted almost at once, were devoured by a public hungry for literature establishing a pre-planned purpose in the historical events of their time. For a society born of almost continual religious revival since 1858, the ultimate Bible code had been broken. In *Light for the Last Days*, published in 1887, and *The Divine Programme of the World's History* in 1888, Henry Grattan claimed for the first time that all the evidence pointed to 1917 as a key year for Jewish restoration to the Holy Land.

His astronomical tables, the third of the three volumes

which made up *Light for the Last Days*, became standard reference in observatories throughout the world, earning him a fellowship of the Royal Astronomical Society. Dr Dreyer, Director of the Armagh Observatory, stated:

> The tables will be of great practical value to chronologists and historians, who can find from them the day of the week and the age of the moon, corresponding to any date. Particularly to students of oriental history, they will be invaluable, as the moon is the clock hand of Eastern nations. But they will also in many cases be of great use to astronomers as a ready means of finding by a mere glance the whereabouts of the moon in the sky at any time during the last three thousand years.[1]

Inexplicably, the more successful his writing, the more his preaching appeared to suffer. For Henry preaching was an art, and like any artist he relied on the spark of inspiration to kindle the dry wood of the discipline of his craft. But inspiration began to escape him with increasing, yet arbitrary, regularity. At some insignificant gathering he would enthral his audience with his message, but when a particularly memorable address was required, he could be suddenly lost for words. Harry accompanied him one Sunday to a small church near Victoria Park where he preached a marvellous sermon to a sparse congregation. The same evening, in a packed East London Tabernacle, he stood in the pulpit stuttering and stammering, unable to marshal his thoughts. For months after, whenever he thought about it, Harry would feel the sweat pricking the back of his neck.

The doctor prescribed complete rest – preferably in a milder climate. For Henry this seemed the perfect opportunity for a prolonged trip to the USA. The hostility of thirty years ago had long since vanished. His books had been published there to great acclaim, earning him an honorary doctorate from Browns University which he wanted to receive in person. And besides, his friendship with Moody could open almost any door.

Even before this extended tour Henry Grattan Guinness's influence had pervaded the country. Many influential American ministers remembered his preaching and dated their own conversion and calling from that time, among them A. B. Simpson, Pastor of the New York Tabernacle.[2] In 1882, Simpson, in the Tabernacle magazine, called for an American Bible College, based on the East London Training Institute, for all the reasons Henry and Fanny had opened Harley College. There were established theological seminaries in the States. Henry and Fanny had spoken at Mount Holyoke about the Congo in 1884. But a large number of potential ministers and missionary candidates were denied access because they came from a background which could not supply them with the necessary education or the funding. On their criteria Hudson Taylor would never have been accepted for training and his China Inland Mission would have collapsed for lack of personnel.

There were several attempts to form non-denominational colleges in the States in the 1870s, but Simpson's New York Missionary Training College was the first formal US Bible School, a pattern for many others throughout the USA and Canada, including the Prairie Bible Institute in Alberta.[3] Even the later Pentecostal schools were based on Simpson's model, inspired by Harley College.[4]

Throughout history, lessons which could have been learned from the prototype have been ignored. A rather extreme brand of pietism led Simpson's first students to set off for Africa without adequate medical supplies in the naïve expectation that God would protect and provide. They died like flies. Guinness was appalled, and said so. In an attempt to reduce costs the Americans were also committed to the idea of establishing 'agricultural missions' up the Congo, small farms which would make their missionaries self-supporting as quickly as possible. The Guinnesses knew from experience that it was impracticable. African labourers had to be paid with goods, and that proved more, not less expensive.

By the time Henry Grattan Guinness arrived in the United States in 1889 these problems were being resolved. At least Simpson had missionary candidates, unlike the American Baptist Missionary Society. Henry and Fanny were desperately disappointed with its inability to develop the work they had started. There had been no further advance into Zaire. When he met the Director, Adoniram Judson Gordon, Henry suggested he train his own missionaries, and by the time he returned to England, Gordon had opened the Boston Missionary Training Institute.

In Minneapolis Henry Grattan encouraged Dr Henry Mabie to start a similar college there. He did, but it only lasted a few years. Lucy, who had accompanied her father, stayed on at Minneapolis with the Mabies, and while he travelled, took on speaking engagements of her own at a number of women's colleges, founding many new branches of the Student Volunteer Movement.

The new wave Bible Schools attracted a fair amount of criticism in the press. Surely they could only detract from the first-rate theological education provided by the 'higher schools'. Gordon defended himself so well that he turned the attacks into free advertising which produced a burst of applications.

Henry Grattan also had a hand in the founding of the most important Bible School in the history of faith missions. In 1873 Moody had asked Emma Dryer to organise some follow-up to his missions. He promised to find her a house as soon as he returned from Great Britain six months later. But he was so successful in Britain that he stayed two years and forgot about his commission. Emma Dryer did not. In 1886 she tried to persuade Moody to let her extend the two-month summer courses she had set up into a full-blown college. It was another three years before Moody decided to buy a plot of land for a residential college, with money given to him by C. T. Studd for missionary work in India. He left Emma Dryer to sort out the practical arrangements of setting up the 'Bible Institute for Home and Foreign Missions of the Chicago Evangelisation Society'. Emma had spent some time at Mildmay in England and seen the work of Harley College. Discovering Henry Grattan Guinness was in the USA she invited him to come and give her the benefit of his wisdom. The new college was called the Moody Bible Institute.

It was an extremely fruitful year for Henry. His preaching ability returned in full force. Men like John R. Mott, a founding father of the World Council of Churches, would look back at his visit and say that to Henry Grattan Guinness he owed the inspiration for his own worldwide travels. In later years Henry Mabie wrote:

> I feel the deepest gratitude to God that I ever came into contact with this gifted man of God. His vision of things celestial seemed immediate; his wondrous eloquence on the platform at times overwhelmed me; a man richly endowed with impressive presence, with rare preaching gifts, capable of lofty flights in imagination, of great heart power and with a faith never daunted – he is an outstanding figure among the limited number of the spiritually sublime men that I have known. He seemed to me ever literally and almost visibly communing with God. He felt terribly the coldness and apathy of the Christian Church. He believed, and inspired me to believe, that if the Church would give itself to prayer in a more earnest way, and if men and women would not withhold their own children from personal service on the high places of the field, the Kingdom of God on earth might yet be

extended with a volume and power not hitherto dreamed of.

While Henry was away, Fanny remained quietly at Cliff, but it was not in her nature to be inactive. Whitfield, who went up to Caius College, Cambridge, known affectionately as 'stinks', to study medicine, wrote to Geraldine, 'Mother is writing another missionary book about the Upper Congo. How she does work! As far back as I can remember, it is always Mother writing away late at night, by the light of a green-shaded candle lamp. Darling Mother, may God keep her strong and well.'

Following a well-established pattern, Harry imposed his ever-expanding vision on Harley College, while Annie took care of its practical application. She gave birth to their first child, Annie Geraldine, known as Gene, in 1888, then John Frith Grattan in 1889, while administering a business which was rapidly expanding to include a soup kitchen, medical mission and dispensary, midwifery school, maternity hospital and children's home. When she returned home, Lucy joined them, taking over the Berger Hall Night School, but more importantly, producing a monthly magazine to keep supporters informed about the ever-increasing ramifications of their industry.

Literature was the only real means of communication on a widespread scale, a resource the Guinnesses tapped from 1874, when Henry Grattan took over as editor of the *Illustrated Missionary News*, a religious, quasi-geographic, popular version of the glossy, fashionable *Illustrated London News*. Full of anecdotes, stories, biographies and correspondence, with graphic illustrations, it had developed an interested, committed readership in the eight years of its existence. Henry felt it could achieve more. It was an opportunity to write some of his most stirring prose, to 'call out the unused gifts and resources of Christian men and women in these enlightened lands, on behalf of those who still sit in darkness and in the shadow of death'.[5]

Every month Fanny wrote a special report from the East London Training Institute. It grew to such an extent that by March 1877, the *Illustrated Missionary News* had become an insert. Even then space for Harley news was insufficient and in 1878 Fanny decided to begin her own magazine, *The Regions Beyond*, first as an 'occasional paper', then as a quarterly journal, and finally as a monthly magazine. Lucy became its editor in 1888.

In her hands *The Regions Beyond* progressed rapidly from being a means to touch the readers' hearts and purses into one of the foremost polemical journals of its day, with a circulation beyond her wildest dreams. Eugene Stock, editorial secretary of the Church Missionary Society, claimed, 'Lucy Guinness is the finest Christian editor by far in the British Isles. There is none like her.'[6] No social injustice escaped comment, be it the miners' strike which left thousands homeless 'under pitiless wintry skies', the fifty thousand unemployed in London alone, or the one hundred and fifty who died of alcohol poisoning every day. No one appeared to care. It was a miracle the working classes did not rise up and shake off the shackles of oppression. Comfortable England teetered on the brink of revolution unawares.

There is no doubt Lucy felt she was the only voice of protest. In pre-litigious, pre-libelous England she attacked whomsoever she chose, at will, often members of Her Majesty's government, 'full of loud futilities and arguments to prove the excellence of its system'. This was especially true in her campaign against the opium trade, spurred on by Geraldine's letters. Was it not enough that imperialist forces had bombarded a defenceless people till the gutters of Canton ran with blood, that we should now destroy the rest with an even deadlier weapon? Jesus-opium, the Chinese called it, because they inherited it from a Christian civilisation.

The government enquiry into the trade was a farce, Lucy declared. Lord Brassey KCB, the Chairman of the Commission, was the director of a company making enormous profits from the drug. Its parliamentary representative, Mr Robert Mowbray MP, had voted in favour of the traffic. Its Indian representative, the Maharajah of Darbhanga, had a large poppy-growing business. The Commission was doomed before it began its research, making Queen Victoria the greatest poison-seller in the world. One day, Lucy swore, Britain would pay the price for its murderous, indefensible behaviour in China.

In the early 1890s her words had the ring of truth. The Indian Mutiny, the Afghan War, the collapse of several building societies sweeping away £50 million of national wealth, the social unrest of the dockers' and miners' strikes, were a judgment on the nation. But even she had no idea how prophetic her words would be, or the disastrous consequences for her sister's fellow missionaries.

Inevitably, in all her polemical writings Lucy had one blind spot. She never criticised the British Government's handling of the Irish problem. The opium trade, the Arab slave trade in Africa flourishing under the noses of British gunboats, aroused her fury. But no cry for justice in Ireland ever came from her pen. Still, once alerted to most injustice, she researched carefully and attacked fearlessly, never ignoring the practical need on her own doorstep.

Under Lucy's supervision regular meals were now provided at the Berger Hall. She never did get used to the daily rush when she opened the doors. The men ate ravenously, having given any money they had to their wives and children. A meat pudding could effect a radical change: 'An altered look – a human look – comes over the men.'

There were few progressive firms like the Guinness Brewery in the East End of London. The provision of health care and midwifery became essential. A doctor's visit cost a shilling, the main part of a weekly wage. The London Hospital provided free medical help, but it was three miles away, too far for a mother with a sick child and no means of transport.

At two thirty every Tuesday and Thursday afternoon the doors of the Berger Hall opens to admit a stream of people, pushing and shoving their way up the stone stairs to get an early place in the queue. A Harley student is waiting to take their particulars and ensure that they really cannot contribute towards their treatment.

'What's your father's occupation?' he asks a young girl.

'A bricklayer.'

'Bricklayer or bricklayer's man?' asks the student, trying to assess the probable income.

'I couldn't say which, Sir. I never sees 'im lay the bricks!' The girl gets the coveted blue ticket which says, 'Patients must attend on Tuesdays at half past two o'clock, and bring a bottle and a galley pot.' The ticket entitles her father to see the doctor for two months for the sum of a penny. A white ticket would mean a charge of twopence. The small charge is a vain attempt to cover the costs of the vast quantities of medicine needing to be dispensed, about seven to eight gallons a surgery. The bottle and galley pot, carried by every prospective patient, are the means whereby the miracle cure is taken home.

By 2.45 the chapel, converted into a waiting room is packed to the doors. The people are still coming and there is half an hour before the doctor arrives. A student takes his place at the harmonium and leads half an hour's hymn singing. The deaconesses move among the female patients, sympathising with the elderly, offering child-care advice to young mothers and spiritual counsel wherever it is needed.

At 3.15 the doctor arrives and patient number one disappears inside the makeshift surgery. In three hours he sees between seventy five and a hundred patients. The most common complaints are arthritis, rheumatism, fevers, asthma and bronchitis, but often a more sinister disease, consumption or cancer, is present too.

It was an invaluable hands-on placement for Harley students. Under close supervision they also ran a dispensary, handling vast quantities of strychnine, prussic acid, arsenic and opium. The experience was a little frightening at first, but they recognised that as future missionaries they would be handing out such substances with little further training.

Known as 'them 'eternity nurses', deaconesses took three months to complete their midwifery training. Such was the wealth of their experience in that short time that all students passed the London Obstetrical Society's examination with little difficulty. Harley opened a maternity ward in 1890, and converted the Bromley Mission Hall into a nursing home in 1894. Most maternity and post-natal care predominantly involved visits to local homes. Of all Harley's work it was the most heart-rending. Women lay in indescribably filthy conditions, on beds of dirty rags with no blankets to cover them, in damp, freezing houses with no money for food or coal. Many were so malnourished or consumptive they produced a stillborn baby. Many more did not survive the birth themselves. The deaconesses could not bring themselves to take an orphaned baby to the workhouse, so Harley opened their first children's home in 1895, Annie's particular interest for many years.

The Harley Institute's commitment to London's poor was by no means unique. It was one of many Christian charitable organisations whose work was a striking feature of the East End in the 1880s and 1890s, forming part of its colour and character. Political socialists accused them of dealing with the symptoms rather than the disease itself, and they certainly lost a voice in government when Lord Shaftesbury died. But on the whole they believed that changing the individual was the only way to change the system. They did what they could, and if they were patronising at times, love covered the sin and earned them an abiding respect.

There were times, however, when aggressive political action became the only resort – as Harry was about to discover.

3.

In China Geraldine's grasp of the language did not improve, and after only a few weeks at Yang-chou, her tutors decided the only way she would ever learn to communicate was by living with the Chinese people themselves. She set off with three other women missionaries in a river boat down the Grand Imperial Canal to a mission station at Tsingkiangpu, scribbling down her impressions on the way. It was almost impossible to convey the sheer beauty of the scenery, the vast expanse of pale grey-blue water, fringed along the towpath with lush green trees, the wide, water-covered rice fields stretching as far as the eye could see, intersected into regular squares and strips by raised brown paths. As she described the wretched living conditions of the Chinese labourers her writing became less spontaneous, more reflective. She knew by now that Lucy was publishing her letters in the *Regions Beyond* magazine, but did not know that in pouring out her ever-increasing passion for China, she had embarked upon her life's work.

Raised on the concept of 'regions beyond', of treading where no missionary had ever trod before, Geraldine was not satisfied with staying at Tsingkiangpu where there were Chinese Christians already. She set her sights on an isolated town called Antung, persuading a Chinese man to arrange for her to stay on a farm. Reliable Lottie with her fluent Chinese agreed to accompany her. 'We're going to live in a real

Chinese home,' Geraldine wrote to Lucy with great excitement, 'and in all ways possible to conform to Chinese customs and manners. We thought we had better begin at once by taking into use Chinese chopsticks and dining in Chinese fashion.'

Reality soon dampened her enthusiasm. Antung was a mere twenty-five miles from Tsingkiangpu, but took ten hours by wheelbarrow. A Chinese wheelbarrow consisted of a large single wheel traversed by a horizontal crossbar with a seat on either side. Passengers clung on to their belongings while a coolie pushed for all he was worth. After ten minutes, let alone ten hours, Geraldine felt as if she would never sit down again. They stopped frequently at villages along the way. Crowds came out to gape and chatter, and demand treatment from the magical medical case.

Late in the evening they arrived at the farmhouse. To Geraldine's dismay, it was the dreariest, dirtiest house she had ever seen. Two brothers, their wives and children, lived in one large room, their sleeping quarters consisting of a corner of the room, partitioned off with a rough blue curtain. Geraldine and Lottie were shown to their own corner, where there was little more than one double bed. It was so dark they could see very little at first, but their sense of smell was not impaired. As their eyes became accustomed to the moonlight struggling through a tiny, barred window, they became aware that a small floor area at the foot of their filthy bed was the lavatory for all the women in the house.

The family was very anxious to please, but unnerved by such unusual company. Adults and children watched the two missionaries in absolute silence. They ate their first meal together, rice and hard-boiled eggs, and Lottie made one or two valiant attempts at conversation but eventually gave up. Several pairs of wide, searching eyes followed their every movement, even as they got ready for bed. Eventually Geraldine begged them to blow their candle out.

Despite the nausea caused by the stench and the filthy bedclothes, Lottie fell asleep. Geraldine waited until she heard the women retire, then balancing a lamp on Lottie's motionless form, wrote in her journal, 'A painful misgiving for a moment crosses my mind as to the advisability of prolonged residence in such a place!' Her misgivings proved correct. The following day she could not stop scratching. But neither woman was prepared to give up.

Their determination paid off. The fear of the strangers gradually subsided. Not only were they accepted in town, but were soon in demand for their medical help. Geraldine, whose medical knowledge was rudimentary, was forced to treat cases which would have tested the skills of a qualified physician. She learned Chinese quickly.

On 26 May, the anniversary of the sailing of the first missionaries to China, designated a special day of prayer by the China Inland Mission, Geraldine rose early and went to a barn where she could be alone. She rededicated her life to God, promising she would go anywhere, do anything he asked. The young woman who could not cope with six weeks at boarding school as a child, wondered if it might not be possible one day to go through the closed doors of Tibet, where no missionary had ever been allowed before.

As she remained on her knees, in the all-enveloping silence she gradually became aware of an inner voice, speaking quietly, but clearly nonetheless. 'Go anywhere, Geraldine? Do anything? Even marry Howard Taylor?' She was stunned. That was the last thing she wanted to hear. The very idea repelled her. But then, as she thought about it, she wondered whether in fact she was not in love with her own romantic notion of self-sacrificial missionary life. Marriage was not such a dreadful proposition. She had said 'anything' after all, and 'anything' it would be.

She shelved the prospect for the time being. There was little she could do about it. And anyway, there were few men whose pride would allow them to propose to the same woman twice. But she told Lottie that if he did, she would not be able to refuse him.

In the hot season the mission ordered her back to Yang-chou. Geraldine never found submission easy, but had to accept its wisdom as temperatures rose to over 106 degrees. A month later she boarded another river steamer, this time bound for a holiday on the P'o-yang Lake in the great province of Kiangsi. A number of Chinese passengers invited her to join their picnic on a little piece of carpet on the deck. It would have been rude to refuse, but Geraldine had not bargained for what followed:

Next came tea, of course politely offered, and I was nothing loathe to accept, but what was my surprise when the elder woman handed me the large teapot bodily, and seeing my momentary hesitation, went on to put the spout to my lips ... But they seemed so pleased when I drank it, and took the teapot myself to facilitate the process, that I really enjoyed it, in spite of the consciousness that we were being watched by at least a hundred curious eyes.

She later discovered that one of those pairs of eyes belonged to the Grand Duke Alexander of Russia, a dignified looking gentleman, and full cousin to the Tsar. Would she have acted as she did had she known, she asked herself, and then decided with satisfaction, that she would.

At Kiangsi, sitting on the shores of the lake, an announcement in *The Regions Beyond* caught her attention.

Dr Howard Taylor, MB, FRCS, has been assisting his father, the Revd J Hudson Taylor, in his present lecturing tour in the United States and Canada. We heartily congratulate both father and son on the entrance of the latter on that co-operation in the China Inland Mission for which he has been so long and so thoroughly preparing, and to which he so unhesitatingly devotes the superior talents, high qualifications and bright young energies which could easily raise him to eminence and fortune at home.

So, he was coming. What would it mean? She decided not to think about it.

As it happened, Howard's elder brother Herbert, his wife and two little boys were taking a few weeks leave at Lake P'o-yang too. They got on well together and Herbert invited her to accompany them to the province of Honan, well known as the 'unreached' centre of the Chinese empire, where fifteen million people were without access to medical, social or spiritual help of any kind. It was too good an opportunity to miss.

The journey in January 1890 across Honan to She-ki-shen, their ultimate destination, was the worse she had ever known. Snow made the roads virtually impassable. A bitter wind howled across the exposed fields, making a trip in a sedan chair an unutterably miserable experience, especially for Herbert's small children. No foreign woman had ever been to the region before, so whenever they stopped at an inn, Geraldine and Herbert's wife were besieged by crowds trying to catch a glimpse of their unbound feet. On one occasion the landlord begged them to leave, but not before scores of leering men had fingered them from top to toe to ensure they really were women and not men in disguise.

In She-ki-shen life was difficult. She was in constant demand for medical help. Mumps, measles and whooping cough often proved fatal. A crude, unskilled and painful version of acupuncture, which involved inserting a variety of long, red hot needles under the skin, was the most common treatment for any illness. Few babies survived the cure. Etiquette forbade women to leave the house at all. Geraldine was unable to visit the women in their homes. She felt she would go mad if she was locked up within four walls any longer and tried to venture out. But large crowds of men would gather around her, poking and prodding her, and jeering as she went. She resented having her liberty curtailed because she was a woman. But this was China, not Africa, not amenable to Western influence. The culture was strong and well established. She had no choice but to submit.

In those tense and difficult conditions an event occurred which would fill her with the most awful wretchedness she had ever known and haunt her for the rest of her life. Herbert Taylor's wife had given birth to a baby girl. It was not easy in their cramped living conditions, but a nurse from another station had managed to get to them in time and the delivery had gone well. Although the baby was strong and healthy, it had taken the mother a while to recover and this put an added strain on Geraldine. She ran the house, cared for the Taylor children and responded to many calls for medical help. Her eyes, once again very infected, were causing her a great deal of distress. When the baby became ill with dysentery it was almost the final straw. One night, at utter exhaustion point, Geraldine made a fatal mistake. She went to pour out a dose of medicine for the baby and in her haste, picked up the wrong bottle. The little one quickly lost consciousness and died.

It was the most appalling shock for everyone. A funeral was out of the question. Baby girls were of no value. Herbert Taylor carried his little daughter to a quiet spot in the Honan countryside and buried her there.

Geraldine was utterly devastated, all the more because Herbert and his wife refused to apportion any blame and bore her no ill will. She did not know where to turn for consolation and wrote to Hudson Taylor, telling him the full story, asking him whether it might not just be possible that his granddaughter had actually died of dysentery. Not a medical man himself, Hudson passed the letter on to Howard and asked him to reply.

The correspondence established a new intimacy between the two. Howard alone knew the guilty secret which gave her no respite day and night. There was no one else with whom she could share her despair. She had forgotten what a dear friend he had always been to her, how strong and sane, how she had always relied on his brotherly comfort in the past.

Some months later, when she went to Shanghai for treatment for her eyes, Howard was standing on the shore of the river waiting to meet her off the boat. One look at his face told her that his feelings had not altered with the passage of time. His attentions embarrassed her, but as he took over her medical care in his usual dignified, unobtrusive way, she was in no mood to resist. She was tired of being independent and brave. Besides, that kind of behaviour was responsible for leading her into a number of disastrous situations.

Howard prescribed treatment for her eyes and left almost at once for language school. As the only doctor in the area he was in great demand. Geraldine was not sure whether she felt relief or disappointment.

Meanwhile, without telling her sister, Lucy had illustrated and edited Geraldine's letters, publishing them in a book called *In the Far East*. A first print run of 5,000 sold out in weeks. It was translated into French and Swedish and the publicity about the effects of opium seriously embarrassed the British Government.

Geraldine described how on one occasion she was called to the bedside of a dying sixteen-year-old. She cradled the girl in her arms while two distressed little sisters, aged ten and eight, clung to her hand, and the mother smoked herself senseless in the next room. 'Heartsick and overwhelmed with grief and shame, I bowed my head beside that dying child. There swept over me an awful realisation of the part England has played in this devil's triumph – the heavy curse of my adopted people.'

Unwittingly Geraldine's vivid descriptions of China had two contradictory effects, on the one hand to raise indignation as she intended to do, on the other, to caricature the Chinese as slanty-eyed, sly and untrustworthy, which she never intended to do. With the intention of repairing some of the damage, Hudson Taylor asked her to write a history of the Mission. She agreed, reluctantly. The idea of being stuck in Shanghai and the discipline of writing was irksome. Still, she could see the value of it.

In May 1890 Howard came to see her before setting off for Honan. Before he left he asked her again to be his wife. She had sensed from the moment he arrived in Shanghai that it was inevitable and had dreaded the moment, never guessing how numb she would actually feel. She had thought that as she accepted his proposal, some emotion, a flicker of romantic love, if not the fire of grand passion, would be sparked in her heart. But she felt nothing.

Howard only heard the word yes and was overjoyed. He cabled home at once and both sets of parents were delighted with the news. Everyone was thrilled – except her. She had a huge panic attack, could not cope with any more congratulations and begged Howard to keep their engagement a secret. He was puzzled by her request but reluctantly agreed as he set off for Honan without her.

He had only just reached his destination when a letter arrived begging him to release her. She loved him as a sister, not a wife. She needed time. Would he continue writing to her as he always had, as a friend, not a fiancé? Howard was more pained than he had been in his entire life, but gave way. He loved her too much to force her into anything so obviously abhorrent. He would wait.

Fortunately, he had no means of knowing how long that wait would be. In March 1892 a cable arrived in Shanghai urging Geraldine to return home to England at once. Fanny had another stroke. This time it seemed it might be fatal.

4.

Throughout the 1890s, while the Grattan empire continued to expand in the East End, social concerns were also uppermost in Sir Edward Cecil's mind. Faced with widespread deprivation on every side, the Harley Institute could do little more than stick a plaster on a gaping wound. Sir Edward had the means to deal with the festering sore itself.

In 1890, although he remained on the Guinness Board as a trustee for his three sons, to mark his retirement from active management he invested a quarter of a million pounds in two trust funds. His utopian vision, extending way beyond initiatives for Brewery staff, was to provide thousands of decent homes for the labouring poor. In Dublin he had already demolished and rebuilt a slum around Bull Alley at a cost of £220,000. The scheme was now incorporated into the Iveagh Trust, to which he added a further £50,000. The Guinness Trust in London received £200,000 to finance a variety of imaginative housing projects. Low rents would ensure funds were replenished so that new homes could be built, and the living conditions of tenants improved, 'without placing them in a position of being the recipients of bounty'.

Encouragement seems to have come from his friend, Lord Rowton, who was impressed with the remarkable achievements of the Peabody Trust, but knew its efforts were a drop in a sea of squalor. Rowton had been Disraeli's private secretary and became a peer in 1880. His mother was Lord Shaftesbury's sister. Shaftesbury evidently realised that Guinnesses got things done.

The familiar Guinness buildings began to appear all over London and Dublin. By today's standards some may seem grim tenements, but in their day they were unique. Facilities for boiling water, community bathrooms and laundry rooms, sheds for costermongers' barrows and spacious yards where children could play in safety, made them a radical improvement on the tiny, back to back shacks they replaced. *The Times* called it 'the most splendid act of private munificence that had been contemplated and carried out in our time by any Englishman'.[7]

For his trouble, and possibly thanks to Rowton's influence, Sir Edward was made a baron. In opting for the name of Iveagh, he unleashed a barrage of unexpected publicity and controversy. Correspondents in *The Dublin Evening Telegraph* and several other leading national newspapers resented his appropriation of the hereditary title of the aristocratic Magennises of Iveagh. Edward stoutly maintained his right to do so by referring them to the work of the genealogist, Sir Bernard Burke. Burke had been employed by Edward's father, Sir Benjamin, when he was made a baronet. From 1814, when the Ulster Herald, Sir William Bethan, had granted Hosea's request to use the Magennis coat of arms, the family had done so with impunity. But Sir Benjamin realised the Guinness ancestry warranted closer inspection. Obligingly, with no more tangible evidence than Sir William Bethan, Burke confirmed the Magennis descent. The public remained unconvinced, but Edward, not surprisingly, was only too happy to abide by Burke's conclusion, and simply waited for the hullabaloo to die down. Whatever his past, he had established the family pedigree for the present.

Fascinated by the debate, Henry Seymour Guinness, eldest son of Henry Guinness of Burton Hall in Stillorgan, Director of the Dublin branch of Guinness Mahon, began a lifetime of detailed research into the family ancestry. His findings were inconclusive.[8]

Throughout the 1880s Ireland's only private bank and land agency had prospered quietly. Occasionally, in its discreet, almost obsequious way, Guinness Mahon had dealings with some of Ireland's well-known characters, among them the woman who had managed to do more damage to the Home Rule cause than any political activist. In 1891 Captain Willie O'Shea divorced his wife, Kitty, on the grounds of her adultery with Charles Stewart Parnell, leader of the Home Rule party. Parnell had broken the unspoken rule of discretion, scandalising the Irish people. Lucy Guinness's adolescent desire for vengeance was visited in full on the national hero. His party disowned him. Prime Minister Gladstone said he had put back any hope of Home Rule for years. He married Kitty, and died three months later, a destitute, broken man. Guinness Mahon were the receivers of the Byrne Estate in County Wicklow, where Parnell had debts of £50 for rent on quarries. No doubt Henry Guinness was aware of the sensitivities of the exercise, when the firm wrote to the poverty-stricken widow to ask whether she intended paying the rent or surrendering the quarries. Her response was not recorded.

The directors of Guinness Mahon, Henry in Dublin, and his brother Richard Seymour in London, kept their heads firmly ensconced in the family business. Richard still failed to keep account books, but they wrote to each other affectionately every day, and the two families met up for summer holidays at the Irish seaside. In many ways their lives were fairly pedestrian compared to their brewing and missionary cousins. There were no parliamentary careers, no clergymen, no great philanthropists or peers of the realm on the banking side of the family. Not yet, at least.

Edward Cecil, however, felt the time had come to find himself an English country seat, suitable for the earldom on which he had set his sights and accessible to the London set. When Elveden Hall in Suffolk came on to the market following the death of the Maharajah Duleep Singh, he recognised its potential and paid £159,000 for it at once.

Once owned by the Earl of Albermarle, the modest

Georgian manor house had been given to the Indian prince in compensation for the annexation of his territory by the British Army. With an unwarranted lack of gratitude, the Maharajah had been out of the country for some time inciting Sikh rebellion against the British Raj. The house, suffering from neglect, was long past its glory, and far too small for the Iveaghs' intentions. But a house was not Edward's priority. The estate was. There was stiff competition for royal patronage, and the 17,000 acres of scrubland were renowned as being one of the best shoots in England.

Buildings, as Dodo knew from a wealth of experience, could be transformed. With her usual panache, she set to work. Duleep Singh had tried to create an extravagant dwelling in the style of an Indian palace, but his sense of interior design appeared to have deserted him at crucial moments. The result was an unfortunate mix of pillared portico Italian Renaissance on the outside, and quasi-Asian temple on the inside. Using photographs from the India Museum, architect John Norton had been instructed to use the Shish Mahal, or Glass Palace, as his inspiration for the drawing-room where tiny slivers of mirror embedded in the plasterwork created a sparkling fantasy. Elaborate pillars and arches in the Mughal style dominated most of the main rooms. And the grand marble staircase with magnificent cast-iron bannisters had been painted a lurid scarlet. The overall effect was of a high-class brothel – not quite Dodo's sophisticated style.

Nonetheless, creatures of their age, the Iveaghs prided themselves in their exotic taste and were keen to preserve the oriental theme. Dodo had to acknowledge that Elveden's most outstanding feature was its sensational, round, snow-white marble ballroom, which took 150 workmen four years to build. An attempt to recreate the Taj Mahal in miniature, it was constructed between 1870 and 1874 around twenty-eight, intricately hand-carved pillars, supporting three levels of galleries, and crowned with a massive copper dome. Dodo ingeniously used the room as the focal point of her new, extended country residence, by building an exact replica of Duleep's mansion on its other side, so that it formed the link between the two, a dramatic 'great assembly hall' with a massive real fire on either side.

The one-hundred-room stately home, with en suite guest facilities, marble baths and solid silver taps, was sumptuously furnished with exquisite tapestries, Chippendale mirrors and oriental rugs. With more than a thousand servants waiting on a brand new servants' wing was needed, connected to the house by a series of passageways. Seventy men were employed in the game department alone. A houseparty of thirty guests would require at least as many household servants, and accommodation for maids accompanying their mistresses.

It was not an easy life for domestic staff. They worked long hours, rising before dawn to clean out the grates and re-lay the coal in the huge Renaissance-style fireplaces dominating the state and drawing rooms. And it was little consolation that the fireplaces were for show. The Iveaghs had installed central heating. At 8.30 in the morning every household member, staff and guest alike, was expected to assemble in the Cedar Room on the ground floor, where Edward Cecil conducted family prayers. They worked all day, and sometimes, during a shoot, it might be 11 p.m. before the maids finally fell into bed. Nonetheless, watching the guests in their finery, their jewels glittering in the firelight as they danced on the mirror-smooth sprung floor to the best orchestras of the day seemed like the stuff of a fairy story. Some could not help but peep through the balustrades of the upstairs galleries, though the penalty for being found out was instant dismissal.[9]

To be fair to the Iveaghs, true to their class, they were largely unaware of life below stairs, and did their best to treat their staff courteously and with respect. Another of Edward Cecil's pithy little sayings was, 'It costs nothing to be polite'. It also cost him little to be generous. While he feathered his own extensive nest he did not neglect theirs and rebuilt Elveden village.

From the outside, the brand new stables erected in the parkland for horse and carriage looked almost as grand as the house itself. Within a few years the invention of the motor car made them largely redundant. Sir Edward was a keen automobilist.

The effort and energy, not to mention the finance, invested in redesigning Elveden paid off, heralding a truly golden era. The Prince of Wales was a regular visitor even after he became Edward VII. So was his son, the Duke of York. The future George V appreciated the facilities more than his father. He at least was a genuine crack shot, whereas his father did not appear to take any interest in the proceedings until lunchtime and the appearance of the ladies.[10] 'The royal suite at Elveden, decorated in coral and green, was the last word in luxury, surpassing any comparable accommodation in the other great mansions honoured by the British monarchs.'[11] Half the peers of the realm were regular Elveden guests. So were the foremost politicians, including the future foreign secretary A. J. Balfour.

Shooting parties usually lasted from Monday to Friday and had their own elaborate, clockwork ritual. Guests descended at Thetford Station from a pre-arranged London train, with servants, trunks and innumerable round black hat boxes. No lady travelled without her 'dress basket', a large wicker receptacle covered in a shiny black fabric, containing her five morning, five tea and five evening dresses. Under no circumstances could she ever wear the same dress twice. Waiting to transport the entire party the three miles back to the house would be a well-organised procession of carriages, brakes, dog-carts and traps. This was a little different from travelling across China in a wheelbarrow, belongings piled high on your lap.

The Prince of Wales and Duke of York were met by a carriage with postilions and a guard of honour supplied by the

Lord Suffolk Hussars. In time, Sir Edward tried to persuade them to use his new motorised toy, but the Prince of Wales never trusted the new-fangled invention and always insisted a second car travel behind in case they broke down on the way.

Every day a luncheon party of non-shooting guests and ladies would leave the house to join the shooters at tents pitched in different parts of the grounds, where boarded floors had been laid, and a magnificent banquet served on best china plates from covered tables decorated with flowers. In the afternoon guests would congregate for tea around the large fireplaces in the round, dazzling white marble room, the ladies in their elegant tea dresses, the men in their tweeds, just back from the shoot. Later, they would gather again in full evening dress to await the formal procession into the dining-room, with its magnificent tapestries and Louis XIV furnishings.

On 14 November 1895, Augustus Hare recorded his own impressions of an Elveden house party. It was lavish, even by his standards.

I floated here in the luxurious saloon carriage of a special train, but felt rather shy, because, whereas all the rest of the party were on terms of Christian name intimacy, I knew none of them except Lord Rowton ... But I was interested to see those who are so frequently part of the royal circle; and liked them all, especially Lord and Lady Carrington; but then, everyone does.

I wonder if you know this house of Elveden? It was Duleep Singh's and he tried to make it like an Indian Palace inside. Much of his decoration still remains, and the delicate white stucco work has a pretty effect when mingled with groups of tall palms and flowering plants. Otherwise, the house (with the kindest of hosts) is almost appallingly luxurious, such masses of orchids, electric light everywhere etc. However, a set-off the other way is an electric piano which goes on pounding away by itself with a pertinacity which is perfectly distracting. In the evenings singing men and dancing women are brought down from London, and are supposed to enliven the royal guest.

Hare had joined the party with the express intention of meeting the Duke and Duchess of York, but to his disappointment the Duke was alone, the Duchess awaiting 'an impending event'. The Duke appeared a 'very unaffected and pleasant' man, good-looking and punctual, which Hare ascribed to his naval training. But he could not help but observe that it must be very boring to be a prince. There was no real discussion in his presence, no one dared to contradict him.

Throughout their lives the Edward Cecil Guinnesses remained a paradox. Everyone agreed that despite their public face, the couple were actually rather reserved. Dodo's extravagance never stretched to her wardrobe. The *Tatler* described her as having, 'an incongruously puritanical appearance', and could only put it down to 'a severe smartness and a proud reserve which can only be equalled by that of our typical grande dame, the Duchess of Buccleugh'.[12] In other words, she thought herself so important she did not need to dress to impress. In fact, she did not particularly enjoy dressing up. Showing off a room was one thing, showing off oneself was another. Dodo had a penny-pinching childhood, Edward's was evangelical. Childhood ghosts were never fully exorcised by lavish spending and haunted them all the same. 'Your parties, if dull, are reckoned to be the most exclusive in London,' conceded the *Tatler*, mastering the art of the polite put-down. The Iveaghs were at heart an old-fashioned pair, wedded to traditional values and deeply conservative. Dodo never invited anyone to a ball if they had not been introduced.

Their lifestyle, away from the social glare, was fairly simple.

Sir Edward enjoyed the company of Mr Blundell, the Rector of Elveden, whose fiery sermons were known to reduce the congregation to tears. He had built the rectory, initially within Elveden grounds. But Blundell's predecessor had been caught snooping through the ground floor windows of the Hall. Sir Edward could not tolerate any invasion of his privacy and built a new one just outside the gates.

His sudden incursion into the art market between the years of 1887 and 1891 was typically anonymous. But two hundred choice paintings by artists such as Rembrandt, Millais, Vermeer, Gainsborough, Turner, Watteau, Vandyke and Canaletto could not disappear for long without someone discovering their destination. One or two claimed it was undertaken with a Philistine rather than aesthetic purpose, but younger family members remembered the quiet, obvious pleasure in Edward Cecil's face as he took them to see his treasures. Later, the paintings were housed at Kenwood and bequeathed to the nation, so that the public could share in his enjoyment. In fact, Sir Edward had the perspicacity to see that in warding off millionaire American competition, he would effectively preserve a collection of priceless art for the British nation.

Chapter 10

1890–1902
Dangerous Adventures Overseas

1.

In 1891 Harry sailed for the Congo. Pregnant with their third child, Annie was in no doubt about the dangers he faced, but even had she the will, there was no way she could have persuaded him against it.

The idea had slowly taken root in his mind from a seed planted three years earlier by ex-Harley student John McKittrick, who had come back from the Congo bursting with tales of horror and barbarism. McKittrick was a genial, enthusiastic Irishman from Belfast. He and Harry had been friends for years. Each was as intrepid and impetuous as the other, and their relationship had been cemented that summer when McKittrick became engaged to Dora Fookes, Harry's cousin, lately returned from Damascus.

McKittrick had spent four years with the Livingstone Inland Mission at its furthest outpost on the Equator, but that had become an increasingly frustrating exercise. The American Baptist Missionary Union had none of Fanny's pioneering drive. The missionaries settled in the lower cataract region with little intention of forging forwards into the unexplored upper Congo. McKittrick balked at such short-sightedness and shortly before his leave, asked if he could go on an exploratory journey up river by canoe to the vast horseshoe bend between Equatorville and the Stanley Falls. This area was called the Lulonga region, home of the Balolo people, rumoured to be one of the most savage and blood-thirsty in Africa. What McKittrick actually saw there made the hairs on the back of his neck stand on end. This was undoubtedly where God wanted him to be.

He knew no one would believe his stories unless they were verified first-hand, and brought a native boy called Bompole back to Britain with him. Listening to Bompole's plea for the white man to come and help his people, Harry became convinced that to support McKittrick in this new venture, Harley College should once again act as a base for pioneering missionary work and in 1889 set up the Congo and Balolo Mission, today the Regions Beyond Missionary Union.

The years 1889 and 1990 were key years for Western involvement in Africa. Stanley published *In Darkest Africa.* The British South African Company was established in Rhodesia. The Church Missionary Society sent an expedition to the unexplored Sudan region. And a national conference of the great powers at Brussels, convened by Lord Salisbury, looked at ways of curbing the slave traffic. The sale of alcohol, guns and gunpowder was banned, a triumph for Lucy, who had been conducting one of her campaigns. In many ways it was too late. The exploiter and the defender of the exploited were already locked in a race against each other, irresistibly drawn by the magnetic powers of that mysterious but deadly continent.

John McKittrick married Dora Fookes in February 1889 and they left for the Congo with a team of six other Harley students two months later. Dora sent Harry a detailed account of their arduous journey, made for the most part on foot. Sudden violent storms turned gentle tributary rivers into virtually impassable torrents, a hazard for the ladies in their respectable Victorian skirts, which clung limply around those potentially provocative ankles. The heat was unbearable, especially in a long-sleeved blouse, buttoned to the neck. Yet despite the discomfort, Dora was dazzled. Africa wove its spell around her. It was more beautiful than she could have ever imagined. Immense flowering shrubs, a riot of colour, wafted their incredible perfume down-river on the breeze, long before the sight of them took her breath away.

Once on board the *Henry Reed,* steaming from Stanley Pool into Lulonga territory, Dora's letters took on a darker tone. 'Every prospect pleases, and only man is vile.' The words of the hymn were the only way she knew to express the horror she felt at the sight of a naked corpse floating down-river, its hands and feet bound to a stake. This was the work of the slavers. Hours later she saw them in broad daylight, their canoes laden with their terrible human booty.

The party could not land at Lulonga as the river bank was lined with hostile natives, armed with knives and spears, ready for the next invasion of slave traders. McKittrick told them to anchor midstream and tried to make friendly overtures, until the jungle drums telegraphed a message of peace at last, and they knew it was safe to go ashore.

The venture was in fact highly successful. The missionaries quickly earned a reputation for peace and fair play, and established four stations in three years, at Boginda, Ikau, Lulonga, and Bogandanga – an impressive record which masked the toll on their emotional health. Dora McKittrick soon discovered that Bompole's account of the cruelty of his people had been a pale reflection of the gruesome truth. Victims of tribal warfare, or even simply tribal customs, would be strung up, their arms and legs broken, and left to die. Human blood sports were a favourite preocupation for this cannibalistic tribe. Knife-throwing, using a human target, throat-slitting, and feeding each other to the crocodiles were commonplace activities. Legs, arms, hands, boiling in a pot or dry roasted were great delicacies. The macabre reality of life in Lulongaland tore Dora's nerves to shreds. Reading her letters, Harry knew it. That was why he finally decided to go and see for himself. How could the secretary of the Congo Mission represent the missionaries, or support them adequately while he stayed in the safety of his own home?

There was another good reason for the trip. In 1890 a young Congo Christian by the name of Mandombi arrived at Harley College suffering from sleeping sickness. He had made the long journey at his own expense in the hope that English doctors might find a cure for a condition which radically diminished the quality of life of his people. Harry never could resist a challenge and having recently completed his MD in tropical medicine, decided to conduct his own research – in the Congo itself.

Annie accompanied him part of the way, then took their children to Tasmania to visit her mother, while Harry went on to Boginda to meet up with the McKittricks. He and John began to prepare for two exploratory journeys almost once, one north and one south, as a feasibility study into the setting up of new mission stations. The north was inhabited by the fierce N'gombe tribe, given to a particularly nasty form of cannibalism. They would go there first, double back, pick up Dora and continue south. But nothing turned out as they planned.

They set off in good heart, Harry with his treasured tripod and large box camera with heavy metal plates. The art of photography, still in its infancy, was an invaluable means of arousing interest in audiences at home. It was also one of his favourite hobbies. They carried guns as a protection against wild animals, never to be used on human beings – not even in self-defence.

Initially, the beauty and tranquillity of his surroundings lulled Harry into a false sense of security. He began to wonder whether some of the tales he had heard were not a little exaggerated. One evening however, putting in to the shelter of a wood, they came upon the burnt-out ruins of a village recently raided by the N'gombe. Harry was confronted with the sight of a decapitated, frightfully mutilated corpse of a young boy. That first experience was always the worst. He managed to overcome his nausea enough to take a few photographs. Anyone at home who doubted his account would be forced to see what he had seen.

On 22 August 1891, they arrived at a village called Bosi Dikolo. The natives were extremely friendly and delighted in very close contact. They ushered the white men into their meeting place, a low-roofed contraption supported by a few posts, and kept pressing in on them until the perspiration poured down Harry's face. A 'palaver' was duly called for the following morning.

It began with the presentation of the ritual goodwill offering, a 'dash' of plantains, fowls and a goat. The chief's first minister then expressed the hope that the white men would act as arbitrators in their dispute with a neighbouring N'gombe village, Bongwonga. Bateko, Harry's interpreter, said they would be delighted to try and re-establish peace between the two villages but would not accept the goat until they had succeeded. He then offered their dash to the chief – two tin plates, two tin spoons, some blue beads, cowrie shells and two pieces of cloth, and set off for Bongwonga.

Harry, naïvely, expected a similar warm welcome there, but the natives thought they were representatives of the Belgian State authorities and prepared to defend themselves. A heavy, flesh-creeping silence greeted their arrival. The terrifying experience which followed would haunt Harry for years to come.

When we reached the enclosure we found the gate shut and before we could mount a little ant-hill to gain a view of the interior, we heard the unmistakable war-cry within!

McKittrick leapt on to the roof of a house, and shouted out that we were come on a peaceful errand, whilst a number of us passed through an open space that separated the house, into a kind of wide street, three hundred yards long. The moment I could take in the situation I saw it was one of critical danger. A scout had evidently warned them of our advent; the women had fled to the wood, and the men, painted in hideous guise for the battle, and armed with spears and shields, presented a horrible spectacle.

Leaving the rest of their party well behind, Harry and McKittrick walked slowly towards the 'dancing demons', completely unarmed. Then they simply sat down on the ground and waited. The natives, disarmed by such unusual behaviour, gradually stopped their war cry and went to inspect the men, still holding tightly on to their spears, waved within a centimetre of Harry's nose.

Bateko shouted, 'See, I am unarmed, I come for peace, not war', whilst an old N'gombe man they had brought with them jumped repeatedly backwards and forwards over his spear, a sign of friendliness. He then took some leaves and stuck them to its point, a way of saying, 'May I be killed with this spear if we do not keep the peace.' At that moment a bright execution knife flashed in the sun very near the old man's head, and Harry was convinced he was dead. But the slightest move would mean certain death for the rest of the party, so he remained absolutely still, 'composed and fearless, thank God'.

The old man was unharmed, but it was another tense half hour before some of the warriors were prepared to shake hands.

We established ourselves in a little house and lunched as well as might be expected under the circumstances. Towards the close of the meal one of their most prominent men, a powerfully built fellow, with cicatrices the size of a calabar-bean in front of and below each ear, yelled out at the top of his voice, 'They love me! Come here. Come here', and by degrees a good many gathered round us and we did a pretty brisk trade in purchasing fowl and eggs.

Just when they thought the crisis was over and began to let down their guard, the natives suddenly sprang back into line and began brandishing their spears all over again. There was nothing for it. Harry and McKittrick took their chairs and sat down outside in the middle of the path as before. 'It was a trying time, far more than I can tell, or you understand. A cruel death threatened us at every instant.'

Finally, the old N'gombe man from Bosi Dikolo managed to convince the natives they meant no harm, and a big palaver to discuss peace proposals was promised for the following day. The old man would sleep in the chief's tent that night as a sign of goodwill.

As darkness fell Harry began to shiver. He had developed a fever and only wanted to sleep. McKittrick, sensing all was not well, spent a tense night beside the camp fire, jumping at the slightest sound. Suddenly, at five in the morning the old N'gombe man appeared waving his arms frantically. The natives were coming to kill them all. They must flee.

They escaped into the forest, the enemy in hot pursuit. McKittrick fired into the air to frighten them, but Harry was so weak he could hardly hold his rifle. On and on they ran, McKittrick dragging Harry along, until at last, Bosi Dikolo came into sight and they knew they were safe. Their ordeal was over, but for the two villages it had barely begun.

One of their men who found his way back to Bosi Dikolo some time later, aroused such fury with his account of what happened that the villagers went out and killed sixteen Bongwonga hunters in revenge, carried off their heads and ate them. So much for negotiating peace terms. Harry's expedition had been a disaster, all the more so when news of the killings reached the state authorities. Officer Peters had his own solution to the native problem. He took a party of his men to Bongwonga and thirty-four N'gombe died at the muzzle of a gun. Superiority belonged to he who wielded the magic weapon.

Harry gave up any idea of a second journey. He was suffering from recurrent bouts of fever. The tribes in the south were at war and he had learned his lesson. Diplomacy could be a dangerous game. Instead, he stayed at Boginda where Dora, who had learned the language from Bompole, had started a simple school.

In November the three decided to take a fun trip down-river, to try out the SS *Pioneer*, a brand new gift from the Irish YMCA. John McKittrick took a boyish delight in captaining the steamer. As they set off he was brimming over with life, full of his usual Irish banter, but to Dora and Harry's profound shock, he was struck down overnight by the sinister blackwater fever. It gave no warning, but rendered its victims completely helpless, mercilessly destroying their red blood corpuscles in hours. No one knew its cause, or its cure.

By the time Dora got her husband home to Boginda the fever had abated and he seemed a little better, though he was by no means himself. He was prey to sudden, inexplicable terrors and would not let her out of his sight. He repeatedly got up and tried to get dressed but was too weak to pick up his clothes. Two days later Dora noticed a sudden change, and in a panic, ran to find Harry. One look at the comatose figure on the bed confirmed Harry's worst fears. He fell to his knees, took McKittrick's hand and whispered, 'Be with our brother in the hour of his death.' Only then did Dora fully comprehend what was happening. She was utterly devastated. 'Africa kills all her lovers,' one of the missionaries wrote home to England. Few had loved Africa as much as John McKittrick.

Harry stayed on to baptise the first five Balolo converts, then set off for home, taking Dora with him, and another Harley missionary, called Luff. All three went down with blackwater fever. Dora lingered on the point of death for days, but finally rallied. On 29 January 1892, the family in England were shocked to receive a telegram which read, 'John McKittrick died November 22nd. Luff died December 19th. Dora and self returning.'

A month later, when Fanny had a second stroke and her life hung in the balance, they were relieved to know Harry was on the way home. By the time he arrived it was evident Fanny would live, though whether that was a blessing none would ever be able to say. She regained some of her speech, but half of her body was paralysed and useless.

Harry was too ill to be much of a comfort, or to enjoy his new son, Henry Reed Guinness, whom he saw for the first time, or even enter into the family reunion with Geraldine back from China, Annie from Tasmania, and Lucy from the United States. But he did send off a detailed report on sleeping sickness to Dr Patrick Manson. Manson wrote to tell Fanny that her son's research was invaluable. Had he not come back alive, his journey would not have been in vain.

2.

News had travelled and when Geraldine first arrived home her night-class students bombarded her with questions about her intended. Was he handsome? Was he kind? All they could get out of her was, 'You would love him.'

'You'd be jealous if we did, Miss,' Matilda replied, and the girls shrieked with laughter. Not a flicker of a smile crossed Geraldine's face. Her relationship with Howard was far too serious a matter.

She travelled extensively, researching her history of the

China Inland Mission, and was in England long enough to witness the book's immense success. Full of sentimental deathbed scenes, it cloys by contemporary standards. But the Victorians loved it. And the self-sacrifice of the early missionaries was undeniable.

Geraldine was never entirely sure at what precise moment, during those two years apart, she knew she had fallen in love with Howard Taylor. She only knew she wanted to marry him the moment she arrived back in China. Leaving Fanny at Cliff in the capable hands of adopted daughter, Leila Dennison, was a terrible wrench. It pained her beyond measure to see her fine, active, competent mother reduced to a dependent, twilight existence. Her father's distress was almost more than she could bear. But had she stayed it would have upset them even more. At least Fanny had the satisfaction of watching her children live out her dreams. Harry was fit again and his family continued to expand. Lucy was in demand as a speaker, particularly at the large holiness conventions in Keswick. Whitfield was a doctor at the London Hospital, gaining practical experience before he too left for China.

In April 1894 Geraldine docked at Shanghai. Howard was waiting for her on the quay, as he had done so many times before. But this time she allowed their eyes to meet and walked off the boat shyly towards him. He ached to touch her hand, to take her in his arms, but Chinese propriety did not permit it. He had loved her since she had opened the door to him nearly twenty years earlier, a gawky twelve-year-old in pinafore and pigtails. Seven years had passed since he had first proposed. He had waited almost all his life for this moment. And all he could do was stand and look at her. But his expression said it all.

They were married in traditional Chinese costume on 24 April by Bishop Cassels in a crowded, flower-filled Shanghai Cathedral. Geraldine's dress was pale grey as white was a sign of mourning in China. Her two bridesmaids were in mauve

302

silk and had real flowers in their hair. As she walked down the red-carpeted aisle the organ played Mendelssohn's setting of 'Oh, rest in the Lord, wait patiently for him, and he shall give thee thy heart's desires'. The words from Psalm 37 had sustained Howard through some of the darkest moments when he was tempted to doubt that this day would ever come.

The honeymoon was a three-week trip by houseboat up the Imperial Grand Canal. Friends had the forethought to convert the cabin of a fairly basic junk into an attractive, cosy little nest, draped in red cloth. When they pulled the cloth back they discovered huge cracks in the woodwork separating the cabin from the boatmen's living quarters, large enough for several pairs of prying eyes. But the curtain did give them a certain sense of seclusion, and other wedding presents, a lamp and a miniature tea-set laid out on the table, made Geraldine feel as if she were playing at married life. The canal banks were a mass of spring flowers. It was an idyllic time as far as Howard was concerned, making up for the many lost years and over far too soon.

Back in Shanghai they were quickly catapulted into a major crisis. Howard discovered his parents had just left in a very agitated state. Fifty Scandinavian associates of the Mission were threatening to resign over Chinese allegations of improper behaviour and Hudson Taylor had set off on a long cross-country journey to try and help them come to terms with the culture. Howard and Geraldine chased after them. The Taylors were too old for such a punitive expedition. Their health would not stand up to it. But when they finally caught up with them, Hudson refused to change his mind. Neither his sense of responsibility nor his determination had diminished with age. Howard realised that if he could not stop them, he had no alternative but to join them.

In eleven days the four travelled over twelve hundred and eighty miles, mainly by wheelbarrow. On the twelfth day they arrived at such a steep hill that Geraldine was determined the coolies would not push her. To their utter astonishment she and Howard leapt out and chased each other to the top of the hill, where for a few moments of glorious abandon, they threw off the shackles of an alien culture, ran around laughing together, revelling in the exhilarating view, the softness of the air and the sweet scent of the wild flowers. Just as suddenly, the moment was over. They collected themselves and stiffly, with great dignity, walked side by side, a proper distance apart, back to the wheelbarrow. 'Oh, China, China,' lamented Geraldine, 'We could not stand near together, or sit down side by side to enjoy the beauty and the stillness . . . Was there ever such a country for a wedding tour?'

The inns were not quite up to Geraldine's standards of hygiene, but she had taught herself to cope – or so she thought – until the day the landlord sprinkled sugar all over her rice balls with a pair of the filthiest fingers she had ever seen.

'Oh Howard,' she whispered, 'I can't eat it now.'

'Don't tell him they're dirty,' Howard whispered back cheerfully. 'No doubt he thinks they're much cleaner than most people's and quite fit for use as sugar tongs.'

Geraldine looked up at her landlord doubtfully and this time caught him licking the offending fingers with relish. The look on her face doubled Howard up with laughter. No wonder Hudson Taylor had nick-named him 'The Lifeboat'. His son was unsinkable.

Howard's indomitable spirit kept them all going through the weeks of torrential rain, continual drenchings, and impassable flooding. Howard was her inner strength in the awful aftermath of her first miscarriage. Geraldine would only have one more chance of motherhood, and again, the bumpy roads, continual joltings and miserable conditions of barrow travel brought about the sudden, heart-breaking termination of her pregnancy. For the remainder of her child-bearing years she would have bouts of longing for the two children she never bore, until the day when unforeseen, unwelcome circumstances gave her the joy she thought would never be hers.

By the summer Hudson Taylor had successfully completed his mission and was ready to return home. By day the temperature rose to an unbearable 140 degrees and the coolies were almost dead on their feet. Night travel was only a little easier, for they were at risk from brigands and from wolves, whose darting, flashing, yellow eyes and continual howling rubbed Geraldine's nerves raw.

One night, on a forsaken country road, two mysterious gentlemen suddenly materialised out of the shadows. Tense and watchful already, Geraldine nearly died of fright. But one was Mr Hoste, a missionary, and the other, the legendary Pastor Hsi, come to escort them safely to the next town.

Pastor Hsi, whose story Geraldine would write, was one of the foremost leaders of the indigenous Chinese Church, at great personal cost. Given a growing mistrust of the imperialistic foreigner, the missionaries had long since recognised the importance of handing over their work to the indigenous Chinese as quickly as possible. 'We have to be most particular not to give anything to the Christians or enquirers which would attach them to us,' Geraldine explained. She loved Pastor Hsi like a father from the moment she met him.

Mr Hoste had an ulterior motive for coming to meet them. In a country where a man was not allowed to look at a well-bred woman, let alone speak to her, he needed them to propose to Taylor's niece, Gertie Broomhall, on his behalf. Geraldine thoroughly enjoyed acting as a go-between in a real live romance, and fortunately, Hoste was accepted. The couple joined the party so that they could be married in Shanghai as soon as possible.

Gertie only just survived to see her wedding day. As a little luxury the two younger women travelled for part of the journey in an enclosed mule-cart. All was well until they came to a ford that was considerably deeper than anticipated. The mules panicked and broke free, leaving a horrified Gertie and

Geraldine trapped inside the litter floating rapidly down-stream. The more they struggled the more the litter sank. Hoste and Howard dived in and swam after them. Hoste finally managed to force open a door, lift his fiancée out and carry her to safety. By that time it had sunk too far for Howard to reach Geraldine. The muleteers arrived back in the nick of time, hauling her to shore with ropes. It left her badly shaken.

She and Howard came to the end of their journey with little regret, left their parents in Shanghai and set off almost at once. Howard was anxious to return to Honan where he was the only doctor in a province the size of England and Wales combined, with a population of thirty-five million people. He had decided they would settle in the ancient prefectural town of Cheng-chou. By tradition the people were so set in their ways that the philosopher Confucius had been unable to cope with their rigidity. No missionaries had ever lived there before.

Howard went on ahead to find suitable rented accommoda-tion, and rushed back to tell her he had found a perfect home, the walls freshly covered in mud, the windows newly papered. Geraldine was in her element – until she saw the dirty little cart-inn with four rooms, a dilapidated roof that leaked and a dark, prison-like courtyard enclosed on all sides by high walls. Still, she had to agree with the irrepressible Howard that after the accommodation of their recent travels, this was luxury.

She worked hard to make it home and it soon became a refuge, not so much for them as for the masses who flocked to Howard day and night to make them well, and for a motley assortment of stray animals. One day a little dog slunk into the courtyard, had a good look round, then curled up in a sunny corner and went to sleep. After that he came every day. He was a nervous, cowering creature at first, but gradually his tail came out from between his legs and curled right over his back. He would run to greet Geraldine wagging it furiously and she rejoiced in his new confidence. In a strange way he seemed to symbolise all her dreams for the Chinese women, subjugated by the expectations of their culture.

One day, however, he crept in quietly in a desperate state. Some boys had doused him in scalding water. Shivering and moaning, he dragged himself to the only place where he had known peace and security, and in his own sunny corner, lay down to die. Geraldine wept bitterly for her faithful little friend.

Though he was a warm, open man, Howard was often puzzled by his wife's emotionalism. Their relationship was never straightforward, but the unnatural environment of Cheng-chou did not help. They were completely dependent on each other, intellectually, emotionally and spiritually, and they were very different. Geraldine was excitable and impulsive. Howard was more rational and sensible. She was given to great swings of mood. He was steady and even. If her impetuosity bewildered him, his slow methodical reasoning grated on her.

Geraldine had always had her doubts about the advantages of marriage for a woman. Even Howard's calm consideration, his concern for her well-being, began to cramp her style, curb her freedom, curtail her independence. It was all too stifling. But there was nowhere to escape and no one to alter the dynamics. Gradually it occurred to her that she still had a choice. She could let the relationship asphyxiate her, or submit to the discipline of sharing her life with another person. She would never change him, and, after all, he had by far the nicer temperament, so she forced herself, through gritted teeth at first, to harness her wilfulness and give way as generously as she knew how. And in time, over many years, they learned to complement each other. But Geraldine never found it easy.

Though their main base was at Cheng-chou, they also hired rooms at Kai-feng, gravitating between the two, and leaving the smaller station in the hands of two missionary women, Ruth Brook and Mary Hodgson, when they were away. At Kai-feng they experienced their worst trauma in China, a taste of the horrors to come to that turbulent empire.

There had been one of the worst droughts for years. Poverty and destitution were driving the people to despair. A Buddhist nun, jealous of the missionaries' popularity, spread the rumour that they had large sums of relief money to give away and every person who called at their house would receive a generous handout.

Barrows, carts, crowds began to arrive, demanding money they thought was theirs by right. Howard and Geraldine spent the day apologising, explaining politely that there had been a mistake. The disappointed crowds dispersed, but their disgruntlement lingered on, and rumour and suspicion slowly fanned ill-feeling to a flame.

The single women were upstairs, Howard in the courtyard treating patients, and Geraldine in the guest-hall when a large mob arrived, howling for revenge, smashing and looting everything in their path as they made their way through the house. Mary Hodgson managed to slip away into a neighbour's property, but Ruth Brook was beaten and her clothes violently stripped off her back. Geraldine ran to her help, but a woman hacked at her with a hoe and split her head open. As the blood poured down her face and neck, she stood, waiting for the next blow, marvelling at her own sense of calm, when her attackers suddenly froze. An impressive Chinese gentleman Geraldine had never seen before had taken command of the situation. His presence had a sobering effect on the mob.

'My name is Wang,' he said to her, as he pushed his way to the front.

'I hope, sir, that you will stay with us until help comes,' Geraldine whispered, taking a quick look at her deliverer, which was improper conduct for a woman. But then, with her clothes hanging off her back, her hair trailing over her shoulders and blood smeared on her face, she was not in any position to worry about propriety. She was however desperately worried about what the attackers had done to Howard.

'I will not leave you,' Mr Wang replied reassuringly.

True to his word, he waited until the Mandarin arrived with his men. Most of the mob fled at the sound of the Mandarin's arrival, but he managed to catch four of the perpetrators, and taking two in each hand, shook them until their teeth rattled. Twenty-four were placed under arrest. He was a fine young Manchu, very zealous about enforcing law and order, apologetic about their ordeal.

Geraldine found Howard tied to a post in the courtyard. The Mandarin's arrival had only just saved him from being stoned to death.

That evening they bathed their wounds, sorted out the dereliction of their home and ate the hot meal delivered by the Mandarin's servants. The following morning fresh clothes and a cart and mules arrived, so that they could travel back to Cheng-chou in comfort.

A month later they were invited back to Kai-feng and received with full civic honours, bands, banners and a triumphal procession worthy of royalty. At the city gate they passed the twenty-four prisoners kneeling in chains by the roadside, awaiting their sentence.

Howard went straight to the Mandarin's residence and begged for their release. The young man was immensely disappointed. This was a great moment. He intended making an example of the culprits and told Howard he would grant him any other request he pleased. Howard insisted he had no other request and finally, the twenty-four men were led under armed escort to the mission courtyard and made to kneel in a row. For one awful moment he thought they were to be beheaded before his very eyes, but the Mandarin turned to Howard and held out the key to their padlocks. As they cowered in front of him, he walked slowly over, unfastened their chains and lifted them to their feet one by one. They were beside themselves with relief and joy.

Watching carefully was Mr Wang, Geraldine's mysterious protector. He approached Howard, bowed and told him that if this was Christianity, this strength and dignity he had witnessed so closely, then it was a noble and worthy calling, one to which he was willing to dedicate his own life.

One Sunday morning, exactly a year later, while Howard was lying dangerously ill with a fever, Geraldine went out on to the verandah to watch nineteen men being baptised in the courtyard below, on the very spot where her husband was almost beaten to death. 'I returned to my husband's bedside and knelt in silence. As we listened to those songs of praise, I think we scarcely knew whether we were on earth or in heaven.'[1]

3.

Harry's photographs of the Congo aroused considerable public interest. No one had seen such horrors before. Stanley's vivid descriptions still left a great deal to the imagination, but the camera was a major step towards shrinking the boundaries of the world. The missionaries turned legend and fairy-tale into reality with their illustrated magazine articles depicting the strangest-looking tribes and their extraordinary way of life. The particular contribution of the Grattan Guinnesses was the breadth of their vision, and remarkable drive, always propelling them further than others had gone before. But visionaries rarely work well as part of a team. Some, largely within the major denominations, criticised them for it, accused them of individualism, of setting up their own societies because they were unable to work with anyone else. Others feared their forcefulness, and resented their criticisms of the British government for exploitation of the poor at home and imperialism abroad. For their part, they simply believed they had no choice but to respond to the inner voice speaking through whatever need presented itself.

The balance between preaching Christianity and respect for other traditions was a fine art. How to deliver the opium-eater from his deadly habit without making him a European, how to save the African from the slavers and the worst excesses of tribalism without destroying his identity – these were constant dilemmas. The Guinnesses may not always have achieved the delicate equilibrium between religion and culture, but unlike the state authorities, the British army, and many denominational missionaries, they recognised the problem, and tried to find a solution. The international student population of Harley College with its work in the poverty-stricken East End, kept their students earthed in reality, and gave them an insight into other ways of life. Wherever they went they made a conscious effort not to import English-style religion or English-style churches.

Whitfield Guinness always found wearing Chinese dress a trial. The long, wrap-round gown with its heavy sleeves, the cumbersome shoes which would not stay on his feet, cramped his athletic style, and made riding a bicycle extremely difficult. He also balked at shaving the top of his head, allowing the rest of the hair to grow long enough for a tight pigtail, but his vocation demanded it. Harley missionaries were taught to live as simply as possible, identifying with the local people, laying down their lives when the cause required it. They were the 'guerilla' priests of their day, protecting the indigenous population against imperialist aggression. Never was that more so than in Harry's fight to free the Congo from Western oppression.

The Congo had been annexed as a Belgian colony in 1884 by an apparently magnanimous, philanthropic King Leopold. Rumour of government atrocities towards the local people had begun to filter back to Harley, but the King's performance as a defender of civil rights was so convincing that Fanny begged Harry to keep an open mind. Any abuse he might see on his visit was probably perpetrated by local officials and not the direct responsibility of the King.

The trip convinced Harry that the authorities were establishing law and order with far too heavy a hand. The massacre of the N'gombe had appalled him. Over the next few years, however, tribal warfare declined dramatically, the Arab slave trade almost ceased, and officials treated his missionaries with courtesy and respect. The General Act of Berlin, the Magna Carta of the Congo, signed by the world super-powers in 1885 when suzerainty was granted to Belgium, had guaranteed the natives total freedom. Commercial transactions were to be honourable, on the basis that the land belonged to the Africans and its produce was their property. The discovery of enormous quantities of rubber overturned international rhetoric in an instant. The highest human principles crumbled beneath a barrage of human avarice. Thousands of natives were driven off their land, their villages rased to the ground to provide rubber plantations for the agents of the King. The Africans were reduced to the status of squatters with an absentee landlord, 'a landlord who has developed within sixteen years the absolutism of a ruthless despot, in place of the philanthropy of a material and moral regenerator'.[2]

The initial problem facing the new Belgian plantation owners was how to collect the precious sticky substance exuding from the vines of the forest. No white man would ever perform such a menial task in the hot, humid conditions. The barrel of the gun soon persuaded the native to give his labour free of charge.

The first authentic stories of the outrage being perpetrated on the African people reached Harry and Lucy at Harley House in 1895 with a visit from the Rev. J. Murphy of the American Baptist Mission. They were confirmed the following year by Mr Sjoblom, a Swedish missionary and former student, who provided Harry with written documentation.

312

On December 14th, 1895, my friend Mrs Banks had been crossing the Station Compound at Bolengi when she saw a woman being beaten by a native sentry, and on her enquiring what was the matter, the sentry replied, 'She has lost one.'

'One what?' enquired Mrs Banks.

'Why, one of the hands,' said the sentry. And then Mrs Banks noticed that *the basket on the back of the woman was filled with human hands.*

She immediately called her husband and Mr Sjoblom, and the hands were counted in their presence. There were eighteen in all, and the angry sentry still asserted that there ought to have been nineteen. Some of these smoked hands were those of children, some of women, and some of men.

'Where are you taking these?' asked one of the missionaries.

'To the white man, the State man, to whom I have to prove that I have been diligent in pushing the rubber business, and who would punish me if I did not compel the people to bring in sufficient quantity.'

Harry was so incensed with the report that he set off for Belgium immediately, determined to speak to no one less than the King himself. He was received by King Leopold's private secretary, sent to vet a possible extremist, but who, in the end, was genuinely concerned about what appeared to be indisputable evidence of cruelty on the part of the Congo administration, and promised to arrange an audience for the following day.

The King was genial, gracious. 'You are an excellent young man,' he said, patting Harry on the shoulder, 'but you mustn't believe all the natives tell you.'

'It is not a native report, your Majesty,' Harry insisted.

It suddenly occurred to Harry that a direct appeal to self-interest might be the only effective way to proceed. He dared to suggest that exercising discipline in this ruthless way was bound to be counter-productive in the end. It could earn the King disapprobation once it became widely known. Furthermore, since the native was the only means available of collecting the rubber, gunning him down and cutting off his hand was destroying the proverbial goose which laid Belgium the golden egg.

To Harry's relief the King began to listen. He was asked what reforms Harry envisaged. Harry had five suggestions to make: an immediate independent enquiry, fair pay for the natives, the removal of the police authorities, a total ban on guns, and an end to murders and amputations.

The King gave way. He promised an immediate enquiry and asked for the names of any officials the missionaries thought should be removed. Harry was overwhelmed. Looking back, he realised that gaining concessions as easily as that should have made him a little more circumspect. But scepticism was not in his nature and he went home well satisfied.

Meanwhile the new Congo and Balolo Mission began to have a more positive impact on the lives of the natives, at immense cost to the missionaries, most of whom were Harry's friends. Of the thirty-five who followed McKittrick out to the Congo, only six survived to see the new century. But their achievement was recorded for posterity by an unexpected admirer, the writer and journalist, Edgar Wallace. Wallace was not a religious man and had little sympathy for the missionary cause before he saw Harry's Congo Mission for himself.

For me, Bongandanga represents the end of a long and trying journey, a journey that has left me heartsick and bewildered ... What the State has done for the Congo

314

and its people, posterity shall judge. What missionaries have done, I am seeing with my own eyes, and seeing, I am prouder of my fellow countrymen and women than I have ever been before. Every work the Congo has seen has owed its inception to, and has been brought to fruition by, these fine people. If from the depths into which the natives have sunk though oppression and neglect, men and women have been brought to the level of good citizens, the missionaries have done it. All that is best in this land is the work of missionaries.

Already, the Congo is to me a dreadful nightmare, a bad dream of death and suffering . . . when every law of man and nature is revolted and the very laws of life are outraged. A bad dream, save only this, that mingled with the bad delirium of lawlessness comes a brighter theme. It is of men and women living their lives and dying their deaths at humanity's need; who are creating a manhood from a degraded race. Hard, bitterly hard is the work . . . Somebody down river told me it was difficult to get men and women for missionary work in the Congo. I wouldn't be a missionary in the Congo for £5,000 a year. I am grateful to the missionaries for this, that they have made me ashamed of my futile life.

4.

By the end of the nineteenth century Guinness was beginning to encompass the globe. The brewing Guinnesses began to expand their enterprise to the West Indies, the banking Guinnesses were beginning to look into investments overseas, but for breadth of scope, spirit of adventure and audacity, neither branch of the family could match their Grattan cousins. Their interests stretched way beyond China and the Congo.

315

For a while Lucy had become fascinated by South America and what she believed to be a basic denial of human rights there. This was potentially controversial territory. South America had been dominated by Roman Catholicism since Pizarro, the Spanish conquistador, had ravaged the fabulous Inca Empire four hundred years before. Was it not therefore a Christian continent already? The daughter of Henry Grattan Guinness stoutly maintained it was not, in a book entitled *South America, the Neglected Continent,* published in 1894. 'Every page is crowded with facts, or bright with diagrams and illustrations, the whole presenting an artistic and panoramic view of the state of that continent,' her father said, as he sat looking at it wistfully, some time after her death.[3] He, in his writings, always described the institutional Roman Church as 'the beast' on seven hills in the New Testament book of Revelation, an apostate church. The continent was therefore a prime mission field, but its constitution forbade religious liberty. Non-denominational Protestant missionaries were denied access.

A few Harley students had settled in Lima and Cuzco nonetheless, in the only capacity they could, as shopkeepers. Local priests informed the authorities and though the missionaries had strictly adhered to the law, they were thrown out. Intelligent Peruvians deplored the persecution of foreigners by an increasingly oppressive regime and the government offered the men £200 compensation, a public admission of guilt which stirred up further national sympathy. The missionaries wanted to stay in Peru, but it hardly seemed possible without the means of earning their living and with no organisation to back them.

With Lucy's encouragement, Harry had begun to consider expanding his Regions Beyond Mission to another continent. If he seriously intended doing so, now was the moment to strike. Never one to let an opportunity pass him by, Harry set off for Peru in July 1897, at his own expense as ever, stopping off in the United States on the way, so that he could enlist the support of the famous preacher Campbell Morgan, to whom he referred as 'the brightest ornament on the Keswick Convention platform', and Dr A. B. Simpson, founder of America's most dynamic Mission, the Christian and Missionary Alliance. His aim was to re-establish the work of the Peruvian missionaries, then link them up with other, independent Harley men working in Brazil and Argentina so that they could support one another. The visit took all the skills in diplomacy he possessed, but by the end of it he had managed to resettle the men into their same old shop at Cuzco. This was the first, crucial step towards the passing of a bill which would give Peru its religious freedom in the new century.

By the time Harry reached Peru, Lucy had sailed with her father for India, yet another of her 'neglected' continents, and one which more than any other had a claim on England's help. Kipling had made the English very empire-conscious, but his writings could not prepare Lucy for the impact of India on her sensitive, artistic mind. Her soul, like a butterfly, was in constant motion, never settling for long on any one of a variety of causes. But India trapped and held it spellbound for some months.

In *Across India At the Dawn of the 20th Century*, published in 1898, she recaptured the towering heights of the Himalayas, the sweltering plains of Madras, the mighty flood of the Ganges, the crowded, dusty streets of Poona, the dark-skinned, turbaned natives thronging the busy bazaars, the overcrowded trains, colourful Hindu temples, and wretched, heart-rending poverty of the people. Standing side by side with her father on a wooded brow of Darjeeling, seven thousand feet above the plain of Bengal, she had watched the transfiguration of the snow-capped peaks of Mount Everest from their first crimson glow at daybreak into a golden then silver skyscape, before they vanished from view in the rising late afternoon mists.

Whatever her ulterior motive, Lucy and her father were true Victorians in their love of travel.

One newspaper review referred to her book as 'A most useful and instructive volume, beautifully illustrated . . . one of the best Christmas gift-books we have ever seen'. It ended with its usual challenge. Workers were urgently needed for the new Bihar and Orissa Mission, another Harley enterprise founded in 1899. Edith Fookes, still single despite Fanny's repeated attempts to marry her off, was one of the first volunteers.

Fanny never witnessed her departure. For six years she had sat quietly by the fireside at Cliff, enjoying from her window the view of her beloved Derbyshire hills, crowned with wonderful sunsets and the brightness of the evening stars. She could do little for herself, and although she never complained, life had become an increasing burden. But she still insisted on being kept up to date with every new development of the work at Harley, dictating long, loving letters to her children wherever they were on the globe.

In thirty years she had watched the tiny acorn of a house in Stepney Green grow into an enormous oak, its branches spreading out in every direction, way beyond her wildest dreams. For the sake of those dreams she had given everything she had, not withholding that most precious treasure of all – her own flesh and blood. When Whitfield, her baby, came to say goodbye to her before leaving for China in 1897, it was the hardest parting of all. She wept as he went out and closed the door, knowing she would never see any of her children again on this earth. She died on 3 November, 1898 and was buried in a quiet corner of Baslow churchyard.

Only two of her four children were present at her funeral, Harry and Lucy. It took months for news to travel across China. Lucy stayed on in Derbyshire for a while to see to her mother's affairs. Fanny's death seemed unreal. She had almost become an institution in her own right. Her presence seemed to fill the house. As she wandered round the building, a thousand childhood memories floated back into Lucy's consciousness – Fanny organising picnic teas in the summer house by the river, enthusing in the observatory about the secrets of the stars and the burnt-out craters of the moon. Everything was the same at Cliff, the flaming tints of autumn, the silent drop of yellow leaves, the last, lingering flowers, the ridge of purple moorland and the red sun westering over the hills. How could Fanny not be there to enjoy them all as she always had?

Henry was bereft. In the past six years he had travelled extensively, in some ways as an escape from seeing her as she had become. His bereavement had been prolonged and agonising. Though marriage to Fanny had not found its fullest expression for some time, she was still his favourite companion and soul-mate. There was always comfort and understanding in her presence. Only now that she was gone could he allow himself to remember what she had once been and grieve for what he had lost.

> As a wife she was exceedingly companionable. Her mind was clear-sighted and capacious, her power of expressing her thoughts unusually great. Her words were always full of good sense and right feeling. Free from exaggeration, from petty selfishness and vulgar egotism, her thoughts and emotions seemed naturally to work on a broad and noble plain. As the months and the years went by, her intellect grew in capacity, and became more and more richly furnished, while her piety took a deeper tone.[4]

At the moments when inner burdens threatened to engulf him Henry had always found travel a pleasant diversion. He had a great desire to see the Holy Land again, to visit the places he had not seen since his honeymoon. An invitation to speak at the International Zionist Conference in Jerusalem provided him with the perfect opportunity. Originally, he planned to travel alone, but at the very last moment persuaded Lucy to accompany him. She needed a temporary escape, a distraction after an unfortunate entanglement with a high-profile gentleman, the recently widowed Mr Hoste, home from China and the new director of the China Inland Mission. There had been a public announcement of the engagement, greeted with general jubilation, but Lucy had known almost at once that it was a dreadful mistake. Calling it off, so soon after the trauma of her mother's death, had played havoc with her mental health. Lucy was always highly strung.

At thirty-four she was long past the usual marrying age and had convinced herself that Mary and Maggie Reeds' teasing prophecy of spinsterhood had come true. She was completely unaware of her attractions for the opposite sex. In his recollections, Eugene Stock, Director of the Church Missionary Society, recalled a remarkable young woman who, when she spoke, turned a deadly dull meeting of the Leicester YMCA into a major event. To watch her play the piano was pure enchantment. There was intensity and passion in her playing. Her very soul, her mind, her heart seemed to be poured out through her fingers. Inevitably, several of the Harley students worshipped her from afar and basked in her aura. Some thought themselves very much in love with her, and there were several proposals, usually from men too young and immature to be suitable. She tried, often successfully, to arrange more sensible relationships for them. But the mature Mr Hoste had been a very different proposition.

As she and her father set off across Europe, an invitation arrived from Prince Bernadotte of Sweden inviting them to pay him a visit at his royal palace in Stockholm. The gracious regent entertained them royally. As he showed them around his palace, a large portrait of a lovely young woman caught Henry's eye. The Prince told him she was the daughter of close friends, so close he regarded her as a niece. Her name was Jane af Sandeburg, and despite moving in the best social circles, despite having Stockholm's finest and richest young men at her feet, she had decided to become a missionary in China. 'My youngest son is a missionary in China,' Henry commented. He made a mental note to write to Geraldine and Whitfield to ask whether they had come across the lady in question.

Several weeks in Palestine, galloping on an Arab steed across the wide Plain of Esdraelon and on the breezy heights of Mount Carmel, helped blow away the vestiges of Lucy's unfortunate emotional attachment. The Kaiser had visited the country recently and said he found it a disappointment. 'If you come and go in a sandstorm like the Kaiser, whirling through a sirocco, and grudgingly bestowing the blink of an eye on the Shrine of the Universe, you needn't expect to enjoy Palestine,' Lucy wrote home disparagingly. She loved it.

While Lucy rode and explored, Henry Grattan spoke at countless meetings. According to Harley student David Baron, the impact of his talk to the Zionist Congress could still be felt in Jerusalem ten years later.

After three months they decided to travel on south through Egypt. Henry had been concerned for some time about the vast unreached areas of the Sudan and wanted to see whether access to this immense, largely unknown territory was possible from North Africa. One evening in May they left Alexandria for an oasis called Fayoom, the 'Garden of Egypt' on the edge of the Sahara. According to a letter from Lucy to Geraldine, they had been joined by a 'guide, interpreter and general protector', a certain Mr Kumm, who worked with the North Africa Mission. 'We are flying down the Delta in a quiet, dreamy light, half grey, half green, half misty blue.' Geraldine, who knew her sister's usual meticulous attention to detail, must have been bemused by the reference to three halves. Did she suspect that they and the 'dreamy light' might have something to do with the mysterious new protector?

321

As they travelled slowly across the desert by camel, exploring the mysteries of the pyramids together, Lucy had plenty of time to study their guide from behind the heavy veils attached to her wide-brimmed hat. And the petite, dark-haired Englishwoman soon fell under the spell of the gentle giant from Markoldendorf in the Harz mountains of Germany.

Born in 1874, and therefore nine years younger than Lucy, Hermann Karl Wilhelm Kumm was born into a family proud of its Hanoverian descent and opposed to the militaristic spirit of the new Prussian-German Empire. They were also strongly Lutheran. Karl was one of five children, three girls and two boys, and showed an unusual flair for languages from an early age – a gift which would stand him in good stead in later years, when he became an international figure, speaking English, French, Egyptian and African dialects with equal ease. As a postgraduate, after study at Heidelburg, Jena and Freiburg universities, Karl visited England, where one night he was taken to hear John Glenny, Superintendent of the North Africa Mission. From that moment Africa was his whole life.

He stayed in England and spent some time at Harley College, preparing for the future, though it does not appear that Lucy remembered him. When they met he was studying for a doctorate in Egyptology and she was deeply impressed with his learning and a great deal more besides. In physical appearance he was not unlike her father, tall, powerfully built with a strong, handsome face and thick mane of hair swept back from a commanding forehead. The facial structure was, however, more angular, the jawline square and determined, and there was no hint of a twinkle in his clear, blue eyes. This was a man who would never be distracted from his purpose, who would be utterly single-minded about the task at hand. Karl Kumm was forceful, mature beyond his years and immensely attractive to women. Only a few months earlier a young woman had turned up with a ring at the Mission headquarters claiming Kumm had asked her to marry him.

He for his part was captivated by Lucy. She was so contained, so feminine, so interesting, a woman who enjoyed music and travel and could engage his mind. She also had the added attraction of her pedigree. She was the daughter of Henry Grattan Guinness, his old teacher. Karl was ambitious and knew only too well that the name, in missionary work, would open virtually any door.

Lucy had been waiting for a man to sweep her off her feet, someone strong and masterful, with a passion and vision to match her own. Karl managed to combine those qualities with an extraordinary childlike innocence, and a naivety which appealed to her mothering instinct. By the time he escorted them back to Cairo, she was hopelessly, irrevocably in love.

In Cairo all three stayed at the same hotel as Lord Kitchener, fresh from his fight against the Mahdi and about to distinguish himself further in the Boer War. Henry watched him with acute interest from their nearby dinner table. But the main object of Lucy's attention was the intense young man at her side, who was about to take his leave of her to make an exploratory journey up the Nile Valley into the Nubian region. Before they parted they made a trysting-place. If in the next months her feelings for him remained unchanged he would be waiting for her at Luxor at the turn of the new century.

Lucy returned to England and continued their romance by letter. Unlike many of her female contemporaries, she appears to have had no qualms about expressing the intensity of her emotion. Whenever she was overwrought, writing would always be a safety valve. 'Where is my wandering boy tonight? I wish I were in his arms.'

Karl felt that at this important stage in their lives, honesty was more important than passion. He warned her what her life would be like if she married him. 'I must be true to God and my conscience all my life. Are you willing to bear separation if the Lord shall cause it? If I have to work night and day you will not think me selfish? There will be very little "drawing-room" time in my life.'

Had she been a little less in love Lucy might have considered more seriously the warning in the words. This was not a contract for a marriage. It was a licence to stay single within the married state. Karl, whose hero was Livingstone, was wedded to his work, to the freedoms and challenges of the outdoor life, to missionary exploration and pioneering, which he saw as a man's unique prerogative. It seems extraordinarily disparaging to suggest that a woman like Lucy Guinness should want or expect a 'drawing-room' existence for her man or herself. She had never sat and crocheted in her life. The daughter of Henry Grattan Guinness had never expected to be treated as less than an equal, a co-worker, a fellow pioneer. But he had never seen her in her home environment, and she never appears to have questioned his views on the role of women, so startlingly clear in the letter.

In January 1900, having terminated his contract with the North Africa Mission and completed his responsibilities, he made his way back down the Nile to Luxor, wondering how she had responded to his letter, not knowing whether she would be waiting for him or not. But she was there, just as she promised. They were formally betrothed in Aswan in the traditional Sudanese way, joining their hands over the entwined, dark-skinned hands of the two native Bischareens who were teaching Karl their language. In later years Karl would claim that on that very day the Sudan Pioneer Mission was born. 'On that dear, beautiful day on the Nile,' Lucy wrote, 'we stood in Africa. We stood for Christ in Africa. What can we do for him in Africa?'

A month later they were married in Cairo, at a civic ceremony at the German Consulate, followed by a service at the American Mission Church taken by Henry Grattan. The wedding breakfast was a tea party for 300 soldiers to whom

Karl had been acting chaplain, and the honeymoon a return trip to Aswan in one of Thomas Cook's discarded Nile steamers. Lucy still did not find domesticity easy, but she 'learned to cook potatoes splendidly, and to make the most delicious soups (out of tins)'. It was the longest time she and Karl would ever spend together throughout their married life, and even that was a fact-finding exercise for the new mission. When she married Karl Kumm she married the Sudan, and that left little time for anything else.

5.

At the end of the nineteenth century, political tension in China rose to fever pitch. Encouraged by an enlightened group of reformers, the young Emperor Kuang Hsu had tried to bring the provincial Mandarins to heel, so that he could transform China into a modern constitutional monarchy. But the powerful reactionary opposition, led by the diehard dowager Empress Tzu Hsi, overthrew the young Emperor and placed him under house arrest. As ruler of the country, she and her followers, known as 'Boxers', needed a scapegoat. They did not have to look far. The foreigner in their midst was regarded with suspicion and hostility and for very good reason.

When Henry Grattan had stopped off in China on his way home from India two years earlier, meeting up with Geraldine and Howard, and a newly arrived Whitfield in Shanghai, the strained relations with the European powers were already apparent. Henry Grattan was ashamed of Britain's unwarranted aggression on a peaceful nation in its own commercial interests and wrote to Geraldine when he reached home:

I suppose you see by the newspapers what is going on in what they call 'the scramble for China' ... Germany seems bent on making acquisitions in the East, and Russia has practically taken over the control of Corea, and has ensconced her fleet at Port Arthur . . . There are probably great changes pending. The victory gained by Japan in her struggle with China has proved to Europe the weakness of the great Chinese Empire to resist the forces of civilisation . . .

The German Emperor's brother is on his way out to the province along whose coast we sailed together on our way to Chefoo. The Chinese authorities must be perplexed at times by the contending interests and conflicting proposals of the 'barbarians', whose naval and military power make them so formidable, and who will have their own way and pay no attention to long-cherished usages.

At that time Geraldine put the worrying political situation out of her mind. She had an exciting distraction, escorting Whitfield to Honan. 'I brought him up, you know,' she said proudly to everyone they met. She was thrilled to be able to introduce the little brother she had mothered to the language and customs of the people she loved.

In many ways the Chinese had a highly sophisticated culture, largely unrecognised by the European powers who took their superstitions as evidence of ignorance. But Whitfield was anxious to please. A newcomer to a missionary station was always a source of interest to the Chinese Christians and a welcome feast was organised in his honour at She-ki-chen by Ch'en of the Pearly Wave, a retired Mandarin and distinguished scholar. The banquet was a trial. Whitfield did his best to comply with local customs, but did not quite succeed, which became clear a year later when the hospitality was repeated and Mr Ch'en was overheard to say:

Now that Dr Guinness, it is really wonderful how he has improved since last coming to Honan! Last year, when

he dined with me, he was gauche in the extreme. He
hardly knew how to make himself presentable (in Chinese
dress); he could not handle chopsticks properly and was
unable to reply to a polite remark. But now, in a little
more than a year, he is becoming quite a gentleman!

But if Whitfield's reputation as a gentleman took some time to
establish, his fame as a doctor was made overnight. One day
a huge crowd arrived at his door dragging along a tailor who
had swallowed his needle. A long piece of thread still attached
to the eye was dangling from his mouth, but attempts to pull
on the thread only drove the needle deeper into the poor
man's gullet. His employer was irate. He would be responsible
for funeral expenses, not to mention ridding the workplace of
the man's ghost.

By the time Whitfield examined the tailor's throat it was
raw, swollen and bleeding. Since this was his first case of
needle swallowing, he could not think what to do. Suddenly
inspiration came. He sent one of the crowd for an india-
rubber tube, passed a piece of strong silk through it which he
attached to the thread in the man's mouth. Then, he slid the
tube gently over the thread and down the swollen throat until
it reached the needle. With a little pressure the needle was
dislodged and dropped into the stomach where it could dangle
freely. To the incredulous gasps of his admiring audience,
Whitfield pulled gently on the thread and drew the needle
safely out through the rubber tube.

It was an immense relief to Geraldine and Howard to have
another doctor in the province. Howard was prone to bouts of
fever and dysentery. Sometimes he was too weak to sit up and
had to be carried into the courtyard stretched across three
forms so that he could attend to his patients lying down.
When an invitation to holiday in Mount Pleasant in Tasmania
with Henry Reed (who had married Geraldine's adopted
sister, Leila Dennison) arrived, it seemed like a gift from

327

heaven. Now that Whitfield was in Honan they could set off with an easy mind.

They stopped en route in Australia, where Geraldine, the more gifted speaker of the two, had accepted several engagements. In Adelaide, on the first evening after her talk, she was approached by a gracious elderly gentleman who offered her his deep condolences on the occasion of her bereavement.

Geraldine was puzzled, then suggested there had been a mistake. 'Thank you,' she said lightly, 'but my dear mother is getting on quite nicely, in spite of the paralysis.'

Clearly disconcerted, the elderly man, with a profound apology, finally managed to stutter, 'Haven't you heard? Your mother died over a month ago.'

Stunned, Geraldine broke down. Howard escorted her quickly away.

Blissfully unaware of the political rumblings and growing resentment of the foreigner, Whitfield enjoyed life at the station in She-ki-chen, shared with a missionary couple, the Conways, and Miss Watson, a single woman. His bicycle arrived and was a source of fascination to the Chinese people who had never seen one before. Their final judgment was that since it provided no shelter and sometimes, instead of carrying its rider, had to be carried itself, it was not nearly as practical as a mule and cart.

By the turn of the century drought and famine in China were severe. The Boxers turned public attention to their usual scapegoat, and in June 1990 the Dowager Empress decreed that all foreigners should be destroyed. On a sweltering July day word reached the little party in She-ki-chen that the locals were planning to kill them and they must flee for their lives. That was easier said than done. The waterway to the sea was completely dried up, and overland, a thousand miles of Boxer-infested country separated them from the coast. To make matters more difficult, the Conways had a six-week-old baby. It turned out to be their salvation, for the baby's nurse, a local woman, had foreseen the emergency and managed to persuade their neighbour, Li Ch'uen-rong, whom Whitfield had attended in a near-fatal illness, that he owed his life to the missionaries and must offer them protection should they need it.

At five o'clock in the morning the rioters arrived. As they began to smash down the barricades the missionaries had erected, Whitfield, Miss Watson, the Conways and their baby slipped out of the back door, clambered up a ladder and over a ten-foot wall, ran across their neighbour's courtyard, and climbed another ladder into the relative safety of his attic. As they sat catching their breath they could hear the murderous shouts of the mob, the crash of falling timber, and finally, the crackling of flames, leaving them in no doubt about the fate of their home.

Then the shouts grew louder, closer, as Mr Li's house was overrun by hysterical crowds screaming, 'We must kill them! We must kill them!' They heard the nurse shout back, 'Kill them? You'll have to kill me first!' and realised that she and Mr Li were all that stood between the mob and the trapdoor.

After a protracted argument there appeared to be sulky acquiescence from the crowds, followed by the sound of retreating footsteps and shouts gradually dying away in the distance.

Their relief was short-lived. The trapdoor was pushed up and a pale, trembling Mr Li appeared. 'You can't stay here,' he said. 'This is my servants' quarters. They will soon be coming up and I can't rely on their secrecy.' He could not think of an alternative hiding place, until Mrs Conway pointed out a deserted-looking building in the back courtyard, adjoining the mission-house. That, he said, was his haunted loft. They were welcome to it.

'The more haunted the better!' Whitfield chortled, as they ran across the courtyard under cover of darkness into what appeared to be a disused granary. They managed to build a contraption of wooden boards across mountains of wheat, held in place by strong cocoa-matting, then, balancing a ladder against it, heaved their way up into a tiny, filthy loft. The loft was certainly haunted – by an insect, not a ghostly army.

They were barely settled when the trapdoor suddenly lifted and tea and bread were pushed through. After twenty-four hours of heat and high humidity with nothing to eat or drink it was a feast. A stranger suddenly surfaced behind the food and urged them to follow him. He had been sent to escort them safely out of the city. They were almost out of the courtyard when Mr Li came rushing after them. Their guide was the leader of the rioters, a decoy sent to lure them out of hiding. And now the dreaded chief of police was on his way.

They ran back to the granary as fast as they could, and as the trapdoor closed after them, the officer and his men arrived.

The warehouse was ransacked, the matting slashed apart, the wheat cascading across the floor.

'Now search the loft,' the officer commanded.

The men refused. 'It's haunted,' they whispered.

'Nonsense!' the officer said.

One of the men fetched a beam and began to ram the trapdoor.

'Rigidly fixed!' he shouted, with relief. 'Quite immovable!' Whitfield, sitting with his full weight on the trapdoor, felt it move beneath him. Mrs Conway rocked her baby gently. The tiniest cry would seal their fate. As they waited, holding their breath, sweat dripped from their faces and trickled down the back of their necks.

After a while there was silence. The officer and his men appeared to have abandoned their search.

On Tuesday, 10 July, the rioters set to work early, smashing everything in their wake. They poured on to the granary roof, peering in the loft window for any sign of life. Whitfield had the presence of mind to discover that one tiny corner of the loft was invisible from outside and there they crouched

together against the wall while the uproar went on around
them. And baby Nora still did not cry.

Whitfield managed to take a peek out of the window, and
saw men in the courtyard below piling up wood, grass and
bundles of straw around the granary beneath them. Their fate
appeared to be sealed. But just as the crowd was about to set
the granary alight Mr Li's farm-workers arrived in high
dudgeon. Killing foreigners was one thing, destroying all their
hard work was another. Disgruntled, the mob conceded. One
man went and fetched a ladder instead and the little party in
the loft heard the sound of footsteps climbing up towards their
window. At any minute they would be face to face with their
assassin. But the ladder was too short. The man could only
reach the window by pulling himself up by his hands for a few
seconds. He quickly scanned the room, and though Conway
felt his breath on his cheek, never saw the people hiding in the
space right next to him.

They hid in the loft for six days with little food or drink.
Every time the trapdoor opened their hearts stood still. On
one occasion, to their amazement, two packets of post were
pushed through. Postman Lu, grateful for treatment for a boil
on his foot, had offered his help in the only way he knew. But
the post brought newspapers reporting the Dowager Empress's
edict and the terrible realisation that the Boxer uprising was
so widespread that to stay in hiding was their only hope.
Whitfield wrote home on a scrap of paper:

It is the sixth day of the riot, and we still lie on a dirty
floor. The ladies are worn and sick; Conway done. I am
well enough thank God, but don't see quite how we are
to get away. Clouds lend a hope of rain. If it fell, it would
make all the difference. Continual firing against thieves
and plunderers goes on. We have no change of clothing;
and day by day in a temperature of 90-100 you may
imagine our condition – all four in one room with a baby.

The Lord grant it may be soon over.

That night they heard an unmistakable pitter-pattering on the roof. It grew louder and louder until a torrential downpour drowned every other sound and they were able to leap around for joy. The trapdoor opened and Mr Li's head appeared. 'Truly,' he said, 'your God is wonderful. Only this night I have made terms with Mr Wang, and now under cover of this rain and darkness, I will get you to his house.'

Mr Wang was a leading businessman in the city, probably the only man who could get them away to safety. But crossing the city to his house was extremely dangerous. The party was split up. Old clothes and blankets were wrapped around their heads and the baby taken from them. The rain had turned the paths into a metre of mud, and as her guide pulled her long, Mrs Conway kept slipping and falling over.

After a nightmare journey Whitfield and the Conways finally arrived at their destination, splattered in mud, but there was no sign of Miss Watson or the baby. Mrs Conway was almost beside herself when one of Mr Li's farm labourers struggled up the ladder into their new attic with a bundle in his arms. 'Truly this baby is good,' he whispered. 'Had it cried when I was in clerk's office, all would have been spoiled.' The labourer, it appeared, had blundered by mistake into one of Mr Wang's offices.

Miss Watson arrived some hours later. She had lost her shoe in the mud and went back to look for it – in vain. That turned out to their advantage, for when the Boxers found it, it convinced them the foreigners had escaped from the city.

The rainfall was insufficient to fill up the waterway so no escape was possible for the next few days. Suddenly, on their eleventh day in Mr Wang's attic they heard excited shouts below. 'Ai-ya! Ho-li-kan, fah shui liao! Amazing! The dried-up river fills with water!' They could hardly believe their ears. How could the river rise when there had been no rain? They waited in an agony of expectation for two hours until a jubilant Postman Lu climbed up to their attic shouting, 'Have you heard the news? The river has actually risen to half its banks!' Far back in the hills, rain must have fallen.

The danger was far from over. That night they crept stealthily out of hiding, clambering over soldiers asleep on mats in the courtyard. The baby started to be uneasy, but Mrs Conway managed to quieten her. Wang had arranged for a cart to take them to the river where a boat was waiting. To get to the river they had to pass through the city's iron gates which were heavily guarded. Lying in the cart covered with old blankets and matting, they held their breath while the driver negotiated his way out with a bribe. Finally they heard the gates swing open and were soon steaming their way to freedom.

The five-day journey took ten days. They spent it shut up in the cabin in the heat lest they be seen from the land. Every province had its own bureaucracy, its own Department of Customs. Each border encounter was a potential disaster. The women covered their feet and hair and pretended to be asleep. 'Your travellers are very silent,' an official said to their escort, poking and prodding them, but he let them through none the less.

At last the foreign settlement of Han-k'ou came into view. They kept their heads well down, and the boat glided rapidly downstream past the final Customs depot until they were out of Boxer territory at last. Dirty and unshaven, without his Chinese gown, Whitfield went on ahead by rickshaw to the China Inland Mission house to inform them of the arrival of a Honan party, thirty days after the riot.

His arrival was greeted with immense joy and utter amazement. Gently, it was explained to him that seventy-five fellow missionaries and twenty-two children had perished. They had held out no hope for him or his colleagues. He could hardly take it in. Why was his life spared? That would be a source of bewilderment for the rest of his life.

A short while later in Shanghai, where he was recovering from his ordeal, he noticed a lovely young woman, tall and slender, with a mass of fair curls caught at the back of her neck. Both were struggling to come to terms with the terrible events of the last months. They felt drawn to each other and spent hours talking about their experiences. But the budding relationship had to be curtailed. She decided to go home to Sweden to spend some time with her family. Her name was Jane af Sandeburg.

6.

While Whitfield was caught up in the Boxer uprising, his twenty-five year old cousin, Rupert Lee Guinness, was experiencing his own first, great adventure – the Boer War. In Rupert a new brand of Guinness had been born to the Lee or brewing side of the family, a Guinness, who in his penchant for travel, innovation, scientific discovery, and ultimately, in his identification with the poor, could well have stemmed from Henry Grattan rather than Edward Cecil's line. Gentle, sensitive, intuitive, there seems little doubt he was a surprise to his father who regarded him as a bit of a misfit. Years later, convinced he must nonetheless be a product of his genes, particularly in his passion for the sciences, Rupert wrote to another Fellow of the Royal Society, the distinguished scientist Sir Ronald Aylmer Fisher, of Gonville and Caius, Cambridge, who had married Dr Harry Guinness's daughter, Eileen, to ask him whether there was anyone in the family he might take after. Fisher told him about his own father-in-law's research into tropical diseases, and described his wife's grandfather, Henry Grattan Guinness. 'He was a mathematician and an astronomer, but I believe his astronomical interests became centred in the interpretation of biblical prophecies.'[5]

The family of the third Earl of Bantry (on the left).
His daughter, the formidable Lady Olive, and her husband,
Sir Arthur Guinness, Lord Ardilaun, are on the far right.

Dr Harry Guinness and his wife Annie with the first five
of their ten children. Harry's worldwide travels to end the
exploitation of natives in the Congo rubber trade
meant he had little time for his family.

'Only a factory girl': Lucy Guinness with the accommodating maid, Sarah, takes on her disguise.

Dr Howard and Geraldine (Guinness) Taylor. He gave up his career to promote hers, a 'new man' before his time.

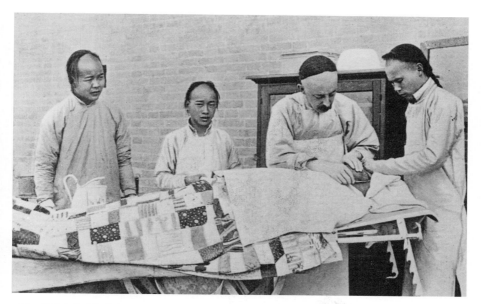

Dr Whitfield Guinness operating in Honan, China. He shaved his head
and wore a pigtail to be indistinguishable from the local people.

Henry Grattan Guinness, DD, Fellow of the
Royal College of Astronomers, whose work on the co-relation between
the stars and biblical prophecy made him one of the most celebrated
writers and preachers of the nineteenth century.

At the age of 67, Henry Grattan Guinness married Grace Hurditch, forty years his junior. According to the newspapers, it was a 'marriage of considerable interest to non-conformists'.

Henry Grattan Guinness' second wife, the lovely 'Gracie'.
She gave him a new lease of life.

Harley House on the Bow Road, the East London Training Institute.

Cliff College in Derbyshire, a summer bolthole for the Grattan Guinnesses. It housed an observatory for Henry's telescope.

Rupert and Gwenny, the second Lord and Lady Iveagh, brewers,
agriculturalists and politicians.

Walter Edward Guinness, DSO, the first Lord Moyne,
who was assassinated on 6 November 1944 after a
distinguished military and diplomatic career.

Bryan Guinness, the future second Lord Moyne, marries society beauty
Diana Mitford, daughter of Lord Redesdale. After their divorce
in 1934 she married Sir Oswald Moseley.

The Honourable Arthur Ernest Guinness with his wife
Cloë and daughter Maureen, whose first husband, the Marquess of
Dufferin and Ava, was killed in action in 1945.

The heiress Lady Henrietta Guinness. Even marriage to a poor Italian could not save her from the curse of her inheritance.

Father Jack Guinness, CR, a quintessential Guinness and a monk.

Throughout his lifetime some thought Rupert saintly. C. H. Allcock, his headmaster at Eton, said, 'I think that his character is one of the most perfect I have ever met with in a boy here and I can hardly think it possible that he could ever do anything discreditable.' Remembering the parents' priorities, he then added sadly, 'I wish his ability approached his character in excellence.'[6]

A speech impediment caused by surgery to his tongue made him hard to understand at times. Combined with dyslexia it condemned him to the pigeonhole marked 'dunce'. Rupert never allowed his handicap to defeat him. He got into the habit of doing without the written word when forming his opinions, depending on observation and experience instead. When, to his great delight, he was eventually made a Fellow of the Royal Society, he remarked wryly that he was probably the only member who could not spell. An apocryphal story claims he once spelt wife 'yph', but this was probably deliberate self-parody.

One teacher at Eton, R. F. W. Talham, lamented not being of much use to the boy, but went on, 'I am sure that he has developed qualities of manliness and self-reliance that are perhaps the best products of life at a public school.' In other words, fortunately for him, Rupert was a champion oarsman, and rowing would take him far. He had the perfect build for the sport, small, yet stocky like his father, with broad shoulders and good strong muscles. In July 1895 he beat the national champion Guy Nicholls in the Diamond Sculls at Henley and became a popular hero overnight. In 1896, on the basis of this particular merit, he went up to Cambridge, won the race again and was hailed the undisputed national amateur sculling champion. But doctors diagnosed a heart murmur, wrongly it later proved, and his father ordered him to stop. Rupert left Cambridge. Without rowing there was little reason to stay on.

Although Edward Cecil had given his eldest son £5 million on his twenty-first birthday, Rupert showed little inclination to jet set into high society. The lavish entertaining of his parents, the balls, the parties, had little attraction for the shy, retiring young man. Denied sport, he turned his attention instead to his other great love – scientific experiment – spending hours alone with his microscope.

In 1891 Jim Jackson, an Elveden stableman, had been bitten by a rabid dog. The only treatment for rabies was the newly invented course of forty injections into the stomach, available only in Paris at the Institute of Louis Pasteur. Research in England by Jenner and Lister had been curtailed for lack of funding. Lord Iveagh sent Jackson to Paris for treatment, and the stableman survived and lived to a ripe eighty-nine. Meanwhile, Rupert persuaded his father to accompany him to Paris so that they could see Pasteur's work for themselves. As Rupert guessed, the trip convinced Lord Iveagh of the need for a Jenner Institute in Britain and he endowed it with £255,000. Over the years the Lister Institute, as it became, led the world in the fight for a vaccination against smallpox, dyptheria and typhoid. Today it exists only as a trust fund, giving vital grants for pioneering research into cancer, rheumatism, and even DNA coding.

Despite Rupert's obvious scientific ability, Edward Cecil could not see how his eldest son could ever develop the cerebral qualities vital for running a successful business. Fortunately he had two others, both at Eton, who appeared to exhibit more of the necessary fibre. Ernest was as well-liked as Rupert, 'most excellent boys and their influence is always on the side of right and their example of steadiness of great value', and Walter, the youngest, with all of his eldest brother's intelligence, and none of his handicaps, was already in the process of reforming the Eton Society, re-instituting debates and making a quota of sixth formers statutory, so that the Society could not be merely athletic.

In 1899, despite his father's reservations, Rupert became a Brewery director. Edward Cecil, unable to supervise his beloved company from afar, had rejoined the Board in 1898. He had his reasons. In 1895 Claude Guinness, a brilliant managing director in every respect, suddenly took leave of his senses and had to be carried away from Brewery premises in a straitjacket. The incident was quickly covered up, the page for that day torn out of the log book.[7] He died at the early age of forty-three some weeks later. According to rumour his death resulted from general paralysis of the insane, the final stage of syphilis. He had, however, two healthy daughters, Marjorie, born to his first wife, Gladys Rowley, who died in 1891, and then Grace, known as Bubsie, born only two years before his death to his second wife, Zoe, daughter of the third Baron Nugent, whom he had married in 1892. Curiously, and probably by pure coincidence, over the next years, his sister, Lady Iveagh, began to behave a little oddly, succumbing very slowly to what appears to have been premature dementia.

His social life contracting slowly, the Brewery in obvious need of direction, it was almost inevitable Edward Cecil should turn his attention back to the business. Reginald Guinness succeeded his younger brother Claude for a time, combining the roles of chairman and managing director, but quickly fell from favour.[8] Where his baby was concerned Edward Cecil appears to have found it very difficult to delegate his authority.

With the outbreak of war against the Dutch Afrikaners in South Africa Rupert had more pressing concerns and, within weeks of his appointment to the Board, set off for South Africa escorting a field hospital endowed by Edward Cecil. Rupert persuaded his father to let him act as chief of staff to the Irish Hospital, supervising its journey to the commanding officer, Sir William Thomson, past president of the Royal College of Surgeons. He simply had to ensure the safe arrival of seventy-five Brewery staff, eight tents with eight beds apiece and twenty small tents for stores and supplies, all drawn by twenty-one wagons and mules. No medical knowledge was necessary.

From a diary Rupert kept in shorthand and inadvertently left behind at Norham Castle, it appears his war was fun at first. On the ship out he served his country as Treasurer of the Entertainments Committee, organising dances and a fancy dress competition. Rupert dressed up as a baby, complete with a large rattle. At twenty-five, a long way from home, without the constraints of his upbringing, he had his first experience of 'social life', and an opportunity to try out his charms on the ladies, whom he found quite 'agreeable'. With one he spent a 'very odd evening'. She felt ill, and 'we consoled her. I am glad there were not witnesses!'[9] Especially his father. These were not the class of women his parents would want for Rupert.

In March 1900 he was in Cape Town when the news arrived that Kimberley was relieved. The Mount Nelson Hotel was so full of jolly old Etonians that it felt like home from home and Rupert had to sleep in a camp bed in Sir William's room.

Gradually he began to experience the real horror and misery of war, lamenting his lack of medical knowledge. In March 1990 the Irish Hospital was the only first aid unit to accompany Kitchener to Prieska. From there he travelled on with the general to Bloemfontein. It was backbreaking work. The wagons were continually stuck in the mud and Rupert had to help heave them out. The supplies were inadequate for hundreds of wounded men, not to mention the thousands suffering from dysentery or enteric fever. It was not long before Rupert succumbed to the fever himself, but he refused to give in. By June the hospital had a more permanent base in the Palace of Justice in Pretoria, and Rupert went home to receive the Companionship of the Order of St Michael and St George, for services to his country.

7.

In that same summer of 1900 news of the Boxer massacres reached Hudson Taylor in London where he was recovering from a slight stroke. It broke upon him like a tidal wave on a tired swimmer. His devastation was total. Fearing for his sanity, his wife took him straight to Davos high in the Swiss mountains. Howard and Geraldine, numb with shock and desperate for news of Whitfield, joined them there.

The telegram announcing Whitfield's amazing escape brought Geraldine only momentary relief. As the scale of their losses became apparent it seemed a waking nightmare. Hudson Taylor paced the floor of his room, hour after hour, day after day, tears pouring down his face, saying nothing. His agony was too deep for words. He felt personally responsible for every death. He had believed implicitly in special protection for every one of his workers. They had sacrificed so much already. Why had God removed his hand? And even if the parents had to die, why should children be allowed to suffer?

Geraldine, in the middle of a biography of Pastor Hsi, worked quietly in his room, while he paced up and down like a demented animal. One day he suddenly walked over to the table where she was writing and said, 'I cannot read. I cannot think . . . I cannot even pray.' She looked up at him with deep sorrow, not knowing what to say to comfort him, but after a long pause, he said quietly, 'But I can trust.'

By the end of the year a letter arrived from Whitfield saying he was going to Chefoo, four days north of Shanghai, to the CIM school for missionary children. Many of them had been bereaved. Hundreds of refugees were pouring in daily from the interior in need of medical help. The resident doctor had had a complete breakdown. Whitfield was needed urgently.

Though not fully restored, Hudson Taylor was well enough to be left, and Howard and Geraldine set off for a speaking tour of the United States with a view to raising extra funding and support for world missionary work. Wherever they went Geraldine, rather than Howard, was the centre of attention. He was shy to the point of self-effacement. She exerted an unmistakable magnetism. She had presence. In America, her beautifully modulated English voice and refined English-rose appearance added to her attractions. She was the quintessential Englishwoman.

This, then, was the future pattern of their lives, Geraldine in the limelight speaking and writing, Howard in the background looking after her. Every book she wrote added to her fame. Though formal and a little stilted by today's standards, they were still thrilling missionary adventure stories. Her heroes were brave, her heroines beautiful, selfless and flawless. The Victorian reader demanded idols worthy of his adulation. Nothing less than perfection would do. Blemishes had no place in Geraldine's portraits, partly because she thought it uncharitable to dwell on the weaknesses of another, partly because she happened to be blessed with a generosity of spirit, which saw only the good in others.

One of Dr Harry and Annie's boys remembered years later that as a child he once told his Aunt Geraldine that a master at his school suffered from asthma. 'I hope the boys are kind to him,' Geraldine said earnestly. Annie laughed uproariously and said in her matter-of-fact way. 'Don't make the boy tell lies, Geraldine dear.'

She was a woman of her time. The suffragette movement had created a vogue for unusual women speakers. There was a certain intellectual snobbery in being part of a following. In America and Canada hundreds of young women heard her speak and volunteered for missionary service. One of her young admirers wrote,

I met Geraldine in Montreal in my early teens. Even at that age she was my model because of what I knew from

her book, *In the Far East.* She so fulfilled my highest
ideals, I longed to be like her, so much so that, having
seen her, I attempted for some time, by standing before a
mirror, to make my mouth to the expression of hers.

The tendency to lionise Geraldine continued throughout her
life and was often counter-productive, both for the imitator
and the imitated. Such was the power of her personality that
living up to her proved an impossible strain for those who
tried. Geraldine herself found it hard to cope with the limitless
demands thrust upon her by the image she projected of perfect
Christian womanhood. Howard alone knew her through and
through, knew that the real woman was often tired and weary,
could be petulant and difficult, struggled with the disappointment of not having children and with the sense of inadequacy
which had dogged her from childhood. Without a question or
word of complaint he gave up his career in medicine to care
for her. He saw to it that she took daily exercise, went to bed
early, ate properly and regularly. She was not allowed to
decide these things for herself. Like a child she became
completely dependent on him, but sometimes she exerted her
independence and with a mischievous twinkle in her eye,
broke free and played truant. But when she was wilful Howard
was hurt. 'Darling,' he once said to her after a particularly
fierce quarrel over something he refused to let her do, 'where
would you have been by now if I hadn't been taking care of
you?'

'In my grave long ago,' she admitted ruefully.

While Howard and Geraldine were at Davos, Lucy joined
them there. Karl sent his wife to her sister to be looked after
so that he could get on with his work. She was pregnant and
desperately sick. Thirty-five was old to become a mother for
the first time.

If Howard Taylor nurtured and encouraged his wife's
vocation at the cost of his own, Karl pursued his career at the

341

cost of his family. His determination could brook no hind-
rance. A wife and children would always be a restriction to his
freedom. He was so absorbed in the task, so single-minded,
that even writing was too much trouble.

In the first few months of their marriage Lucy had worked
at his side in Aswan. She too was completely committed to
the task. For more than ten years her father had produced a
little paper called *The Sudan*, an attempt to alert prospective
missionaries to the three thousand miles of territory, including
French West Africa, Nigeria, the Cameroon, Sierra Leone,
Senegal and the Ivory Coast, 'from the heights of Abyssinia to
the wide, sweeping flood of the Atlantic – 100 lands, 100
languages – all, non-Christian to this hour'. It was vital to
reach the people before Islam did. It was a race to end all
races – with the souls of the Sudanese as the ultimate prize.
The face of one dark-eyed Bishareen, a lithe sinewy desert
ranger, proud, bold, free, appeared to haunt Karl, symbolising
all the people, driving him on through ancient empires, cities
and schools, mosques, ports, caravan routes, rivers, mountains,
lakes, empty wadis, desert and green oases, palm-fringed
villages and wells, looking for ways of establishing the work.
'The eyes that look at us from that one silent face are eyes
innumerable, hopeless eyes of slaves, anguished eyes of
tortured women; keen eyes of clever traders and the proud
glance of chieftains; others dull, bewildered and shadowed by
life's miseries, unlit by any of heaven's rays.'[10]

On one trip with his father-in-law, to their utter amazement,
they came across an old Harley student working behind the
counter of the post office in Shellal. Samuel Ali Hussein, a
young Nubian, had been taken to Geneva by Swiss Christians
as a boy. After two years at Harley he had returned to his
village in Nubia as a farmer, fled in the tribal war, joined Lord
Kitchener's army as an interpreter during its fight against the
Mahdi, and ended up eking out a living in Shellal. To Samuel
it seemed he had simply been awaiting the two visitors. When

Henry Grattan asked him if he would like to work for the new mission, he could hardly believe the chance had come at last to return to a devastated Nubia to see what he could do. Girgis Yacoub, an Egyptian Copt, was also engaged to start a school in Aswan.

With two workers, the new mission now needed an official European base, and proper funding. Germany seemed the obvious place, and in the summer of 1900 Karl and Lucy set up the headquarters of the Sudan Pioneer Mission in Eisenach. Karl now needed to travel extensively to establish a network of support. Lucy, suffering from nausea, could only hold him back.

She found the separation harder than she had ever imagined. And it never became any easier. 'I do love you so,' she wrote, 'and long to creep into your arms ... come back soon to both of us.' When he failed to appear, her letters took on a chiding, petulant tone. The baby she carried began to move inside her and she wrote to Karl, 'He's a nice little darling to come and cheer me when naughty Husbie keeps so far away! Naughtie Husbie said he was coming on the 10th and now today is the 11th and never a word to say when he will come or how, at all, and yesterday no letter! Naughty, naughty, naughty, naughty.' In her more rational moments she remembered the promise she had made before they were married, 'Now, I know you understood, when we first talked of working hand in hand and I told you I never would hinder but always set you free to serve.' But as the separation continued, Lucy's sense of duty was in ever-increasing conflict with her sense of need.

Their first son, Henry, was born at Wiesbaden, Karl's home, at the end of February 1901. Karl was in Wiesbaden for the birth but set off on a fact-finding mission to Wadi Halfa before the baby was a month old. Normal domestic life was at best a trial to him. The urgency of the task required sacrifice – but it was Lucy who paid the price. Rather than stay among strangers, she returned to her father at Cliff, in theory to regain her strength, in practice to raise support for the new pioneer mission in the Sudan. From Cliff she wrote Karl a love letter expressing the overwhelming desire she felt for him, eliciting a similar response from him, almost as if she fears that time and separation are robbing her of its reality.

Dearest precious Sweetheart
Best of all my life, crown and light and joy and Treasure – HOW I long for thee. I sit alone in my dim room; the fire burns low and red; white and cold and silent and frostbound lies the valley with its naked trees.

Husbie I want you; come to me Husbie – take me in your arms, Dear Light, beautiful joy, hide me again in your big heart like the old days when you took me there first – in my dream of Paradise.

Not a dream: It was true once. Tell me it all again, Darling. Write to me that I may have it always – write me a little every day – just as you remember it all.

What was life to me then, before I saw thy face? Yet how blindly I walked on. Never thought any perfection could be. Never dreamed anything better could come than a poor make pretence of love. Truly I thought so. Believed so. And yet loved love so beyond words that I had seriously come to the conclusion that to go alone always would be worse than to have a ½ empty heart, and someone to hold one's hand sometimes, and . . . make believe.

– Oh Husbie!

A great cry rings through all my heart when I think of what I was snatched from, what God would not give me, tho I prayed for it. Husbie, if I had married him – and then had – had met you . . .

No, it is all unspeakable. All quite beyond words. But tell me a little of it, Darling. Tell how we met each other, how my own darling found his *little one.*

What Karl replied remains unknown, but such intensity must have been suffocating at times, particularly for someone who appears to have been more emotionally reserved.

Apart from a few servants, Henry Grattan had lived alone in his apartment at Cliff since his return from the Middle East. It was a lonely existence for a man who still possessed the energy and intellectual powers of someone half his age. He was glad of Lucy's company. He was facing a major crisis and needed her support.

The Boer War had robbed the Institute of volunteers and severely depleted its funds. In 1901 the old Queen died. Her passing marked the end of an era and the entry of a new age. King Edward VII, with his many mistresses and hedonistic lifestyle, symbolised a new joviality and affability undermining religious devotion. There was an almost instant reaction against the sobriety and strictness of his mother's reign. The people threw off their restraints. The Edwardian age, epitomised by the golden lifestyle of Elveden, was gracious and carefree. Interest in missionary work, funded largely by society's well-to-do, died almost overnight.

Henry Grattan insisted that the only option was to close Cliff College. Harry was horrified at the suggestion. What would his mother have said? For thirty years Cliff had played a vital part in their lives. But he contracted typhoid during a preaching tour of Ireland and the recurrent bouts of fever left him severely weakened. Heart-breaking though it was, closing Cliff College and giving up the lease now seemed inevitable. Much as he loved it, it was far too big for Henry Grattan to justify living there alone.

The first bid came from the Jesuits. Henry Grattan was horrified. He could not let his beloved Cliff fall into the clutches of Rome, the Scarlet Woman of the apocalyptic books. He begged Lucy to persuade Karl to take over the property as a potential centre for their new mission. The idea appealed to her enormously. Her heart was at Cliff. She felt tranquil there, at peace among so many happy memories. But Karl was dubious. It was hopelessly impractical, far too big for their purposes, and they had no money to run it. Besides, Karl knew from experience how easily people were dominated by the powerful personalities of his wife's relatives. Cliff was Henry Grattan's throne. Would he really abdicate or would Karl have to submit himself and his mission to a benevolent autocracy? The latter was unthinkable to his proud Germanic spirit.

In the end he had little choice. Lucy was pregnant again and needed a base while he was in the Sudan. Furthermore, it had become abundantly clear that the parting of the ways with the new German Board was already imminent. Its members, respected church leaders in Germany, were nonetheless conservative, worried about Kumm's inexhaustible drive and determination, his reckless single-mindedness. They could not understand his dream, enter into his vision. Missionaries traditionally spent their lives in an isolated village, put down roots, learned the local language, built relationships. This man had no intention of staying in any one place. He wanted to press on far too quickly into every part of the territory. He was headstrong, independent, possibly a liability, certainly unresponsive to their control.

Saddened, Karl announced his intention of establishing new mission headquarters in England. They would take over Cliff on a temporary basis.

It was there that little Karl was born in 1902. Separated from the husband she adored, Lucy lavished all her affection on her two babies. They were a precious gift she thought would never be hers. Feeding them was one of the greatest satisfactions of her life. As a teenager bound for Tasmania she had turned up her nose at the 'fits, convulsions, teething or one of the many mysterious maladies to which I understand all babies everywhere are subject'. Now she sat for hours with her baby in her arms, marvelling at the exquisite workmanship of the tiny features, startled by the penetrating gaze of those two large trusting eyes fastened upon her. The belated blossoming of her mothering instincts was poured out into poems and prose celebrating the wonder of this new experience with an emotional impact which had taken her by surprise.

As long as there are babies in the world the age of miracles will never cease.
All mothers know this.
To look at the dainty, breathing, moving creature lying in its curtained cot with its own energy and volition, its own world and life, its private joys and sorrows, pains and satisfaction – to look at it and think that a few months ago it had no existence and that to you and another its presence on earth is due, is to realise yourself in the presence of a miracle compared with which all but one other pale. For this to which you have given birth is a life which will go on. How far? How long? And whither?

The poems, 'long withheld as too sacred for publication', did not reach the general public until 1929. Though steeped in Victorian sentimentalism they manage to convey something of the mystery of life itself. Scanning them quickly is like barging into a shrine without removing one's shoes, for Lucy's love for her children is hallowed ground. It seems she sensed she had found a treasure too precious to keep, for she confronts her fears of death and separation repeatedly. Perhaps her feelings were born of her experience of marital love, a grand passion granted only to evade her possession continually. Or perhaps she simply had a sense of what was to come.

In 1903, to Karl's immense relief, the Wesleyans approached the Kumms and asked if they could have Cliff as a training college for Methodist ministers. From Henry Grattan's perspective, the Wesleyans, though not as sound in their interpretation of biblical prophecy as he might have wished, were angels of light compared to the Jesuits. And Cliff would still be training men for the ministry.

The Guinnesses had until the end of the year to vacate the premises and find new accommodation. Lucy rented a small cottage in Castleton in the Derbyshire hills near Sheffield where the Sudan Pioneer Mission had held its inaugural English Council meeting in upstairs rooms in the YMCA on 13 November 1902, with Dr Grattan Guinness in the chair. 'Mount View' became the Mission's British headquarters. But where was Henry Grattan to live? She wrote about it to Geraldine, who replied, 'I know how perplexing the question seems about Father's future home. We cannot fully see how the needs are to be met.'

But Henry, to his children's surprise, found a most ingenious way of solving the problem.

Chapter 11

1902–1908
Life in the Edwardian Age

1.

On 14 August 1900 Henry Grattan had scribbled the following words on a piece of paper, which he then kept folded in his wallet.

> After a quiet day of prayer in the woods at Eisenach, had a very vivid dream in the night. I had prayed that God would bring me a wife suitable for me and had endeavoured to trust him to do so. Dreamed she came to me in the night, and sat on my knee and kissed me – with a bright smile, her own act. Not given to dreams! Will wait, and wait on God. Through his grace.

Three years later the following postscript was added in a woman's hand: '. . . and Grace came and sat on his knee and kissed him! My own act. 11th June 1903.'

For a respectable young woman to sit on a strange man's knee was remarkable by the standards of propriety of Edwardian England. That Henry Grattan was sixty-seven and she twenty-five makes the event extraordinary by any standards.

Henry's dream was fulfilled at Wilton House in St Leonards. He was house-hunting for Lucy, and the House of Rest for Christian Workers belonging to his old friend Charles Hurditch was an ideal place to stay. On the morning of Wednesday 11 June he called to book a room. Summoned by the bell, Grace Hurditch went to deal with his request. As she walked down the staircase into the hall their eyes met and there was instant, mutual attraction.

Grace was the seventh and youngest child of Charles Russell Hurditch, converted under Grattan Guinness's preaching in Exeter, a leading light in the Plymouth Brethren and professional supporter of worthy causes. Grace wrote later:

> My parents were born in the great revival of 1858. In point of fact this was their Second Birth, but it was an event in their lives of such unparalleled importance that they hardly ever troubled to mention the first, and we children might have been forgiven for imagining that they had leapt into existence Athene-like in that fervid hour, full-grown and spiritually armed, had it not been for a list of dates in the large family Bible, and a small collection of miniatures, oils and daguerreotypes scattered over the walls of our home.[1]

Although, in true Brethren fashion, life was rather serious and austere at home, hers was a warm and loving family and the Hurditch children found ways and means of indulging their high spirits. Since only games of a religious nature were allowed, they held mock adult baptisms. By suspending sheets from the bedsteads a four-poster bed was converted into a baptistry, into which the candidate was 'plunged' by an 'elder' balanced precariously on a bedside table. 'I must confess that somewhat unholy mirth accompanied the proceedings when occasionally elder and candidate together suffered total immersion.'

Since their father was much too preoccupied with philanthropy to supervise his children, and their mother was a sweet, shy woman with an implicit trust in her children's natural inclinations towards righteousness, they were left to their own devices. Musical evenings, the only entertainment they were permitted, rapidly expanded into full-blown music hall and Grace's exceptional talent for mimicry earned her pride of place on the billing. The victims of her impersonations were usually revivalist preachers or members of their mission-hall congregation, whose idiosyncrasies she had plenty of time to observe during the long Sunday services. Her reputation soon spread and she was offered an opening on the stage at a starting salary of fifty pounds. It was a fortune for those days. 'I'd rather see her in her grave,' her father was reported to have said.

But Grace grew up to exercise a freedom of choice and independence of mind unusual in a woman of her background and generation. At twenty-six she had evaded all attempts to marry her off and had chosen a career in nursing instead. Shocked by the ignorance of her contemporaries in the basic workings of the human body, and equipped with specimens of animal viscera obtained from the local butcher, she delivered a series of lectures in elementary human anatomy:

I would then proceed to demonstrate the fascinating action of the valves of the heart by pouring water into the auricles and ventricles, and show the workings of the lungs, which I inflated by means of my bicycle pump; when suddenly there would be a thud, thud, thud, as one after another of my audience fainted away at these 'ghastly sights'.

After nursing for several months in the poverty-stricken East

End of London, Grace had to abandon her work when, with a legacy bequeathed him for missionary purposes, her father bought Wilton House at St Leonard's, Sussex, and turned it into a 'rest home' for Christian workers. In all his philanthropic schemes Charles Hurditch expected the support of his two unmarried daughters, Grace and Beatrice.

Grace loved Wilton House with its heavy Victorian furnishings and gracious air of comfortable solidity. Mr Hurditch would permit no rules or regulations to mar its home-like atmosphere. Massive gilt-framed pictures hung on the walls, lending an air of quality and richness. They were painted by an artist of repute, a Fellow of the Royal Water-Colour Society, whose chief merit in the eyes of the Hurditch family was his membership of the Plymouth Brethren.

When Beatrice sustained a serious injury as a result of a riding accident, Grace ran the house on her own, experimenting with new management principles. Ruth, her favourite sister, was a missionary in Africa and on 11 May Grace wrote to tell her how it was going:

> Amidst the many reforms the entire domestic staff were swept off the premises! The new lot were not brought in until the following day. Well, my dear, for twenty four hours we were domesticless and you never in your life heard such peals of laughter as emanated from these premises in that twenty four hours. All the visitors helped. There were twenty six of us.

Of the twenty-six, several, it appears, were men who took advantage of the occasion to flirt with the vivacious Grace. Intelligent and teasing, exceptionally pretty with an oval face, large, mischievous eyes and a mass of light brown curls held against their will in a bun at the nape of a long and graceful neck, she was never short of admirers. But, she went on to tell Ruth, she had no time for suitors or people who said stupid things about 'ought to be married'. Not until a fortnight later when Henry Grattan Guinness walked into her life.

Her next letter to Ruth, dated Sunday 27 June 1903 was radically different in tone.

> My Ruth, my darling sister
> At last! The awakening has come, and your little Grace is transformed, and she is really in love. Oh my darling Sister, how I have longed to cable this to you, or at any rate the date of our wedding. July 7th, and yet I dare not for fear it would come as too much of a shock to you just now. But the relief to sit down and talk to you about it, knowing that you and Bee will at least understand it all, and so what do I care for all the other criticisms. Fancy, Ruth, that Dr Grattan Guinness (he is 67 darling!) has been the one to break down the barriers I was building round my little life, barriers I thought insuperable until I met him here just 2 weeks ago.

Henry Grattan Guinness was not a total stranger to Ruth. It was at Geraldine Guinness's farewell in 1887 that Ruth, a teenager at the time, decided she was called to be a missionary herself. In time the formidable Ruth was to prove more intrepid than her heroine, becoming the first white woman to climb Mount Kilimanjaro, delivering all five of her babies herself and confronting the legendary Tippu Tib over his slaving activities.

But, as Grace knew only too well, admiration and respect for the Grattan Guinnesses was one thing, marriage to the elderly patriarch another. Some detailed explanation of her extraordinary choice of fiancé was required:

> Well, his magnificent presence appealed to me very strongly, his clean-shaven face and white hair brushed back off that great forehead of his. He tells

me his first impressions of me were, 'What a sweet girl', and from that moment we felt most strongly drawn to each other. He watched me a great deal at lunch. Harvey Harte was sitting next to me and noticed it. Edith Greenhill sat at the head and of course she noticed it.

Well after lunch we had tea as usual, and everyone went out but the doctor and me, and strange to say I did not feel in the least afraid of him as the great Dr Guinness, as everyone else seemed to be. And then he took my hand and asked me a little about myself and what I was doing here, after which he gave me a kiss – such a kiss – and I loved him and felt I never wanted to leave him, but never for a moment thought that he would care for me like that. Such a thought never crossed my mind. I only knew that it was an exquisite day to be with him then and the future never occurred to me.

The next day he was with me a great deal, coming to meet me as I came from dressing a wound of one of Dr Berry's patients and taking my hand and walking up and down with me and talking all about his travels, and how he would love me to see these places and how it would develop me. Then Friday night, darling, he asked me to come and have a talk with him in the office and he drew me to him and told me how he loved me right from the first, and how for five years he had prayed God to bring him this love, which I had awakened in him, love he tells me such as he has never known before.

If Grace was not afraid of the great Dr Guinness, she was still flattered at having a man of his reputation declare his love to her:

Really, darling, I could not have thought it possible to be

so happy, yet so humbled, for Ruth I cannot understand why he loves me. Such intellect, and such a soul. I tried to tell him of all my faults, but he only kisses me and says he has never known such love before ... Now, my darling, how I shall need your prayers, for I long to be worthy of my high calling, and he wants to teach me so much ... He is just now completing a marvellous book on the historical sequence of the Apocalypse (and I don't even know how to spell it!) ... I think I must give you a most exquisite little poem he wrote me just before he went away after our engagement. Somehow I don't like that word and I wouldn't allow him even to give me a ring, for we were so completely one, and from the very first he called me his little wife and there was nothing for us to wait for, and so you see that is why we arranged to be married so soon.

The immediacy of their wedding day, less than a month from their first meeting, meant that Henry had to return straight to Cliff to sort out his affairs and make the necessary arrangements. Saying goodbye to Grace, even for a few weeks, was a wrench, but under the inspiration of her love he wrote a poem especially for her:

> She has come to my arms, she has come to my heart,
> And the dream of my soul is fulfilled,
> And the love that unites us shall never depart,
> Nor the love that our union has willed.
>
> O thanks to the Giver, O thanks for the gift,
> From the gift to the Giver we turn;
> From the bliss he bestows to Himself we uplift
> The hearts which with gratitude burn.
>
> There is heaven below, there is heaven above,
> And they answer like ocean and sky;

For heaven is found in the bosom of love,
In spirit to spirit made nigh.

In his absence a present arrived at Wilton House almost every
day, a compressed cane travelling trunk, a canteen of cutlery,
two buckles for waist belts, a long string of pearls and a purse
with silver corners. 'I have told him I don't care a bit about
these sorts of things but he loves me to look pretty fancy,' she
wrote with undisguised coquetry. As the prestige of marrying
a famous man began to dawn on Grace she began to feel a
little pride in her conquest. After all, her Henry was even in
communication with the Foreign Secretary. 'Balfour has
written to me,' Henry told her, 'to say that he is so interested
in my books, and has studied them closely.' The full significance of these words did not strike Grace in that summer
of 1903, nor would it for another fourteen years. The growing
Zionist interest within government circles was not exactly
uppermost in Henry's mind at that moment either. He wrote
to Grace from Cliff on 17 June:

My own darling Grace, my very own
I have read and re-read your last letters, which I found
on my arrival here last night, with such love and joy,
answering to your own – my wife, my life – in anticipation, and in heart, intention, spirit, in reality, how
wonderful is the relation – love's secret hidden for
a season in the heart, and then, slowly or suddenly
bursting into bloom!
   Lucy rejoiced when I told her of my appreciation of my
darling. She will leave her two babes here, and come to
our wedding, so all my children will be there ... How
soon they will know that you have ceased to be Miss
Hurditch! Changed your name, while remaining yourself,
will you know yourself my darling? When your pure, sweet
life is blended with the riper life of the one you love? ...

I write from my quiet study at Cliff, with beautiful memories. I was in the garden this morning and the park, and wanted to gather the best of all the flowers and send them to you. I plucked the leaves of fragrant thyme, or rather lavender and roses and wanted you to have them all. You must come here with me after Switzerland, to see the place where we have lived for so long.

I hope you will have a happy Sunday at your father and mother's house, I will not say your home, for your home, darling, is with me.

I am your own loving husband that is to be. Henry.

Although it was fairly accepted convention for a young woman to marry a much older man, the age difference of forty-one years caused quite a sensation, and Grace refers to 'not caring for all the criticisms'. Whatever the judgment of the mass of evangelical piety, the two families were genuinely pleased. Geraldine wrote from Switzerland to the future step-mother who was fifteen years her junior:

Gracie dear

How can I write to you from so full a heart? Though we have never met, I love you dearly because of your love to him. And I long to make you feel how real is our joy in the thought that so soon you will be ours!

Only this morning father's letter reached me bringing the first news of this happy event. Of course it is a great surprise, but most welcome! And Father tells me that all is arranged and even the day decided upon ... It is very good and sweet of you to consent to its being so soon. I am glad on dear Father's account.

For he loves you Gracie! I wish you could see his letter to me about it. He has so much to give. The wealth of his great soul and tender heart. And it is yours, all yours. Oh such a heart Gracie! You will explore your treasures as the days go on. And you have much to give dear, your fresh young life and love. But he is worth it all. How did you find out so soon?

You will tell me all you can when we meet next week – DV. Meanwhile, with deep thankfulness to God and warm, welcoming love,

I am your own Geraldine.

It took Charles Hurditch and his wife some time to overcome their initial shock. 'The events of the past few days have fairly taken the wind out of our sails whilst your craft seems to be sailing over calm and sunny seas,' he wrote to his daughter. But once they had recovered they began to find the whole thing 'too romantic', but not so romantic that they neglected their parental duty. 'In spite of all the criticisms that may be passed, and under the special circumstances these may be expected', Hurditch gave his willing consent to the match, with prayers that God would preserve his future son-in-law for many years yet. Then he wrote to Henry Grattan reminding him to adjust his will.

It was decided in the circumstances to keep the engagement as quiet as possible, but news travelled. When at the end of June Henry kept a prior appointment to speak at a public meeting at Harley College, the gardens were packed to capacity. Everyone thought Grace would be there and were dying to catch a glimpse of her. But she never appeared, no announcement was made and the disappointed crowds had to be satisfied with excited chatter and speculation.

2.

Hastings Observer, 7 July 1903:

A wedding of considerable interest to Nonconformists

took place on Tuesday at the Robertson Street Congregational Church, the contracting parties being Miss Grace Russell Hurditch, daughter of Mr Russell Hurditch (founder and director of the Evangelical Mission, London), and the Rev. Grattan Guinness DD (founder of the East London Training Institution, Harley St, Bow).

The marriage service was conducted by the Rev. Charles New. After the ceremony luncheon was partaken of at the Queen's Hotel, at which attended only the immediate relatives of the bride and bridegroom. Afterwards the happy couple left by train for Folkestone, en route for the continent, where the honeymoon is being spent.

Mr Dick Russell supplied the carriages.

From Brussels Grace wrote to Ruth filling in the details of her wedding day. It was a rather more traditional affair than Henry's Quaker marriage to Fanny forty-three years earlier.

Such a wedding, darling, simple and quiet, just the plain marriage service read by Mr New, with Harry and his eldest child, Whitfield, Geraldine and Howard Taylor and Lucy on one side, and Mother, Phil, Harry, Lil and Auntie Maud on the other in the choir stalls at Robertson St. The whole service was over in half an hour and finished with his giving me a lovely embrace. There were a few outsiders there, who managed to find out where the wedding was, in spite of our endeavours to keep it quiet. We then drove to the Queen's Hotel, where a lovely lunch was provided, with white flowers all down the table.

In case no one tells you what I wore, here goes. The palest dove grey gossamer voile dress made over silk, with a real lace berthe, a black velvet bonnet, with white net strings, and long pale grey gossamer veil down the back. Everyone said, darling, that I looked rather sweet.

My beautiful bouquet was composed of tiger lilies and lilies of the valley. After a bright, happy cheerful time at luncheon we drove off to Westons to be photographed, sweet Geraldine and her husband coming too, in order to pose us (both are very artistic), then we went back to the hotel where Mother and Edith were waiting to get me into a Bolton-tailor-made pale grey coat and skirt. (I am sticking to a bonnet. It becomes me as Mrs Grattan Guinness!)

Then off we went to the station and had a loving send-off from Geraldine, Howard and Lucy. The two families had stayed at the Queen's the previous evening with their father and did a hundred and one little nice things for me, finishing touches to his toilet. He looked perfectly exquisite in frock coat and white tie and waistcoat and top hat, so absolutely aristocratic with his magnificent face and white hair and upright figure. Really it's not surprising that people stare at us both. We are a little out of the ordinary! And whenever we go into a shop he manages to say something about his 'petite femme' so as to see the looks of approval!

The only cloud to cast a shadow across an otherwise perfect day was poor Bee, still lying in bed after her riding accident. Some months earlier Beatrice had been jilted at the altar. Like Dickens's Miss Haversham she kept her precious lace wedding-dress in a box, taking it out occasionally to caress its limp folds. Dr Berry felt that Grace's wedding would be too much for her and kept her sedated at home. Grace popped in and out of her room at each stage of her wardrobe and marvelled at Bee's unselfish enthusiasm and excitement.

The early days of her marriage were more wonderful than Grace had ever dared to hope. In a letter to Ruth dated 11 July, with a rapture unfettered by the usual prudery of her generation, she wrote about the intimate details of their relationship:

360

How can I write to you old girl of all my happiness –
this wonderful new life – isn't the love, protection,
guardianship, sympathy, affection of a good man the
greatest blessing that can come with a woman's life? My
beloved husband has opened up a new world to me. His
love has just touched the spring of that secret chamber
which I never knew existed and my happiness is
complete.

Ruth, you don't know how humbled I feel when I think
of the way God has honoured me, for my darling is so
good and clever and wonderful and his marvellous
intellect! He reads to me and is educating me all day, but
at numerous intervals, whether in the 'Grand Parc de
Bruxelles', or under the palms on the Hotel verandah,
impresses his ideas on me with a kiss, such a kiss, followed
by some exquisite expressions of his love . . .

I remember old girl, the first letter you wrote to me
after your marriage you said it was all so natural and no
wonderful changes had come. Well, darling, that is just
about the truth of it. It is just the most natural thing in the
world to be with our kindred spirit, and I'm sure you
would have thought that no change had come to me, if
you had seen me this afternoon in a marionette tea gown
reciting to my dear Grattan, who greatly appreciates all
my little funs and frivolities. Don't be afraid of his con-
verting me into some sedate little saint, for he loves me
just as I am, at least so he says!

I am keeping a short diary, just writing down the places
we visit, because we hope to travel much and it is bound
to be an interesting record . . . While I am writing this
there are about a dozen Americans twanging away nineteen to the dozen they are talking such a lot of nonsense
and in such loud tones, evidently wealthy people by the
way they are talking about their travels. How trivial even
travel becomes when done in this way, whereas with my

Grattan it becomes an education, creates an interest and leaves a lasting impression.

In the four weeks prior to their wedding, Grace, aware that marriage to Henry Grattan would require more than the usual domestic skills, had taught herself photography and typing so that she could be a proper support and companion. From a letter to his mother-in-law, dated 23 July from Aix-la-Chapelle, it would appear that her new husband appreciated her endeavours:

Dear Mrs Hurditch

You ask me in your letter to Grace what I think about your darling child now! Well I could write eloquently on the theme, if I could only trust myself to speak out all my appreciation, I fear I should seem extravagant! We are more happy together and more united to each other than I could have conceived we should be.

She is bright as sunshine, and sweet as a spring day, practical, energetic, clever and deft in her ways, and helps me marvellously well! writes for me, reads to me (and I to her) took down an article for me today for the press on 'The Holy Roman Empire' and its connection with Aix-la-Chapelle – looks after my things! and is the most loving companion that could possibly be . . . I will not add, but only say my heart overflows with gratitude to God and I am doing all I can to care for my sweet treasure, your dear child, and make her life happy.

Give my love to your dear husband and believe me, dear Mrs Hurditch

Yours affectionately, H. Grattan Guinness.

As Grace imagined, they travelled much, more than she anticipated. With his new young wife at his side filling him with fresh energy and vigour, Henry decided to fulfil a lifelong ambition to visit former Harley and Cliff students all over the world. Now that Cliff had gone he had no roots in England. After a short stay in Switzerland with Howard and Geraldine so that Henry could complete *History Unveiling Prophecy*, they set off for the United States. The honeymoon turned into a world tour. It would be five years before Grace saw her parents again.

Forty-five years had passed since Henry Grattan last visited Philadelphia. In the great revival of 1859 thousands had flocked to hear him preach. He found it strange to stand in the same pulpits, to meet the children and grandchildren of those converted through his preaching so long ago.

For several months, as they toured the United States, Henry maintained an exhausting preaching schedule. He was more popular than ever, and they were feted wherever they went. His books had sold in their thousands. *Light for the Last Days* was reprinted over and over again. To Grace's immense concern he became overtired. A few days recuperation at the Moody Bible Institute in Chicago were exceedingly welcome. Moody had always encouraged Henry to regard the Institute as his American home, but Henry never managed to take Moody up on his offer in his lifetime. The American preacher had died in 1899 and the College was run by his son, Bill.

With pressure from Grace, Henry realised at last he was not as young as he felt and began to accept the limitations of mind and body. That was clear from a letter he wrote to Geraldine. Like her father she was constantly pushing herself. Her biography of Pastor Hsi appeared to have been a success and had already been translated into six languages, but writing under pressure, with so many other engagements to fulfil, had worn her out. Full of loving concern, Henry could be quite sharp when his children's emotional well-being demanded it.

How well I understand that nervous breaking down from which you have suffered. Let it be a warning. There is a limit you should not attempt to pass in exhausting labours. It is not easy to fix it, but experience shows pretty clearly where it is. I have been beyond it at times, when all the foundations of life seemed gone. I cannot express what that means, and hope you will never know. Most people have no conception how thin the foundations are which keep them above the abyss, where the interests of life exist no more. I tell you this, for you need to be warned. Learn to say 'No' to invitations or calls or labour which destroy the power to labour and the possibility of service. I do think Howard, as your husband – and doctor – should say 'No' for you, and forbid suicidal toils absolutely, firmly, finally. Tell him that with my sincere love.

In Australia news reached them of the death of Tom Barnardo. It was a blow to Henry. He had never managed to make many intimate friends in his lifetime. Barnardo was one of the few, and their affection was mutual. At the end of his life Barnardo had written to Lord Radstock:

I feel dreadfully alone so far as human friendship is concerned; all my old friends and counsellors have passed away; hardly one is left; one dear old man who lives abroad is my only link with days gone by. His love seems quenchless and my own gratitude to him is the answering tie. Of those my own age who have survived, almost all have either withdrawn their friendship or are so absorbed, I suppose, in other matters that old friendships seem to have died out. Dear Grattan Guinness is the one surviving like at home with days gone by, whose human love, brotherly kindness and personal devotion to Christ are to me a source of refreshment and blessing.[2]

Henry Grattan sent a letter of condolence to Barnardo's widow Syrie:

> Beloved Dr Barnardo with his beaming face, cheery voice, broad brow, big brain, glowing heart, indomitable courage, tender sympathy, intense philanthropy, unwearied activity, and marvellous practical ability – when shall we see his like again?
>
> . . . The memory of our friendship is sweet and fragrant now, a friendship never overshadowed by even a passing cloud. My only regret is that I did not see more of him in later years, but our absorbing occupations stood in the way of this. Now that he is gone, I feel that I have lost a dear, personal friend, and a precious link with the past which none can replace. And the world is the poorer for his absence; a beautiful life is ended, a fair and shining light has been extinguished, and I mingle my tears with those of the children, the thousands of rescued children, who have lost by his removal a father and friend. Earth is poorer, heaven is richer!

From Australia Henry and Grace travelled via Japan to China, returning to Japan later for four months, so that Henry Grattan could teach a course at Tokyo University.

In the early hours of a chilly November morning they caught the sight of the outlines of Shanghai. Streams of muddy brown water intermingling with ocean-green indicated their entry to the great Yangtze River. Passengers and baggage were transferred to a river steamer for the remainder of the journey and suddenly Whitfield's familiar face materialised on the quay. With him was his new wife Jane, whom Grace had never met. Whitfield had waited five years for Jane to return to him, and when she did, they were married almost at once.

One of Henry Grattan's first priorities was a visit to the

cemetery where Hudson Taylor's remains were buried. A few months earlier Howard and Geraldine had brought him out to die in his beloved China so that his remains could lie peacefully beneath its hallowed soil.

But this appeared to be China's only peaceful spot. In a letter home Henry spoke of:

> Meetings, meetings, walks through the malodorous Chinese cities, walks among the graves (graves every-where), outside the city, sedan chair rides in and out, in and out, round impossible corners, between high blank walls, opium shops, dust heaps, courtyards, with Chinese eyes scrutinising, speculating, admiring, scorning, sus-pecting, pursuing, all round – pigtails swinging, clothes flapping, signs swinging, cries ringing, odours pervading, poverty pleading, idolatry repelling, necessity calling – voices, voices, multitudinous, like the sound of many waters – waves which have been rolling and breaking since far distant times, anteceding all European civilisa-tions and almost all memories of mankind . . .

The highlight of their visit was an opportunity for Henry to speak to the Shanghai Zionist Association in the Royal Asiatic Hall. A large number of influential Chinese Jews were present, complete with pigtail, and for over an hour he held them spellbound with one of his most eloquent addresses on 'Zionism from a Christian standpoint'. The entire text appeared verbatim in a local Jewish newspaper.

At 9.15 p.m. on the day of their departure, Henry noted sadly in his diary: 'Said "Goodnight" to Gershom and Janie.' Some years later Grace wrote underneath, 'It was their last "Goodnight".'

By the time they travelled back to Australia via Japan in 1906, Grace was five months pregnant. She decided to stay on in Sydney while Henry travelled on alone. It was their first time apart and an experience he did not much enjoy.

Newcastle, New South Wales. 26th May

My darling
I am lonely – no one I care for near me – none to go to –
none to talk to – no face to smile on me with love – no
echo to my heart – because you are not with me – out
more than 100 miles away, and I am among uninteresting
strangers, kind in a way, but with no heart for anything
that stirs the soul within me. Why should I write all this?
Well, I want you to know how I feel when days away
from you. If you were not with me, I should not stop long
in Australia, but with you I could stay as long as I wanted.
Strange is it not? But such is the heart.

I feel fresher today – I rose at half past five, and
watched the day dawn, and had a walk since, and now
am writing on the verandah of the house – the children
playing about – and there's the sound of a distant train,
and I wonder whether it is going to Sydney and you, and
how I should feel if I was going on it!

Monday morning and I'm off from Newcastle with
pleasant prospects in view. This is not an interesting place,
but somehow Sydney is, especially the top storey of No 1
Glen St!

Well – farewell – it is no use to say come and kiss me –
for you are too far off.

God keep you – my pet wife, and bless you.

Ever your loving husband.

Henry was back in Sydney in time for the birth of John
Christopher who weighed a magnificent nine pounds. The
Australian midwife had never seen such an enormous baby –
nor such an easy first delivery. Labour lasted a mere six hours,
and as Henry telegraphed the world, Grace, looking radiant,

fed their infant son. At seventy, Henry was as excited as if he had become a father for the first time. He took endless pleasure in the baby, noting every development with enormous pride and tenderness. 'He would delight to carry him out into the warm Australian sunshine, and to pick the flowers from our garden, and see the child's appreciation of beautiful things,' Grace noted in her diary. 'It was a wonderful preparation for the heavy blow that was so soon to fall.'

3.

1903 was a bumper year for Guinness weddings, each, like Henry and Grace's, attracting a share of newspaper attention. All three of Lord and Lady Iveagh's sons married into the British aristocracy, delighting the public with three grand society occasions. In June the Honourable Walter Edward, twenty-three, the youngest and most dashing of Dodo's boys, married Lady Evelyn Erskine, third daughter of the fourteenth Earl of Buchan. Walter, equally public-spirited and more military-minded than his eldest brother, had abandoned plans to study biology at Balliol College, Oxford, and followed Rupert out to South Africa so that he could fight the Boers, where he was wounded and mentioned in despatches. In later years he would show his children the mark where the bullet entered his cheek, narrowly missing his brain. Had it not, they would not be there.

Since his return, he had served on the London City Council, prior to being elected Member of Parliament for Bury St Edmonds in 1907.

In July, twelve days after his cousin Henry Grattan created a stir in the nonconformist ranks by marrying a woman forty years his junior, the reserved, rather conventional Arthur Ernest married his complete opposite, the vivacious socialite

Marie Clotilde Russell, known in the family as Cloë, daughter of Sir George Russell. They set up home at Glenmaroon, next to Farmleigh and Knockmaroon on the Phoenix Park side of Dublin, an area of elegant mansions and sweeping lawns, rapidly becoming a sophisticated Guinness enclave, so that Ernest could be within easy reach of the Brewery. In 1902 Edward Cecil had once again taken over as Chairman on Reginald's retirement, sharing the power with the formidable new managing director, C. D. La Touche. Though not given any formal management position or status, Ernest was spending an increasing amount of time at the site, fascinated by the brewing process. He had in fact exceptional flair in engineering and technology, combined with a highly inventive streak, which would lead to the vital modernisation of brewery equipment. Gadgets were one of his greatest loves. At Glenmaroon he installed a mechanical electric organ.

The following October, the Honourable Rupert Edward Cecil Lee married Lady Gwendolin Onslow, eldest daughter of the fourth Earl of Onslow. Since his return from South Africa, most of Rupert's time had been taken up with sailing and military service. The sea and sailing was an abiding passion for all three brothers throughout their lives. Each would develop a singular devotion to their boat, each set sail on exotic, sometimes hair-raising adventures overseas. In 1901 Rupert built a ninety-foot, ninety-eight-ton racing yacht called the *Leander*. It won the King's Cup, beating both Sir Reginald Bulkeley's *Britannia* and the Kaiser's *Meteor*. 'Will you ever forgive me?' Bulkeley is supposed to have said to his wife. 'Never,' replied the lady in her humiliation. The *Leander* went on to win several more prizes, including the Vasco da Gama Challenge Cup, but crashed during the Kaiser's Cup in 1902, subjecting Rupert to an ignominious rescue.

From Rupert's perspective the Territorial Army was a serious business, not merely a pastime for a wealthy, bored young man who liked playing with guns. The Admiralty seemed largely unaware of the growing German military threat. Rupert was in no doubt about the Kaiser's intentions and saw the vital potential of a well-trained regiment. For a while he was captain of the London Rifle Volunteer Regiment. His enthusiasm and dedication to training gradually turned a bunch of amateurs into a regiment worthy of acceptance by the Royal Navy in the crucial year of 1913.

Lady Gwendolin Onslow had been intrigued by the Guinness family for some time before she and Rupert were formally introduced. The daughter of William Hillier Onslow, Governor General of New Zealand, formerly Minister of Agriculture, she had been filled with a passion for social justice from early childhood. In 1896 when she met Lord Iveagh for the first time she was fifteen and, despite a sheltered up-bringing at Clandon Park in Surrey, was 'very full of ideas about social reform and, having consumed much literature on the subject, was impressed by the great gulf between the rich and the poor and the misery and squalor of the slums'. Lord Iveagh's reputation for philanthropy had captured her adolescent imagination. He was the living expression of her ideals.

Eventually she received the coveted invitation to Elveden. But at close quarters she found the Iveaghs rather disap-pointing, formidable and distant, and the house over-whelming, 'luxurious beyond any dream'. Of the sons of the house Rupert caught her attention from the first. Walter, endowed with the most obvious charm, was 'too mature for his years', aged by South Africa and that scar across his face. Rupert, on the other hand, acting as his father's secretary, courted by many ambitious mamas with marriageable daughters, was unlike any other debutantes' delights she had met. He had lost none of the gentle, thoughtful qualities lauded by his schoolmasters. Quiet and unassuming, devout like his mother, whose high churchmanship he found appealing, his tastes were simple and unsophisticated. He was as uncomfortable with the ostentation of Elveden as Gwendolin, preferred walking, and could talk sensibly about issues that really mattered. 'We had a long and enjoyable discussion on mentally defective and crippled children,' she noted, though it was hard to converse seriously on any matter, since conversation was drowned by the din of the electric piano.

They met regularly at shooting parties and, to her father's horror, the relationship deepened. He is reputed to have said to her, 'Never mind the money; don't marry a brewer.'[3]

It was made clear to Gwendolin that she was welcome to lunch at any time at the Iveagh's London house in Grosvenor Place. But to be received at Elveden or Farmleigh or St Stephen's Green she must await an invitation. She never felt completely relaxed with her future in-laws. Although Lord Iveagh was often described in the newspapers as scholarly, Gwendolin found him rather dapper, albeit modest and reserved, considering his great wealth. Lady Iveagh was continually suffering from recurrent bouts of 'ill health', a euphemism for the strange obsessions which afflicted her mind from time to time. When she did make an appearance she was 'well-corseted' and not very fashionable, though she played and sang charmingly.

For their part the Iveaghs thoroughly approved of Gwendolin. 'I consider you a very nice girl, my dear,' Adelaide said to her one day, patting her hand, 'and I only like to have nice girls here.' In fact they must have heaved a sigh of relief. It was rumoured that their eldest son was embroiled with a not-so-nice young woman he had met on a train who had borne him a child. The mistress, if she existed, suddenly disappeared from the scene thanks to the intervention of Gwendolin's father, and never, throughout his long and happy marriage, was there ever the faintest whiff of infidelity attached to Rupert, unlike brother Ernest, who had rather a reputation as a womaniser, and Walter, with his very public dalliances.

The society gossip magazines, *Vanity Fair* and the *Pall Mall Gazette*, approved of the match, solemnised in a crowded St Margaret's, Westminster. The future George V sent the groom a tie-pin. For their honeymoon the couple travelled abroad – by car, not carriage, an adventurous choice in its day, but neither Rupert nor Gwenny could resist a challenge.

Shortly after their marriage Rupert was adopted as the Conservative candidate for the Haggerston division of Shoreditch, an area of high economic deprivation, hardly likely to choose a Conservative as its MP, let alone one with immense wealth and a title. Neither set of parents thought it the best place for Rupert to launch his political career. They were even more horrified when Rupert and Gwenny chose to set up home at 266 Kingsland Road in the heart of the constituency, the only way they felt they could contest the seat with integrity. Lord Iveagh, who had bought the happy pair a house in fashionable St James's Square as a wedding present, was beginning to discover of what mettle his son was made. Rupert had chosen to live in the midst of the slums he had spent his life trying to eradicate. When Dodo had criticised Henry and Fanny all those years ago for raising their children in the East End, little did she guess her own son would one day choose to live there himself. Even the press was approving, though puzzled. 'It speaks well for dis-interested public service in this country that a man whose recreations are yachting, rowing, shooting and golf, and whose clubs are the Beef-steak, Leander, Carlton, Garrick and Royal Yacht Squadron should be ready to work for the weak and needy.'[4]

Working for the poor, living among them for some of the time, did not necessarily imply a complete change of lifestyle. Rupert was after all the eldest son of a peer, and Gwenny was presented at court, dressed in soft white chiffon, her gown trimmed and hemmed with wide bands of white lace embroidered with silver thread, her silver train trimmed with silver cords and tassels. The couple also bought Pyrford from Lord Onslow as their country seat and bolthole, and Rupert took great pleasure in redesigning the house.

In fact, until he met Gwenny, Rupert showed little political promise or party enthusiasm. His first public speech, reported in the *West Suffolk Advertiser* in 1902, deserved two out of ten for originality. It was a hotch-potch of basic patriotic values – the need for a strong navy and empire – spiced with just a hint of the ideals which Gwenny would mould into a motivating force – a plea for better education and housing. 'The Conservative Party', he said, 'had always been the working man's friend.' Seven difficult years in Shoreditch were the anvil on which the metal was hammered into shape.

Rupert taught Gwenny to drive their sixteen-horsepower, four-seater Dietrich. In 1906 she was involved in a car crash, and though unhurt physically, lost the baby boy she was carrying. He was born prematurely and lived only thirty-six hours. It took her a long time to come to terms with the loss of their first-born.

For a long time she was edgy and nervy, given to anxiety states and bouts of depression. Rupert, with his even good humour, provided the rock-like foundation which enabled her to find her feet and encouraged her to exercise her gifts. Because her mercurial, shrewd, penetrating analysis of every situation often eclipsed his more measured, cumbersome approach, not everyone realised how much she depended on him. She helped him assimilate information, wrote his letters and his speeches, and was a constant hive of mental activity. He drove away the darkness, raised her spirits, and in time encouraged her into her own political career.

Temperamentally they were complete opposites. Yet theirs proved to be a mutually liberating and complementary union. While he was gentle, chivalrous, invariably kind and generous, she could be imperious and temperamental. She never did learn to suffer fools gladly. Her mental powers were far too alert, though she did mellow in time and become more approachable. Rupert's greatest gift was his ability to put people at ease. They would tell him their life story in five minutes, Gwenny claimed. His ability to make her feel safe and cherished was always his greatest attraction for her. A close relative suggested their relationship was built on devotion rather than passion.[5] But that is an artificial divide. Devotion is a powerful emotion. If the heart strings still twang when the other walks into the room, passion has not died. And Rupert and Gwenny were lost without each other.

With Gwenny's support, Rupert worked hard on the London City Council. As Chairman of a sub-committee on special schools, he introduced a number of humanitarian reforms in the treatment of 'backward' children, with whom he felt a special empathy because of his own childhood struggles. In a visionary move by standards then, £¾ million was spent on employing educational psychologists responsible for organising small classes at ordinary schools so that children with special needs could receive individual attention.

In 1908 his patience was rewarded when he became MP for Haggerston in a by-election. He and Gwenny were in Canada little more than a year later when news reached them that there was to be a General Election and he must return to London, 'to submit to that degrading process, a contested election in the London slums for the second time in 12 months, and the fifth time in five years'. He was heartily sick of being attacked for his background, of being snubbed for his upper-class associations. The voters abandoned him, as he knew they would. He had given so much, but received little back. Enough was enough. He had served a reasonable apprenticeship, moved into St James's Square and accepted the candidature of a safer seat.

Enthusiastic imperialists, Rupert and Gwenny had been deeply impressed by the wealth of opportunity for enterprising British immigrants in Canada – if they were adequately prepared for conditions out there. In 1912 they bought Working Park Farm, 550 acres of land near their Pyrford estate, and set up the first emigration training establishment. No fees were required, simply token board and lodging costs and a deposit on the fare out. Students were to adhere to a strict code of conduct – no swearing or gambling, no smoking on duty. By the summer of 1912, seventy-five men had left for Canada. The similarities with the subsistence farming programme Henry Grattan Guinness had established at Cliff College forty years earlier are striking. The old genetic code appeared to be playing games once again, linking Lord Iveagh's son to his grandfather's late cousin.

In 1912 Rupert became the MP for Southend-on-Sea, a seat he retained for fifteen years, until he inherited his father's peerage and moved into the House of Lords. But his pedigree, and the snobbery it invoked, pursued him to the Commons. In the 1914 debate of the Inebriates Bill his absence was duly noted with cries in the House of 'Call for Stout'.

But whenever they looked back at their time in Shoreditch Rupert and Gwenny would always see that no matter how difficult they were, those were the most formative years of their lives.

4.

While Henry and Grace were touring the world and Rupert and Gwendolin were setting up home in Shoreditch, Lucy lived with her babies at Mount View, her Castleton cottage. Karl came and went like the Cheshire cat in *Alice in Wonderland,* and Lucy's letters followed him about with news of any support she had managed to raise for the Mission and detailed accounts of the development of their two boys. In one letter she described a light contrivance, which costs about 2/6d and has 1000 charges. It is quite a little thing. You can carry it about in your hands and it has no outside battery connection or wires. You press a button and it shows a bright electric light, which appears as long as you keep the button pressed down and when you want to put it out, you raise your finger. I have so wished for one of these, as it would be an immense help with little Bab at nights. One need not strike a match or fumble with a candle, but one can just put a light weight on the button of the box and instantly have light enough to attend to him.

The torch was evidently an exciting newfangled invention.

Throughout 1903 Karl and Lucy travelled the United Kingdom separately, trying to establish the work of the Sudan Pioneer Mission,[6] speaking at countless meetings, setting up thirty-two local support groups known as 'Lightbearer Leagues'. While Karl completed his doctorate at Freiburg University, Lucy visited senior Christian ministers in person, making unashamed use of her name and her network of contacts. Childhood lessons learned from watching Hudson Taylor and her parents stood her in good stead. Nonetheless, raising support was harder than she ever imagined. Despite concern for the Sudan region, every existing British missionary society was stretched to the limit. Competition for funds was fierce. Few church members seemed to share her sense of urgency in halting the march of Islam. Well-respected ministers like F. B. Meyer told her it was unwise even to consider another nonconformist mission at that stage. Lucy was undaunted, but the new SPM was forced to run on a shoestring. By the end of 1903 there was only £230 in hand. Dr Kumm, the Council was informed, would not draw a salary. His services were free.

Despite warnings that they must be prepared to face 'loneliness, hardship and danger', potential candidates began to come forward and since the Council felt operations should begin in Northern Nigeria, Karl was sent to Tripoli to learn the Hausa language. While he was away Lucy managed to convene a crucial meeting of eminent Scottish supporters in the Session Room of the Free St George's Church in Edinburgh, among them the church's minister, the elderly Dr Alexander Whyte, one of the great pioneer explorers of the Sudan. On hearing him for the first time, the writer Sir James Barrie had said, 'He came to announce his discoveries with a greater joy on his face than I think I have ever seen on the face of any other man.' At that first Scottish Council meeting on 15 June 1904, Dr Whyte proposed that the SPM change its name to the Sudan United Mission, since it was the only nonconformist missionary society working in the Sudan, and could provide a united denominational front. The decision was a turning point. It established the SUM as an accepted, viable proposition.

The first London Council meeting on 27 June 1904 authorised the decision to send Karl on a risky fact-finding expedition to the unknown Bauchi Hill Country on the Upper Benue River. On 23 July a pioneer party of four set sail from the Liverpool docks for the mouth of the Niger with a commission to set up a church there. There were no funds for the journey, but when Lucy arrived home from the farewell, a gift of £1,000 was waiting for her.

In theory she accepted the inevitability of another long separation. In practice her emotions were becoming severely strained. The writing and travelling continued at a frenetic pace. She attended all council meetings in Scotland, Ireland and two in England, and often wrote the minutes. She interviewed prospective candidates, collected lantern slides and delivered hundreds of lectures on the needs of the Sudan. She could not relax or rest, and when she was at home the baby meant broken, sleepless nights. In one letter to Karl she tells him that Evan Roberts, the young miner whose preaching has triggered the Welsh revival, is tired out and forced to take a fortnight's rest. 'Lucky fellow! I envy him and hope for quiet days in the Blessed Beyond.'

It appears that at some very deep level she found it necessary to prove herself to Karl. In March, while he was in Tripoli, a woman had applied to go to the Sudan and was rejected on the grounds that the Mission was not in a position to accept women, men pioneers being needed first. To the minute book Lucy added in pencil, 'It was hoped she might go on later.' But it was several years before Karl recognised the possibility of a woman's contribution to his work.

Lucy was left to imagine what it would be like to be able to share completely in Karl's work.

> I write in a stuffy noisy restaurant near the Law Courts, where I have come in from the grind of the noisy street. Deft waiters pass and repass. Electric light shines on me. I write on a white tablecloth amidst glistening knives and silver. And will this reach thy dear hand in Africa? In Africa? Oh my dear – *would* I might come with it!

The more she demanded to be let into his life, the more he held her at arm's length. The more he guarded his space, the more desperate she became. It was a vicious circle. From the earliest separation she adopts a pleading, almost childish tone, referring to him as 'Husbie' and herself as 'Lulu'. 'Shall I say I will come when my Darling has finished his task? When should I come?'

Everyone complained that Karl was a bad letter-writer. He became so completely absorbed in the task that he failed to keep in touch, and letters were the only means of following his progress. Lucy took this failing personally. When he ceased to write regularly it almost broke her heart. She had not missed one mail day since he left.

Oh my naughty darling, why have I no letter from thee for over five weeks now again? What prevents just one post-card from reaching thy little waiting one? Has my Heart's Dearest been ill? and he doesn't tell me? Maxwell (one of the team) actually says that you said that you couldn't write to me – you were 'busy'. He says you said you sent me your love.

But Karl was too preoccupied to hear, too single-minded to understand how hurt she was, and Lucy would not even admit to herself that she could not cope, let alone hold him back. He was too perfect a hero to be dragged down by her inferior needs. She had constructed a pedestal for him and there he must remain, adored but unobtainable.

But she had her babies. They at least ensured her some short interludes of playfulness, though they continually asked for their father.

Babs is so sweet and funny. This morning, lying in bed, I was having little jokes with him and asked, 'Who is this in Mummy's bed? A horsey?' 'No,' he solemnly replied in his deep voice. 'A moo-cow?' I asked. 'A chick-chick?' 'No.' 'Is it a fish? A doggie?' To everything he answered, 'No,' till I asked, 'What is it then?' and the tiny atom answered, 'A MAN.'

Almost at once the relaxed, unguarded moment is over and she is reading to Henry from the Book of Daniel, because she believes it is vital he should grow up with a knowledge of biblical prophecy. After all, he could well see its fulfilment.

The rapid succession of the seasons as she waits for a few snatched moments with her husband oppressed Lucy with a strong sense of brevity of life. 'Autumn weather has come today. The beautiful Indian summer has gone and the rains have broken. The birds flew South last night . . . a great cloud of them . . . and I longed to go too – to you, to you – in the far South.' The passage of time had always filled Lucy with a wistful yearning for the irretrievable. Now every fleeting moment is a sacrifice of time they could have spent together. In October she tells him the children have enticed her into the churchyard where they play happily and she gets on with her writing, until, 'In the still grey evening the hands of the clock in the Church tower point towards five and another day is almost gone. Sitting here, one realises that our day too must vanish. Such a beautiful day of life you have made mine, so full of unutterable beauty, wealth and joy.'

Christmas approached and Lucy wrote to Karl, 'In the dim faint hope that possibly you may appear, I am actually beginning to practise a piece of Chopin (his ballade No.3) which appeals to my mind at present. Always at special seasons of life, there come to me special pieces of music, musical expressions of the thoughts of the time. The present one is very beautiful.' Karl did arrive home to Derbyshire for that blissful Christmas of 1905, 'the people of the village coming to rejoice with us under the Christmas tree'. But around the little family, revelling in moments of rare togetherness beneath the Christmas lights, the shadows were beginning to lengthen.

A few weeks later Karl left for the United States and in April 1906 set up the American SUM headquarters in Germantown, Philadephia with Charles Kurthalz as the director. Speaking invitations poured in and it began to look as if this might be a long trip. Henry Mabie, Secretary of the American Baptist Missionary Union, who had not seen Lucy since her visit with her father thirteen years before, encouraged Karl to send for her and the boys. Her gift at public speaking would be an invaluable asset, particularly over the summer when thousands of young people converged on the Moody Conference Centre at Northfield for the annual convention weeks. Bill Moody offered the Kumm family the use of a delightful chalet within easy access of the main auditorium, hidden away from the crowds in a secluded spot in woods high above it, with magnificent views of the surrounding countryside.

Lucy loved it. She wrote to Geraldine:

Here at Northfield that you know so well, in the midst of a beautiful forest, with fir trees, birches and sycamores around us on three sides, and a lovely view of distant country stretching away from our hillside in front, we are living in a pretty little cottage or bungalow – an earthly paradise.

As I write the boys are playing steam-engine, running and calling to each other round and round the house. They tremendously enjoy their free, open-air life up here.

Our cottage is only one sitting-room and three bedrooms, besides kitchen and bathroom; just a tiny spot of a place one storey high, with a wide verandah in front leading straight out to the woods and hillside. We are close to the auditorium but out of sight of visitors and meetings. Unless we care to go down the hill, we need not see anything of crowds or conference, and feel quite out of this world. How I wish you could be here to see our cosy corner and enjoy its beauty with us.

Shortly before she left England Harry had told her of recent, shocking information he had received from the Congo about the way natives were being oppressed and exploited by the Belgian rubber slavers. Lucy, as ever, was incensed and anguished at such injustice and decided to use her summer retreat at Northfield to alert the public. It would be the strongest piece of polemic she had ever written.

At five in the morning on 2 July she got up early to say goodbye to Karl. He was to spend some time in New York, return to England to speak at the Keswick Convention, then travel on to the Sudan, probably not returning for at least two years. Karl thought she seemed more positive than usual at his departure, committed to her writing project, talking enthusiastically about the possibility of staying on in the States for a year or so, as she had received such a warm welcome. The summer break at Northfield was evidently doing her a great deal of good. She and the boys accompanied him into the woods a little way, then waved him off.

From that moment she seems to have been filled with a sense of foreboding. She began to write desperately, in an agony of mind, the anguish of parting from her husband fuelling her indignation for the world's oppressed.

As she was busy writing on 18 July she felt an excruciating stab of pain in her lower abdomen and began to bleed heavily. A doctor was called to see her the following day and suspecting a miscarriage, told her she needed immediate surgery to deal with 'septic endometritis'. Lucy refused. She had more important things to do. It appears from a letter she wrote to Mrs Penrose, wife of Judge Penrose, with whom she had stayed five weeks in Germantown, that she had no idea of the real nature of the problem. She asked Mrs Penrose if she knew of any remedy for the loss of blood, as her doctor wasn't doing her any good.

On 22 July, by sheer force of will, she gave an inspired, impassioned appeal for the Sudan in the packed, great auditorium. Mabie later wrote to Geraldine,

> although I had heard her in previous years, and knew her gifts in that line, this particular address delighted and astonished me beyond measure. It moved on with telling and dramatic power, as she portrayed to us with the aid of a map beside her, the great Soudan, and Christ knocking at the door of his church to find who of his people were willing to go. It was a marvellous address and will never be forgotten by anyone who heard it.

She collapsed immediately afterwards and had to be carried home.

On 27 July a second doctor strongly advised immediate curettage, but she still refused. It seems she was unaware that she was having a miscarriage until 4 August, when the obvious remains of a baby were lost. For a while the pain disappeared and she toiled on with her writing day after day, night after night, often in bed, until 7 August, when the pain suddenly returned with a vengeance and she scribbled her final sentence. 'It is done. Now they can do what they like,' she said to Alice Thompson, the children's nurse.

In Castleton on 8 August Karl received a cable, 'Ill. Operation today. Lucy'. 'Shall I come?' he cabled back.

Curetting, a relatively new operation, was performed in the cottage under ether. During surgery it became clear that an ectopic pregnancy had ruptured the fallopian tube. The pain must have been unbearable. How Mrs Kumm could have continued with her work, the doctors hardly knew. They simply hoped that the local peritonitis would not spread to the rest of her body.

She regained consciousness three hours later. The Moodys offered her their own home, but she was too weak to be moved. The slightest noise disturbed her. But it was difficult for Alice Thompson to nurse her and care for the children in a holiday chalet. 'Helmy and Karl are just as good as can be,' Alice wrote to Geraldine.' 'They are so gentle and quiet when in the house, which is not often. We have been mercifully favoured with fine weather so they are able to live outside all day long.'

Lucy seemed to rally. 'Unnecessary,' she cabled Karl in response to his question about whether he should come. 'But I hope he does come soon,' Alice wrote to one of Lucy's friends.

Karl never came. A second cable from Alice on the 9 August, 'Probable recovery. Improving', was reassuring. But two days later he wrote to Geraldine, 'Our darling Lu is seriously ill. When I left her she was perfectly well. In her last letter she says she may have to undergo an operation . . . You may well understand that I am exceedingly anxious. Do join me in prayer. I am so busy with the mission, and now our little one ill.'

By then Lucy's condition had deteriorated alarmingly. The peritonitis had become generalised and there was little more the doctors could do. A further operation offered one possible last chance. For the children's sake she consented. At six o'clock in the evening she calmly set about ordering her affairs. Moody's daughter, Emma Moody Fitt, acted as her amanuensis. She dictated one last love letter to the husband she had so adored. She reassured him that she regretted and resented nothing. He had been the light, the joy, the glory of her life. In her will she left her few possessions, her journals, books, a watch, her sonnets on motherhood and a small sum of money, 'enough for the journey home', to Karl and the children.

To Geraldine she bequeathed her most precious treasure, her two boys. She explained to her sister that one day Henry was to have her own big Bible, while her father's Bible, with notes in his hand, was to go to little Karl.

I want him to study Daniel, and Revelation and the Lord's closing prophecies of the three Gospels. If he will do that for Mother's sake, when he is fifteen to sixteen, he will understand afterwards why I wanted him to do so much. When he is old enough I should like him to know all the time before he was born I had one prayer, one longing, one hunger – that he should continue Father's prophetic studies and research, and in the later days, when he lives he may perhaps see the restored Jewish state, in those unutterable days, he may understand and tell. He is only four now, but I see, I know he is a seer, a thinker. He will look more into the heart of things; will live, I hope, in those days, and he must understand. I wish he could have access to Father's library when he is old enough to hunger for it, to need to know what it contains.

Henry, my angel boy – he does seem that to me, with just an angel's heart, sympathy and devotion – will want to help the suffering, and put wrongs right. He is more called to that I think; perhaps to be a medical man. But that I do not know. Perhaps rather a preacher. Possibly both. I should like that. I must not write more. I am very restful, very happy in God. How wonderfully good He has been to us – the boys – how can I thank him? My husband, God's gift, blessed and beloved beyond words; and then you, Father, Harry, Annie, Gershom and darling Janie, whom I have never seen. My love, my heart to all of them, AND TO MY SONS – MY SOUL.

Good night, dear heart,

Without fear, yours, Lucy.

Finally she dictated one last message for her boys:

I am leaving you, darlings. I am waiting for you with Jesus – waiting till you come. Don't be lonely, darlings. You will come. It is only a little while. I want you to be brave.

I want you to have Auntie Geraldine for your Mamma. She has no little boys or girls, but she is waiting for you. She will be your Mamma – only very, very much better than I have been. Ask Papa to let her be your Mamma – for a little time at least.

And now – you both belong to him. He will safely lead us home. Good-bye, darlings – heart's darlings. I am waiting for you – There.

At seven the operation was performed. Her last words to the

doctors were, 'I know that my Redeemer lives.' A raging thunderstorm suddenly broke over Northfield, shattering the hush which had descended over the conference centre since Lucy's condition had become known, shaking the great auditorium where many had gathered in silent prayer. According to Alice the lightning 'was playing around us all the time'. Lucy never fully regained consciousness and died five hours later at one o'clock on 12 August. It was 'Missionary Day' at the August conference.

In the early morning a brief service was held at the cottage, led by Dr Torrey and Dr Campbell Morgan, two of the most respected preachers in America, speakers at the conference. Then the coffin was hoisted gently on to the shoulders of Moody's two sons, Charles Kurthalz, Harry Mabie, and two ex-Harley students, and carried carefully down the winding path through the woods to a hearse on the road below. It was deposited in the Moodys' vault to await her husband's arrival.

That evening thousands packed the great auditorium for a memorial service. Dr Campbell Morgan and Henry Mabie both spoke briefly, Mabie explaining what the Guinness family stood for in the world of missions, 'and of the part your dear sister had taken in editorial and other practical labours,' he wrote to Geraldine, 'and of her absolutely fearless and radiant crossing of the river when she reached it'.

Henry and Karl had been taken to Emma Moody Fitt's house. They desperately wanted to go back to the cottage to see Mamma, and Alice did what she could to make the bereavement as bearable as possible.

We thought at first that it was best not to tell the little fellows, but they asked about Mamma so often that I had to prepare them by asking them if they wouldn't like Mamma to go to heaven where she wouldn't have any pain. But they said they would like to go too. We talked a long time about it and then I read the letter to them that she had dictated. When I had finished reading Helmy said, 'Has Mamma died?' He was almost heart-broken. But he is happy most of the time. Only first thing in the morning and last thing at night he asks about her.

A distraught Karl Kumm arrived ten days later and Lucy was finally laid to rest as the sun set in the Northfield village cemetery. He described the scene to Geraldine and Howard:

I am sitting by darling Lu's grave. All is silent except for the rustling of the birch leaves and the sighing of the branches in the breeze. I might be in the dead, silent desert. No human habitation is in sight. To the left the quiet fields of Connecticut valley, before me the wooded hills, and to the right the grey-white graves of the cemetery.

Shadows play on Lu's tombstone as the boughs of the trees bend to and fro. I would like to stay here altogether and always. Oh how she loved me.

Six years and six months we were married but less than a year we actually had together.

What a difference that year has made in my life, what a depth of fellowship and soul communion.

Only now did Karl appreciate what he had lost, but even then it was, 'Oh, how she loved me', not, 'Oh, how I loved her'. Her belief in him had given him the impetus to carry on, however difficult the circumstances. And they often seemed impossible. 'Vorwärts' was a common leitmotiv in her letters. How would he carry on without that measure of love and trust undergirding all he did?

But Lucy could not have lived life at that intensity much longer. While she was in Germantown Mrs Penrose was horrified to find her writing at 10 p.m. one night, obviously worn out, with little Karl in the middle of the bed. Her kindly hostess made a bed up for her right at the top of the house and insisted she had at least one good night's rest. 'She told me her mother had killed herself with work. I said, "My dear Mrs Kumm, you are doing just the same." "Yes, I know," she replied.'

When the precious manuscript which cost her so much effort was finally placed in Harry and Annie's hands, they made the appalling discovery that it was virtually unpublishable. It was too subjective and emotive. Some of her descriptions were so horrendous, her accusations against the Belgian authorities and British government so outrageous they would have alienated any support Harry hoped to rally. For several years the manuscript lay on a shelf at Harley House, gathering dust.

For some people intensity is a fairly minor handicap like colour-blindness in an otherwise rich and colourful personality. In Lucy it was a fatal flaw which eventually cost her her life. But she died as she wished, not sitting primly on her womanly Edwardian dignity, leaving fire, courage and passion to the male of the species. She had her adventures, her causes, her dreams. She had an undeniable impact on her world, left books of poems and hymns enjoyed in their time, founded a missionary society called 'Action Partners' today, still working in Africa. Mabie thought her a prophet, but that did not mean she was a plaster-of-Paris saint. In her tiredness she was often stressed and sometimes irritable. Certain individuals got on her nerves. 'Oh, darling, you know what she is,' she once wrote to Karl. 'There are times when I feel I cannot endure her another moment, and just take refuge in silence.'

Into her forty-one years she tried to pack another hundred, but her physical and emotional being could not take it. Like a meteor Lucy, the Light, burned herself out.

5.

Like Karl, Howard and Geraldine were shocked beyond words when they heard that Lucy was dead. The last telegram had reassured them she was improving. At Castleton Karl had received a telegram at 6.35 on the morning of 12 August which simply said, 'Mrs Kumm died midnight after operation here. Insistence peritonitis. End peaceful. Cable instructions. Christian sympathy. Moody.'

Karl contacted the Taylors at the China Inland Mission home in Barnsley at once. 'Come immediately Castleton. Lucy gone.' On 14 August, when Karl had left for the States, Geraldine took it upon herself to inform all their friends, including the Sudan United Mission councils and supporters.

> One week ago we did not even know she was ill. Now her stricken husband is on his way across the Atlantic to bring home the little sons who alone, of all her own, were with her.
>
> It is hard, and would be well nigh impossible to write about it, as you will understand, were it not to ask you, dear friends, to bear him up in prayer in his hour of need, and to remember my dear Father, Dr Grattan Guinness in Sydney, (it was on his seventy first birthday our loved one passed away) and my dear brother Whitfield in China, to whom the news will come as a terrible shock.
>
> You will know what it is to our hearts that none of us were near her.

But life would go on. There were now five missionaries in the Upper Benue. Five more would join them soon. She ended her letter with Lucy's recurrent cry, 'We must go forward'.

She and Howard were waiting at the Liverpool docks when Karl arrived back in England with the children.

Never shall I forget Karl's face as he came down the long flight of steps by which they had to cross from the vessel to the landing stage, carrying the little one in his arms and leading Henry by the hand. The children were pale and tired with being up so late and looked almost as pale and wan as he did and their whole dress and appearance so pitifully told the lack of a mother's care.

They all went to Mount View in Castleton to sort out the remainder of Lucy's personal belongings.

Geraldine was impressed by Karl's relationship with his children.

I have learned to know him and love him as never before, and to see something of the power and sweetness of his character. He is unusually gifted and loving, He will be able, yes, even single-handed to carry on the work. He is devoting himself to the children and finds his chief comfort in them. They love him and cling to him in a most beautiful way and it is a great comfort to see how thoroughly he understands and how well he can manage them.

It was a rude awakening when she realised Karl had no intention of leaving the children with her. It pained her most of all that Lucy's last wishes were not to be fulfilled, but Howard in his usual wise and patient way urged her to keep quiet and wait. An argument at this stage would only hurt the children. And after all it was Karl's right to decide. The Taylors bowed to his wishes and left for Switzerland, where Geraldine planned to write an epic biography of her father-in-law.

Worried as ever about his wife's overpowering relatives, Karl had sent to Germany for his sister Amanda. But caring for two strange children who did not speak her language in a foreign country was not an easy undertaking. 'She is going to spoil the children altogether,' Karl wrote. 'She simply lets him have their own sweet will in everything.'

The idea was doomed from the start. Amanda could not create a home for the little family. She was terribly homesick. As soon as she heard that their mother was ill she insisted she must return to Germany at once. Karl was desperate. He was due to speak at a huge convention in the United States. There was no other alternative but to send an urgent telegram to Switzerland. Howard wired back immediately, 'Send the boys to us,' and set off for London to collect them.

It seemed to Geraldine that her two dream-children, the children she had never managed to bear, had materialised at last. Nevertheless the enormity of the responsibility, of Lucy's sacred trust, made her nervous. She and Howard were approaching fifty, the boys only four and six – how would it work out? But the mothering instincts so long repressed rose naturally to the surface. 'I loved them just as I had loved Phoebe and Agnes – there was something special about it.' With the boys she and Howard were young again. They romped and played as they had never done before.

One day the boys arrived home full of a story they had heard about a mother who had left her baby on a bus. 'Do you think a mother could forget a baby like that?' she asked them, intending to teach them about God's love from the verse in the Old Testament which said, 'Even a mother may forget, but I will not forget you'. Henry looked up at her, his eyes full of love and trust, and said, 'I don't know if a mother could, but I'm sure an auntie-mother couldn't,' and somehow the moral of the story slipped out of Geraldine's mind.

She spoke to them of Lucy often, determined they would never forget her. Small as they were, they remembered her playing the piano. Everyone always did. And whenever Geraldine wanted to hold up a model of perfect manhood she always told them they could do no better than to be as kind and considerate as their Uncle Howard. Watching this sweet and courteous man, they knew she was right.

6.

Henry Grattan received the news of the death of his beloved Lucy only a month after the birth of his son, John Christopher. 'I shall never forget his tearless grief as he read the cabled message of sorrow,' Grace noted in her journal. He wanted to be alone and went for a walk along the shore of a quiet bay in New South Wales. The pain of losing Lucy was almost more than he could bear and he sat for some time on the sands listening to the mournful roar of the ocean. Burying his head in his hands he began to weep. Suddenly he felt the gentle pressure of a hand on his shoulder. He raised his head slowly and found himself looking up into the radiant, wrinkled face of an old Aborigine woman. In a strange, halting accent she whispered, 'Let not your heart be troubled, neither let it be afraid . . . in my father's house are many mansions.' He turned away from her momentarily and sat looking out to sea, trying to absorb fresh meaning from those familiar words. When he turned back a few seconds later she had vanished. He stood up, looked in every direction, but there was no sign of her. For the rest of his life he would wonder who she was and where she had come from, and whether she was not some angelic visitation.

The arrival of John Christopher meant that Henry and Grace's companionship could never be quite as unbroken as it once had been. Finding suitable accommodation for a wife and baby was a continual problem for an itinerant preacher and Henry frequently had to travel on alone, leaving Grace in a rented flat and returning to her as often as he could. It was not an ideal arrangement. Although Grace was fairly resourceful, he fretted for her and tended to overwork to avoid loneliness. Knowing their time together must inevitably be short made separation hard to bear. But what were they to do? He was much in demand and his calling must come first.

My own darling Wifie
How precious you are to me! You grow more and more dear as the days go by.

It has been an easy and most beautiful journey thus far. Only lonely! I seem to miss you most when there is something beautiful to see or hear or tell!

I wish I could find words strong and tender enough to tell how much I love you!

The Lord graciously grant that you may soon be strong again. And guide us where to be for the next few months.

Gladly and devotedly
Your own fond
Lover

While Grace stayed in Las Palmas in the Canary Islands, Henry went on alone to South Africa, preaching to huge mixed black and white congregations, standing on the seat of an open carriage.

Money seems to have been a constant worry. The bills he received from Las Palmas horrified him. The expense was 'ruinous'. '£10 a week is frightful. £80 for 8 weeks, I hope it will not be that.' But it was, and in the end they were both more than glad to be returning to England.

When they finally reached home in February 1908, Grace was pregnant again. Seeing England after an absence of five years was little short of heaven, though she had forgotten how ugly London could be. They steamed down the Thames on a grey, smoky, chilly winter morning:

Steamers, schooners, barges, were plying up and down the river, and then, a small boat came into view. We

393

could scarce discern its passengers, but some strange impulse bade us respond to the waves of welcome. Yes, we were right. There were Dr and Mrs Taylor, Mrs Harry Guinness and her daughter and later on at the railway station, my dear father, mother and eldest sister.

The press was also waiting for them. Grace was now accustomed to the fact that Henry was a source of public interest, but couldn't stomach 'the newspaper reporter, with his photographic apparatus, insisting on getting the travellers' impressions of the world in a ten-minute interview'. Ten minutes is luxurious by today's standards.

In five years London had undergone enormous change. It was an exciting, frightening new world with its crowded streets, and 'all the modern innovations of motor traffic'.

Needing a rest they settled for a time in St Leonards, enjoying the refreshing sea breezes of the quiet coastal town where their adventure together had begun. There in May their second son, Paul Ambrose was born, 'a child of energy and purpose, whose vivacious temperament helpfully balances the quiet, more meditative tendencies of his elder brother', Grace noted. At seventy-two Henry Grattan was the proud father of two small boys. His joy was complete. He bought a house in Bath and for the first time settled down with his young family to a life of tranquil domesticity.

While he and Grace were abroad on their extended honeymoon, Henry Grattan had also acquired four new grandchildren. Whitfield and Janie had a daughter, Isabel Gordon, known as Joy, in 1906, and a son, Henry Whitfield, in April 1908, a month before Paul was born. Harry and Annie's family had also continued to grow. Since the birth of their third child in Tasmania, there had been seven more, Alexander Fitzgerald in 1893, Margaret, known as Meg, in 1896, who died shortly before her second birthday, Victor Noel in 1898, Ruth Eileen in 1900, Gordon Meyer in 1902, and Howard Wyndham in 1903. By the time Robert Desmond appeared in 1905 his eldest sister Gene was seventeen.

In 1907 Gene accompanied her father to Peru and the book she wrote describing the trip, illustrated with her father's photographs, was an instant bestseller, making her Britain's most precocious travel writer to date.

But despite many preoccupations elsewhere, Harry's heart was still bound up in the Congo. By the turn of the century it was clear that the independent enquiry promised him by King Leopold back in 1895 had been nothing more than a placatory gesture, an attempt to 'throw dust in the eyes of Europe'. The officials Harry had named were simply moved elsewhere, the atrocities against natives worse than ever. When Sjoblom, whose original report had first sent Harry to the Congo, had complained to Governor-General Wahis he was manhandled himself and threatened with five years' imprisonment if he did not stop interfering. Harry was incensed and passed Sjoblom's account on to Sir Charles Dilke and other important MPs. He also contacted Reuters to ensure the story would appear in the European press.

Then, for several years, he did little more. At the Regions Beyond Mission stations some improvement had been noted and Harry wanted to believe it was due to King Leopold's direct intervention. But in 1902 Mr H. R. Fox-Bourne of the Aborigines' Protection Society published a document called *Civilization in Congoland*, and from that moment, Harry wrote, 'it became obvious that the policy of the entire State was one of rapine and cruelty, and must be publicly and determinedly exposed'.

Weekly articles on the Congo in the *West African Mail* by its correspondent E. D. Morel galvanised the British Parliament into action and they sent the consul, Roger Casement, on a tour of investigation. His report of the atrocities he had seen shocked the House of Commons,[7] and led Harry to believe the time was ripe to set up a pressure group.

The Congo Reform Association came into being in March 1904. Harry was the only committee member with the freedom to engage in full-time propaganda work, but his drive and charisma made him the ideal man for the job. He compiled a catalogue of evidence of brutality. Natives were chained, beaten, mutilated, starved and arbitrarily shot. With the compliance of white officers, native soldiers were allowed to eat their victims.

He took his evidence with him around the British Isles on a three-year tour, illustrating his lectures with a set of stomach-churning lantern slides. His most successful meeting, on 8 June 1904, was a public debate with a representative of the Congo Government, chaired by Lord Kinnaird at the St James's Hall. Many of the audience were totally unaware of the issues. Harry delivered irrefutable proof of Belgian maladministration, holding up the chicotte, a whip made of hippopotamus hide, which had been used to beat a native woman to death because her husband had not collected enough rubber. The government representative was rendered speechless.

Convincing the British public was not enough. Reform could only be accomplished at a diplomatic level, so Harry went back to see the man who had turned the Congo into 'an inferno'. King Leopold received him twice and Harry did not mince his words. The King could not help but admire the man though he did not care for what he had to say and promised little.

Undaunted, Harry laid carefully prepared memoranda before the Foreign Secretary, Lord Lansdowne. But the British Government seemed unable to exert any pressure on Belgium. In 1907, on his way to Peru with Gene, in one last desperate bid to arouse international concern he crossed the Atlantic and demanded an interview with the President of the United States, Theodore Roosevelt. It was granted. Harry reminded the President that America was the first to recognise Belgian supremacy in the Congo, supervising the signing of the Berlin Act by all the European powers. The President was not only entitled to remonstrate with the head of the Congo Free State if the constitution was not upheld, but had a responsibility to do so.

How Roosevelt reacted to being told his duty remains unknown, but since there were no obvious results, Harry was forced to continue his campaign with the pen as his weapon. In 1908, the year the Nigerian government gave its full support to Sudan United Mission proposals to build the Lucy Memorial Freed Slaves Home, Harry produced *The Congo Crisis, Rubber is Death* and *Slavery*, and at last began to see the fruits of his labours. On the evening of 19 November 1909 the Albert Hall was packed to capacity for a huge protest meeting, with the Archbishop of Canterbury in the chair, and the Bishops of Oxford and London among the speakers.

A month later King Leopold was dead and his successor, King Albert bowed to the strength of public protest and instituted immediate reforms. By 1912 the reforms were complete and the Congo Reform Association had the satisfaction of dissolving itself, its aims and objectives fully achieved.

After such a long struggle Harry found it hard to believe the campaign was over. He desperately wanted to see the results for himself. His doctor warned him against it. His strength had been taxed to the full. The strong, athletic young man with the robust constitution, ready for any adventure, had become rather frail and ailing in middle age, exhausted by physical and emotional strain. But he ignored the doctor's advice and went to the Congo anyway in April 1910.

He was laid low with a mysterious wasting disease three months after his arrival and had to return home. But three months was enough to see the fulfilment of all his hopes. In a circular letter to his supporters he was able to write with enormous satisfaction:

You will be glad to hear that the conditions of slavery which characterized the old regime in the Congo are disappearing, and as far as I can judge there is a genuine desire to deal fairly by the natives. Speaking to an exceedingly intelligent native at Stanley Pool the other day, I asked him his feelings in regard to recent changes at Leopoldville. His reply was unhesitating. 'The old, bad times are past, and to-day we are free!'

Chapter 12

1910–1918
The End of an Era

1.

Retirement never entered Henry Grattan's head. Preachers did not retire and the demands on him, at seventy-two, were almost as great as they had ever been. Besides, the new century had heralded many exciting new inventions and developments. There was still so much he wanted to do and see, exhibitions to visit, books he intended to write.

With his thick mane of white hair swept off his high forehead, and the small moustache he had taken to wearing, he cut an impressive figure in his dark frock-coat and high winged collar. His marriage seemed to have endowed him with eternal youth. He was as adventurous and as enthusiastic as ever. His grandchildren found him a stimulating, charming companion and he enjoyed seeing the new world through their adolescent eyes. On 4 July 1908 he wrote to Grace from Harley House:

Just now is the height of the season in London. The weather is lovely, and there is much to see. I am going this afternoon with Geraldine (Junior,) to see the great Missionary exhibition at the Agricultural Hall, connected with the London Missionary Society. You may judge of its magnitude from the fact that the exhibits fill that vast hall, and that there are 10,000 stewards.

Then on Saturday I have promised to take Geraldine and Dora McKenzie to see the wonderful Franco-English Exhibition. They say it is 'a perfect dream', that is – people say so – 7 miles of roads and palaces! I shall wonder if it eclipses the St Louis Exhibition.

Meanwhile I am getting on fast with writing work, as I have access to the books I need. It is sweet to think of you and our darling children. I long to be with you.

With a thousand kisses.

Your ever loving Henry.

From time to time Grace tried to remonstrate with him. She begged him not to over do things, but he was incorrigible. One letter began, 'You will see from above address that I am at Cliff.' Grace was unaware of his intention of going up to Derbyshire and had waited up for him until 3 a.m. After enthusing about the wonderful improvements made to his old home by the new owners, he apologises profusely for causing her such anxiety and promises faithfully to wire her about his movements in future. 'Don't be anxious about me,' he underlined, and enclosed a cheque for £5 towards household expenses.

Henry was still, it would appear, easily distracted from his domestic responsibilities, but Grace, more than Fanny, managed to bring him to heel. She could be coquettish and winsome, and he was a much older man, more easily tired and more susceptible to the lures and comforts of his home. Aware that he needed a hobby to occupy his active mind, she encouraged him to take up painting. He had never painted before, but it was abundantly clear, as soon as he picked up a brush, that he had inherited his mother's considerable talent both in water-colour and in oils. All his life he had loved nature. Reproducing its form and shape, its light and shade, its marvellous blend of colours, was a source of immense satisfaction.

When Grace went away, leaving him behind, he felt utterly bereft. He was as anxious about her as she about him. On two occasions, when her father died and she went to clear the parental home, and then when she masterminded their move to Bath, going on ahead to supervise the arrival of their belongings stored in boxes for the last five years, he wrote with grave concern:

> My darling
> All goes on well and quietly here. The children are flourishing. Only I am lonely – without you – not a soul to speak to. I read and write and go out and come in and pine to have you back.
>   So you are at last getting on with the house at Bath, cumbered up, books and boxes up to the ceiling. But my fear, my dread, is that you should lift weights and severely injure yourself. You know how shocking this would be in its effects. So for the children's sakes, and mine, as well as your own, don't do that.
>   Remember!

Throughout 1909 speaking invitations continued to pour in. People flocked to hear the old preacher. He could still pack the St James's Hall in London to capacity, as well as an overflow hall in the Polytechnic. Grace had no desire to curb Henry's active life, control his exuberant nature or inhibit him in any way, but was very aware of the strain it involved. He began to sound weary. 'London is very lonely to me – more than any other place I was ever in – such multitudes and you know nobody. Your mother seems well and contented here, and says she is never lonely. I suppose we are differently constituted.'

Separation became an increasing trial. He depended on Grace. He had always been dreamy, but his absentmindedness was becoming hazardous. On one occasion, taking a train journey with a young couple with a baby, he failed to see the precious bundle his friends had deposited on the carriage seat. They had only just put their little daughter down, when the great man, his thoughts on higher matters, lifted his coat-tails and was about to lower himself. They caught his arm just in time. In years to come, whenever the mother recounted the story she would look at her daughter, sigh, and say with a twinkle in her eye, 'It would have been a heavenly end for her!'

Grace's anxieties were well founded. Following a series of Advent lectures on the Second Coming of Christ, delivered in St James's Church, Bath, which attracted great crowds and were reported in detail in the *Bath Herald*, the doctors warned Henry that his heart was severely overstrained. If he continued to tax himself in this manner it would prove fatal. Henry had no regrets that his public ministry had cost him his health, but realised that for Grace's sake and the boys he must cancel all engagements for the following year.

On 29 December 1909 he wrote the last letter he ever sent her:

Darling Grace
John arrived safely with Bessie last night. I went to meet them as the night was fine. It was a great joy to get the dear boy back safe and sound. He slept in our bedroom, and today has had a good outing, and a merry evening romp and stories with me. I have seen no one else, and long to have you back, it is lonely enough now you are away.
    Take care of yourself.
    Karl was to have reached London today. I feared winter fogs and thought it best not to go up to town to meet him,

as we may have a visit from him here.

I have been reading and writing and had a walk on the top of Coombe Down today. It was lovely up there in bright sunshine. I think many thoughts but pen and ink are poor media of communication.

Ever darling, Your loving husband Henry.

A month later he set out on a cold, wet night to fulfil an obligation to the postman who had begged him to go to his house to say a few words to a gathering of his friends and relatives. Grace was loath to let him go, but he insisted. A promise was a promise, even to the postman. He caught a severe chill which quickly turned to pleurisy and pericarditis.

Henry weakened slowly, but though in intense pain, and unable to lie down, he was as mentally alert as ever. Aware that the end was creeping close, in a desperate bid to catch hold of every precious moment, Grace noted down everything he said. There was no fear whatsoever. He had once written a book called *On This Rock.* Now he reassured her, 'Gracie, can I sink through a rock?' Would He who had never abandoned him throughout his earthly life not take him safely through its close?

Howard and Geraldine, Henry and little Karl came to England to be near him, renting a house in Bath. To Geraldine's loving care Henry committed his beloved wife and children. 'What more fitting that my only daughter should be a guardian to you and the children. You cannot find a better friend than you would have in Geraldine. She is like me. I was very like her as a younger man and I am glad she loves my darling boys, I want her to be an influence in their lives.'

On the evening of 20 June he and Geraldine had a long discussion about the World Missionary Conference meeting at that very moment in Edinburgh under the leadership of his old friend and student, the American visionary, John R. Mott.

It was the first large international, truly ecumenical conference of its kind. Both Henry and Geraldine had dreamed of such an event and were excited about the potential of a conference which would one day form the basis of the World Council of Churches. As she was about to leave the room Geraldine turned back to her father and was very struck by his face. As he smiled back at her in the evening light it almost seemed transfigured.

Later that evening Grace noted:

We wheeled the invalid couch from the drawing-room, where he was during the seventeen weeks illness and as he spoke to me he was facing that lovely extensive view over the city of Bath which he loved to see from his study window. He smiled at me and said, 'I am too weak to talk, but have strength enough to meditate. I think over the history of the world, the history of redemption, the progress of Christ's kingdom, the important issues of this great Missionary Conference at Edinburgh. Then of our own missionary work in the world and all that has grown out of it, work in America, on the Continent, in China and Africa – and I think of what my dear ones have been enabled to do, and of my own life with its shortcomings.'

Someone came into the room, and he still smiled that beautiful smile, which so often illuminated his face; and throughout the day we noticed it, the light of his soul shining through. It was the last time we were alone together.

On 21 June 1910 she wrote: 'This beautiful midsummer day my precious Henry passed peacefully and quietly to rest at 10.45 this morning. I was not with him at the end, nor was Geraldine. Strange after we had been with him so constantly. It seemed as if we were not to say goodbye.'

Howard had been alone with him in the room when he

died. He said his father-in-law suddenly sat bolt upright in bed and with a rapturous expression on his face raised his arms to heaven. He kept them raised for some time, which was extraordinary, given the fact that he had been too weak to lift them at all the previous day. Then he let them fall, lay back on the pillow and was gone. He died, as he had been born, in the year of Halley's Comet, a happy coincidence for one who had spent so much of his life studying the signs in the heavens.

Grace wired the Edinburgh Missionary Conference with the news, and Dr Mott read the telegram to the vast audience assembled in the main auditorium. Almost every delegate present could claim that Dr Grattan Guinness's ministry had touched their lives in some way or another. The entire congregation rose spontaneously to its feet, and after a minute's silence, with a volume which almost shook the building, sang, 'For all the saints who from their labours rest'. The conference which was the fulfilment of so many of Henry Grattan's dreams was the scene of the public announcement of his death.

After a service in St James's Church, where he had recently delivered his series of Advent lectures, Henry Grattan Guinness was buried in the Abbey Cemetery overlooking the city of Bath, his grave sheltered by a large, solitary copper beech tree. Like Barnardo and many of his nonconformist, evangelical contemporaries, he had returned to the bosom of the Church of England in old age.

Obituaries appeared in *the Times*, the *Daily Express*, the *Daily Telegraph*, the *Westminster Gazette*, the *Yorkshire Post* and the *Sheffield Telegraph*, as well as in many other local and religious newspapers. They described his distinguished career as a writer, preacher and founder of missions. Some referred to his brewing connections and to the old story of how his mother's first husband had been killed at the hands of Daniel O'Connell. Many harked back fifty years to the days when he had preached to thousands from an open carriage in Northern Ireland. All paid tribute to his breadth of vision and achievement. Along with Spurgeon and Moody he was hailed as one of the three greatest preachers of the nineteenth century.

> The doctor's commanding figure will no longer be seen about Bath, which he made his residence for the last two years or more, and Bath will be the poorer, for Dr Guinness was a man of intensely human and wide sympathies, a member of all churches. One who knew him well has described him as a great thinker, a powerful writer and forceful preacher, one who gave up his life to missionary work and found in it the greatest happiness.[1]

Despite the simplicity of his lifestyle Henry Grattan Guinness was, nonetheless, a quintessential Guinness. He had all the drive, industry, energy, initiative, flair and philanthropy of his cousins. He also had their touch of austerity, their ruthless integrity, and the Guinness presence which made itself felt whenever they walked into a room.

From the moment he gave his legacy away, Henry Grattan's path diverged from that of his brewing cousins, while remaining strangely parallel in the building of their respective empires. When Sir Benjamin Lee died in 1868, the Rev. Dr Leeper praised the work he had carried out at St Patrick's Cathedral, 'a temple on whose every stone, on whose every shaft and cornice, on whose every embellishment his nature is inscribed'. Henry Grattan never built a monument in his own memory – though he had ample opportunity – unless St Sava's in Belgrade can be counted.

In 1895, Francis Harford Mackenzie, missionary, philanthropist and bachelor, converted in his youth by Henry Grattan in Paris, left his old mentor his entire estate, including 12,000 square metres of land in the centre of Belgrade. The land had particular significance for the Serbian Orthodox Church, for it was there on top of Vracar Hill in 1595 that the Turks publicly burned the relics of St Sava, Serbia's patron saint. In 1895 the Serbians started a fund-raising drive to build a cathedral on the spot, and in 1898, to enable them to do so, Henry Grattan Guinness gave them the land. In the cathedral, – not yet completed – the name 'Henrikh Gratan Gines' is inscribed in Cyrillic gold letters on a marble plaque.[2]

No one would have been more surprised at the dedication than Henry Grattan himself, for he never attached any importance to 'earthly' belongings. When Cliff, his 'palace', became a financial burden he let it go. The lease was a temporary gift, valued in its time, but never truly owned as a symbol of increasing social and temporal power. His only real treasure there, the eight-inch-diameter telescope, was transported back to Harley for the use of the students.

A stone Irish cross was erected over his grave. On one side Grace had Fanny's name inscribed. The other side she left blank for herself. In later years, looking back, she saw that it was fitting that there had been no formal farewell between them. For Henry the afterlife was a vivid reality, divided from this world by such a tenuous thread that death involved no real separation for those who truly loved each other. Knowing how soon their physical relationship must come to an end, he left her a poem to comfort her when the moment finally came, to remind her that the love they had shared would never die.

> Love links the living with the dead,
> The dead who only are departed;
> For lingering still when joys are fled
> Love binds around the broken-hearted
> a sense of that which never dies
> A tie that reaches to the skies.

For from beyond the shadowy veil
Sweet voices cry, we love you still,
For heaven-born love can never fail,
Or cease the holy heart to fill,
And souls that love are sundered never
But one on earth are one forever.

Grace was thirty-three when Henry died. She lived a further fifty-seven years, and did not marry again. He left her £4,000, the most money he had personally possessed in his entire life, but not enough to keep her and the two boys. Unlike many middle-class women of her day she worked as a nurse and school bursar so that she could support herself and the children. With her thick hair swept up into a bun, curls escaping rakishly around an elegant throat, she attracted a great deal of masculine attention – in vain. Henry's real legacy to her was of a different kind. In seven years he had provided her with enough romance and passion to last the rest of her eighty-nine years.[3]

In old age she would sit ramrod straight, reading his poems and letters over and over again, the cameo he had given her fastened to the front of a ruffled collar which framed a face still bearing traces of its former beauty. As she did so her face would light up and she would be a young woman once more, deeply in love with the only man who visited her in her dreams. In many ways he had never left her. 'Even now,' he once wrote, 'softly falls the whispers of the departed, as they stand in the cloudless light on the other side of death's dark portal, saying, "We wait for you here – we love you still."'

2.

In the summer of 1912 the Grattan Guinnesses held a grand family reunion. With their father gone, Harry and Geraldine feared the next generation of cousins would have little to bring them together and had an idea to recreate the idyllic summers at Cliff, renting a large house in Newquay for the entire month of August.

Everyone was there: Harry very much the patriarch, Annie organising the whole event, as efficient as ever, their nine children and first grandchild, Karis, daughter of Gene, who was married to Ian Mackenzie, the son of her parents' closest friends; Grace, by far the most liberated of the party, her skirt tucked into her waistband and hair streaming down her back as she paddled with her two boys; Whitfield and Janie on furlough from China with their three children, Joy, Henry and little Mary Geraldine, known by her Chinese name, Pearl; Howard and Geraldine with Henry and Karl; Karl Kumm himself with his new bride, a charming, petite Australian called Gertrude Cato.

For Howard and Geraldine, Karl and Gertrude, it could potentially have been a very difficult holiday. It was Gertrude's first real introduction to Karl's rather overpowering tribe of in-laws and she was very conscious of having taken Lucy's place. She was also acutely aware that her presence might cause Geraldine some difficulty, but if it did, Geraldine was far too gracious to show it.

The news of Karl's marriage had been a shock. A letter furnishing them with all the details of his engagement to Gertrude had never arrived. The first they heard of it was in a telegram which read simply, 'We are to be married at once, and are coming home via the United States.' Karl wanted his boys back.

For six years Henry and little Karl had been Geraldine's life. She and Howard had moved around a great deal and the boys had always gone with them, accompanied by a governess, secretary and the sixteen trunks of papers which were the background Geraldine needed for her biography of Hudson Taylor. She often rose and started writing before dawn, so that she could give the best of the day to her precious children. After six years how could she hand them over to a complete stranger? Yet her only real choice was to relinquish them joyfully or reluctantly. The latter, Howard reminded her, would only cause pain all round. She must trust that Karl would choose a good mother for his children and prepare them to love and welcome her.

A few days later photographs and newspaper cuttings of the wedding arrived and Geraldine decided they would share in the happy occasion by having their own celebration. Eleven-year-old Henry wrote to his new stepmother:

My dear new Mother

I hope you had a very nice wedding. We had a lovely wedding tea – lots of cake and jam and Devonshire cream; flowers and bouquets for each of us, and all of us made speeches in honour of the occasion. Please don't stay in America too long, because we are longing to welcome you home to England.

Please give dear father a kiss and tell him we are so glad.

I send you both much love from your little son, Henry

PS. We are having honey for tea tonight in a beautiful piece of honeycomb, because it is your honeymoon you know.

The letter reveals the magnanimity of Geraldine's character, her generosity of spirit. She could be prim, she could be strait-laced, but she was never petty or small-minded. The children had been hers – but only for a time. There was no subtle attempt to hold on to them, no malicious or underhand remarks which would hurt the children in the end. She wanted only the best for them and her total lack of self-interest enabled them to cope with a very unsettling situation.

My dear Father
I am looking at a little picture we have of Mother. She does look nice! I can quite believe she is very much like an angel and that she makes your loneliness go away. That was the piece I liked best in your letter – that part too about how you thought she was like our own Mother come back from heaven. I long with all my heart to see her and you again.

Karl and Gertrude had in fact booked tickets for the Titanic's return voyage, but several days before they were due to sail Karl developed appendicitis and was forced to stay in the USA for urgent surgery.

The day of their arrival finally dawned. With sinking hearts and the bravest of faces, Howard and Geraldine took the two boys down the station to meet them. 'You can imagine what it was like waiting for the first sight of her,' Geraldine later said to her niece, Joy.[4]

The boys were my very soul. The train came in, Dr Kumm jumped out, and turned to hand his wife down. As soon as I saw her I knew all our prayers were answered. I saw at once what Karl meant when he said she was like Lucy. She was small and graceful like her, but she was prettier than Lucy. She had a lovely gracious spirit and my heart went out to her.

However serene Geraldine's public face, her inner pain was almost unbearable. She watched the expression on little Karl's face as he looked up into the eyes of his new mother and knew that a special bond had been made. It was all she had hoped for, but cost her more than she could have ever imagined. 'When I parted from them something died within me. There is a peculiar joy in having children of your own. You live outside yourself, and when it is cut off, you are very solitary. It

411

is different to parting from anyone else.' Only Howard fully understood how she felt, for he shared her pain.

The final separation was postponed by the family holiday in Newquay. The children were not aware of any tension among the adults despite the almost ceaseless rain. There were still plenty of games, walks and endless tales of real-life, hair-raising adventures in faraway places. Geraldine, wisely, sublimated her feelings by cultivating close relationships with her two little half-brothers and other nephews. Gordon, one of Harry's three youngest sons, adopted her completely and decided that he too would be a missionary one day. Time proved him wrong, though he did become a well-known clergyman and canon of Winchester Cathedral. Desmond, Harry's youngest son, half-terrified by Whitfield's tales of the Boxer uprising, decided he would never go anywhere near China. Time proved him wrong too.

In a remarkable way, time proved Lucy right. Henry, and little Karl, shyly cementing their relationship with their new mother, would grow up to fulfil Lucy's prophetic instincts, Henry as a physician specialising in the treatment of Yaws' Disease, Karl as an Episcopalian minister. What she could not have known was that her father's life work in Jewish–Christian relations would be continued, not by her own son, but by Paul, the little half-brother born after her death.

Nor could any of them have guessed that Paul's older brother, John, Grace's six-year-old son, romping with his mother across the sands, would one day meet Karis, the baby in the cot, on a ship in the mid-Atlantic, two strangers apparently drawn together by chance, who then discovered that they were related and had once met, many years before, at a reunion in Newquay. When they married, Karis became her own mother's half-aunt, one of the anomalies created by Henry Grattan Guinness siring two separate families so far apart in years. Although intermarriage had become a fairly regular occurrence on the brewing and banking sides of the family, this was the first opportunity for Grattans to produce a line of double-barrelled Guinnesses.

Of the sixteen cousins playing together in the house at Newquay, two would become missionaries in China and six would be ordained in the Anglican ministry. In the twentieth century there was no sign of any tailing off of the clerical calling in the Guinness dynasty.

But that was all hidden in the future. Before the unfolding of the young cousins' destiny, came an event which would turn their lives upside down. Like a vast bulldozer, the Great War would demolish every remaining nineteenth-century value. The world in which the new generation made its mark was very different from the secure and tranquil world of Newquay in the summer of 1912.

Harry was already facing some very difficult decisions. The Harley empire, which had started to crumble with the handing over of Cliff, was on the point of collapse. It was as well he had his Congo triumph to sustain him. All else was bleak. Although the annual income had risen, most of it was going to the Regions Beyond Missionary Union, to ever-increasing expenditure in the Congo, Peru, Behar and Argentina. Harley College bore the brunt of the deficit.

Furthermore the grounds had been leased from the London County Council (of which Rupert and Walter Guinness were members), on condition that a new college be built by the year 1908. There was little choice but to rebuild, but the mountain of debt grew with the new building into menacing proportions, ready to topple at any moment. In their attempts to stem the inevitable avalanche, the committee was in total disarray. Retraction had been unknown. It was contrary to the Harley ethos. It seemed faithless, yet there was no alternative. The student course was cut from four to two years, and the much-respected Principal Jackson resigned. The charitable work in the East End dwindled, a ghost of what it had been in former days. Harley students offered themselves less to the

China Inland Mission and Regions Beyond Missionary Union, more to the big denominational missions which would guarantee them a regular salary. It soon became abundantly clear that Harry would have to make a choice between his missionary society and the college, and with a heavy heart, he finally decided to close the college.

For years after, friends remembered Harry's announcement that the new college would have to be sold to cover outstanding debts. He was desperately sad and seemed to feel that he was in some way to blame. 'Never get into debt,' he warned. He had tried to listen carefully to what God wanted him to do, but must have misheard somewhere down the years. The cost of it in terms of bitter disappointment, a sense of failure, and strained relationships on the committee, were all hard to bear.

The new college building was temporarily leased to the London Hospital as a nurses' home. Harry and Annie moved their family into a large, rambling house called Mount Hermon in Sydenham. The last few students moved into their vacated home, but when war broke out they volunteered and classes finally came to an end. Harley House, home of the Grattan Guinnesses for half a century, was requistioned as a home for Belgian refugees. Doric Lodge, the deaconesses' residence, and Bromley Hall, the maternity home, were also shut down.

Annie was more philosophical than her husband. In the end, the war, not their debts, was the final avalanche which swept the Harley empire away, and there was little they could do about that. Besides, she had worries enough of her own. Two of their boys were in the trenches, and she had begun to realise with a sickening certainty that Gene's six-year marriage to Ian Mackenzie seemed unlikely to survive. Divorce was anathema to Harry and Annie. It was scandalous in the times in which they lived. How could their beloved, brilliant eldest daughter, who had been an acclaimed writer at the age of nineteen, live with such a stigma for the rest of her life? She was barely twenty-seven and her future was over. This simply did not happen in their family. It is ironic that divorce, so prevalent in a later generation of brewing Guinnesses, should nonetheless have started with the Grattans. An arrangement was reached. Little Karis stayed with her father, the new baby daughter with Gene, and both sets of grandparents drew a veil over the whole affair.

In the early morning of 26 May 1915, Ian's parents arrived in London. They had travelled overnight from Scotland, not to see their son, but because Harry had persuaded his old friend to help him administer the work of the Mission. No one was at the station to meet them. They waited for some time, becoming increasingly annoyed, when a complete stranger rushed up to them, grabbed their bags, muttering something about an upheaval at the house. Harry had died in the night.

He had never been well since his return from the Congo five years earlier, but the symptoms were elusive and un-treatable. Long after his death rumours circulated that he had died of a broken heart. It is probable that disappointment weakened his ability to fight infection, but it also appears he picked up a mystery virus on one of his many trips abroad. His doctor, a leading London consultant and close friend of the family, recommended surgery. Most operations were still performed at home. Annie found homes for the younger children and three operations were carried out. Huge growths full of pus were removed, but there was no guarantee they would not grow again, and no final cure for his condition. He was only fifty-three.

When he was told that he was probably terminally ill, he accepted the news quietly. Asked whether he was glad, he replied, 'How could I be?' then added, after a long pause, 'And how could I not be?' Then he muttered to himself, 'Still young – life has been short – I might have had another thirty years.'

The younger children each saw their father for the last time to say goodbye and receive his last blessing. It was an awesome, rather than a sad occasion. They revered rather than loved him. He had always seemed a little distant. Their mother had always been the real anchor in their lives.

After the funeral she disappeared for three long, bewildering days, then emerged from her room, just as suddenly, in long black widow's weeds, her mourning done, ready to supervise a move into the serene suburbia of Upper Norwood.

3.

The Grattans were only one of the three branches of the Guinness family to lose a patriarch in the year 1915. Lord Ardilaun had died on 20 January, aged seventy-four, not as deeply lamented in the land of his birth as he might have been, had his resistance to Home Rule not been quite so blinkered and obsessive.

In Ireland the vacuum left by Parnell's disgrace had been filled by a brilliant journalist called Arthur Griffith, father of Sinn Fein. The British Government, anxious to be more conciliatory, had passed a Land Purchase Act in 1903, permitting large-scale transfers of land from landlord to tenant, facilitating the growth of the enlightened Unionist Sir Horace Plunkett's agricultural co-operative movement. It was an obvious way of making Irish farming more viable, supported by most clear-sighted Irishmen including his brother Edward Cecil. Lord Ardilaun would not have any of it. Bountiful to a fault to his own pet causes, but with a blind spot which seriously restricted any political vision, he stood in the House of Lords lambasting the government for weakness, defending Irish landlords as over-generous towards the peasantry and badly served by the unjust new laws. To ensure himself a platform in Ireland he even went as far as buying up

416

four Dublin newspapers, including the *Daily Express* and the *Evening Mail*, and still failed to comprehend why his younger brother, and not he, was made a Knight of the Order of St Patrick.

Lord Ardilaun's will, drawn up in 1902, left most of his land to Lord Iveagh, 'fearing that the care of my estates would impose too much upon my wife'. Nonetheless, upon his death, Lady Olive inherited their London house in Carlton Terrace, the Dublin house in St Stephen's Green, and St Anne's, Clontarf. She sold the Carlton Terrace house at once to Lady Iveagh's cousin, Benjamin Seymour Guinness of Guinness Mahon, and retired to eke out her days in her beloved Ireland.

St Anne's, Sir Benjamin Lee's elegant two-storey, pseudo-Palladian house, had been doubled in size by the Ardilauns to make it comparable with mansions being built in the USA by people like the Vanderbilts. But the grand entertainments for which it was a suitable backdrop had come to an end with the passing of viceregal society. Once the epitome of good taste, the house was now past its prime, damp and dingy inside like a mausoleum, far too big for one solitary inhabitant. To her cousin, Katherine Everett, Lady Ardilaun seemed a 'tall, slight figure, flitting across a cavernous hall'.[5] She was lonely, childless, 'and feeling the old life shattered around her'.

Nonetheless, in Dublin she was still a force to be reckoned with, a regal, rather formidable character, buttoned so tightly from waist to chin that her head was held rigid and erect, with eyes that could fillet flesh from bone with one look.

She was a creature of strange contrasts. The epitome of nineteenth-century restraint, she was nonetheless a radical in her support of the arts. At her salon in St Stephen's Green where she entertained the cream of artistic society during the particularly tense era between the Easter Uprising of 1916 and the civil war of 1918, officers from the castle rubbed shoulders with leading members of Sinn Fein. W. B. Yeats read his poetry, leaving the entire company wildly enthusiastic, but completely bewildered.

Unlike her husband, Olive Ardilaun was never hidebound by political considerations. As the major patron of the new Abbey Theatre, she seemed unaware of any anomaly in supporting a venture so openly nationalistic in tone. When the Black and Tans commandeered the castle she had inherited from her father in Macroom, she was put out, to say the least. When Republicans burned it to the ground, she despised Westminster for being too lenient with militant Sinn Fein, but she despised the Black and Tans more for provoking an unnecessary attack.

There was a large cache of warmth hidden behind the austere façade. Charity work was more than a mere gesture. When her sister-in-law became the chief benefactress of the Adelaide Hospital, Lady Ardilaun took on the Mercer Charity Hospital, visiting the patients regularly, sitting at the end of a bed, regaling them with tales of her glorious past. The tradition began when Sinn Fein was stealing cars. Looking out of the window of an upstairs ward, Olive Ardilaun observed that she couldn't see hers. 'What should we do if it has been taken?' she asked.

'But, my lady, the tram passes your gate,' piped up an old man from one of the beds.

'I've never been in a tram,' she replied, causing a sensation on the ward.

'How would you be going then?' the patients asked her, and she explained that she had always had a coach, a head coachman, horses, and a reserved carriage on the train if she had to travel as far as London.

For most of the patients it seemed unreal, a fairy tale, and they begged her to tell them more, which she did, on each successive visit, with increasing Irish verve.

'Tell us, my lady, did you ever see the King?'

She said she had, at various garden parties and dinner

parties. She had attended the jubilee, and two coronations.

The patients were always loathe to let her go. 'Did you ever see Queen Victoria?'

'Yes, of course, often in London; but the old Queen didn't treat Ireland too well. When she was young she and the Prince Consort came and stayed with my mother's people at Muckross, and about fifty years later she came again and paid me an afternoon visit.'

'Did you give her a cup of tea?'

Olive laughed. 'Yes, and a bunch of flowers.'

'She'd like a cup of tea as well as any old woman, wouldn't she?'

Olive Ardilaun's fierce exterior was a veneer imposed by her aristocratic breeding. The poor managed to draw responses her peers never saw. She regularly visited them in the tenements, and after she died, one old woman said to her cousin, 'God rest her soul for she was good. She would sit here without a proud end on her; she was a friend to the sick and the poor.'

One anecdote in particular typifies her sensitive, imaginative approach to charity, and explains why the popularity of the Guinness family survived their politics and position. She always went to a great deal of trouble to ensure that the regular tea parties she laid on for the poor were as perfect as if she were entertaining the King himself. On one such occasion for fifty repatriated prisoners-of-war, she ordered her butler, with the unlikely name of Millions, to fill the prize cups on the sideboard with plenty of flowers. In the dining-room the tables were elegantly laid out with plates of wafer-thin slices of bread and butter, butterfly-sized sandwiches and sugar-coated petits fours. Olive's cousin, Katherine, was perplexed.

'Don't you think the men would be happier in the servants' hall with more substantial food?' she asked her.

'No!' Lady Ardilaun replied adamantly. 'They are going to

have our sort of tea with us, and the servants to pour it out, and hand round the cream and sugar, and the best china is to be used.'

Lady Ardilaun was vindicated when after the tea, one of the men rose to his feet and said:

> My Lady, I speak for all present, for every one of us wants to tell you what you have done for us today. You have sat down with us, you have eaten with us, and all your servants have waited on us, and we feel you have wiped out the shame of having been spitted on in the streets of Berlin when we were handcuffed prisoners.

As they were taking their leave, Olive Ardilaun grabbed her cousin's arm and whispered, 'You need not worry about their not eating much at tea because I have arranged for them all to have a good, solid dinner directly they get back to Dublin.'

Unlike future generations of her family, Lady Ardilaun never resented her wealth, though it did at times cramp her style. 'I should have enjoyed doing some actual work,' she once said, 'but it wasn't possible.' Reluctantly, she was even forced to relinquish her one great love – gardening. 'Once I pulled up a weed or two, but my dear old head gardener met me in the act and looked very pained and hurt, and the next day there were men and boys in every border and by-way hunting stray weeds like sleuth-hounds.' Her strength was her ability to accept the limitations of her position, while using its possibilities to their full potential, as imaginatively as she knew how. Wealth, when undeserved, brought responsibility and she took that seriously to the end of her life. She lived another ten years after the death of her husband, and with her passing the Ardilaun peerage became extinct.

The third Guinness patriarch to die in 1915 with Dr Harry and Lord Ardilaun was the eighty-nine-year-old Richard Seymour Guinness, son of the founder of Guinness Mahon, and head of the London branch, he who never kept a ledger to the day of his death. In their youth Harry, Geraldine and Lucy had played tennis at his house with his five sons and four daughters. Four of Richard Seymour's 'boys', Robert Darley, Gerald Seymour, Arthur Eustace and Benjamin Seymour, had joined the modest, yet solid family business at their offices in 28–29 St Swithin's Lane. Their first clerk was engaged in 1894.

In 1901 the leasehold of 80–81 Lombard Street was bought from Brook's Bank for £17,000, and Guinness Mahon moved in with a staff of five clerks, and their first female typist, Miss Martin. The London office began to keep its own books at last, rather than relying on Dublin to do so. This was progress, but it was not fast enough for Benjamin Seymour, the youngest son and real capitalist in the family. His early training opened his eyes to the lucrative potential of Wall Street, and after several trips across the Atlantic he had managed to become a senior partner in the formidable Ladenburg, Thalmann and Company, opening the way for considerable business between his firm and his brothers'. Profits were substantial enough for the three brothers at Guinness Mahon, London, to retire from the business on their father's death in 1915, handing over the reins to their cousin, Howard Rundell, at the Dublin office. Benjamin Seymour was granted the right to take over the London branch for two years after the termination of the war, should he want to do so.

He never did. There was no financial need for him to do so. Indeed, he was well on the way to becoming fabulously rich. It is indicative of the rise in wealth and social status of this branch of the family that he was able to buy 11 Carlton Terrace from Lady Ardilaun in 1916, stepping straight into her high-class slippers. From that time on the four brothers were known to their brewing cousins as 'the Benji Guinnesses', their rivals in the social stakes.[6]

As international banking slowly ground to a halt during the

Great War, Howard Rundell in Dublin had no real cause for concern. It was a relief not to have the worry of the London office, which would have become moribund anyway. As it was, Guinness Mahon remained in a fairly comfortable and consolidated position in Ireland, ready to sit out the long, dark years.

4.

The war which brought the Harley College and Guinness Mahon empires to a standstill, did not spare the gracious world of Elveden. For almost three decades to 1914, despite two changes in monarchy, the routine there continued much as it had always done. The new King George V paid an annual visit to Elveden for the shooting. His host had become his sovereign's unofficial advisor in all matters relating to Ireland. When the King went to Dublin with Queen Mary in 1911, it was Lord Iveagh who escorted them round and took them to see the Guinness Trust housing project and Lady Iveagh's new nursery and play centre.

Elveden had also become the glamorous, glittering focal point of an extended family network, the house parties a coveted venue for a new young generation of Guinness cousins intent on making their mark. An invitation represented acceptance in the clan, an opportunity to meet the rich and impressive, to see and be seen. Lord Iveagh was hospitable not only to his own immediate family, descended from the first Arthur Guinness, but also to his wife's less well-endowed Guinness relatives. Beauty, grace and wit, possessed in full measure by Dodo's two nieces, Mabel and Katy, the penniless daughters of her wayward elder brother, were an obvious asset. But a medley of poor, plainer nieces and nephews were caught up from time to time in the dazzling orbit and given their chance to shine.

'It was a well-ordered, formal life, leisurely but disciplined, regulated by the shooting season and untroubled by any suspicion of its essential impermanence. Looking back on it now, it seems like one long summer – the last summer but endlessly drawn out.'[7]

It could not last indefinitely. Events outside Lord Iveagh's control began to encroach upon the ordered world he had created. Lady Iveagh became increasingly incapacitated, her public appearances sporadic. Her behaviour had been erratic for several years. At times she seemed well and in her right mind, but those occasions became less frequent as the dementia increased its grip over her mind. The depth of Edward Cecil's pain and embarrassment can be gauged from the fact that it was the family's best-kept secret. No one was ever allowed to speak of it. She was left to her twilight world in a private wing, largely content, playing games of hide and seek with the maids and valets. Her elder sister, the elegant, gracious Geraldine Kerr-Pearse simply slipped into Dodo's role as hostess. Geraldine, whom Dodo had always adored, had been widowed for the second time in 1900, when Beauchamp, overcome by the pain of kidney stones, had shot himself, a deeply shocking act for a clergyman. With typical resilience, 'Aunt G' weathered the personal pain and public scandal to become family matriarch as well as hostess. She and Edward Cecil had always been close. He came to rely on her more and more. It was she who drew all the nieces and nephews into the Elveden orbit. And they loved her as fiercely as they disliked Lady Iveagh.

In the end political rather than personal circumstances brought Elveden to a standstill. In 1914 many of the estate workers volunteered and went to the front. The shooting parties ceased and were never revived. Nor was the lavish entertaining.

Lady Iveagh finally died in 1916. Her illness compounded the emotional distance between Dodo and her children. In her lifetime Rupert hardly ever spoke of his mother, and after her death, never.

Lord Iveagh was a lonely man without her. He stayed at his stately home alone during the last two years of the War, worrying about Walter who was serving in the trenches. For company, and because she was ill, he took in Walter's wife, their two eldest sons, Bryan, aged eleven, the sickly Murtogh, aged three, and a governess.

Used to fairly noisy family Christmas parties at Elveden, Bryan was not in awe of his grandparents. On the contrary, he had seen a softer side of them reserved only for the grandchildren. When he was a small child Dodo had taught him to say his prayers and read to him from a book of spiritual homilies for children called *Peep of the Day*. Lord Iveagh was an indulgent grandfather, taking him out into Hyde Park in a four-in-hand coach, allowing him to hold the reins as if he were driving. He grew up treasuring the toy donkey called Neddy his grandfather had given him when he went to tea with him one day, telling him he was sometimes called Neddy himself.

It came as a shock to discover the more austere, punctilious side of his grandfather's character. One day Bryan was summoned and reproached for not having answered a letter. 'I thought I was on very easy terms with him. I thought he was joking and laughed, which understandably made him cross. I very much minded his minding. It was all over in a few seconds. He only said, "You're not the nice little boy I thought you were." '[8] Despite the misunderstanding Bryan remained fond of his grandfather and always believed the grandeur of Elveden overshadowed the real man.

By that quiet, tense summer of 1916, the great era was almost over. The few inhabitants rattled around the building like ghosts of former days. When they left, most of the rooms were closed, the furniture covered in dust sheets. Elveden, the epitome of all that was serene and self-confident about

424

Edwardian England, had fallen asleep.

5.

London, June 1917. General Sir Beauvoir de Lisle KCB, KCMG, DSO, on leave for ten days from his command in the trenches, was reading *The Times* over breakfast, revelling in a temporary return to his normal home routine, when an announcement caught his eye. His old friend, Field-Marshal Sir Edmund Allenby, had been appointed Commander-in-Chief of His Majesty's forces in the Middle East.

This was not a comfortable sinecure. The British intention was to establish supremacy in all territory around the Suez Canal, and Allenby's brief was to deliver the Holy Land from a hundred years of domination by the now crumbling Ottoman Empire. Those who thought it a relatively simple task after the conquest of the Sinai Peninsula had been forced to change their minds. With German support the Turks held on to their precious treasure with the iron grip of a drowning man. The Allies had fought a long and bitter campaign under Sir Archibald Murray, suffering a humiliating defeat at Gaza.

Few would envy Allenby his appointment, or rush to congratulate him, but Beauvoir de Lisle had a rather different perspective on the situation and thought it might encourage the new Commander. He dressed quickly and went with his wife at once to the Grosvenor Hotel where Allenby was staying. This was how he later described their conversation.[9]

'No cause for congratulation,' Allenby said in his gruff way. 'Had to give up a jolly fine army to take over a rotten show. Archie Murray is a good man and if he could not succeed, I don't see how I can.'

'My dear Allenby,' I replied, 'you are on velvet. You may make all the mistakes in tactics or strategy, but nothing can prevent you from being in Jerusalem by the 31st December.'

'How do you make that out?' he asked.

I told him of the book *Light For the Last Days* by Dr Grattan Guinness in 1886, in which he had stated that the interpretation of the three prophecies in Daniel, Ezekiel and Revelation all pointed to the same year, 1917, as the end of the Gentile times, a period of 1260 years – Time, times and a half a time. 'At the same time,' I added, 'don't forget your big guns.'

Beauvoir de Lisle had said his farewells and was at the door, when a sudden thought occurred to him and he turned back. 'When you get to Jerusalem, Allenby, I hope you will not ride in state, for that is reserved in the future for One higher than you.'

The significance of the year 1917 had not passed unnoticed in the national press. In January, at the advent of the year, a correspondent in the *Daily Mail* reminded readers that Henry Grattan Guinness had written, 'There can be no doubt that those who live to see this year will have reached one of the most important, perhaps momentous, of these terminal years of crisis.'

Light For the Last Days was reissued for the sixteenth time in July and had to be reprinted in August. Guinness's words provided a glimmer of hope in the fourth year of a disheartening world war.

In his lifetime Henry Grattan knew that the politician Arthur Balfour had read his books. Balfour, Foreign Secretary in 1917, had also been a regular guest at Elveden once Rupert was helping to put the guest list together. On 2 November he signed a historic Declaration:

His Majesty's Government views with favour the establishment in Palestine of a National Home for the Jewish people, and will use their best endeavours to facilitate the achievement of this object, it being clearly understood that nothing shall be done which may prejudice the civil and religious rights of the existing non-Jewish communities in Palestine.

On 11 December Sir Edmund Allenby rode at the head of his victorious troops right up to the gates of Jerusalem. Then he stopped, got down from his horse, and holding her by the bridle, walked into the Holy City.

Geraldine Guinness Taylor opened her Bible and read to her fourteen-year-old nephew, Gordon, words he never forgot. 'Therefore say to the house of Israel, "Thus says the Lord God, it is not for your sake, O house of Israel, that I am about to act, but for the sake of my holy name. For I will take you from the nations, and gather you from all the countries, and bring you into your own land." '

With her dying words Lucy Guinness Kumm had said her boys would live to see 'those unutterable days', and she was right. But Henry Grattan Guinness had alluded to even later dates. The last, scribbled in pencil beneath the final paragraph of the book of Ezekiel in his large black Bible, was 1948.

Chapter 13

1918–1939
Upwards and Onwards

In a modest terraced house in Chiswick, in her ninetieth year, lives the sprightly Paddy Ullstein, daughter of Henry Seymour Guinness, Governor of the Bank of Ireland from 1922 to 1924, and eldest son of Henry Guinness, who managed the Dublin side of Guinness Mahon after the death of his father, Robert Rundell Guinness. Paddy's brain is like a Guinness file in a computer. Insert a name, an event, an anecdote about virtually any member of the family and she has perfect recall of almost every detail. It's a passion inherited from her father, who spent years researching the family roots, following up the adventures of the various branches, producing the first family tree and pedigree. She still remembers hundreds of notes and names carefully laid out on the billiard table at her childhood home, Burton Hall in Stillorgan. Her own recollections provide a fascinating insight into what it was like to grow up in the shadow of Ireland's 'Troubles'.

At the end of the nineteenth century the Guinness Mahon land agency was fairly undistinguished, though profitable enough for Henry Guinness senior to buy the Carman Hall Estate in Stillorgan, where he built a white, nine-bedroomed, two-storey mansion called Burton Hall. There he installed his wife, Emmelina Brown, daughter of a Dublin merchant, and the five sons and seven daughters they had produced. Two of the younger sons, Howard Rundell and Richard Noel, followed their father into the land agency, but Henry Seymour, the eldest, had more adventurous notions.

As a child Henry Seymour had been deposited at Rose House, a private prep school in Geneva, and never came home again. Henry and Emmelina were not insensitive parents, they simply wanted their eldest son to have all the advantages of the education his father had missed. Few educational establishments in Ireland satisfied Protestant aspirations, so Henry Seymour was packed off to Switzerland, followed by public school at Winchester.

In 1876, pursuing a career in engineering, he set off for Burma to work on the newly developing railway system, returning to Dublin in 1893 after the death of his father, when he fully expected to take over as senior partner of Guinness Mahon. But Howard Rundell, who had taken a tight hold of the reins long before his father died, had no intention of loosening his grip.

'What do you know about banking?' he asked his elder brother. 'You can join the company if you want, but as a junior partner.'

A sanguine Henry Seymour simply 'went over the road', according to his daughter, to the Bank of Ireland, where he appeared to know enough about the profession to become a director in 1910, and Governor in 1922. His most satisfying contribution was the introduction of the first female employees, an innovation which necessitated the employment of a women's welfare superintendent too.[1]

No lasting animosity developed between the two brothers. On the contrary, they remained on very close terms, each marrying a Mary who liked to be known as May, distinguished from each other by the addition of their husband's first name. Howard Rundell's marriage to May Howard (Mary Alice Guinness) represented yet another intersection of the brewing

429

and banking lines. She was the daughter of a clergyman, William Newton Guinness, who had taken his third wife to Australia where he became Vicar of St John's, South Yarra, near Melbourne. According to Howard, she was so beautiful that men came from miles around and stood on the pews just to catch a glimpse of her. They were evidently wasting their time. A deeply devout low church Protestant, rigid in her views and scathing of worldly nonsense, May Howard would dismiss her husband's romanticisms with one of her biting remarks. 'Beauty unadorned adorns the most,' was one of her favourites. Make-up and jewellery were ungodly embellishments. A strict disciplinarian with all of her five boys, except for some reason the irascible Bobs, whom she indulged shamelessly, eventually to her cost, she demanded manners at the table, prayers in the home, and punctuality in church attendance, however long the walk to get there. Roman Catholicism was anathema to her, an unfortunate animosity given her geographical circumstances.

Henry Seymour's home at Burton Hall, inherited from his father, was relaxed and happy by comparison. His wife, 'May Harry', whom he married in 1900 when he was forty, was thirteen years his junior. They had four daughters who were allowed to romp freely in the relative seclusion of their extensive grounds with tennis court and croquet lawn, trimmed regularly by a horse-drawn mower. With six servants, theirs was a serene, comfortable existence at Burton Hall, though it did not compare in grandness with the lifestyle of one of their father's closest friends, his distant cousin Lord Iveagh.

As one particular visitor, the forbidding Lady Ardilaun, frequently lamented, society had vanished with the passing of the viceregal court. Well-to-do Dublin families were penalised by their own wealth and Ireland's lack of it. They lived in isolation in large houses outside the city, six, seven and eight miles apart with no means of transport except a horse and carriage. Henry Seymour bicycled to Stillorgan station every morning, took a train into Dublin, then bicycled to the Bank. But family attendance at an evening dinner dance or ball, dressed in best finery, was a major, lengthy expedition, not to be undertaken on a regular basis.

Nonetheless, the immediate family spent a great deal of time in each other's homes, Howard Rundell's five boys arriving in school holidays with Nanny Scarborough, known as Nanny Scar, in a jennet-drawn trap. A jennet was half-horse, half-ass. The girls found their eldest cousin, Sam, shy and rather boring. Ned was fun, Arthur fairly nondescript, and Bobs an absolute terror, one of the naughtiest little boys they had ever met. Brian, or Bim, was simply the baby. Occasionally they paid a return visit to their Uncle Howard and Aunt May, but it was a bit of an ordeal. Bird-watching with Uncle Howard was fun, but the unpredictable and rather tyrannical Aunt May soon quelled any boisterous spirits. Woe betide the child who was caught with her elbows resting on the table. An almighty thud would make the silver cutlery bounce a clear six inches in the air and land with an ominous clatter. Children, even when seen rather than heard, were only barely tolerated.

Uncle Noel who ran Guinness Mahon with his brother Howard, and for whom banking was simply a means of funding the real passion of his life, sailing, lived at the wonderful Ceanchor House in Howth with its a magnificent view over Dublin Bay. He and his Mary, known as Molly, sister of the well-known Irish surgeon Henry Stokes, had two children, Margaret and Henry Eustace. Molly's language was, however, a little too 'brisk' for May Harry's liking. The two women never got on and visits were irregular.

By complete contrast, the four sisters were invited from time to time to Glenmaroon, the home of cousin Ernest, whose three girls, Aileen, Maureen and Oonagh were of a comparable age. They travelled by train into Dublin station, where

431

Ernest's large car would be waiting to take them to a house which was luxurious beyond their wildest imaginings. It had an indoor swimming pool, its own cinema, and an electric organ which started to play as if by magic. His daughters' clothes, their wonderful selection of toys, even their nanny, were, undoubtedly, vastly superior. Henry Seymour Guinness's girls were quite overwhelmed.

Occasionally, Ernest appeared, austere, forbidding in frock-coat and striped trousers. He had no idea how to relate to children. But the dazzling, elegant Cloë at his side in long, floaty dress and tiny lace cap was more inclined to be indulgent. Never far from either of them was the tall, rather plain, put-upon 'Aunt Gunn' – a poor Guinness relation who had compounded her shortcomings by making a bad marriage, had been adopted by the Glenmaroon family and become an indispensable maiden aunt, performing all the matriarchal duties Cloë found too onerous or too boring. Cloe often complained of ill health, but was not too indisposed, it seems, to take a long-term lover.

On the whole, the four girls preferred their tranquil, relatively simple existence at Burton Hall. Every summer, the London lot, or 'Benji Guinnesses', descended en masse with their well-heeled wives and children for three weeks, as they always had since they were children themselves. Henry Seymour was extremely fond of Benjamin, but less so of Benjamin's three brothers, who became increasingly snobby with their burgeoning fortunes and waistbands. Marriage to suitable women of good breeding did not prevent them turning over the plates to check the make of the china.

In 1911 Burton Hall was extended. May Harry decided she could not cope with the dust and took her four small daughters with governess off to France for a year while the necessary alterations were made. They stayed in a flat near Henry Seymour's black sheep of a brother, Geoffrey, the children's favourite uncle, who had been banished to South America for his misdemeanours, and had married a fifteen-year-old French girl called Severine who took her doll to the wedding. Flats in Paris had no bathroom. The children learnt to wash themselves down with water from a bowl, then once dry, to rub themselves all over with cologne.

Sepia photographs of life at Burton Hall taken shortly after the First World War, suggest an unspoiled rural idyll for the four teenage girls in sailor-suits and straw boaters, a constant round of tennis parties, picnics at nearby Bray, and swimming in the river. What they do not show is the relentless strain of living under the spectre of sudden violence. The political temperature in Ireland was rising to boiling point. In 1921 Henry Seymour was appointed a Senator of the Irish Free State, becoming an obvious target for terrorism almost overnight. Paddy's eldest sister's engagement that year was the last decent do at the house. In October 1921, William Moore, the gardener, a known Protestant and freemason, who lived in one of two staff cottages on the estate, opened his front door and was shot dead by the IRA at point-blank range.

'The Troubles' cast their shadow over every well-to-do Protestant home. Many were rased to the ground. The well-to-do like Henry Seymour and Ernest Guinness sent their daughters to England to private schools for safety. One day early in 1922 Henry Seymour arrived home from work and calmly told his wife to pack up anything of value. The vans, he said, would arrive in the morning to take the bulk of their furniture and belongings to England. They would keep just enough for their basic needs. It was abundantly clear to May Harry that her husband had been warned that his home was on an IRA hit list.

The following day, hours after the last van had left, Thompson, the steward at the lodge, looked up to see a gun at his head. Three masked men escorted him up to the house, where, the gun still pressed to his temple, he knocked and asked Mary, the kitchen-maid, to open the door and let him in.

Family members and servants were rounded up in the main hall. 'Is everyone here?' one of the gunmen asked. Mrs Morissey, the cook, said, 'No, Christina, the laundress, is still over in the laundry', and was promptly dispatched under escort to fetch her. But Christina, who was partly deaf, did not understand the seriousness of the situation and refused to come down. The gunman raised his weapon, debated whether to go up and shoot her, then, with an impatient shrug, manifestly decided she was not worth the effort, and hustled Mrs Morissey out to join the rest of the party.

The entire household was shunted down to the lodge. Once they were in, the doors were locked behind them, and the men went back to burn the house. But within minutes, Thompson's son who happened to be away for the day, arrived from the train station. May Harry sent him back to the station at once to telephone through to Dublin for the fire brigade.

When the Army arrived half an hour later the house was burning, though not enough to make it uninhabitable. Cans of 'Irish cheddar', home-made explosives, wired up and planted all over the building, had not had time to explode. The family simply cleaned up and went on living at Burton Hall for a further two years, by which time May Harry decided she had had quite enough of living with the strain.

Howard Rundell had already transferred the centre of Guinness Mahon operations to London, and had moved into the lodge of the Earl of Onslow's Clandon Regis estate in Surrey.[2] With them went Nanny Scarborough and her husband, who was given work at the London office, and their small 'daughter', Patricia. Patricia in fact belonged to Bobs who had disgraced himself by producing a child out of wedlock. It was a best-kept family secret, even when he married Nora Shelton in 1925, and would have remained so, were it not for a heart-rending, potentially tragic irony. Years later Bobs' teenage son, Michael, happened to fall in love with a girl from the village, Patricia Scarborough. At which point Bobs quickly removed his family to South Africa.

Long before that sad event May Harry decided the time had come for all sensible people to take themselves off to England. 'I have given Ireland twenty-five years of my life,' she said, 'and I am never going back.' She was true to her word, despite the fact that her husband had now acquired an interesting new job in Dublin and was unable to join her.

In 1924 Lord Iveagh had approached his old friend about 'a very delicate matter'. The 1920s were a low period for Guinness sales and he was deeply concerned about it. Ever whimsical and easily threatened when it came to the Brewery command, he was looking for a scapegoat. Sutton, the managing director, was his cypher. But Ernest, the vice-chairman, was another matter. His son's skills as an engineer were unquestionable. The variety of innovative new technology Ernest had introduced simplified and speeded up the brewing process beyond imagining. But Ernest's reserved manner made relationships difficult and Lord Iveagh was not convinced his son was coping with the delicacies of management and marketing. He had it in mind to replace him with 'an older, wiser man'.

As he grasped the implications of the conversation, Henry Seymour became increasingly uncomfortable. Edward Cecil's intentions, on the face of it for business reasons, represented an attempt to oust his own son. It was a dreadful thing for a man to do and Henry Seymour told his cousin so in no uncertain terms. Not only would it irreparably damage their relationship, but it would look very bad in public. Eventually, he agreed to become one of four assistant managing directors, working with, not instead of Ernest.

Burton Hall was sold and Henry Seymour took a flat in Dublin. But he was not a young man and the work was taxing.

In 1930, when he was seventy-two, May Harry finally coaxed him into retirement, and he joined her in Hayes in Kent, moving to the safety of Tunbridge Wells during the Second World War for the last years of his life, where he continued his life-long study of the Guinness family pedigree.[3]

2.

From the 1920s the story of the Guinness family begins to read like a quasi-epic Greek tragedy. The doomed romance of Michael and Patricia was only one of a number of unfortunate circumstances which cast a malign shadow over the family down the next decades, threatening the succession both at the Bank and the Brewery. Henry Seymour's brother, Howard Rundell, broke his neck in a riding accident and was left a paraplegic. The management of Guinness Mahon in London passed to his eldest son, Sam, and in Dublin, to Noel's son, Henry Eustace.

Sam was married to Alfhild, a beautiful blond Norwegian with a wonderful soprano voice. They had met and fallen hopelessly in love when Sam was nineteen and a student at Balliol College, and she only seventeen. Howard Rundell refused to allow them to marry. They were far too young. Besides, his son was being groomed for the Bank. But he finally relented, and they married four years later in 1913.

There were four children, George, their only son, and three daughters, Helga, Marit and Ingrid. Marit and Ingrid were both born with cleft palates. During the long walk to church from Clandon Regis endured in turn by all the grandchildren when they stayed with their grandparents, Howard Rundell would tell them they must do their best with their speech to be a credit to the family. Marit, already showing signs of the red-haired beauty she would become, bitterly resented his references to her weaker points, and thought him rather cruel.[4]

In fact, her grandfather, like Rupert Guinness, had been forced to overcome a speech impediment himself in order to make the family business the success he intended.

Sam was also a man who knew what he wanted and was determined to have it. Walking with the children by the Thames, he would point to Cheyne Walk in Chelsea and tell them that one day he would be rich enough to buy them all a house there, a dream fulfilled in 1928 when he bought number 6.

Three years later, sixteen-year-old George was cleaning his gun in an outhouse. It was supposedly filled with blanks, but as he got up, he tripped and fell and the gun went off, killing him instantly. A devastated Sam lost his only son and potential heir, not the first or the last Guinness to be robbed of the succession to the family business. Rapidly becoming a superior, successful enterprise since its move to Corn Hill, the London side would eventually be run by his younger brother Arthur Rundell's children.

George's death changed Sam. He had been rather grand, very much the successful businessman on his uppers. George's death pricked any inflated notions he might have entertained about his own place in the universe. He became less pompous and aloof, more approachable, more mellow, a positive outcome of the immense pain he shared with Alfhild. Their utter devotion to each other was a source of great inner strength. He called her 'Fluff', but as she grew older and stouter, pressing her ample form into her favourite blue lace dresses, anyone less like fluff was hard to imagine. In 1949, when they arrived in Los Angeles, an *LA Times* journalist asked him if he was taking a second honeymoon. 'No,' he said, with a twinkle in his eye, 'I'm still on my first.'

He was a fond and doting father to his three lovely daughters. There was a great deal of satisfaction in seeing Helga and Marit become debutantes. (Ingrid decided on a world-trip and got married instead.) To their father's surprise the two girls proved themselves capable of more lasting and meaningful achievement. Inheriting their mother's creative gifts, they were the arty members of a branch of the family only distinguished so far in the material world of high finance. Helga married Sir Hugh Carleton Greene, a future governor of the BBC, divorced him in 1948, and became a successful literary agent in her own right, acting for novelist Raymond Chandler, according to her ex-husband, to 'escape the stifling appurtenances of wealth'.[5] Marit, who had flaming red hair, thanks to a recurrent and dominant gene on the banking side of the family, became one of the country's leading enamellists, her exhibitions attracting a great deal of international attention.

Sam's greatest achievement was to turn a small, successful family bank into an international enterprise. He travelled the world clinching new deals for the company, and felt particularly at home in the USA, where the 'nouveaux riches' were the new royalty, lauded and admired, free to be as benevolent as they wished without appearing tasteless or crass. Sam loved making money and giving it away. Why should he apologise for the fact? In many ways he was the quintessential pre-war American business magnate, unlearned, but generous to a fault. When Helga married he gave her a limousine and a real-life chauffeur as a wedding present. Acutely embarrassed, the young couple gave the human component of the gift his freedom as soon as they possibly could. Despite the meteoric rise in their fortunes, the whole family remained unpretentious. An abundance of high-flying friendships, including that of King Haakon VII of Norway, did not put a stop to Alfhild's regular sallies into the London slums, giving away food to the poor.

In his youth in the pre-war days, when he was courting Alfhild, and there had still been the hint of the snob about Sam, he had warned her of the social disadvantages of changing her name to his. 'There's a Brewery in the family,' he said, 'but you needn't worry, they never advertise.'

3.

Advertising, almost as great a social no-no as brewing, was a bone of contention in the family. The first Lord Iveagh did not exactly disapprove of it, as some assumed. He simply said Guinness should sell on its own merits. The quality of the product was so important that Guinness brewers were required to have a first- or second-class honours degree from Oxford or Cambridge.

But when he died in 1927, the second-wealthiest man in the British Isles, business was in the doldrums. The lucrative USA market had eluded capture for a hundred years. It presented a host of difficulties: how to prevent the distributors circulating forgeries, how to transport the commodity successfully without sacrificing the taste, how to convince well-to-do Americans that beer could be an acceptable national booze. Just as the climate began to change and American taste buds began to awaken to a hundred years of missed opportunity, the Great War put paid to Guinness's great cross-Atlantic trading future, and Prohibition prevented any chance of a reawakening.

Absolute monarch almost to his dying day, Edward Cecil's last gesture, two days before his death, was to make Rupert Chairman of the company. Rupert had always been a director, but had never been encouraged to take a real interest in the business. Ernest, on the other hand, had been a vice-chairman for years. But Edward Cecil doubted Ernest's abilities and Ernest had three daughters. Walter was otherwise occupied as Minister for Agriculture. The line of command must pass through the eldest son, though the controlling financial interest was to be divided between all three. Their father, in true Guinness patriarchal fashion, had dictated the firm's future from beyond the grave.

Lord Iveagh had effectively split the company three ways, a policy rejected by his forefathers for fear of weakening it financially. There was no danger of that any longer, but the decision did have long-term repercussions, weakening family interest in its own way and time.

The three brothers were close. They worked together well. Rupert was easy-going and approachable, Walter a shrewd politician and diplomat, and Ernest a real brewer with hands-on experience of life in the family firm. In the historic tradition of industrial capitalism, the family reigned while professional managers were employed to do their bidding. Initially, the arranged marriage worked well as it had for countless other Edwardian family businesses. Well into Lord Iveagh's lifetime, there had always been loyal, loving and upright Pursers to keep an eagle eye on the actual money-making process. They were followed by a succession of managing executives who might not have shared the Pursers' Moravian values or their place in the family heart, but who understood the logistics of the relationship.

Whether that could survive the next generation was another matter. There were ten offspring. As well as Ernest's three girls, Rupert and Gwenny had four children, Honor born in 1909, Arthur, Viscount Elveden, born in 1912, Patricia, known as Patsy, in 1918, and Brigit in 1920. Walter had added a daughter, Grania, to Bryan and Murtogh. None grew up with much notion of what brewing, or even business, involved, yet all would expect their shares to entitle them to some say in the running of the company. Gradually, over sixty years, the marriage of proprietor and manager would become an unequal partnership. A struggle for supremacy ensued with divorce as the inevitable conclusion. But the seeds were sown at the death of the first Lord Iveagh.

Rupert inherited his father's peerage, as well as his mantle, and moved into the House of Lords. In the resulting by-election in Southend Gwenny was elected in his place. One of only seven women MPs in the country, she had a distinguished political career of her own, increasing her majority substantially at each succeeding General Election, until she retired from the Commons in 1935, handing over her seat to her son-in-law, Henry 'Chips' Channon. Effectively the seat belonged to the Guinness family for eighty-five years.

The eldest son also inherited his father's favourite property, which for Rupert and Gwenny was rather a booby prize. Neither were emotionally attached to Elveden. Its upkeep was almost too horrendous to contemplate and they were both fully committed elsewhere, Rupert to the Brewery, Gwenny to her political work. Pyrford was their home. There was no question of selling Elveden. One thousand employees depended on it for their livelihood. Besides, at his first meeting with Rupert after Lord Iveagh's death, the King offered his condolences, and said with remarkable tact and altruism, 'I hope you're going to keep up the shooting at Elveden. I shall hope to come next year and I think the Queen would like to come too.'[6] A wish from a monarch is as good as a command, though it made their hearts sink. They had other plans in mind. Nonetheless, in 1928 they opened the house for one last shooting party, an Indian summer, a sentimental close to a chapter in the Elveden book, before setting in motion a wildly ambitious agricultural experiment.

Convinced of its importance in combating TB, they had been producing tuberculin-tested milk from their herds at Pyrford for some years. Now they planned to extend the scheme, reclaiming eight thousand acres of barren Elveden shrub land in an attempt to prove that what appeared to be wasteland could be effectively used in the production of food.

Destroying the rabbits creating the breckland was a first priority. That was followed by the introduction of effective drainage, using new, experimental techniques, and then the slow ploughing in of acres of lucerne. It was a long, tortuous process, punctuated with constant set-backs, but by the 1950s it catered for the largest dairy farm in England, producing half a million gallons of milk a year. Rupert could tour the burgeoning fields, as he often did, with immense satisfaction. His little Citroen had a horn designed to imitate the sound of a mooing cow. When they heard it, all the cattle would get up and go to him. He had their names and numbers on cards in his pocket. Gwenny became even more proficient at recognising each one.

The project's success was largely due to his absolute determination to improve British agricultural methods. 'One could hardly imagine a more socially beneficial use of a private fortune which is a by-product of the capitalist system. The failures and disappointments which are inevitable before a scientific investigation is crowned with success are debited to private account. The final results are a gift to society.'[7] Rupert's pioneering work earned him an array of honorary degrees, and during the Second World War Elveden proved an invaluable example in agricultural reclamation.

The house itself had become an anachronism. Rupert and Gwenny referred to it as 'the mausoleum', and preferred to live in a five-bedroomed cottage in the grounds. Apart from one last time in 1938, when the marble hall was opened up for their daughter Patsy's wedding to the rising young Tory star, Alan Lennox-Boyd, it remained shut.

Gwenny occasionally used a wing of the house for her committee work. As Chairman of the National Union of Conservative and Unionist Associations, she entertained her political colleagues there. She was fairly progressive, slightly ahead of the rest of the party in some issues, for example in promoting the independence of India, where her brother-in-law, the future Earl of Halifax, had been viceroy, but deeply conservative in others. Typical of a woman who could afford the domestic and child care which enabled her to work, she believed women should vote, but that their first call was to their homes and families.

As an orator Gwenny was past master, holding audiences spellbound with her beautiful well-modulated voice and impassioned, polished performance. Her maiden speech in defence of the new Anglican Prayer Book was hailed as the best speech ever made in the House by a woman – praise indeed! It was probably one of the most carefully constructed, powerfully delivered speeches made by any MP for a very long time. The Archbishop of Canterbury commended its excellence. Yet her only plea in thirteen minutes was that the bishops should not be hampered in their task of 'making the Church a real and living entity in what I believe is a deeply religious nation'. The granddaughter of the renowned Dickensian actress, Julia Fortescue, had inherited the histrionic gift, and it would always be a welcome source of pleasure to her listeners. With Lord Onslow, her brother, and Walter, her brother-in-law, in the Cabinet, the trio exercised a powerful influence in the House. It upset Gwenny that, unlike them, she was denied access to the atmosphere of the smoking-room – for no reason other than that she was a woman.

In the House she always wore black. Her son-in-law, Chips Channon, despaired of her dress sense. He tried to encourage his in-laws to become less austere, more stylish. Rupert was so old-fashioned that his clothes came back into fashion before they wore out. But Rupert was a gentleman farmer, un-interested in elegance and chic. He did not particularly enjoy going out to dinner and was at his happiest in an old tweed jacket and corduroy trousers, pottering around his property, chatting to his cows. But wealth destined him inevitably for some participation in the social round.

Though a fluent speaker, an achievement in itself given difficulties with his speech, Rupert was not an orator. He preferred to work behind the scenes and began to invest a great deal of energy in the Brewery. Boosting static sales was a first priority for the new Chairman. In 1926 there had been an unprecendented levelling off of sales. Quality of brew was apparently not enough. Steps needed to be taken to get it off the shelves. An elderly Lord Iveagh had issued the Board with a clarion call. 'I believe very firmly that a business either goes forward or it goes back – it seldom remains stationary, and when it arrives at that point, something ought to be done to get it moving again.'[8] He never lived to see that 'something' become the most famous Guinness innovation, a policy which would make Sam Guinness eat his words – the introduction of advertising.

It caused some temporary tension between the three brothers. Ernest was opposed to the idea, Walter for it, and Rupert supported the exceptionally gifted new managing director, Ben Newbold, who was convinced it was the way forward. In the end it was probably the single major contributing factor to the company's success in the 1930s and survival through the war. It certainly prevented fossilisation. S. H. Benson, the advertising agency responsible for the success of Colman's mustard and Bovril, was invited to come up with a catchy slogan. 'What have you got for us, Mr Benson?' Rupert asked him when he reappeared weeks later at the Board. 'Just this,' he replied, removing a small slip of paper from his pocket. It said, 'GUINNESS IS GOOD FOR YOU.'[9]

The first advert, which appeared in the national newspapers on 7 February 1929, gave no suggestion that Guinness might taste good, or even make you feel good, especially after a pint above the recommended dose. It simply did you good. The first two Arthur Guinnesses would have approved. It was entirely in keeping with their nonconformist philosophy.

When one indignant peer complained in the House of Lords that everywhere he went he was unable to enjoy the beauties of the British countryside for billboards proclaiming 'Guinness is good for you', the Earl of Iveagh rose to his feet, and made his one and only 'speech'. 'Guinness *is* good for you,' he shouted back.

The slogan continued for many years, right up to the 1950s when the Labour MP, Baroness Summerskill, a herald of advertising standards, asked whether the health-giving properties could be proved. By then, other promotional ideas had been equally successful – the brightly lit 'Guinness Time' clock in Piccadilly Circus, and at other focal points in major cities, so prolific in Dublin they almost recreate the atmosphere of the Blackpool illuminations, the animals at the zoo which pinch the keeper's pint to a lament of, 'My goodness, my Guinness'. Most famous of all the animals was the toucan, appearing in 1935 with two pints and a clever slogan penned by Dorothy L. Sayers, the crime writer and religious playwright, during her time working for Benson's.

> How grand to be a Toucan
> Just think what Toucan do

Since the Guinness Brewery had never been involved in the tied-house system, and never owned their own public houses, it was imperative they maintain nationwide demand in all outlets. Advertising, promoting a funny, familiar, homey, attractive image, enabled them to do exactly that.

The second most important decision made in those vital pre-war years under Rupert's leadership was the establishment of a British brewery, and it was taken in the end for political reasons out of a very real fear that beer might be priced out of the market by Irish import duties following the establishment of the Irish Free State. There was some debate about using land already in Guinness possession at Trafford Park in Manchester, but in the end, transporting stout via the Manchester Ship Canal was too slow a process. In pre-refrigeration days, ensuring the best keeping qualities was a high priority. Access to a road and rail network was essential and the Board opted for a site at Park Royal, just outside of London.

The building programme was shrouded in secrecy, initially not to give offence to the Irish, but also out of desperate concern that the punters might not take kindly to the notion that their pint was no longer brewed by the magical Liffey waters, but in a London suburb just off the A40.

But the legend survived. So did Guinness. And Gwenny sent a herd of sixteen Pyrford cows to graze on Park Royal grass, regularly enquiring after their individual welfare.

4.

While Bank and Brewery consolidated and expanded through the 1920s and 1930s, missionary enterprise had far from ceased in the Grattan line with the closure of Harley College. Annie's first and third sons, Jack and Gerald, managed to return from the trenches physically intact. Her second son, Harry, had escaped the trauma by emigrating to his grandmother's home in Tasmania at the age of seventeen before war began. Victor, the fourth son, delicate and spoilt, ran a taxi service on Salisbury Plain for soldiers.

Life for their mother was very different from the one she had known before the war. Annie was nearly fifty when Harry died and still had young children to care for, including a granddaughter. Undaunted, she moved them all into a smaller, more manageable house in Upper Norwood, now that her older children had left home, with a kitchen on the ground floor, not in the basement. Domestic help was hard to come by and for the first time in her life, she had taken to doing the cooking herself – with varying degrees of success. The three youngest boys, Gordon, Howard and Desmond, almost a separate family, greeted her scones with demands for a hatchet, and fed her semolina to the chickens. Keeping livestock, providing shelter for several missionary children, and unsuccessful attempts to cultivate a plot of spare land at the back of the house to feed them, were Annie's particular contribution to the war effort.

She was also the first woman in Upper Norwood to attach a one-and-a-quarter horsepower motor to the back of her bicycle so that she could deliver home-made soup to a larger number of housebound elderly neighbours. One day the children came home to find her stretched out in bed with a blood-soaked bandage tied around her head. The autocycle had got stuck in a tramline and thrown her headfirst into the road, where she had lain unconscious until a policeman found her and brought her home. The indomitable Annie was back on her cycle almost as soon as she could stand. The moral of the story, she told her boys, was to master the art, not give it up.

Raising three fatherless boys alone was a heavy responsibility and Annie felt they needed a firm hand, with the regular help of a hairbrush. Her older children had not turned out as she might have wished. By the end of the war Gene was divorced, Jack had married Ursula, was ordained in the Church of England, but had abandoned his evangelical, as well as his nonconformist roots, Victor was vain and egocentric, and the precocious, rebellious Eileen had married at seventeen, far too young to Annie's mind. Eileen had taken advantage of her mother's wartime trip to Tasmania to begin a heavy, adolescent flirtation with Ronald Fisher, a young science student. The marriage in fact turned out well. Fisher became an eminent Caius don, a Fellow of the Royal College of Scientists, and a friend of Rupert Guinness.

Gerald was Annie's greatest heartache. As a medical student at Guy's Hospital he had fallen into bad company and started drinking heavily, keeping his penchant well hidden from his mother. He took a practice in Plymouth and married Inez de Charriol, whose father was the French Consul in Calcutta, hoping that medicine and marriage would put him back on the right track. Inez was a Roman Catholic and the family did not approve of the match. They were horrified when Gerald converted. Only Annie attended the wedding.

A short time later she went to visit the couple in Plymouth. At 10 p.m. on her first night there was still no sign of Gerald. At 11 p.m. Inez' nerve broke and she told her mother-in-law it was a waste of time waiting up for him. He went out drinking most nights and she never knew what state he would be in when he arrived home. Annie waited up for him that and every subsequent night of her visit, but her remonstrations did no good. His medical career was already in ruins. He was forced to leave Plymouth, and Rome, and Durban, settling finally in a backwater of the Veld. At last, in extremis, alone and abandoned, he remembered some of the miracles which he had seen accompany his father's preaching when he was a boy, got down on his knees and prayed his father's God would save him. The prayer was answered, but Annie did not live to see it.

Gerald's 'problem' was never mentioned in front of the three younger boys. The rudiments of child psychology escaped Annie and most other parents in the first half of the twentieth century. Unable to see how unsettling the last years had been, with the move from Harley, Harry's death and the war, she decided discipline was what they needed, and asked her mother for the money to transfer them from their prep school at Dulwich College to the Leys School in Cambridge. Gordon and Howard were both highly competitive and settled in well.[10] Desmond, the youngest, was miserable, and withdrew into himself. When his mother fell victim to the flu epidemic which swept across the world after the war, claiming more lives than the actual fighting, Desmond convinced himself she would die.

One evening in chapel, in a state of panic, not caring what the other boys thought of him, he sat with tears pouring down his face. As he rose to sing Cowper's old traditional hymn, 'God moves in a mysterious way', he was suddenly overwhelmed with the awareness of God's supreme control of his life, and the sense that all would be well. For decades after, he would never hear the hymn without being transported back to the school chapel with its peculiar smell of newish oak pews, and remember, as if it were yesterday, that feeling of utter desolation slowly giving way to peace and calm.

The boys had been introduced to Anglicanism when they first moved away from Harley House, simply because Christchurch, Anerley, had a reputation for the best preaching in the area. And preaching was everything – the greatest privilege on earth. Annie told the boys their grandfather had been used to convert thousands, their father hundreds. The achievement of their forefathers was an unspoken expectation hanging over their heads during their growing years, pursuing them relentlessly throughout adulthood. Living up to the family name was as hard for the Grattan Guinnesses as for the other branches, harder in some ways, since successful preaching put more onus on individual public performance than banking or brewing.

Every Sunday in Eton suits and boaters the three boys had been frogmarched two miles from Upper Norwood into pew number 21. Chanting canticles and psalms, reciting state prayers, churchwardens in morning-coat, disapproving looks at their raucous hymn singing was a shock to their non-conformist systems. 'Rude people turned round to see where all the noise was coming from. Even the vicar's wife used to turn round – bad manners we were told – and the Guinness boys would stare her out (very bad manners).'

Neither the formality of their church, nor school chapel predisposed them to any sympathy with what their mother believed was their obvious calling, but Crusader Boys' Clubs, and summer camps on the Isle of Wight did. As teenagers the boys discovered a faith which eventually led all three of them to ordination, along with friends like Max Warren, Brian Green and Stafford Wright, leading evangelical Anglicans in the 1940s and 1950s.

But the world in which they exercised their ministry was very different from the world of their predecessors. The last flickers of religious revival were finally doused by a blanket of post-war scepticism. There was little evidence of the existence of a compassionate deity for those who had survived the trenches and for those whose loved ones would never return. What public religiosity remained was rigid and formal, enshrined in ritual and traditionalism to ensure it remained suitably remote, well removed from possible close examination. Robust evangelicalism with its absolute certainties and demand for commitment was no longer fashionable. Liberal theology was in the ascendancy – particularly in the Church of England.

Gordon, Howard and Desmond had the same missionary zeal as their forefathers, but it was anathema to their own generation. Outside and often inside the Church, they found themselves with their backs against the wall, defending their religious principles, more certain the more they were questioned, scorned by the upper classes for whom piety had become a private matter, ignored by the working classes, for whom religious practice, particularly Anglicanism, was largely an irrelevancy in a class-ridden society.

Nonetheless each of the three brothers made his own mark, though the defensiveness of their position took its toll on their personal lives. Evangelicals had to be faultless, successful, super-spiritual. Achievement was measured in souls converted. Gordon established a reputation for taking on dwindling congregations and building them into the most vibrant in the city, became a canon in the Winchester diocese, but spent his life working himself to a virtual standstill. Howard was sent by his fellow London University students to Canada in 1928 to form a Christian student movement like the British Inter-Varsity Fellowship. They collected enough money to buy him a one-way ticket and a new overcoat. He completed the job and went on to pioneer evangelical student movements in Australia and New Zealand, but his insensitivity as a clergyman in Britain earned him the enemies which eventually forced him permanently abroad. And Desmond, the only one of Annie's children to become a missionary, never found a woman spiritual enough to marry.

That her youngest had taken up the call was a source of immense satisfaction to Annie. Now, she said, she would not be ashamed to meet her Maker. She died in 1933, shortly after Desmond sailed for China. His choice of destination was due, inevitably, to the influence of Aunt Geraldine, who kept a weather, almost patriarchal, eye on her fatherless nephews and two half-brothers, as well as on Henry and Karl Kumm.

In middle age Howard and Geraldine were still having adventures of their own. One of their escapades captured the newspaper headlines for several weeks and was the subject of major diplomatic negotiations.

The war period passed them fairly quietly. Geraldine was writing the second half of her biography of Hudson Taylor. The first volume had been a huge seller and her public eagerly awaited the end of the story. It was a major blow when the publisher demanded she reduce it by two hundred pages, but she complied and it took another year to complete.

Henry and Karl still came to her for school holidays. Karl Kumm senior had refused to deny his German citizenship during the war and rather than be treated as an enemy alien, had emigrated with Gertrude to the United States, leaving the boys in boarding school. By 1919, when the China Inland Mission asked Howard and Geraldine if they would be willing to go on a lengthy tour of China, encouraging missionaries in the furthest outposts, the boys were old enough to leave behind.

Howard and Geraldine spent three years in China, travelling thousands of miles in carts and sedan chairs, staying in dozens of uncomfortable, vermin-infested inns, rising before dawn, and journeying long after dusk. It was a punishing

451

existence for a couple in their late fifties, their difficulties compounded by the fact that Howard was so profoundly deaf he heard little without the use of an ear trumpet. But whatever they faced, never, for one moment, did she forget Lucy's charge, and wrote to her boys daily.

Their first Christmas in 1919 was spent with Whitfield and Janie in Kaifeng. In her journal she wrote, 'No notes. I was absorbed in dear little Mary's life story.' Whitfield's youngest daughter, her namesake, Mary Geraldine, had died the previous year at the age of nine. The beautiful little girl with the mass of golden curls, whose Chinese name was Pearl, had a very real faith of her own, and her aunt decided to record it there and then for posterity. She had never written a children's book before, but the response to *Pearl's Secret* was overwhelming. It was translated into more languages than any of her other books, and young readers from all over the world wrote to tell her how much the book had meant to them.

A year later, one cold December night in Lanchow, Howard and Geraldine were sitting around the fire in the sitting-room of their missionary hosts when a strange disturbance began.

It seemed to be outside and overhead, like the thundering toward and then above us of a train on an elevated railway. It was bewildering and almost overpowering, but for the moment we went on praying. Then the floor began to move – and we knew! The parents rushed for their children, while the building rocked and the floor swayed so that it was difficult to reach the door. Outside the courtyard was rolling like a rough sea. Sounds of creaking timbers, falling walls, and that indescribable groaning of great roofs continued. As we stood, an amazed and silent group in the middle of the courtyard, it went on through minutes that seemed interminable. Yet we were calm, strangely calm and were able to reassure the servants and others who had run out of their rooms in terror. Then gradually the earth under our feet steadied, the deafening roar passed away, and the worst was over.[11]

Two hundred thousand people lost their lives in the earthquake that night. Thousands more were left homeless in bitter winter weather, watching the floods sweep away their possessions, leaving a desolate, unrecognisable landscape behind.

They stayed a further five months to help with the salvage and relief work, then set off on their travels towards Yunnan in the south, much of their journey through brigand-infested mountains. In January 1922, Geraldine wrote to young Karl at college:

Imagine a wintry day, with mist and snow and sleet, and the worst road you ever saw, threading valleys, crossing mountains – up and down again by long flights of steep stone steps, frightfully slippery, as the whole road is, with mud and slush; and two sedan chairs plodding on from daylight to dark, the bearers wearing irons under their straw sandals to keep them from falling, and you have our circumstances as I write. The snow is drifting into my chair, and my hand is so cold I can hardly hold my pen, but my heart is happy in Jesus, and warm with thoughts of you.

A month later, almost at Yunnenfu, they were ambushed and taken hostage by brigands.

The brigands would in fact have been very happy to make off with Howard on his own, but Geraldine insisted they should not be separated because of his deafness. They were held for two days at the brigands' headquarters in a courtyard in a nearby village to await the arrival of the leader, P'u Kiang-kuin. There was little food and no covering to keep out the penetrating cold of sleeping on the ground, but otherwise, they were not harshly treated.

When P'u arrived after midnight on the second day, he made it clear that he would kill them if Government troops advanced on his men, but release them if certain terms were met. The following day he decided that Geraldine should go on alone to Yunnanfu to negotiate. Parting from Howard was extremely painful for her. Blinded by tears she said goodbye for what, for all she knew, might be the last time.

For five weeks there was no news of him. Geraldine worked tirelessly for his release, begging local officials to take some action, but they seemed so unprincipled, so motivated by avariciousness and personal gain that her sympathy for the bandits grew by the minute. The British Consulate intervened but was equally powerless in the face of a dispute between the 'law', and the outlaws of a Chinese provincial government. British newspapers carried the story daily.

She wrote to him one evening:

How it goes to my heart that another night is closing in and you are still out there on the mountains. It is a month today since we were taken. A whole month you have been herded together with the brigands – eating their food, breathing their atmosphere, and never alone day or night. The Lord would never have allowed it if he had not some special purpose of blessing. He will not fail us.[12]

A week later a reply managed to reach her. She was not, said Howard, to overestimate his trials. Suspense, opium fumes, crowding, vermin, the monotonous loitering and being unable to hear his possible fate were causing him some discomfort. But on the other hand horse riding, open-air life and a compulsory diet had much improved his figure and he had never enjoyed such rugged health in his life. The submarine, it appears, was as unsinkable as ever.

Several weeks later changes in China's highly volatile political life made Howard a redundant captive. 'Do you want to go tonight or tomorrow morning?' P'u asked him. A close friendship had developed between the two men. Howard said it wasn't for him to decide. P'u insisted politely that he must suit his own convenience, so Howard left for Yunnanfu that night.

This was their last experience of the interior of China for many years. Inevitably Geraldine wove it into a little booklet called *With P'u and the Brigands*, a sympathetic portrait of a group of pathetic young rebels who were simply looking for a better life. Through Howard's influence P'u in fact became a Christian.

It was her more detailed account of those three long years of travel, *The Call of China's Great North West*, which ten years later fell into her nephew Desmond's hands and led to his decision to become a missionary in China.

After Howard's release they settled in the United States, travelling and speaking on behalf of the China Inland Mission, watching the political situation deteriorate from a distance.

In the hospital in Honan which Whitfield had built, the first in the area, he and Janie were driven to the limit of their resources. As law and order broke down, murder, pillage, looting and rape were widespread. Their hospital wards were filled with the wounded and dying. 'Janie wondered at a patient's lack of interest in her new-born baby,' he wrote to his sister in America. 'It's a bandit baby, came the explanation.'

In 1926 as the southern army descended on the northern troops holding Kaifeng, Honan was like a walnut in a nutcracker. Colleagues remember that Whitfield was his old self, calm and unruffled, playing his violin for his medical students to help them relax, enjoying an occasional game of golf or chess.

I remember his being so amused over some fresh expression of slang heard for the first time – rubbing his hands and looking just as he always did. He stooped a little more than formerly, but his hair was as black as ever, and in response to an outside call for help he would go off on his motor cycle just like a young man.[13]

But he was very glad that the children, Henry and Joy, were safely away at school, though he missed them terribly. In the end there had been no option. Life had always been hard in Honan where the Yellow River often flooded its banks, spreading infection and disease. At two young Henry had contracted tuberculosis and persistently suffered from dysentery. Whitfield and Janie made the most painful sacrifice of their lives, and sent their children to live with an aunt in the pure clean air of Sweden. By the time he was ready for secondary school, Henry was tri-lingual in English, Swedish and Mandarin.

Though he had seen little of them, Whitfield adored his children and wrote almost daily.

Feb 6th 1927

Tomorrow we open the hospital again after the Chinese New Year, but who knows how long we can carry on? . . . Consular telegrams urge the ladies to leave. Still we wait. We do not want to yield to any spirit of panic, and at present things are quiet here at Kai-feng. The great fact is, God is with us, so all will be well . . .

The city is upset with crowds of Northern soldiers billeted here. They look more like bandits than soldiers, commandeer everything, go into homes and take possession – and there is no redress. Mother bravely keeps on, also Dr McDonald and Miss Soltau, and others out here.

This afternoon I took the old jumping pole and taught the students to do the high jump, or rather pole jump. They greatly enjoyed the fun. I drew the line for myself at a little over six feet, as I am too old now, 58 in April! But I remember doing eight feet six at Cliff years ago.[14]

A few days later guns could be heard in the distance, and the wounded began to arrive in droves. When there was no more room at the hospital, Whitfield nursed them in his own home. One night a man arrived at his door obviously suffering from typhoid fever. Whitfield was in a dilemma. It was a freezing night and he could not turn the man away. But nor could he risk an epidemic. A fellow missionary offered to prepare a hut nearby, and Whitfield stipulated that he alone would take care of the patient.

By the time the order to evacuate reached Kaifeng, Whitfield was seriously ill. General Mi made a box car available on a special train to Peking. It was not intended for passengers, but better than nothing. For two days with Janie at his side, he travelled day and night on a camp bed through the war-torn state, conscious, but in a high fever and very confused. When they finally reached the Union Medical College in Peking on 8 April, it was Eastertide, the first day of Holy Week, and Whitfield had slipped into a coma. Janie wrote in her diary: 'My heart is breaking with sorrow, but full of peace. I stand by his side and praise God for all the love of these twenty two years. Such perfect happiness. There is peace in this little room and Whitfield is too ill to feel any pain . . . He put his hand between mine this forenoon.'

On 12 April she wrote:

My dearest has passed through the sufferings of death and is so near the Homeland – how can I, dare I, call him back, or even wish him back? From weakness, pain and death he is going to liberty, joy and life. Heaven is calling

457

and I let him go. For myself and our precious children, we are in God's keeping.

He was buried on Easter Day in the English cemetery in Peking. Geraldine was speaking at a conference in Australia when the news reached her.

> We are in the midst of a great conference of young people, some four or five hundred. We have had to speak several times, and now, today, are packing to leave for our next engagement. There has been no time really to think. A wave of pain and desolation sweeps over me at times, and then again a great and wonderful gladness ... just long to get away somewhere, quietly, and try to realise what has happened – I mean to realise *his* joy.[15]

Geraldine was Henry Grattan Guinness's last surviving child by his marriage to Fanny. The other three had all died before the age of sixty of conditions directly related to their missionary service. Whitfield's death seems to have galvanised the China Inland Mission into the realisation that they could not take their brightest stars for granted. After years of faithful service the Taylors needed a complete rest. A cottage was rented for them for six months in exclusive La Jolla in California. For the first time in their lives they were free to do as they pleased. Geraldine tried her hand at cooking. 'I am very much interested in it and Howard appreciates my efforts!' They spent a great deal of time in Passiflora with Karl and Gertrude Kumm and their three children, and were delighted when Henry Kumm married Joyce Beale, of Beale's department store in Bournemouth. Joyce was Grace Guinness's cousin on the Hurditch side, and the couple had been introduced at Gracie's house in London.

By 1930 the Taylors were facing their seventieth year, but there was no question of permanent retirement. They loved living in the States, and went on travelling extensively, speaking at large youth gatherings and summer conventions like Camp Diamond. As skirts became shorter, and necklines plunged, Geraldine continued to wear neck-to-ankle dresses. It did not seem to antagonise her young audiences. No one could conceive of her in anything else.

When Gracie's younger son, Paul, now in his early twenties, arrived in the USA to study at Dallas Theological Seminary, and needed preaching opportunities to earn his living, Geraldine arranged them for him, introducing him to bemused audiences as 'my brother'. She looked more like his grandmother.

He was engaged by then to Jean Elliot of Montreal, whom he had met when he was a speaker at the Canadian Keswick Convention. Jean, the daughter of strict Baptists and a real rebel, had an aversion to these powerful Guinnesses. As a teenager she had been left by her parents alone in a room with Howard Guinness, the well-known student evangelist with an ego to match. This could only mean one thing. He had been encouraged by her parents to convert her or propose to her. Fortunately it was the former, but whichever, she had already determined to send him away with a flea in his ear. He was far too pushy for her liking.

Nor was she in any mood to accept the advances of another member of the clan, but then Paul was a different matter, tall, broad, mouth-wateringly handsome, with the same penetrating eyes as his father, the legendary Henry Grattan Guinness. There was the same aura of saintliness, the same gift of oratory, the same presence, though Paul had been only two years old when his father had died.

After their engagement he took his fiancée to meet Howard and Geraldine. Howard, she said, was 'a perfect pet', so deaf she would have to repeat her inanities *molta voce* into his ear trumpet, but Geraldine, taking her duties as the family matriarch seriously, aware of the demands involved in marrying into the clan, interrogated her in depth. 'Jean, dear,' she asked, 'can you cook? Jean, dear, can you sew? Jean, dear, can you type?'

'What a cheek!' my mother-in-law would say indignantly years later. 'She had never done any of those things in her life. She had always had someone to do them for her.'

It was a huge blow to both Howard and Geraldine when the Mission instructed them to return to England for their retirement. They were almost eighty and the year was 1939. Hardly the best time to arrive.

Chapter 14

1939–1960

A Murder, a Mystic and the Mystery of the Succession

1.

The last significant date noted in Henry Grattan Guinness's Bible was 1948. On 14 May 1948, sitting in her armchair in her room in the retirement home where she had lived for three years since a stroke, Geraldine Taylor heard on the wireless that the independent Jewish State of Israel had been born. She was eighty-five and it seemed she had waited all her life for this one moment. She picked up her pen and to her niece, Joy, who was writing her biography, wrote, 'From a full heart words will hardly come this morning; yet I long to write to you. It is like trying to express the inexpressible.' On her deathbed, Lucy Guinness Kumm had known her boys would see 'those unutterable days', and hoped they would have a part to play. Her prophetic vision was only partly correct.

On a troop ship mid-Atlantic in the early days of the Second World War, two army chaplains, cousins, had met by apparent chance, one British, one American. For Paul Guinness it was an extraordinary occurrence, too strange to be pure co-incidence. He had always wanted to meet Lucy's younger son,

Karl. 'Do you', he asked him, 'feel it is your ministry is to fulfil your mother's last words, to explain the relevance of Grattan Guinness' work in the history of the Jewish people?'

Karl said he didn't, and Paul heaved a sigh of relief.

'I'm glad,' he said, 'because I do.'[1]

News of the creation of the state of Israel may have been the culmination of Geraldine's hopes, the fulfilment of her father's vision, a sign she could die in peace, but there was little joy in it on the brewing side of the family. On 6 November 1944, Walter Guinness had been assassinated in Egypt by Jewish terrorists intent on freeing Palestine of British domination.

The youngest of the first Lord Iveagh's sons, charming, discerning and astute, Walter had carved out a hugely success-ful career for himself in politics. According to his grandson, he was 'too cool and open-minded to be a real party man', a diplomat rather than a Conservative, and therefore invaluable to successive prime ministers. For outstanding service as a staff officer during the First War he earned the unusual double honour of a DSO and a bar. The diary he kept is a grim account of the horrors of the trenches. His ordeal was as harrowing as any endured by his missionary cousins at the hands of the Boxers, Chinese bandits or Congo natives, and he did not care to speak of it much afterwards. In his memoirs, Anthony Eden, who met him there, paid tribute to his extraordinary courage. But it was Walter Guinness, the shrewd, level-headed strategist, who managed to survive and triumph over experiences which would have destroyed a weaker man, to become Under-Secretary of State for War, Financial Secretary to the Treasury, and from 1924 to 1925, Minister of Agriculture.

In 1932 he was offered a peerage, but was reluctant to accept it because he felt he could be of greater public use if he remained in the Commons. In the end he conceded and picked the name Moyne for his title from a map of Loch

Corrib, near his uncle Arthur's Ashford estate. It designated a small islet – and it was plain and short. The supporters for his coat of arms were a pair of macaque monkeys. The geographical and scientific inquisitiveness in the Guiness genes also affected Walter in large measure. He was an inveterate traveller in Asia Minor and Africa, using his ocean-going yacht, *The Rosaura*, to collect anthropological data and unusual animals. Even so, Lady Evelyn could have done without the monkeys on her crest.

Winston Churchill respected Walter Guinness as a colleague and found him 'a most agreeable, intelligent and unusual friend'.[2] In the late summer of 1934 Winston and Clementine joined him for a month's holiday in the Mediterranean on *The Rosaura*. The relationship was a happy one, for the following year they were both invited to accompany Walter on a four-month round-the-world trip to bring back a live giant 'monitor lizard', and 'komodo dragons' for the London Zoo. The long sea journey did not appeal to Winston, but Clementine was so taken with the idea that she went without him. The trip was one of the most memorable experiences of her life.

Some of the 'specimens' Lord Moyne collected were of more public interest than others. On one occasion he picked up the Prince of Wales and Wallis Simpson in the South of France. This was their first holiday together, and despite the presence of Wallis' ubiquitous chaperone, Aunt Bessie, and Moyne's extreme discretion, tongues began to wag.

In 1938, recuperating from a long bout of illness, Clementine Churchill joined Lord Moyne once again on *The Rosaura* for his fact-finding mission as Chairman of the Royal Commission on social conditions in the West Indies. She loved the Caribbean, but the cruise was a strain because of major political differences among the passengers. When Lord Moyne remained silent in the face of Lady Broughton's criticisms of Winston (Lady Broughton was Moyne's mistress), Clementine went to her cabin, packed, and took the first ship home.

The tension between Lord Moyne and the Churchills was short-lived. In 1940, when Churchill became the leader of a nation at war, Lord Moyne succeeded Lord Lloyd as Secretary of State for the Colonies, and from 1941 to 1942 was Leader of the House of Lords. In 1942 he joined the Cabinet as Minister of State in Egypt, and in 1944 became Minister resident in the Middle East, responsible for an area stretching from Tripoli to eastern Persia. He went alone. Lady Evelyn had died in 1939.

Though a prestigious appointment, it was an unenviable one. Tensions in British-controlled Palestine were reaching breaking point. This was the era of 'the Exodus', when thousands of Jewish refugees fleeing Hitler's death camps in Europe were arriving in 'coffin boats', desperately seeking safe haven in the land of promise. The British government, protective of the indigenous Arab population, with whom relations were cordial, yet appalled by early stories of Jewish persecution emerging from Europe, was faced with an impossible dilemma. The extent of the Holocaust was not yet widely acknowledged.

Bryan Guinness, Lord Moyne's son, was convinced of his father's sympathy for the Jewish cause. In the early 1930s Bryan had been married to Diana Mitford who divorced him to marry the British fascist, Oswald Moseley. He remarried in 1936, and was posted to Damascus during the war, near enough to visit his father from time to time. He claimed they never discussed diplomatic issues, though he does say, 'I have a vivid recollection of my father's intense anger once expressed to me before the war at the indignities and atrocities inflicted on the Jews in Austria after the Anschluss and before the onset of the genocide.'[3] Lord Moyne's sympathy, however, was based more on anthropological principles than genuine affection. Before the First World War he had alerted the public to the plight of the Kurds. During his later travels he was the first to discover the stone-age Aiome Pygmies. He was interested in the rights of peoples, in the preservation of racial identity, and in that context, made certain comments about Jewish racial characteristics which appeared patronising at the least, downright antisemitic at their worst. To make biological remarks about an unknown species of pygmy was one thing, to speak of the Jews in similar terms, when dealing with statesmen like Chaim Weizmann, Lewis Namier and Isaiah Berlin, was quite another. Moyne's cool objectivity was leading him into dangerous territory.

According to his son, 'He used to see and hear with sympathy Dr Weizmann and Lewis Namier and Isaiah Berlin. I cannot give you chapter and verse for this however. It is founded on impressions in talking to these two (presumably the latter two).'[4] Nonetheless, in the early part of the war he made a speech suggesting Jews be brought out of Nazi control to *anywhere* in the world. The memory of it lingered on, a festering sore re-opened when he was appointed to oversee the British policy of limited Jewish immigration to Palestine, a policy which to many Jews, escaping the Holocaust, amounted to a cruelty worse than the one they had left behind.

On 4 November 1944, Chaim Weizmann, the future first President of Israel, then a lecturer at Manchester University, was invited to lunch with Churchill at Chequers. The Prime Minister wanted to discuss the possibility of partitioning Palestine into two independent states, Jewish and Arab, with Jerusalem as a free city. Moyne had apparently been involved in delicate negotiations with Arab and Jewish representatives. Weizmann appears to have been genuinely delighted that his dream of a Jewish homeland might yet become a reality. As he was about to leave for Palestine, Churchill suggested he broke his journey in Cairo to visit Lord Moyne and see for himself how the man had 'changed and developed in the past two years'.[5]

Two days later, before Weizmann had left England, Lord Moyne was dead. He was returning home from the British

Embassy in Cairo to his residence on Gezira Island, separated from the city by the Kasr-el-Nil Bridge across the Nile. He was sitting in the passenger seat of the black Humber limousine, a perennially elegant figure in a white suit, Dorothy Osmond, his secretary, and Andrew Hughes-Onslow, his ADC, in the back. The car drew up at the front door of the house. Onslow jumped out and ran to open it, while the chauffeur, Corporal Fuller, went to open the passenger door. Two young men suddenly appeared with revolvers in their hands, one trained on Onslow, one on Fuller. 'They're going to shoot us,' Moyne shouted, as the terrorist pointing at Onslow suddenly turned, thrust his gun through the driver's window and fired at almost point-blank range, hitting Lord Moyne in the neck and the stomach. Fuller was gunned down by the other assassin and died almost at once. 'Be still, don't move,' they shouted to Onslow, who stood helplessly on the doorstep. Then they made their escape on push bikes. Onslow gave chase, then alerted the police. Both assassins were arrested shortly after on the bridge by an off-duty policeman. Had they crossed, it would have been almost impossible to catch them.

Parliament was informed at once, but eleven days passed before Churchill could trust himself to speak of it in public. When he did, his words were barbed. 'If our dreams of Zionism are to end in the smoke of the assassins' guns and our labours for its future to produce only a new set of gangsters worthy of Nazi Germany', then we would have to 'reconsider the position we have maintained so consistently and so long in the past'.

British colonialism was a generic part of Churchill's make-up, however sympathetic to the Jewish cause he thought he was, and Lord Moyne had been the supreme symbol of British control of the Middle East. But no assassination could have caused the Jews more embarrassment. They distanced themselves from the actions of the Stern Gang as far as they could. *Haaretz,* the most influential Jewish newspaper in Palestine, said, 'No more grievous blow has been struck to our cause.' Chaim Weizmann denounced the killing and sent condolences to Bryan Guinness, referring to 'personal kindnesses' received. Bryan agonised over his reply, then asked him for his help in putting an end to terrorism, for 'without the terrorised acquiescence of the population of Palestine such crimes would not be possible'.

Bryan escorted his father's body home for burial. As the two coffins were taken to the airport, the people of Cairo were moved to see the cabinet minister and the corporal receive the same military honours. They landed in Oxfordshire and a padre sent to welcome the plane, said to Bryan without the greatest military or pastoral sensitivity, 'You've a corpse on board, haven't you?'

'Yes, my father,' he replied.

In 1985, looking back at those events, Bryan Guinness wrote, 'It can be no more than speculation to suppose that if my father had not been murdered by Stern Gang terrorists, and if he could have achieved agreement before the end of the war on a partitioned Palestine . . . the many cruel wars that have since beset Israel and her neighbours might have been avoided.'[6] But as his forefathers had foreseen only too well, a partitioned Ireland was no guarantee of peace.

2.

Walter Guinness's death was not the only tragedy to beset the brewing side of the family in those war years. Weeks before the end, Rupert and Gwenny's only son and heir, Arthur Onslow Guinness, Viscount Elveden, was killed in action at Nijmegen. Their devastation was total. They had lost their only, much beloved son, and the succession at the Brewery was put in jeopardy. Ernest, the vice-chairman, also had daughters, and Walter's son Bryan was never taken seriously. He was arty, a writer and poet, not cut out for business.

Viscount Elveden had in fact three children by his marriage to Lady Elizabeth Hare, daughter of the fourth earl of Listowel, a son, Arthur Francis Benjamin and two daughters, Elizabeth and Henrietta. From the moment of his father's death eight-year-old Benjamin was groomed for his inevitable, inescapable destiny, his grandfather remaining chairman of the company, resolving any intermediate problem with the blessing of longevity. He lived to the age of ninety-three.

Nonetheless, there was a shortage of good Guinness material to prime the pumps at the Brewery once again, and when Edward Guinness turned up out of the blue at Holmbury St Mary's, his godfather Ernest's Surrey house, it must have seemed as if opportunity were knocking at the door.

Edward was a grandson of Dodo's black sheep of an elder brother, Cecil Guinness, the remittance man who had been sent to Australia and had charm enough to marry into money. He and Marion Forlonge, the sheep baron's daughter, produced two girls, Mabel and Katy, and to launch them in society, eventually moved back to England, set up house in the modest Warwick Road in Maida Vale, and lived off Marion's money until it ran out. Marion was continually and chronically ill and Mabel and Katy were raised largely by their adored 'Aunt G' Kerr-Pearse. Fortunately for them they were exceptionally vivacious and beautiful which made them great favourites with their Iveagh aunt and uncle.

In 1882, when she was eighteen, Mabel had an exclusive society wedding when she was married by Uncle Beauchamp Kerr-Pearse, who had also conducted the Iveagh's wedding ceremony, to Walter Lang, a wealthy, worldly Bombay merchant and exchange broker twenty-four years her senior.[7] Lang owned race horses and was a great gambler, but it was not until his sudden death in 1912 that Mabel discovered that her cousin, to whom she had always been so good, was in fact his mistress. The year before Lang's death, Edward Cecil stayed with them when he went out to India alone for the Delhi Durbar.[8]

In the same year that Mabel married Walter, her stunning red-haired elder sister Katy eloped with John Brennand, a penniless northerner. Brennand turned out to be a man after Lord Iveagh's heart – thoroughly self-made. Within a few years he became the hugely wealthy owner of Buckley and Brennand's cotton-bleaching business in Lancashire. At their charming, but cold and draughty house, Baldersby Park near Thirsk, where deer roamed freely in the park, the Brennands held shooting parties which may not have matched Elveden, but were the envy of the wealthy northern mercantile classes nonetheless. In 1907 they bought the first motor car in the area.

Three years after her girls married, Marion Forlonge died. A combination of drought and bad investment caused her Australian sheep farming father to go bankrupt and Cecil was left destitute. He turned, naturally, to his brother-in-law for financial support. Dodo adored her brother and tried to ignore his faults, but even she balked when Cecil remonstrated with her husband for signing himself 'Cecil Guinness' when that was his sole prerogative as the elder of the two. They were probably quite relieved when Cecil took up the life of a remittance man again and set off for America. But their relief was short-lived. In New York he met a pretty barmaid called Agnes Gilchrist, married her, then died suddenly in 1898, leaving her in penury with two small children to support. Inevitably, she appealed to her husband's wealthy relatives for help. Lord Iveagh instructed her to bring Cecil, aged eight, and Mildred, aged five, while they were young, 'so that they could not come and claim relationship later when he did not know them'.[9]

But unlike their beautiful elder half-sisters, Mabel and Katy, Agnes' children were never made to feel a full part of the

Elveden family. Dodo was forever going on about how good Marion had been, and how beautiful Mabel and Katy were. Though Aunt G thought Aggie 'nice and respectable', she dropped her aitches, an unforgivable sin as far as Dodo was concerned. With no other means of earning her living, Agnes was forced into domestic service. Dodo always referred to her as 'that dreadful woman'. Aunt G alone gave the little trio her wholehearted acceptance, took Mildred under her wing, and insisted she be included in the Elveden family houseparties.

Though striking with red hair and blue eyes, Mildred was altogether too big to be described as pretty, and no matter how hard she tried to be an equal, was made to feel she should be compliant and grateful. Even before her disastrous five-year marriage to alcoholic Eric Gunning, she became an indispensable companion and helper to Cloë, paid for her services in family sufferance. It was a role she played to perfection, ingratiating on the surface, resentful underneath, jealous of Mabel and Katy's popularity, desperate for a share of the Guinness glamour, but always in the background of Elveden family photographs. Cloë put upon her shamefully, using her to chaperone her three girls whenever it suited her, though in fact Mildred was only eleven years older than Aileen, their eldest. It was a small price to pay for acceptance.

Ernest and Cloë moved from Glenmaroon in Dublin to Holmbury St Mary's in Surrey during the Troubles in the 1920s, but they still returned to their Irish home three times a year, at Christmas, Easter and in the summer for the horse show. Glenmaroon was the scene of a particularly tragic family accident in 1934. Aunt G's son, Bertie Kerr-Pearse, was spending a few days at the house with his daughter, Elizabeth. Ernest, a hardy and seasoned yachtsman, who had taken his wife and three teenage daughters safely around the world in 1923 on a 600-ton, four-masted yacht called *Fantome*, simply took his guests out for a turn on the lake in his speed boat. During a very sharp manoeuvre he managed to overturn the boat. Bertie was knocked unconscious when he fell out. Though Elizabeth was not a good swimmer she managed to hold on to him for a while, but eventually lost her grip. He disappeared under the water before help reached them and never resurfaced again. The first his wife Lillie knew of the accident was when the press besieged her London flat. Ernest never spoke of it again and it was quickly relegated to the annals of forgotten history.

Though she followed Ernest and Cloë everywhere they went, Mildred nonetheless came into her own in the 1930s, working with Schreiber as an interior designer. Tall, imposing, with a mass of red hair and a very large bosom, she made a formidable quartermaster at the Auxiliary Hospital on Ernest's land at Holmbury St Mary during the war. She finally managed to persuade Cloë to play Lady Bountiful and make a formal visit.

'How have you come to be here, my man?' she asked at the first bed. 'Is it because of shrapnel?'

'No, I got kicked in the testicles, ma'am,' the patient replied. The genteel Cloë had be led away.

For Ernest one major irritation of the war was being denied the use of his autogyro – his helicopter – which he kept in a hangar nearby. His choice of Holmbury, an ugly house, disliked by the three girls, had been decided by the proximity of the airport. His autogyro was one of his special 'toys', one of his larger 'gadgets' or inventions which magically appeared, moved, told the time or forecast the weather at the push of a button. He had been the oldest man in England to acquire a pilot's licence, adored flying almost as much as he loved sailing, and was broken-hearted to see his pride and joy rotting before his eyes, a victim to moths and decay.

But his automobile kept going. He attached a charcoal-burner to the back to ensure it would get him to the Brewery several times a week and after the war turned his attention to inventing a gas-run car. Cloë meanwhile became a martyr to her digestive system and an early devotee of colonic irrigation.

In later years Mildred bored her friends half to death with tales of her important Guinness connections and French cousins, referring to the descendants of the Duc de Montebello no less. She achieved her ambition of a flat in Mayfair, kept a companion called Alan and was devoted to her nieces and nephews who adored her, finding her invariably generous and kind, a steadying source of affection when they needed it, particularly for some of the younger, more sensitive Guinness children like Henrietta.

Mildred's brother Cecil was left to make his own way in the world, and support his mother as best he could. His step-sister, Katy Brennand, twenty-five years his senior, rescued him from a dreary job on the railway and provided him with an apprenticeship at their booming Pilsworth bleach works. Cecil did not want to seem ungrateful to his half-sister, of whom he was exceedingly fond, but the work was drudgery. The First World War postponed any difficult decision, and on his return, after being wounded three times, he discovered John Brennand had had a stroke and, since his sons had been raised to be 'huntin', shootin', fishin' ' gentlemen, the business was moving rapidly towards bankruptcy. Their friends and thriving rivals, Davies and Eckersley who owned the Eckersley Bleach Works in Adlington, recognised his ability and snapped him up. So did the company daughter, Betty Davies. The couple produced five children and Cecil saved every penny to provide his children with the education he had been denied. Edward was the eldest.

With her usual insistence on the importance of making the right connections, Aunt Mildred had encouraged her brother to ask Ernest to be his first child's godfather. Ernest had agreed, but his only acknowledgment of the role had been the gift of a pair of binoculars at the child's christening. Otherwise he seemed oblivious of Edward's existence.

At the end of the second war, Edward, a young officer cadet

with a broken arm, found himself with a day's leave of absence from the rehabilitation hospital in Aldershot where he was posted, and wondered whether it might not be time to re-establish contact with the missing godfather who lived nearby. The first phone call was unpromising. He introduced himself as 'Ted', which sounded very much like 'Ned' down the crackling wartime line. Since Ned was a Guinness relative who was *persona non grata*, Edward was given a polite, but firm brush-off. But persistence paid off. 'My appearance in army hospital "blues" was a slight shock to the Jeeves-like butler, Lapham, who received me at the door but only by a faint twitch at the corner of his mouth did he betray this and I was given the friendliest of welcomes by both Ernest and Cloë.'[10]

They invited him back for a weekend, and he managed to contrive a thirty-six-hour pass, arriving at Holmbury House one Saturday afternoon. This time Ernest quizzed him in depth about his schooling and army career, even asking to see his school reports. When Gwendolin and Rupert Iveagh turned up at Sunday teatime on some contrived pretext, Edward was left in little doubt that the visit was not merely a social occasion. And though he could not engage in informed conversation with Rupert about milking machines, a letter inviting him to go for interview to Park Royal arrived within days of his return to Aldershot.

On 1 October 1945 he worked his first 2 p.m. to 10 p.m. shift, a junior brewer in overalls and wellington boots, helping the process workers clean out the enormous mash and fermenting tuns, coppers and vats, all done by hand in those days. This was the start of forty-three years with the company, the last fifteen as managing director of Harp, Guinness's lager offshoot. From that first day he was conscious of being part of a family firm with a reputation for integrity. Apart from his brother, who to this day is manager of the Runcorn branch, Edward was the last family member to understand the brewing process. He was the last to hold an executive position on the

Guinness Board – a strange irony considering the way the family had treated his grandmother, father and aunt.

3.

Geraldine Taylor's joy over the establishment of the state of Israel was modified in succeeding months by news of the Communist takeover of her beloved China. When a letter reached her telling her of the destruction of Kaifeng and the appalling carnage in the city, she wrote, 'My heart is silenced. I know not what to say. Words will not come in face of so terrible a tragedy.'

Whitfield's son, Henry and his wife, Mary, were still in the country and in grave danger. His father's sudden death in 1927 had made Henry take stock. At eighteen he decided to bypass university and go straight to the Bible Training Institute in Glasgow so that he could prepare to leave for China as quickly as possible.

No one was more surprised than his housemaster at St Lawrence College in Ramsgate. Henry was full of tomfoolery, never could resist a dare and had narrowly escaped expulsion after a night-time exploit left him so wet that the noise of his squelching socks gave him away as he tiptoed back into school. In China his daredevilry would enable him to survive.

He sailed from Tilbury with seventy other new recruits, including his cousin, Desmond Guinness, in 1931, starting his missionary career in the same rural prefecture as his parents – Honan. Walking or cycling between villages, he would stop on street corners, wearing local costume as his father had always done, and play his silver cornet, the family heirloom he taught himself to play in Glasgow. Then he would preach to the intrigued, assembled crowd.

His ability to speak cultured Mandarin was a huge advantage. It opened doors into schools, universities and hospitals. Having loved summer camps when he was a boy and never really growing up himself, he took groups of youngsters away for a few days, enthralled them with his ability to make pin-hole cameras and aeroplane propellers, and used the opportunity to lead discussions on, 'Why should we believe in the Bible?'

The country was yet again in political turmoil. By the time the Japanese invaded Shanghai in 1933, civil war between Chiang Kai-shek's Nationalists and the Communists had weakened the Chinese army's ability to defend itself against foreign onslaught. Taking advantage of a new outbreak of anti-foreign feeling, Communist soldiers began to vent their anger on Christian missionaries. Some were taken captive. Two, John and Betty Stam, were executed in 1934.[11] Others were forced to trudge thousands of miles on Mao's infamous Long March.

One night, after holding a meeting at an inn, Henry overheard a plot to put him down a well. Despite having TB as a child he was now extremely fit, thanks to the typical British boarding-school regime of cold showers and cross-country runs, now an ingrained and regular habit. With an instinctive nose for danger, he had taken stock of the place before preaching and noticed a small niche in the courtyard wall, one solitary, possible foothold. Walking nonchalantly across the courtyard in the direction of the toilet, he suddenly scaled the ten-foot wall, jumped down the other side and outran his captors and their dogs to the next town, four miles away.

In Kaifeng, his childhood home, there was such opportunity for evangelism that he was desperate for help and prayed God would send him a co-worker. That night a burglar broke into his house. Henry greeted him in pyjamas, invited him to sit down, and read him John's Gospel. Within a short time the thief decided to become a Christian. Henry prayed with him and the next morning left him in charge of the house with instructions to prepare the lunch. When he came home from his visits, the house was immaculate, the meal waiting on the table. Henry invited the erstwhile thief to become his co-worker and never regretted it.

He married Mary Taylor, the daughter of CIM missionaries, in 1938. Mary, a qualified doctor, worked at the hospital her father-in-law had founded in Kaifeng. A gentle, practical, unpretentious woman, she was as brave and resourceful as her husband, with indomitable inner strength and a twinkle in her eye, invaluable character traits given the trials that lay ahead.

After the bombing of Pearl Harbour and the threat of a Japanese invasion they lived in Xiangcheng where life was unbearably hard. Drought, famine and flood were followed by a plague of locusts of almost biblical proportions. Raging inflation meant that money bought nothing but a little rice. Starving local people discarded their youngest children and the Guinnesses took them in, sharing out their own meagre supplies with an ever-expanding family.

Between 1940 and 1943 they had three boys of their own, Gerald, Oswald and Reginald – the common ending to their names an established Chinese family custom. But conditions in Xiangcheng took their toll and Gerald died of dysentery when he was only two. Reginald, born shortly after the death of his brother, died at seven months and was buried alongside him. There was no time to grieve. The Japanese were closing in and they had to flee the day after Reginald died, carrying Os, their remaining toddler, in a basket on a pole the three thousand miles to Bombay and the boat home.

For three years they represented the Mission in Dublin until a telegram arrived from Chinese friends in Honan, begging them to go back. Communist thought was gaining ground, but many students and intellectuals wanted to hear about the Christian faith. The Chinese Student Christian Movement, founded in 1944, was the largest in the world. In 1947 huge numbers had gathered in Nanjing for the Chinese

Inter-Varsity Fellowship conference, addressed by Madame Chiang Kai-shek herself.

Leaving Os with Gordon Guinness and his family, Henry and Mary went out to Nanjing where they started a Bible study group which grew as fast as the political vice tightened. Indoctrination meetings were followed by mass shootings outside the city gate – 300 people at a time, every day. The presence of foreigners became increasingly untenable. Chou En-lai said ominously, 'While China is putting its house in order, it is undesirable for guests to be present.' They were becoming a threat to the safety of their Chinese friends.

When Mao came to power all foreigners were finally expelled from the People's Republic. Henry and Mary, who had moved south, held out as long as they could and were among the last to leave in 1952.[12] They spent most of the three years under house arrest on meagre rations – tea on Sundays, water the rest of the week.

During that time news reached them of the death of Henry's aunt, Geraldine Taylor. Her last years were not easy with increasing ill health and the war, but Geraldine soldiered on despite rheumatism and the bombs, an inveterate writer and crusader to the last, cared for by her old friend, Matilda. Her nephew Gordon was a vicar in nearby Tunbridge Wells. He and his family visited regularly. As a boy, Garry, one of Gordon's sons, remembers a striking-looking old lady with flowing white hair and a seraphic face. He thought she was an angel.

Henry Seymour and May Guinness had also retired to Tunbridge Wells. Discovering she had other, less familiar Guinness relatives in the area, Geraldine decided to get in touch, and was invited to spend the afternoon with them. Henry Seymour was delighted to meet one of the intrepid Grattan cousins whom he had researched so carefully for the family tree, and whose adventure with Chinese brigands he had followed in the newspapers. So was May Harry, at first.

But as they took a turn around the garden together, Geraldine turned to her and asked, 'Do you walk with the Lord, my dear?' May, who was not exactly a regular churchgoer, but thought herself a committed Anglican nonetheless, was extremely put out.

In 1944 Howard and Geraldine shared their Golden Wedding quietly together, moving into a retirement home with adjoining rooms after Geraldine had a stroke seven months later. Every day they sat and chatted to each other for endless hours, recalling their many adventures together. Howard's death in 1947 was a terrible blow. After all, he had loved her for over seventy years. Few women could make such a claim. His, she would tell her visitors, was a devoted, unchanging kind of love, unselfish and ever increasing. But in the last years the man who had always been her support, her mainstay, her lifebuoy, had been racked by agonising depression.

> I couldn't wish him back . . . and yet it seemed as though one's life had ended there. And then, it was all trans-figured. Now, he seems nearer, really, you know, than before. It's more like the old relationship. All the weak-ness and weariness is gone, and there is the same bright, cheery, loving spirit one had come to depend on so much. There is the consciousness that he is there, waiting, nearer, dearer than in far years.

She went to meet him, and more important, the God she had served so faithfully for almost ninety years, on 6 June 1949.

4.

There are no longer Guinness monarchs ruling over its many empires. Modern society rarely produces charismatic giants like the first Lord Iveagh, Robert Rundell Guinness or Henry Grattan Guinness. There are no outstanding Guinness politicians today and no Guinness bishops. Pure genius is much more thin on the ground. Nevertheless, every once in a while, another larger-than-life member of the clan emerges from obscurity to make his or her mark. Such was Jack Clephane Guinness, a descendant of the first Arthur Guinness's eldest son, the Rev. Hosea, the first to opt for the spiritual bonuses beyond brewing.

Through Hosea's eldest son, Arthur, Vicar of Seaton Carew in Durham, this senior branch of the family produced the artist May Guinness, a formidable lady who studied in Paris with Andre Lhotte, joined the French Army Medical Service as a nurse in the First World War, was awarded the Croix de Guerre for bravery, and went on painting to the age of ninety-two. Some of her paintings hang in the National Gallery of Ireland.

Hosea's youngest son, Francis Hart Vicesimus, emigrated to New Zealand in 1852 where his eldest son, Sir Arthur Robert Guinness KCB, became Speaker of the New Zealand House of Representatives. Jack, his great-nephew, arrived in Britain shortly after the Second World War, knowing little of his roots. Discovering his illustrious connections was a revelation. No other member of the family epitomised as he did the delicate balance between the love of glamour and the call of charity. He revelled in the family name, but enjoyed few of its benefits, hobnobbed with the well-to-do, but lived a life of near austerity. Father Jack was a monk.

In 1946 he left New Zealand to join twenty other novices at the Anglican Community of the Resurrection in Mirfield, West Yorkshire. The new boys were a spirited band and Jack quickly became the ringleader with his endless shaggy-dog stories and gift for mimicry. Within days he had mastered the mannerisms of the Novice Guardian, raising his spectacles with a quick sniff. Jack was always at the centre of the sudden burst of laughter which broke the heavy silence in the dining-room, and drew disapproving looks from the Superior. 'Missionary pudding again,' he would sigh when the inevitable prunes appeared on the table. Conspiratorially, he would lean across to any visitor and whisper that they went into all the dark places nothing had ever reached, and did you good. Such was his fund of anecdotes that the Brothers were convinced he not only read the *Irish Digest*, which arrived for him every month, but swallowed it whole.

He soon became intrigued with the idea of belonging to the Guinness dynasty, and sent off to Brian Guinness in Frensham for a family tree. Brian, Howard Rundell's youngest son, had become involved in running boys' clubs in a run-down area, and had been issued with an ultimatum by his father – either he must give up the clubs or the family bank. Brian gave up his work at Guinness Mahon, but took on the unenviable task of compiling the ever-expanding pedigree from his uncle, Henry Seymour Guinness.

As he studied the family tree, Jack could barely control his excitement. Not only was he related to the brewing Guinnesses, but he was a member of the senior line. His branch might have been the Earls of Iveagh had not his great-grandfather, Hosea exchanged his inheritance for the Church. He became so impassioned by his history that the Brothers were convinced they could detect a hint of an Irish lilt in his accent.

Brian Guinness, who became a personal friend, put him in touch with other members of the family. Jack wrote to them and managed to secure several holiday invitations. The protected, sophisticated world of the aristocracy with their stately homes, holiday villas and lavish lifestyles slowly opened up before him. But the high life had no lasting appeal. Perhaps that was why his presence was so welcome, so unthreatening. He was in no doubt of his calling and in 1951 took his final vows of poverty, chastity and obedience. What mattered to Jack was that he had arrived in England not knowing a soul and had found a family – and what a family!

At Mirfield his seniors became aware that behind the fun-loving façade was a man with a deep and gentle humility, shunning the limelight and never pushing himself forward, despite his many, obvious talents. He was patient and thoughtful, vital qualities in an all-male community. Laughter was a safety valve.

In many ways he was the obvious choice for one of the community's most difficult assignments – South Africa. In 1954 he set off for Johannesburg, travelling via Australia and New Zealand, where the press showed a great deal of interest in him. 'A representative of the world-famous Guinness Brewery family was in the city yesterday,' claimed one Dunedin newspaper, 'but according to his own statement, deals in a different kind of spirit.'

In Johannesburg he joined Trevor Huddleston, whose book *Naught for Your Comfort* was having a profound effect in awakening the British conscience to the evils of apartheid. Reading about apartheid was one thing, experiencing it in the raw was another. The exploitation of the impoverished black people of Sophiatown was almost more than he could bear. 'Apartheid does something to you,' he said. It dehumanised its supporters. 'You could strike matches on their faces.'

South Africa broke his heart and his spirit. It eventually broke his health as well, and he returned to the mother house in Mirfield to be 'custos' in charge of the grounds. Trundling around with his wheelbarrow after the gardener, talking incessantly, provided the recuperation he needed.

He also became warden of a community of sisters in Sandymount, Dublin, which meant regular trips to the city to hear their confessions. This gave him the opportunity to visit his cousin, Major Owen Guinness of Tibradden, nephew of May Guinness the artist, who had a gallery in the barn there before her death in 1955. He also made contact with the

Brewery at St James' Gate, arranging for Guinness to deliver a much-needed water-butt to the Sandymount Sisters. And whenever he took a mission in a local church he would plaster the walls with 'Guinness is Good for You' posters, supplied en masse by the Brewery.

On one occasion he and his companion, a tall, impressive-looking black South African brother called Zachary, were invited to St James' Gate for dinner with the directors. The barman pulled a pint for Jack and was about to do the same for Brother Zachary, when the monk whispered softly, 'Orange juice for me.' The barman was rendered speechless, but eventually found enough voice to mutter, 'This Brewery has been making beer for 200 years, sir, and never in its entire history has anyone had the gall to ask for orange juice.'

But Brother Zachary went on drinking orange juice as he accompanied his friend on holidays in the stately homes of his relatives, in Dublin and London, and at their luxurious villas in the south of France. Although Jack had never met her, he referred to Lady Normanby, the sister of the second Lord Moyne, as 'my cousin Grania'. She was at best a very distant cousin. Arriving back on one occasion he informed the Brothers that he was very upset by Ernest's youngest daughter Oonagh's choice of a third husband. Except with Major Owen, a staunch member of the Church of Ireland, religion was never discussed. 'It simply wasn't that kind of environment,' Brother Zachary said. But the family always welcomed them with open arms, and Zachary was under the impression that all Jack had to do was point to his name on the family tree for doors to open before him.

But for Jack, the happy, carefree summer holidays were almost over. The Order had a seminary for black students in Alice and Jack was asked to go and take charge as the Prior. It was the hardest test of his obedience. He would have given anything never to face the sorrow and tension of South Africa again. The Community had already been marked out for observation by the Special Branch because of their involvement in finding defence lawyers for young black people thrown into gaol without charge. It was abundantly clear the phone was being tapped.

Nor did Jack relish the idea of leadership. He knew it meant difficult decisions, conflict and hurt. He felt he was a pastor at heart, not a manager, better at one-to-one relationships than teaching or administration.

His seven years there were every bit as hard and bitter as he feared. The black people were more oppressed than ever. All forty black schools in South Africa set up by the Mirfield Community had been closed down under the new legislation. The atmosphere in the seminary was often charged and difficult. It appalled him that the world seemed to care so little, or perhaps people simply did not understand what apartheid entailed – the loss of dignity, the brutality of the secret police, arbitrary imprisonments and deportations. In the *Church and People* he wrote, 'I cannot see a peaceful solution. Eventually some kind of revolt is bound to take place – you can't treat human beings as cattle. The black man knows time is on his side.'

Despite his extreme reluctance he was promoted to Provincial, in charge of the Order's work throughout the whole area, but once again his health broke down beneath the strain and he was returned to England – not to the quiet, rural house in Mirfield, as he hoped, but to the East End of London, to be Master of the Royal Foundation of St Katharine in Stepney. This was Father Jack's own moment for hobnobbing with royalty. As Patron of the Royal Foundation, the Queen Mother invited him to dinner at St James's Palace. He took a carefully nurtured rose with him and presented it to her, 'from your garden in the East End, ma'am'.

His health continued to deteriorate, but when the cancer he had so long dreaded was finally diagnosed, fear seemed to vanish, but not his sense of humour. When he was told he would lose a nipple he joked, 'I won't be needing that anyway.'

He died in 1975 at the age of sixty, and the Community mourned a man of enormous personal charm who had never worn his piety on his sleeve. A small, but exceptionally bright flame was extinguished that day, yet not completely, for many anecdotes about Father Jack Guinness have passed into Mirfield history. In his cell were his few treasured possessions, two photograph albums, two newspaper cuttings, some books and a copy of the Guinness family tree. No one ever claimed them, so the Brothers kept them safe in the belief that one day one of the family would come for them.

Ten years later my husband Peter, Paul Grattan Guinness's youngest son, became a curate at Normanton Parish Church, a mere ten miles down the road from Mirfield. It was a regular place of retreat for us. As the Brothers placed the family tree in my hands I knew that Father Jack would have wanted me to have it, and that he would have been delighted to have his place in this book.

He is buried in the gardens he loved so much. There is an unmistakable tranquillity about his grave, sheltered by choice trees, an atmosphere reminiscent of Henry Grattan's resting place beneath a large, shady copper beech, overlooking the city of Bath. Could it be that the poorest of all the Guinnesses are in fact the richest?

The Continuing Story . . .

In *The Silver Salver*, published in 1981, Frederick Mullally entitled his last chapter 'A Dynasty Secured'. He could not have been further from the truth. In so far as its relationship with the Brewery was concerned, the dynasty died in 1967, when Alan Lennox-Boyd, the last managing director with direct family ties, resigned in the belief that he had prostate cancer. Twenty years later, Ernest Saunders finished the job.

The end of the era was not so much due to the way Saunders set about disempowering the remaining family members of the Board, the takeover of Distillers reducing their share proportion from 22 per cent to 4.5 per cent, nor even the damage to the company's reputation which resulted from his own arrest and trial. The seeds of its destruction were sown when a family of middle-class merchants-made-good began to acquire aristocratic airs and graces and an unhealthy disdain for the trade which had given them the leg up. Had it not been for Saunders they may even have presided over the death of the goose which had laid them the golden egg. The company was in a very vulnerable position when Saunders began his reign, having diversified into areas where it had little expertise. In the cut-throat business world of the seventies and eighties it was a case of take over or be taken over. Saunders ensured it was the former.

Bryan Guinness, then Lord Moyne, assured me in 1989 that

apart from Lady Ardilaun, there was little snobbery among the Guinnesses, but in the *Sunday Times* in the same year, speaking of Saunders's arrest, one of the family is quoted as saying, 'the whole thing gives the aristocracy a bad name'. Bryan Guinness seemed naïvely unaware of how ingrained the veneer of class had become, how its values would separate his generation from the next, moving them further away from the Brewery. His café-set cousins Oonagh, Maureen and Aileen, Ernest's three fun-loving daughters, though raised in Ireland, had each been launched into London society at a coming-out ball, earned a reputation for chic, sophistication and beauty, and married their way through eight men, three with titles. Each had inherited £1 million and was a celebrated hostess, entertaining on a lavish scale in her Irish stately home.[1]

Shortly after the war Aunt Mildred 'Gunn' engineered a regular invitation for her niece Mary, Edward's only sister, to Aileen's home at Luttrellstown Castle, for the Irish Horse Show. She was very keen that the Lancashire teenager should have the advantages of her connections, should experience the glitter and glamour she herself had known as a young woman at Elveden. Her niece, with the wonderful copper hair of many of Cecil's descendants, needed to be polished, to be launched into society, to meet the right people. It was, Mary remembers, a sophisticated, exciting world, with balls, dinner parties and handsome attendants to dance with every night. The recently widowed Aileen was a generous, thoughtful hostess, if a little distant, and enjoyed providing little treats for her young cousin, including several of the many essential evening dresses Mary would need every night and could not possibly afford. But in the end, Mary set her cap at a local doctor she had met at a badminton club, settled in Wigan and lived happily ever after. Unlike her wealthier cousins.

Rupert's three daughters, less mercurial, less Irish, shunned the limelight by comparison, yet were still among the wealthiest women in Britain. They married well, Honor to Henry 'Chips' Channon MP, the political diarist, Patricia, known as Patsy, to the Right Honourable Alan Lennox-Boyd MP, and Brigid to HRH Prince Friedrich of Prussia, grandson of Kaiser Wilhelm II. Neither Ernest nor Rupert expected their daughters to take any active interest in business.

Despite Gwenny's achievements, women of her daughters' class and generation were expected to be ornamental rather than useful. Trade had no part to play in their exclusive education, a major drawback when they were called upon to take their place on the Guinness Board. Acquiring wealth and a title or two inevitably led to a certain exclusivity which became so deeply embedded that it created distinctions between titled and non-titled members of the family and with the Brewery management. Not surprisingly, in that climate, Ernest Saunders, as a new Chief Executive, felt he had received something akin to the 'Aunt Gunn treatment' when he found himself on a table with 'family retainers' like the company secretary and an estate manager at a Guinness family wedding. The chasm between the dynasty and the dirty lucre which made it was becoming so deep that some were bound to fall in.

In 1967, when Rupert died, his grandson Sir Arthur Francis Benjamin became the third Earl of Iveagh. Benjamin was a shy, retiring, gentlemanly man, dogged by Crones Disease, deeply suspicious of publicity, with an abhorrence for scandal, a cruel irony in the light of the way his family managed to capture the headlines during his possession of the patriarchal mantle.

In April 1966 his uncle by marriage, the Prussian Prince Friedrich, mysteriously disappeared from his German home, Schloss Rheinhartshausen near Wiesbaden, just as divorce proceedings had been initiated by his wife Brigid on the grounds of their incompatibility. Of all the Guinness marriages theirs had appeared the most solid. On 1 May the Prince's body was found in the Rhine near Bingen.

In the same year playboy Tara Browne, Oonagh's twenty-one-year-old son by her marriage to Lord Oranmore and Browne, died when he crashed his sports car in Chelsea during a bitter custody battle for the children of his two-year marriage.[2] For Oonagh who adored her children, the blow was compounded in that she had already lost a daughter, fourteen-year-old Tessa Kindersley in 1946, due to an asthma attack following by a diphtheria vaccination. Both children were buried at Luggala, her magical home in the Wicklow Mountains.

A second tragic family suicide twelve years later convinced the public there was a darker, more desperate face hiding behind the 'beautiful rich people' mask of the Guinnesses. One May afternoon the Earl's youngest sister, Lady Henrietta, crossed the little Italian town of Spoleto where she lived with her husband and new baby daughter, for an appointment at the dentist's. She never arrived back at the tiny, sparsely furnished council house the couple had shared with his parents for the past two years. On her way home she threw herself from the narrow, windswept Ponte della Torri aqueduct into the deep ravine below. She was thirty-five, attractive, warm-hearted, wealthy and loved, a woman with everything to live for.

'If I had been poor,' she once said, 'I would have been happy.' But in the end living like the poor had not been penance enough to lift the intolerable burden riches placed on her spirit. She felt her wealth prevented people from accepting her as she was, from being natural in her presence. When she finally tried to cheat her destiny by marrying the unemployed son of an Italian mechanic and chambermaid it was too late. Her inner life was seriously impaired, starved for lack of affection.

She was only two when her father was killed in action and his death left a huge hole in her life. Her mother Elizabeth was hard on her. She had nothing in common with her brother and found him difficult to get on with.

For a while she ran an exclusive London restaurant called the Louis D'Or with enormous verve and success. But a number of emotional scars transformed a creative, bubbly, bright-eyed young woman into a jaded, restless adult. She never recovered physically or emotionally from injuries incurred when her lover Michael Beeby crashed his red Aston Martin in the South of France. The only major source of affection and stability in her life, Aunt Mildred Gunn, died in 1975, leaving her bereft. In her vulnerable emotional state, alone and without adequate medical support, it was almost inevitable that the birth of her baby daughter would result in severe post-natal depression. The happiness she had sought appeared to have escaped her grasp and she made one final act of defiance and despair.[3]

There have been several Guinness women like Henrietta, intelligent, generous, yet apparently unfulfilled. Contentment was the one gift the fairy-tale magic wand of wealth could not bestow, no matter how hard they pursued it, in a succession of marriages, in filling the social calendar or by the rebellion of unconventionalism.

Seven weeks after Henrietta's death, her eighteen-year-old cousin, Natalya Citkowitz, Maureen's granddaughter, was injecting herself with heroin when she slumped, headfirst, off the toilet seat and asphyxiated herself in a bathful of water. It was devastating for her mother, Maureen's elder daughter, the successful novelist Caroline Blackwood, already suffering from depression and alcohol problems. She never recovered from the blow.

In 1986 Olivia Channon, the bright, attractive daughter of cabinet minister Paul Channon, son of Honor Guinness and Henry Channon, was found dead in her bedroom at Oxford University the morning after an end-of-term party. A mixture of drink and drugs had cost her life.

In 1988 Maureen's eldest son, Sheridan, died of AIDS. In 1995 her attempt to pass assets of £15 million directly to her grandchildren was contested in protracted legal wrangling by Caroline, Caroline's sister, Perdita, and Sheridan's widow, Lindy. Maureen was reconciled to her eldest daughter shortly before Caroline's untimely death in 1996. In 1998 the late Benjamin Iveagh's niece, 31-year-old Rose Nugent, died after being thrown from a horse-drawn gipsy caravan.

The press have long talked of a family curse. But that seems a smug solution for those who cannot cope with the idea of humans enjoying great wealth without incurring the jealousy of the fates. Money brings its own curse, the deserts of those who lose the battle between God and mammon. But it would be untrue to suggest the poor Guinnesses always found happiness, while the rich ones did not. For all their great wealth, Rupert Guinness and Olive Ardilaun lived lives which were full and satisfying, while Lucy Guinness was temperamentally unable to enjoy the moment. The members of the missionary and clerical line of the family were not necessarily more fulfilled than their brewing or banking cousins. Many members of the brewing and banking line were devout members of the Church, while not a few of the Grattans rejected the faith of their fathers. While Rupert and Gwenny read a portion of the Bible together every night before bed, John Guinness, the elder of Henry Grattan Guinness's two sons by his marriage to Grace, abandoned his evangelical faith whilst studying theology at Oxford. With his wife, Karis, daughter of Ian and Geraldine Guinness McKenzie, he set up a progressive, co-educational private boarding school in Kent called Long Dene, where fagging was forbidden, organic food served, discipline minimal, and pupils encouraged to develop their potential by swimming in the nude. His eldest daughter was a Bluebell dancer in Las Vegas. All three girls were attracted to Eastern mysticism.

Any family sprouting into the proportions of the

Guinnesses, be they Smiths or Jones, whatever their achievements, will also have their share of the sad and the bad, eccentrics, drop-outs, suicides and other tragedies. The 'curse' of wealth, if curse there be, is that it can inhibit the discovery of a *raison d'être.* Guinnesses, like Sam the banking pioneer, are invincible when they have a goal or find a cause. Without ambition they perish. That was Henrietta's tragedy.

The demise of the brewing side of the dynasty began during the chairmanship of the second Earl of Iveagh, which is ironic since Rupert and Gwendolin were so committed to family continuity. At a Guinness Trust meeting shortly before she died in 1966, Gwenny spoke so powerfully of family responsibility that Edward Guinness, the distant cousin rising rapidly through the executive ranks, never forgot her words and felt he had been given a sacred trust. When you get to the twilight of your life, she said, you want more than anything to ensure that what you have built in your lifetime is carried on. But as parents who had lost an only son, they should have had the foresight to widen the catchment and encourage other young Guinnesses into the family business. They were unaware that they were placing far too many eggs in one very weak basket. Benjamin, the grandson she and Rupert had groomed for chairmanship, was not a visionary. He introduced little in the way of fresh ideas. Nor did immediate family Board members have the insight, imagination or flair to supplement the lack. Yet in the unknown wider family were a motley of brilliant engineers and mathematicians, shrewd, determined businessmen and skilful entrepreneurs. The genetic strain was alive and well, but since the Brewery door stayed firmly closed in their faces they took their gifts elsewhere.

Today there is Sir John Guinness chairing British Nuclear Fuel (BNFL), Tim Guinness who heads up Guinness Flight Global Assessment Management, Robert Guinness of Straffen who runs an antique steam engine business in Dublin, John

Elliot Guinness who manages his own electricity generating company, Cogen, in the USA, all carrying on the great family tradition for leadership and innovation, like Kenelm Lee Guinness, the first Lord Iveagh's nephew and world record holder for land speed in 1924, who invented the new improved KLG spark plug.

Others, particularly the women, made their mark in education, like Elizabeth Maude Guinness of the banking line, who became Vice-Principal of Cheltenham Ladies' College, or Dawn Guinness of the Grattan line, who became the youngest ever principal of a girls' public school when she became head of Felixtowe College at the age of twenty-nine.

The dynasty has not died – it simply is not brewing. Rupert and Gwenny lacked the impetus to harness that talent. It was as if some genetic memory inherited from the second Arthur convinced them that all distant relatives with ambition were bound to be leeches.

Those who did inherit the titles and the wealth that went with them, acquired their veneer of aristocracy too late, when class structures were already beginning to break down, and there was nothing for the idle rich to do except indulge their whims, and few respected them for it. Olive Ardilaun took her philanthropy seriously. Gwendolin Iveagh was a consummate orator and politician. Rupert had his farming. Ernest was a brilliant engineer. Walter Moyne was a respected diplomat.

But life for the next generations became more, not less restricted. Some found an outlet for their energy in voluntary and charity work. Ernest's daughter Maureen, Marchioness of Dufferin and Ava (all three sisters liked to use the titles they had acquired by marriage, whether still married to it or not!) admitted, 'It's maddening to be written up as a millionairess, get dozens of begging letters, and then, when you send the charity £25, they expect £500, when one is in quite a jam oneself.'[4] And then she added wistfully, 'It was wonderful when one was young. Everything was so much more glamorous in every way.'

Desmond, Bryan Guinness's younger son by his first marriage to Diana Mitford (Moseley), who lived at Leixlip Castle, retreat in the sixties for Marianne Faithful and the hippy brigade, founded the Georgian Society to preserve Dublin's historic heritage. Simon, Viscount Boyd, was Chairman of the Save the Children Fund until 1993, and since then has been Vice-Chairman of the Guinness Trust, still one of the largest housing trusts in Britain. It is chaired by another family member, Antonia, Marchioness of Douro. Guinness-funded projects abound, including research into the causes and prevention of alcoholism.

Though respected by Guinness staff, primarily for history and longevity's sake, Rupert was already a distant chairman, unlike his father, who would suddenly appear at a brewer's side day or night without warning to see how things progressed. He never wrote his own speeches and at the first Annual General Meeting after Sir Hugh Beaver had replaced Ben Newbold as managing director, got to his feet as usual, adjusted his papers, looked up at his audience, down again at his script, and said wryly, 'It appears that my style has changed.' When Rupert died in 1967, family members were already being treated with amused contempt by Guinness staff. Wealth and titles were no longer any guarantee of respect. It had to be earned.

It was a lesson Edward Guinness learned early in his apprenticeship. In 1949, lying in bed one night in his bachelor accommodation at Guinness staff house, he overheard a conversation he never forgot. Just outside his bedroom door Sir Hugh Beaver, a widower, who had just returned from a session with the family, was talking to Norman Smillie, the assistant managing director, who had decided to stay at Park Royal for the night.

'How did it go?' Smillie asked.

'Awful!' the managing director replied. Beaver was utterly loyal to the family, but was immensely frustrated that he could not seem to make himself understood. A chasm between executive members and the family had evidently started to open up, compounded by the sudden death of Ernest Guinness, the last true brewing descendant of the first Arthur Guinness.[5]

For the four years they overlapped at the Brewery Edward went to see his godfather at Holmbury House. They walked and talked about the company for hours. Ernest shared his hopes, his aspirations, his dreams. He treated Edward like a son. 'It was heady stuff. I felt as if he had given me a torch to carry.'

The family remained in overall control. A tradition had arisen that on the eve of a Board meeting the managing director would be summoned to a 'tea party' to give account of his stewardship and hear their views. Sir Hugh Beaver, with the old school respect for the family, managed to hold the two sides together – but Edward knew from the beginning of his career that it would not take much to effect a permanent separation. Times were changing. The executive staff was less inclined to indulge the family. The family was unaware of it. They did not understand that their aristocratic aura might mean they needed more quality of character, more inner strength, more hands-on information about the business to earn the right to be heard.

But Edward worked his way through the company. He was hungry. Unlike the rest of the family, he had a living to earn. He was also a man for whom Christian ethics in the workplace mattered. A sudden death at Park Royal when he was only twenty-six led to a summons from his honeymoon to become Labour Manager. In 1956 he became Head of Personnel, a position he held through the long difficult years of trade union disgruntlement. That strike action was averted was largely due to his skills, his determination that the company tradition of fair play and generosity to those who made the family their fortune should be maintained.

None of the non-executive Guinness Board members with their public school backgrounds appeared to have much understanding of the workforce and its demands, and had little time for the trade union. Trade still carried its own stigma. Edward loved being part of the actual production team, but then he was never strictly 'inner' family. During Saunders's trial, when the defence barrister tried to lump all the family Board members together, Edward was quick to point out the deeper divisions. 'We don't all spring from the same root, and so we're not quite as family as all that.'

In 1960 the incisive, faithful Sir Hugh Beaver had a coronary. Patsy's husband Alan Lennox-Boyd left his job in the Cabinet as Colonial Secretary to take over as managing director, breaking the unspoken rule that 'inner' family members did not accept executive positions. But the youthful Benjamin, feeling his way shyly and reluctantly into the leadership of the company, needed strong support. Viscount Boyd was certainly that. A charismatic personality with a gift for making relationships, he was tipped as a rival with Alec Douglas Home for the Tory party leadership, might even have become Prime Minister had he not sacrificed it for Guinness. When she died in 1966 Gwenny must have thought the family position at the head of the company was secure.

For a while it was. Lennox-Boyd's time in office coincided with the lager phenomenon, a remarkably successful episode in the story of brewing. Created in 1961, Harp Lager sales rose to one million barrels in 1970, two million in 1976. But Alan Lennox-Boyd thought he had cancer, erroneously as it happened, and resigned in 1967, the year of Rupert's death. (He lived to be knocked down and killed by a car in 1983.)

His resignation heralded the end of any real family influence in the company. Under the leadership of successive managing directors there were financial struggles. And without

Viscount Boyd's support, Benjamin could not cope with the chairmanship. Since it is the chairman who holds the ultimate responsibility for company decisions, who sanctions managerial policy and stimulates new initiatives, experience and confidence are vital. Benjamin Iveagh had neither. The thought of an AGM filled him with dread. When acquiring Irish citizenship meant he was not allowed to set foot in England for five years, so that he could no longer chair AGMs held at Park Royal because Guinness was a British-registered company, he must have heaved a sigh of relief. If ever a man had greatness thrust upon him it was Benjamin Iveagh. He could not choose to be a poet or an actor, a doctor, postman – or a missionary for that matter. His destiny was prescribed and that, combined with a crippling shyness and constant illness, led to his early death.

For a time a strong family presence remained on the Board. Benjamin's uncles, Viscount Boyd and Bryan Guinness, Lord Moyne were vice-chairmen. His aunts, Patsy and Maureen, along with Bryan's son, Jonathan, were directors. Peter Guinness of the banking side of the family had been appointed to the Board in 1964. And Edward took his place in 1971 as the managing director and chairman of Harp Lager.

In 1977 tragedy struck once more. The Honourable Diarmid Guinness, a son of Lord Moyne by his second marriage, who had started to work in the company's personnel department, showed real promise, and would have become a useful member of the Board, developed severe abdominal pains during the Silver Jubilee celebrations. He died of stomach cancer two months later leaving four small children. He was thirty-nine.

By the end of the seventies Alan Lennox-Boyd, Bryan Guinness and Maureen had all retired. Patsy followed soon after, urging the family to remember the first Lord Iveagh's injunction not to sell their shares, an irrelevancy in the end. They were all replaced by younger family members who received a cursory introduction or crash course in brewing, had little time for business and were more distant from the centre of command than ever.

In 1979 there was not enough money to renovate the Dublin Brewery which was in serious need of modernisation. In 1980 pre-tax profits dropped from £52 million to £48 million, and then to £41 million the following year. Edward was now Head of Corporate Affairs, a position he did not enjoy. Retirement beckoned and would have been welcomed, had it not been for the appointment of Ernest Saunders.

'How are you getting on with your man Schleyer?' Edward's wife was asked at a dinner party one night in Corfu in the summer of 1984.

Elizabeth did not understand the question.

'I think he calls himself Saunders now,' the woman replied. 'His father was my medical consultant.'

Edward was utterly astonished. Saunders's early background had never been an issue at Guinness. It was never discussed. Yet it explained a great deal. It gave Edward a greater understanding of his new colleague.

The son of an Austrian Jewish gynaecologist who fled with his family from the Nazis, Saunders, though he was only two at the time, like a member of any family which had faced extinction, often appeared haunted by his past. He attended public school, became a member of the Church of England, read law at Cambridge, a process of assimilation which never managed to convince the sub-conscious, or assuage the wounds of rejection. They were sublimated into driving ambition, yet he constantly seemed to feel that the society to which he aspired, conspired to keep him out, and none as deliberately as the Guinnesses. Family eyebrows were certainly raised when he let it be known that he expected special seats for himself and his wife, Carole, at Viscount Boyd's memorial service in Westminster Abbey in August 1983, attended by Margaret Thatcher the Prime Minister and five ex-prime ministers, and almost the entire Cabinet.

Insecurity, however understandable, can be self-fulfilling. He made no attempt to get to know his fellow brewers and it caused a great deal of resentment in the trade. At the end of a Brewers' Society meeting he once turned to Edward and said, 'Any one of these people here would stick a knife in my back, given the chance.'

'That's not true,' Edward said to him. 'They're very anxious that you play your part in the Society as leader of a very important company.' But Saunders remained unconvinced.

Yet he was a man who could inspire immense admiration, particularly for his shrewd, inspirational business skills. Draconian measures to save the company were introduced at once. Even the previous scale of charity money had to be cut as it was not compatible with the profit then being earned. Saunders brought in the young French accountant Olivier Roux as his financial director, and Tom Ward, an American lawyer who had helped him when he was Chief Executive of Nestlé in Switzerland, to handle problems resulting from increasing public pressure against the sale of baby milk in Africa.

Change at Guinness was urgently needed – but the price in human terms was high. In 1984, of the eight original executive directors when he took over, Edward was the only one left, largely because Saunders was perceptive enough to realise that someone had to maintain good relations in the brewing trade, and that, for many years, had been Edward's strong point. It was Edward who was sent in November 1986 to a two-day trade forum in Scotland after the Distillers' takeover, and returned with disturbing information about the evident anti-Saunders feeling across the border following the dismissal of Sir Thomas Risk, the invited head of Distillers, despite promises to the contrary. Edward felt he was like a messenger telling the king his horse was dead. But Saunders took it well and began to make arrangements for Edward to live in Scotland as part of a damage limitation exercise – then he changed his mind.

The failure to re-appoint Risk and the abandonment of headquarters in Scotland were fatal mistakes. Resentment now riddled the company. As a manager Saunders was totally unpredictable. The staff never knew whether the sun would shine on them – or vanish behind a cloud. One moment he could be complimentary, the next cutting to the quick. The night before the takeover of Martins the Newsagents in 1984, Edward was telephoned at 8.30 p.m. and asked to come to a hastily convened Board meeting. His presence was needed to make up a quorum. The decision in hand had been made long before the Board met.

News reached the Chief Executive the following morning that Edward was unhappy.

'Are you trying to rock the boat?' Saunders demanded down the phone.

The next day Edward said to him, 'I feel very sorry that you felt it necessary to speak to me like that. Haven't I always been loyal to you?'

'Of course, of course,' Saunders conceded in conciliatory mood. 'I was a bit hasty.'

Carrying a torch for the old family values was becoming increasingly difficult.

There is no doubt Saunders was dismissive of the non-executive family members. He would sometimes keep the full Board waiting for up to two hours, or disappear to make a lengthy phone call. It appeared that key decisions were made before they met. On 8 July 1986 they were informed that Guinness needed a great deal of ready cash in the USA for future takeover deals. Only later did it emerge that one hundred million dollars had already been invested with the ruthless, soon to be infamous Wall Street 'shark', Ivan Boesky, on 24 May. Unwittingly, on that fateful day in April when Saunders had breakfast with Boesky, he walked into a trap. Boesky was already under investigation as an insider dealer by the American fraud squad. He was wired for sound to catch his contacts. Later he talked. A tip-off to the DTI about his English visitor was inevitable and led to the ultimate un-covering of what the 1997 government report called 'an enterprise of deception'.

Bryan Guinness never approved of the takeover of Johnnie Walker, but Bryan was a writer, unworldly rather than pragmatic. Generations of Guinness brewers had refused to have anything to do with hard spirits. 'It has been painful to see this family tradition shattered.'[6] He in fact blamed Benjamin, whose early performance as chairman was passable.

> It was only later, when the fear of being taken over led to that very thing by arranging our own demise in merging with the bigger Distillers company that he seems to have gone astray from a family point of view. However, the shares have of course gone up; only the family must regret the end of their two hundred or more years of responsibility for the Brewery itself, especially at St James' Gate.

In many ways the family had no choice. The survival of the company was at stake. By 1986, with the acquisition of Bells and Distillers, assets had multiplied from £250 million to £1 billion, and reduced the family share interest to insignificance. Guinness was a major international company, safe and secure, but the responsibilities of the Chairman were now formidable. The family had always relied on a patriarchal figure, a charismatic leader. Benjamin was too gentle, too accom-modating. The inevitable moment arrived when he announced he had yielded to the pressure to stand down and accept the more honorary position of President. For the first time in history the chairmanship passed out of family hands. The Chief Executive, Ernest Saunders, accepted the dual role in the Earl of Iveagh's place. The arrangement only lasted a few months.

The early death of the rightful successor, the production of more daughters than sons, changing social conditions – all contributed to the demise of the brewing dynasty, though Saunders's pride might not like to admit that he was merely a symptom, not a cause. It was remarkable Guinness lasted as long as it did. Few family companies had survived as long. A takeover became vital, but takeovers are too expensive to lose. Frighteningly, Saunders could argue he had not done anything many others had not done before – for the sake of the firm. He was, he claimed, a government scapegoat. But the court decided that the legislation was clear and had been transgressed. The government report eleven years later found a cynical disregard for regulations, the misuse of company funds and contempt for truth and honesty. Arthur Guinness, its founder, would have been the first to say that justice must be done. There cannot be one law for the rich, one for the poor. But whether lessons have been learned in the City from this morality play, only time will tell.

The Brewery weathered the storm. After Saunders's arrest, Edward wrote to Sir Norman MacFarlane,

> I can assure you that my respect and concern for Guinness pledge me to do all in my power to overcome the present problems and when I cease to be an executive director to do anything which may be required of me to rebuild bridges, so that the standing of Guinness in all respects is restored to the position it has enjoyed over a long and proud history.

Today there is a new Board, and Guinness is as popular as it ever was. Non-alcoholic lager has been a major success, a venture of which the Guinness ancestors would have no doubt approved, but when Benjamin Iveagh died in 1992, all family connection with the company came to an end. The only remaining evidence of family proprietorship are the portraits lining the corridors of Park Royal, reminding current employees of the giants of the past who turned a small Brewery into the largest in the world and set new standards in the welfare of their staff.

For years the family resisted any suggestions of changing the firm's name – though immediately after the Saunders affair, some wished they had not. Thanks to yet another major merger – this time with Grand Metropolitan – the company name of Guinness has given way to Diageo, pronounceable in the days of the multi-nationals in any language. The word means 'through' and 'earth', and for its creation Guinness paid an advertising company £250,000. But the beer itself will retain its original name, so no one, for the foreseeable future, will ever nip out for a pint of Diageo.

While the brewing side of the family passed its prime, the bankers came into their own. In 1979 Guinness Mahon Holdings merged with Lewis and Peat Ltd to become Guinness Peat (now ProVen), with Sam's nephew, James Rundell Guinness, as Deputy Chairman in London. It was an immensely successful company, catapulting its Guinness directors to the very heights of high society, enabling their children to marry into the Rothschilds and Barings. And though they have produced no earls or peers, it was Sabrina, one of the 'Rundell' Guinnesses, who ultimately came the nearest to marrying the heir to the British throne.

The smaller, Irish side of the operation was managed in Dublin by Henry Eustace Guinness's younger son, John Henry, a gentleman of the old school with a gentle approach to banking, who with his wife Jennifer lived a life of simple pleasures compared to their London counterparts. It was hard to convince Jennifer's captors when she was kidnapped and held for ransom that they were not personally 'loaded'. Such was the remarkable metal of the woman that she managed to strike up a close relationship with her captors, becoming a godmother to one of their children shortly after her release.

Within years of this trauma, John Henry Guinness, who was attending a conference in Llandudno, went out for a walk in Snowdonia in his trainers, slipped and fell to his death. He was the last family member to hold an executive position with the Guinness Mahon company in Ireland after 152 years.

On the missionary side of the family there are still clergy carrying on the great tradition. Canon Gordon Guinness's three sons are all ordained. Henry and Mary Guinness's son, Os, the toddler who survived the escape from the Japanese in a basket hung from a pole, is a well-known Christian writer and apologist in the USA, though, sadly, his father found it hard to understand what his books were about. Henry himself, despite an unsuccessful hip replacement operation made walking difficult, returned to China in 1994 to try and find the graves of his two other sons. In one of those remarkable crossovers which happened so often between branches of the family, he was accompanied by Dr Frank Guinness, the son of Brian Guinness of Frensham, editor of three family trees and member of the banking Rundell side of the family. The men had been introduced a few months earlier, and despite the age gap, there was an immediate affinity. Frank, a consultant in genito-urinary diseases, had been a missionary with the Church Missionary Society in Uganda for many years, and always took an interest in the Grattan side of the family.

As hosts of the Henan Medical Association, Frank and Henry visited Kaifeng and were warmly welcomed at the Provincial hospital founded by his father. They travelled on to Xiangcheng where he still managed to converse in perfect Mandarin with two old men who remembered him. But there was no sign of his sons' graves.

Time marches on kicking over the traces of former lives. Of the great Guinness houses, a few, like Farmleigh and Knockmaroon, still belong to family members. Iveagh House in St Stephen's Green was donated by Rupert to the Irish Government and is the home of the Department of Irish

503

Affairs, the magnificent ballroom occasionally opened and used for state receptions. Glenmaroon, now the New Hotel, played host to Kennedy when he visited Dublin. Burton Hall, Stillorgan, is a drug rehabilitation centre. Baldersby Park in Thirsk became a retirement home, but is now a school. Elveden is a Centre Park holiday resort. The auction of the contents of the house which Benjamin put on the market raised £6 million. There were bales of chintz and Persian rugs from Harvey Nicholls – all unwrapped. Cliff College is still a Bible College, but Grattan Guinness's first house on Upper Baggot Street has been reborn as Joe Rocket's Diner.

Thousands of Guinnesses now circle the globe. Frank Guinness does not think there will be another official pedigree as the breakdown of marriage is beginning to undermine the concept of a patrilineal family tree. Nonetheless family members will keep popping up all over the place, in the arts, sciences, business and education, wherever the old genetic strain leads them. And genetic strain there seems to be.

Or perhaps it is merely coincidence that my father-in-law, a clergyman, was another Mr Gadget like his distant cousin Ernest, who could make or mend anything – and did, in his lovely retirement home in Ibiza overlooking San Antonio Bay. His two sons both graduated in mechanical engineering and inherited the inventive streak. As soon as his power-generating business in the USA enabled him to do so, John, the eldest, acquired a sixty-five-foot ocean-going yacht which he keeps in Chesapeake Bay.[7] My husband, his younger brother, Peter Grattan, became a clergyman in the time honoured tradition of the Grattan line, and has a life-enhancing ministry to defunct church boilers everywhere. In another life, his inventiveness would have been invaluable at the Brewery. Rupert, the second Lord Iveagh, was told that he had inherited his love of the sciences from Peter's grandfather, Henry Grattan Guinness. Sometimes, as I have written the story of Rupert and Ernest I have laughed out loud. They sound so familiar, so like my own in-laws.

No false humility ever made Father Jack disguise his pride in his family name. It is an invincible pride for all three major family lines, bankers, brewers and clergy, surviving, with a wobble or two, the series of scandals which culminated in the trial of Ernest Saunders. Small wonder they resent the inference constantly made in the media that the only real Guinnesses are directly descended from one of the peerages and are therefore mouth-wateringly rich. 'There is no such thing as a poor Guinness,' said biographer Hugo Vickers in an article by Anne de Courcy in the *Daily Telegraph* recently.[8] 'If any of them do happen to be poor it's because they've squandered their inheritance.' Peter never had an inheritance. It was given away by his grandfather when he became a teetotal itinerant preacher in the last century. You could say, and some family members would, that we are poor – but then it is all relative.

Notes

Prologue

1. In her evidence in the trial, Saunders's secretary, Margaret McGrath, confirmed that she had destroyed certain documents and erased certain entries from Saunders's diary on his orders.
2. This conversation was repeated in court during the trial of Ernest Saunders almost verbatim by Edward Guinness, according to the transcript of the evidence he gave.

Chapter 1

1. The pedigree of the Guinness family was subject to detailed scrutiny by Henry Seymour Guinness in *Richard Guinness of Celbridge*. Only a few copies exist in private circulation within the family.

   Jonathan Guinness, the third Lord Moyne, in his book *Requiem for a Family Business* (Macmillan, 1997), prefers the more common explanation that Richard Guinness was descended from a humble part of the Magennis clan, far removed from the earldom, which dropped the 'Mac' (meaning 'son of') at some point in history, possibly around 1690, to avoid penal laws against Catholics.
2. An anecdote recounted to the author by a Manchester journalist who heard it from a relative of Oliver St John Gogarty.
3. Wesley's Journal, 12 May 1748, quoted in *John Wesley's England*, compiled by Richard Bewes (Hodder and Stoughton, 1981).
4. *Freeman's Journal*, 12 March 1765.
5. Patrick Lynch and John Vaizey, *Guinness Brewery in the Irish Economy 1759–1876* (Cambridge University Press, 1960), pp. 74–7.
6. Letter quoted in Lynch and Vaizey, *Guinness Brewery*, p. 72.
7. ibid.

8. Lynch and Vaizey, *Guinness Brewery*, p. 73.
9. Parliamentary debates of Ireland, 2 February 1792, xii, p. 52.
10. Lynch and Vaizey, *Guinness Brewery*, p. 58.
11. Plunkett Papers, 4 June 1798.
12. Lynch and Vaizey, *Guinness Brewery*, p. 104.
13. ibid.

Chapter 2

1. *Saunders Newsletter*, 12 September 1812, reprinted from *Freeman's Journal.*
2. 1 August 1813: Lynch and Vaizey, *Guinness Brewery*, p. 110.
3. According to local records a John Guinness and Susan Hatton had a son, Benjamin, in Dumfries. It would appear that they too, with their two sons, fled to Scotland to avoid creditors. Benjamin did not survive babyhood.
4. Letter from Richard Guinness Esq to his brother Samuel, 8 November 1811: Lynch and Vaizey, *Guinness Brewery*, p. 109.
5. 14 August 1813: Lynch and Vaizey, *Guinness Brewery*, p. 112.
6. Harry Guinness, *In Memoriam, A Biography of Henry Grattan Guinness by His Son* (RBMU, 1911), p. 3.
7. This account of the duel is based on several newspaper cuttings of the time and later, including 'Grattan Guinness: An Echo of a Great Duel', from *TP's Weekly*, 8 July 1910. The details of their stories vary according to their Protestant or Catholic sympathies. I tend to feel that one of the most accurate accounts appeared in *The Irish Times*, Monday, 1 February 1965, written by Fergus Pyle. Pyle was a descendant of John Norcott D'Esterre's daughter, Amelia, who married Captain John Grattan Guinness's second son, Arthur Grattan Guinness, and carefully researched the story.
8. Harry Guinness, *In Memoriam.*
9. An inaccuracy repeated as late as 1910 by T. P. O'Connor in *TP's Weekly*.
10. W. E. Adams, quoted by S. Blake and R. Beacham in *The Book of Cheltenham* (Buckingham, 1982).
11. Harry Guinness, *In Memoriam.*
12. ibid.

Chapter 3

1. Farmleigh Manuscript.
2. Lynch and Vaizey, *Guinness Brewery*, p. 126.
3. Undated letter to Mrs Jane Guinness, Farmleigh Manuscript.
4. To John V. Topp, 1844, cited in Lynch and Vaizey, *Guinness Brewery*, p. 112.
5. Records of the Battle of Waterloo refer to an English officer drinking a glass of Guinness.
6. Plunkett Papers, 9 February 1816.
7. Plunkett Papers, 12 March 1849.

8. Lynch and Vaizey, *Guinness Brewery*, p. 106.
9. G. Martelli, *A Man of His Time: A Life of the First Earl of Iveagh, KP, GCVO* (privately published, 1957), p. 21.
10. Lynch and Vaizey, *Guinness Brewery*, p. 108.
11. 7 November 1839: Lynch and Vaizey, *Guinness Brewery*, p. 114.
12. Throughout the diary Frederick refers to the second Arthur's single Beaumont daughters as his 'aunts', though they are in fact his cousins.
13. The diary contains an interesting account of the way Fred is amused by his Uncle Arthur Darley, who 'entertained me with a disquisition on the taste of ladies for "colloquing and shannihan" ' – presumably gossiping and chatting.
14. He went on to have a distinguished clerical career as Rector of Trinity Church in New York City. His elder brother, David, was professor of ecclesiastical history at Rutgers University, and at the General Theological Seminary in Manhattan. The clerical tradition in the Guinness family remained strong even in the daughters' line.
15. Alexander to Arthur Guinness, 1842, Park Royal Manuscript.
16. Lynch and Vaizey, *Guinness Brewery*, p. 167.
17. Farmleigh Manuscript, 2 November 1851.

Chapter 4

1. Henry Grattan Guinness, *In Memoriam* (RBMU, 1910).
2. ibid.
3. Letter in the author's possession.
4. John Farquar Shaw, 'A Sketch of the Life and Ministry of the Rev. H. G. Guinness', from *Thirteen Sermons* (1859).
5. ibid.
6. Lynch and Vaizey, *Guinness Brewery*, p. 178.
7. From Frederick Mullally, *The Silver Salver* (Granada, 1981), p. 81.
8. From an Elveden manuscript.
9. F. S. L. Lyons, *Irish Historical Studies* (1962–3), p. 374.
10. J. Edwin Orr, *The Second Evangelical Awakening in Britain* (Marshall, Morgan and Scott, 1949).
11. *Enter Thou, Pages from the Life of Fanny E. Guinness* (RBMU and Paternoster, 1899).

Chapter 5

1. *The World*, 1862.
2. Mrs S. Barnardo and James Marchant, *Barnardo* (Hodder and Stoughton, 1907), p. 17.
3. Dr Frank Guinness, a descendant of the banking side of the family, tells the story of how, many years ago, when he was a missionary with the Church Missionary Society, he was introduced in Kenya to an elderly couple called

Knight, who had retired there in 1922. The old man was ninety. His wife was eighty-seven. She told him her maiden name was Pauline Jameson and that she was a niece of Sir Benjamin Lee Guinness, the daughter of his sister Elizabeth who had married the Rev. William Jameson of Drumcondra in 1844. Before the First World War they had been missionaries for fifteen years with the Japanese Evangelical Band.

4. Other illustrious pupils of the Academy include Richard Brinsley Sheridan, Robert Emmet, Thomas Moore and the Duke of Wellington.

5. Letter in the possession of Edward Guinness CVO, the last member of the family to hold an executive position on the Brewery Board. Richard Samuel was his great-grandfather. Mossy, Richard Samuel's mother, was living in Westport, near Castlebar, Country Mayo, following the death of her husband, Dick, in 1829.

6. Farmleigh Manuscript, 1 June 1862.

7. Farmleigh Manuscript, 1 January 1863.

8. Lynch and Vaizey, *Guinness Brewery*, p. 181.

9. H. Grattan Guinness, *Lucy Guinness Kumm, Her Life Story* (Morgan and Scott, 1907).

10. December 1866: Lynch and Vaizey, *Guinness Brewery*, p. 180.

11. 16 February 1866, from the Hudson Taylor Archives of the Overseas Missionary Fellowship, sent to the author by the remarkable archivist and Taylor's cousin, Jim Broomhall, now deceased.

12. A. J. Broomhall, *Hudson Taylor and China's Open Century*, Book 4, 'Survivor's Pact' (Hodder and Stoughton, 1984), p. 122.

13. Tom Barnardo had decided to stay in England, feeling he needed more time to consider his calling.

14. Fanny E. Guinness, *She Spake of Him, Being Recollections of the Loving Labours and Early Death of the Late Mrs Geraldine Dening* (1872).

15. An obituary of Mrs Geraldine Dening in *The Christian*, Thursday 2 August 1872.

16. *What It Is to Die a Brewer: The Burial of Sir Benjamin Lee*, pamphlet by J. A. Mowatt.

17. From an obituary booklet published on the death of Pastor Claude Degremont in 1912. Degremont, who supported Guinness's ministry, was minister of various Reformed churches in north-eastern France between 1861 and 1894, when he became pastor of the French Protestant Church of London in Soho Square.

     Some of Guinness's preaching in France was shared with the well-known French evangelist, Theodore Monod.

18. From Kate Drew, *The Escape Upward* (Drummonds' Tract Depot, Stirling, undated).

Chapter 6

1. Barnardo and Marchant, *Barnardo*, p. 104.
2. 'The East London Institute, Our First Year, 1872.' Fanny liked to keep their supporters informed. She wrote to them on a regular basis, and her letters were compiled into a series of annual reports.
3. Retaining its Christian foundation, the Mildmay Hospital is today one of the foremost centres in the world for the palliative care of people with AIDS.
4. Farmleigh Manuscript, October 1971.
5. From John Pollock, *Shaftesbury, the Poor Man's Earl* (Hodder and Stoughton, 1985), p. 155.
6. John Pollock, *Moody without Sankey* (Hodder and Stoughton, 1963), p. 82. Reprinted by Christian Focus Books, 1995.
7. Joy Guinness, *Mrs Howard Taylor, Her Web of Time* (China Inland Mission, 1949).
8. These and subsequent quotes are from The East London Institute Reports, 1874–9.
9. Alan Moorhead, *The White Nile* (Book Club Associates, 1960), pp. 83–4.
10. Moorhead, *White Nile*, p. 100.

Chapter 7

1. Introduction to *The Approaching End of the Age, viewed in the light of history, prophecy and science* (Hodder and Stoughton, first published in 1878, with twelve editions by 1896).
2. Over the years a variety of cranks, sects and amateur biblical sleuths have claimed that Henry Grattan Guinness foretold 'the end of the world'. Academics criticised him for it. In an article as recent as 1988 in *The Asbury Theological Journal*, entitled, 'The World Will End in 1919', Professor Stanley Walters of Knox College, Toronto University claimed that Henry Grattan Guinness died in 1910 'without knowing he was wrong'. But Grattan Guinness intentionally never used the phrase 'the end of the world'. The man whose preaching was equated with Spurgeon's knew the biblical texts about the day of the Lord coming as a thief in the night only too well. In *Light for the Last Days* he expressly asks his readers not to use his book in that way.

   He did however describe 'the end of the age', explaining that biblical ages came in and went out over a period of many years. The sign of the gradual waning of the present (Gentile) age would be the return of the Jews to their homeland in Palestine. This was the only future event which fired his imagination, and the two particular years he felt were vital in this respect were 1917 and 1948. In later years Geraldine often spoke of these dates, her eyes on events in the Middle East. No mention of the year 1919, or the end of the world, was ever made within the family.

3. From Piers Brendon, *Head of Guinness* (privately published, 1979, for family circulation only), p. 33.
4. *Whitehall Journal,* 1881.
5. *The Tatler,* 1900.
6. Lynch and Vaizey, *Guinness Brewery,* p. 195
7. Anecdote recounted to Piers Brendon (see note 3 above).

Chapter 8

1. G. Martelli, *Man of His Time,* p. 111.
2. Martelli, *Man of His Time,* p. 92.
3. G. Martelli, *Rupert Guinness: A Life of the Second Earl of Iveagh, KG, CB, CMG, FRS* (private publication), p. 5.
4. Mary Reed's reminiscences of Lucy Guinness are taken from Irene V. Cleverdon, *Pools in the Glowing Sands* (The Specialty Press, Melbourne, 1936). Lucy was in fact a great niece of J. B. Cramer, the acclaimed pianist.
5. A method of soaking lace in saffron-tinted water to dye it a cream colour.
6. *The Regions Beyond Magazine,* 1885, p. 110.
7. J. Guinness, *Requiem for a Family Business* p. 22.
8. J. Guinness, *Requiem,* p. 26.
9. Professor S. R. Dennison and Dr Oliver MacDonagh, '*History of Guinness, 1868–1939*', ch. IX, p. 19. Only two copies exist, in manuscript form.
10. Dennison and MacDonagh, *History.*

Chapter 9

1. Harry Guinness, *In Memoriam,* p. 40.
2. Founder of the future Christian and Missionary Alliance.
3. L. E. Maxwell, who founded the Prairie Bible Institute, trained at the Midlands Bible School in Kansas City, which was based on the New York Bible Institute.
4. See Klaus Fiedler, *The Story of Faith Missions* (Regnum Books International, 1994). Fiedler is one of the foremost academics in the field of nineteenth-century missions.
5. *Illustrated Missionary News,* 1 December 1873, p. 134.
6. From J. Lowry Maxwell, *Half a Century of Grace* (London, SUM, 1954), p. 22.
7. 20 November 1889.
8. Henry Seymour Guinness leans towards the theory that Richard Guinness of Celbridge was the illegitimate son of an English soldier by the name of Gennys, who went to Ireland with Cromwell for the Battle of the Boyne. But his only evidence is hearsay. In his book *Requiem for a Brewing Family,* Jonathan Guinness, basing his theory on the fact that there were Protestant families in Ireland long before William of Orange with the name of Gennis,

Ginnis, Gennys and Guinness, believes that Richard Guinness was probably descended from one of them, and possibly distantly related to the Magennis clan. Since there is little evidence one way or another, I suspect the obvious, albeit the least romantic, is probably correct.

9. A private account given to Piers Brendon and described in his book *Head of Guinness*, p. 149.
10. J. Martelli, *The Elveden Enterprise* (Faber and Faber, 1932), p. 50.
11. Mullally, *The Silver Salver*, p. 43. Mullally relied on the accounts of old Elveden retainers for descriptions of Elveden shooting parties.
12. Martelli, *Man of His Time*, p. 258.

Chapter 10

1. Joy Guinness, *Mrs Howard Taylor*, p. 160.
2. From *The Congo Crisis*, one of three polemical works Harry wrote on Belgian slavery in the Congo. The titles of the other two are *Rubber Is Death*, and *Congo Slavery*.
3. H. G. Guinness, *Lucy Guinness Kumm*.
4. *Enter Thou*.
5. 12 June 1925, in Brendon, *Head of Guinness*.
6. Martelli, *Man of His Time*, p. 13.
7. Guinness, *Requiem for a Family Business*, p. 35. It seems probable that untreated syphilis was the cause of Claude's demise as Jonathan suggests, though it does seem odd that Claude's sister Dodo was also given to bouts of strange behaviour. This too was covered up by the family, but told me by Paddy Ullstein, Henry Seymour Guinness's daughter, who claims that this was why she never met her aunt, the wife of one of her father's closest friends and business colleagues.
8. The reasons for Reginald's fall from grace are unknown, but when he died in 1909, two years after receiving a knighthood for services to the City of Dublin, no mention was made of his contribution to the company in the annual report to shareholders, a fact which did not escape notice by *The Times*.
9. Martelli, *Man of His Time*, p. 24.
10. Karl Kumm, *To All People* (Sudan Pioneer Mission, 1900).

Chapter 11

1. From *Peculiar People* by 'Septima' (Heath Cranton, 1935). 'Septima' was a pseudonym for Grace Hurditch. The book, her autobiography, sold fairly well as an antidote to Edmund Gosse's *Father and Son*.
2. 20 August 1893.
3. Brendon, *Head of Guinness*, p. 75.
4. *The Times*, quoting from G. Martelli, *Rupert Guinness*, p. 43.

5.   In a conversation with Piers Brendon, quoted in *Head of Guinness.*
6.   In 1903 the Sudan encompassed a vast area of the African continent covering about three thousand miles from Abyssinia to the Atlantic, including French West Africa, Senegal, the Cameroon, Libya, Sierra Leona, Nigeria and the Ivory Coast.
7.   Roger Casement was knighted in 1911 for services to the British Consulate. In 1915 he visited Irish prisoners of war in Germany, tried to persuade them to renounce British allegiance and form an Irish brigade in the German army. He was tried for high treason, stripped of his knighthood and hanged at Pentonville Gaol on 3 August 1916.

Chapter 12

1.   *The Bath Herald.*
2.   I am indebted for this information to Dr Michael R. Palairet of the Department of Economic and Social History at the University of Edinburgh, who has written a short biography of Francis Harford Mackenzie.
3.   Much of my assessment of Henry Grattan Guinness's character is based on Grace's recollections. Academics who have written about him recently tend to forget that my husband, Peter, knew his grandmother well. He was eighteen when Grace Guinness died in 1967. He received a first-hand account of a life shared for seven years with his remarkable grandfather.
4.   Joy Guinness, *Mrs Howard Taylor.*
5.   Katherine Everett, *Bricks and Flowers* (Reprint Society, 1951), p. 162.
6.   The eldest, Robert Darley Guinness, a barrister by profession, retired to Wooten Wawen Hall in Warwickshire, where he later became High Sheriff.
7.   Martelli, *The Elveden Empire*, p. 102.
8.   Letter from Lord Moyne to the author, 18 July 1988.
9.   *Reminiscences of Sport and War* (Eyre and Spottiswood, 1939), pp. 229–30.

Chapter 13

1.   The First World War alerted businesses to the value and competence of a female workforce. The Guinness Brewery also began to employ women as cashiers and secretaries, with the proviso that they remained single. No lady could be retained in employment after her marriage. A certain cashier by the name of Miss Tripp concealed her married state from the Brewery until the rule was rescinded after the Second World War – almost twenty years – then held a substantial wedding reception so that her true and long-standing status could be entered into the company's books.
2.   The estate belonged to Gwenny's family.
3.   The first official family tree, the product of Henry Seymour's meticulous and painstaking work, was published in 1924. Three subsequent editions, the most recent appearing in 1985, were compiled by his nephew, Brian

Guinness, Howard Rundell Guinness's youngest son. Henry Seymour Guinness was also responsible for researching the origins of the name Guinness. He was fascinated by all the various branches of the family and followed their progress, including the Grattan Guinnesses.

4.   Graham Hughes, *Marit Guinness Aschan, Enamellist of Our Time* (Starcity Ltd, 1995).
5.   Mullally, *The Silver Salver*, p. 93.
6.   Martelli, *The Elveden Enterprise*, p. 87.
7.   Professor Joseph Johnstone, quoted in Martelli, *Rupert Guinness*, p. 204.
8.   Brian Sibley, *The Book of Guinness Advertising*, p. 38.
9.   J. Guinness, *Requiem for a Family Business*, p. 43, taken from Sibley, *The Book of Guinness Advertising*.
10.   One of their favourite teachers, Mr Belgarnie, was the model for James Hilton's *Good-bye Mr Chips*. Hilton even used Belgarnie's jokes.
11.   *Mrs Howard Taylor*, p. 241.
12.   *Mrs Howard Taylor*, p. 255.
13.   Miss Soltau, in Mrs Howard Taylor, *Guinness of Honan* (CIM, 1930), p. 303.
14.   *Guinness of Honan*, p. 307.
15.   *Mrs Howard Taylor*, p. 275.

Chapter 14

1.   Paul Guinness, Vicar of Christ Church, Ashton-under-Lyne and later Ecumenical Officer for Greater Manchester, spent a lifetime involved in Jewish–Christian dialogue, culminating in his writing a book called *Hear O Israel*, which showed the crucial role his father and other Victorian leaders had played in the creation of a Jewish state.
2.   Mary Soames, *Clementine Churchill* (Penguin, 1979), p. 376.
3.   Bryan Guinness, *Personal Patchwork, 1939–45* (Cygnet, 1986), p. 219.
4.   Personal letter from Bryan Guinness, the second Lord Moyne, to the author, 18 July 1988.
5.   Gerald Frank, *The Deed* (Simon and Schuster, 1963).
6.   B. Guinness, *Personal Patchwork*, p. 219.
7.   The Langs' only daughter, Enid, had her coming-out ball and was married from Grosvenor Square, her godfather Lord Iveagh's house, in 1909. The wedding took up two pages in the *Tatler*.
8.   One of the most popular and enduring Guinness family legends surrounds Walter and Mabel's second son, Lionel, who worked for the Indian service and was the British Resident in Cashmere during the early, difficult days of Gandhi's protests. Lionel was very unhappily married. His wife, Constance, an aunt of the future spy, Guy Burgess, hated diplomatic life and loved to shock. Renowned for her unpunctuality, she appeared late for a state dinner and walked slowly down the central staircase – and here the legend varies – stark naked but for a large fan, or dressed in nothing but a leopardskin.

Either way, it took some time for Lionel's career to recover.

9. This was how it was later explained to Edward Guinness by Diana Wightwich, Geraldine Kerr-Pearse's granddaughter.
10. Edward Guinness, *The Guinness Book of Guinness, 1935–85* (privately published, 1988), p. 41.
11. Geraldine Taylor wrote *The Triumph of John and Betty Stam* (CIM, 1935), describing the death of the missionaries at the hands of the communists, while she was still living in Germantown, Philadelphia. It was one of her most popular books and a lasting success.
12. In 1998 it was estimated that the number of Christians in Honan (now Henan) exceeded several million. The Church is growing rapidly despite the ruthless grip of the state and regular persecution.

The Continuing Story . . .

1. Aileen was mistress of Luttrellstown Castle in Clonsilla, Maureen of Clandeboye in County Down, and Oonagh of Luggala, the fairytale Gothic castle in the Wicklow Mountains.
2. The Beatles' song, 'A Day in the Life of', alludes to the death of the Honorable Tara Browne, who was a friend of theirs and a cult figure in the swinging sixties. After a bitter court battle with Tara's wife, Oonagh managed to gain custody of her two grandchildren.
3. Oonagh, Ernest's youngest daughter, who adored children, tried to gain custody of Henrietta's baby, taking her away from her natural father, a move of which many members of the family disapproved. It generated a great deal of hostile media coverage.
4. *Daily Telegraph*, Monday, 2 February 1987, in an article by Alison Miller.
5. Cloë died four years later in 1953, her stomach so horrifically distended that she hid herself away for the last two.
6. Personal letter, 4 August 1989.
7. Ernest's ex-round-the-world yacht, *Fantome III*, sank off the Honduras in November 1998 with the twenty-one crew, a victim of Hurricane Mitch.
8. Saturday, 20 November 1997.

Bibliography of publications concerning the Guinness family

Barnardo, Mrs S. and Marchant, J., *Barnardo* (Hodder and Stoughton, 1904).

Brendon, P., *Head of Guinness* (privately published, 1979).

Broomhall, A. J., *Hudson Taylor and China's Open Century* (Hodder and Stoughton, 1984).

Cleverdon, I. V., *Pools in the Glowing Sands* (The Specialty Press, 1936).

Dennison, S. R. and MacDonagh, O., 'History of Guinness, 1868–1939' (typescript).

Drew, K., *The Escape Upward*, Drumaronds Tract Depot, Stirling, undated.

Everett, Katherine, *Bricks and Flowers* (London Reprint Society, 1951) (about Olive, Lady Ardilaun).

Fidler, Klaus, *The Story of Faith Missions* (Regnum Books International, 1994).

Frank, G., *The Deed* (Simon and Schuster, New York, 1963) (about the assassination of Lord Moyne).

Guinness, B., *Personal Patchwork 1939–45* (Cygnet, 1986).

Guinness, B. (ed.), *The Guinness Family* (1985) (official genealogy).

Guiness, C. E., *The Guinness Book of Guinness 1935–85* (privately published, 1988).

Guiness, Fanny E., *Enter Thou, Pages from the Life of Fanny E. Guinness* (RBMU and Paternoster, 1899).

Guinness, Fanny E., *She Spake of Him* (Book Society, 1872).

Guinness, Harry, *In Memoriam, A Biography of Henry Grattan Guinness by His Son* (RBMU, 1911).

Guinness, Harry, *The Congo Crisis* (RBMU, 1908).

Guinness, Harry, *Congo Slavery* (RBMU, 1908).

Guinness, Harry, *Rubber Is Death* (RBMU, 1908).

Guinness, Henry G., *The Approaching End of the Age* (Hodder and Stoughton, 1878).

Guinness, Henry G., *Creation Centred in Christ* (Hodder and Stoughton, 1896).

Guinness, Henry G., *History Unveiling Prophecy* (Hodder and Stoughton, 1905).

Guinness, Henry G., *Light for the Last Days* (Hodder and Stoughton, 1887).

Bibliography of publications concerning the Guinness family

Guinness, Henry G., *Lucy Guinness Kumm, Her Life Story* (Morgan and Scott, 1907).

Guinness, H. S., *Richard Guinness of Celbridge* (privately published, 1934).

Guinness, J., *Mrs Howard Taylor, Her Web of Time* (CIM, 1949).

Guinness, J., *Requiem for a Family Business* (Macmillan, 1997).

Hughes, Graham, *Marit Guinness Aschan, Enamellist of Our Time* (Starcily Ltd, 1995).

Jones, Ivy F., *The Rise of a Merchant Bank: A Short History of Guinness Mahon* (privately published, 1974).

Kumm, K., *To All People* (SPM, 1900).

Lynch, P. and Vaizey, J., *Guinness Brewery in the Irish Economy 1759–1876* (CUP, 1960).

Martelli, J., *The Elveden Enterprise* (Faber and Faber, 1952).

Martelli, G., *Rupert Guinness: A Life of the Second Earl of Iveagh, KG, CB, CMG, FRS* (privately published).

Martelli, G., *A Man of His Time: A Life of the First Earl of Iveagh, KP, GCVO* (privately published, 1957).

Mowatt, J. A., *What It Is to Die a Brewer: The Burial of Sir Benjamin Lee.*

Mullally, F., *The Silver Salver* (Granada, 1981).

'Septima' [Hurditch, G.[, *Peculiar People* (Heath Cranton, 1935).

Shaw, J. F., 'A Sketch of the Life and Ministry of the Rev. H. G. Guinness', in *Thirteen Sermons* (1859).

Sibley, B., *The Book of Guinness Advertising* (Guinness, 1985).

Taylor, Mrs H., *Guinness of Honan* (CIM, 1930).

Index

518